The Daily Telegraph

AIRMEN'S OBITUARIES

BOOK TWO

The Daily Telegraph

AIRMEN'S OBITUARIES

BOOK TWO

Edited by

JAY ILIFF

Foreword by Air Commodore

Graham Pitchfork MBE, BA, FRAeS

GRUB STREET · LONDON

Published by
Grub Street
4 Rainham Close
London
SW11 6SS

Copyright © 2007 Grub Street, London
Text copyright © 2007 Telegraph Group Limited

British Library Cataloguing in Publication Data
The Daily Telegraph airmen's obituaries
  Book 2
  1. Air pilots – Obituaries 2. Flight crews – Obituaries
  I. Iliff, Jay II. Airmen's obituaries
  629.1'3'0922

ISBN-13: 9781904943839

Cover design by Lizzie B design

Typeset by Pearl Graphics, Hemel Hempstead

Printed and bound by MPG Ltd, Bodmin, Cornwall

Grub Street only uses
FSC (Forest Stewardship Council) paper for its books.

DRAMATIS PERSONNAE
(in order of appearance)

FIRST WORLD WAR VETERAN
Leading Aircraftman William Roberts

FIGHTER BOYS
Squadron Leader Pat Wells
Wing Commander J G "Sandy" Sanders
Air Vice-Marshal Edward Crew
Squadron Leader Donald "Dimsie" Stones
James Sandeman-Allen
Air Chief Marshal Sir Kenneth Cross
Wing Commander Peter Parrott
Squadron Leader "Buck" Casson
Tim Vigors
Group Captain John Peel
Wing Commander David Cox
Group Captain Tom Dalton-Morgan
Group Captain Mike Stephens
Group Captain Frank Carey
Squadron Leader "Chips" Carpenter
Air Commodore Sir Archibald Winskill
Group Captain Edward "Hawkeye" Wells
Wing Commander "Bunny" Currant
Wing Commander Johnny Checketts
Wing Commander George "Grumpy" Unwin
Wing Commander "Moose" Fumerton
Wing Commander Bobby Gibbes

BOMBER BOYS
Group Captain Mike Shaw
Air Commodore Brian Frow
Paul Hilton
Squadron Leader Ken Brown
Air Marshal Sir Ivor Broom

Lieutenant-General Reg Lane
Air Vice-Marshal Tony Dudgeon
Group Captain Kenneth Hubbard
Group Captain Robert McFarlane
Wing Commander Basil Templeman-Rooke
Group Captain Keith "Slim" Somerville
Flight Lieutenant Bob Knights
Flight Lieutenant Pat O'Hara
Group Captain Dudley Burnside
Group Captain Kenneth Smales
Wing Commander Peter Ward-Hunt
Group Captain Dick Maydwell
Air Commodore Wilf Burnett
Air Vice-Marshal Jack Furner
Flight Lieutenant Wallace McIntosh

DAREDEVILS
Flight Sergeant Alfred Card
Norman Hoffman
Adrian Nicholas
Squadron Leader Ray Hanna
Squadron Leader Michael Casano

SOE
Squadron Leader John Mott
Squadron Leader James "Waggy" Wagland
Air Chief Marshal Sir Lewis Hodges

FOREIGN FRIENDS
Prince Emanuel Galitzine
Joe Foss
Major-General Alois Siska
Colonel Bob Morgan
Air Commodore
Robbert "Bergy" Van Zinnicq Bergmann
Major-General Charles Sweeney
General Stanislaw Skalski

Pierre Clostermann
Major-General Frantisek Perina

THE GIRLS
Air Commodore Dame Felicity Peake
Fay Gillis Wells
Evelyn "Bobbi" Trout
Edna Morris
Iris "Fluff" Bower
Elspeth Green

CIVILIANS
Captain Ronald Ballantine
Captain Ian Harvey
Captain Norman Todd

TEST PILOTS
Group Captain John "Cat's Eyes" Cunningham
Air Commodore Cyril "Cyclops" Brown
David Morgan
Johnny Squier
Wing Commander Dickie Martin
Hugh Merewether
Wing Commander Walter Gibb
Alex Henshaw
Squadron Leader Neville Duke

MARITIME
Air Vice-Marshal David McKinley
Wing Commander Micky Ogden
Group Captain Alan Anderson
Air Commodore E W "Bill" Tacon
Group Captain "Bill" Sise
Air Vice-Marshal John Stacey
Wing Commander Douglas Wilson
Air Commodore Leonard Birchall
Flight Lieutenant Charles Corder

Wing Commander Peter Cundy

ESCAPERS AND EVADERS
Wing Commander Norman Mackie
Wing Commander "Taffy" Higginson
Flight Lieutenant Tony Bethell
Wing Commander Nicky Barr

INDUSTRIALISTS AND ENGINEERS
Sir George Edwards
Sir Frederick Page
Sir Peter Masefield
Stanley Hiller Jnr
Group Captain the 9th Earl of Ilchester
Sir Arthur Marshall

GEORGE CROSS WINNERS
Air Vice-Marshal Sir Laurence Sinclair
Squadron Leader Sidney Wiltshire
Air Marshal Sir John Rowlands

DISTINGUISHED LEADERS
Air Chief Marshal Sir Christopher Foxley-Norris
Marshal of the RAF Sir John Grandy
Air Chief Marshal Sir David Lee
Air Vice-Marshal John Barker
Air Chief Marshal Sir John Aiken
Air Marshal Sir Edward Gordon Jones

FOREWORD

During my years as a regular reader of *The Daily Telegraph*, the obituaries page always provided me with some of the most fascinating and stimulating reading. Those entries devoted to aviators, of course, were of particular interest to me; often they recorded the exploits of boyhood heroes and, in more recent times, they featured distinguished men under whom I had been privileged to serve. I greatly admired the perception and skill of Edward Bishop, who wrote the aviation obituaries for many years, and I was immensely flattered and honoured when I was invited to take over his mantle almost four years ago.

To many, aviation may appear to be a narrow field; yet it can include an astonishing diversity of subjects, and it is a diversity graphically illustrated in this second volume of airmen's obituaries. Inevitably, the exploits of men during the Second World War feature extensively, and in this context we are reminded of the immense debt owed by this country to the men of the Commonwealth, many of whom left their families and comfortable lives to fight alongside their British cousins: men such as Bill Sise, from New Zealand, who led some of the most dangerous strikes against shipping off the Dutch and Norwegian coasts; Reg Lane, the bomber commander who led the first Canadian Pathfinder Squadron; and Australia's Bobby Gibbes, who was recommended for a Victoria Cross for landing in the desert behind enemy lines in his single-seat fighter to rescue a downed colleague.

Others had to flee their countries to resume the fight after the enemy had occupied their homelands. Stanislaw Skalski had to escape three times before reaching Britain, where he became the highest-scoring Polish fighter pilot; the Dutchman Robbert van Zinnicq-Bergmann had to attack the palace of his queen after it had been taken over by the Gestapo; Pierre Clostermann, the Free French fighter ace, was one of the first to land back on his native soil in June 1944; and Frantisek Perina, having returned to Czechoslovakia as a hero, was forced to flee soon afterwards following the Communist takeover of his country.

Among the Americans featured here are Bob Morgan, who flew the Memphis Belle, and Charles Sweeney, who dropped the second atom bomb to end the war against Japan.

Men with distinguished war records rose to the highest ranks of the RAF. Marshal of the RAF Sir John Grandy became the head of his service having earlier fought in the Battle of Britain and in Burma. Air Chief Marshal Sir Lewis Hodges escaped from France before leading the clandestine pilots flying in support of SOE in north-west Europe and in Burma. And Air Chief Marshal Sir David Lee, who first flew on India's North-West Frontier, commanded RAF forces against Indonesian guerrillas following the Allied victory in the Far East.

Some of those who served were professional airmen, but many aircrew who joined for the duration of the war – all of them volunteers – came from very diverse backgrounds. Their careers were often short, but those who helped to win the Battle of Britain included men such as the fish merchant David Cox and the Old Etonian bloodstock agent Tim Vigors. Robert McFarlane, an organist and choirmaster, played a key role in the strategic bomber offensive. James Wagland, a banker, landed in French fields by night to drop agents and pick up VIPs, including two future presidents of France.

The years following the war saw the exploration of the extreme boundaries of flight, and the test pilots of that era became household names. Some already had distinguished war records, among them John Cunningham, one of the greatest night fighter pilots, who later tested the Comet; and Neville Duke, a fighter ace in the desert whose name became synonymous with the Hawker Hunter. Johnny Squier ejected from a Lightning at more than 1,000mph; Walter Gibb set a world height record; and Hugh Merewether did much to pioneer the Harrier vertical take-off and landing fighter.

The extraordinary developments in the world of civil aviation also find their place here. The career of Ronald Ballantine, who flew with Imperial Airways in the 1930s, is featured alongside that of Norman Todd, who flew Concorde's first commercial flight. There is also the story of Ian Harvey, who managed to land his airliner full of passengers after a bomb had exploded on board.

Of course, not all of those who gave such valuable service to aviation were aircrew. No one could fail to admire the work of the women who appear in this book. Iris "Fluff" Bower was a gallant RAF nursing sister who was one of the first women to go ashore on the French beaches immediately after D-Day; and the nurse Edna Morris was one of six "Flying Nightingales" who volunteered to fly into the combat area to evacuate the wounded from France. Elspeth Green won the Military Medal for her gallantry under fire at Biggin Hill.

Stanley Hiller, the American helicopter pioneer, and the RAF's Earl of Ilchester are among those representing the many who support those who fly. Air Marshal Sir John Rowlands was awarded the George Cross for his dangerous work in bomb disposal. And there is the brave, ebullient Michael Casano, the RAF Regiment officer who took his armoured cars – and his dog – deep into the Western Desert and Iraq.

The lives of this diverse group of people – and there are many more in this book – illustrate all that is typical of human nature; but there is also something else, something that sets them apart. Gallantry, fortitude, service and loyalty all spring to mind. Yet, in my experience, the majority would claim none of these qualities, saying simply: "I was just doing my job." So often I have found myself unearthing aspects of these people's lives that have been unknown to others, even to their own families; what characterises them is their modesty and their sense of duty.

Piecing together these short biographies and presenting them in a succinct and interesting way is a challenge. It is also important that they are placed in a historical context, thus allowing their achievements to be fully appreciated. The demands of space dictate that the reviews of these lives are brief, but the obituaries page of *The Daily Telegraph* provides an immensely valuable service, not only to today's readers, but also, through the medium of books such as this, as an inspiration to future generations.

AIR COMMODORE GRAHAM PITCHFORK
MBE, BA, FRAeS

INTRODUCTION

The first *Daily Telegraph Book of Airmen's Obituaries*, published in 2002, was edited by Edward Bishop, the newspaper's RAF obituarist since Hugh Massingberd had taken him on some 15 years earlier. Sadly Ted died in 2003, but his enthusiasm and expertise have been equally evident in his successor, Air Commodore Graham Pitchfork, who wrote most of the obituaries in this new collection and kindly agreed to write a foreword. Most of the entries here date from where Ted Bishop's book left off; none was published earlier than 2001.

As for the selection process, it has been difficult, and inevitably some obituaries I would like to have included have been omitted simply for lack of space. Inevitably, too, fighter pilots have a very prominent showing, but I make no apology for that; it was the fighter pilots who usurped most of the glamour. The Army has the Battle of Waterloo, the Royal Navy has Trafalgar; the Battle of Britain is the engagement that has most resonance in the junior service.

I have followed Ted Bishop's example in dividing the obituaries into categories, because I think it makes the book more reader-friendly. Some of the subjects, of course, could have appeared in more than one category, and those I have tended to allocate on the principle of balancing the numbers. I have also tried to include as broad a range of subjects as possible. There is a section on "Foreign Friends", a gesture to the contributions made by Americans, French, Dutch, Czech, Polish and Russians during the Second World War. There are sections on women, civilian airmen, engineers and industrialists, and test pilots. A couple of skydivers appear under "Daredevils".

The vast majority of these short lives were written by Graham Pitchfork and Ted Bishop, and they received invaluable assistance from the head of the Air Historical Branch, Sebastian Cox, and his staff, Graham Day and Flight Lieutenant Mary Hudson. Charles Owen, our Army obituarist, contributed to the George Cross winners, and here thanks are also due to Didy Graham, secretary to the Victoria Cross and George Cross Association, Martin van der Weyer helped with "Industrialists and Engineers". A cast of characters on *The Daily Telegraph* obituaries desk (known in this context as the 'groundcrew') guided the pieces on to the pages of the newspaper: Andrew McKie, the obituaries editor; David Twiston Davies; Philip Eade; George Ireland; Georgia Powell; Katharine Ramsay; and Roger Wilkes. Until she left us last year we were all kept in order by our editorial assistant, Teresa Moore.

Morven Knowles, *The Daily Telegraph*'s publications manager, has been a source of much-needed good advice; while Matt Adams, the newspaper's operations general manager, and Janet Plaskow, helped me negotiate various technical difficulties.

There have been several editors of *The Daily Telegraph* over the past few years – Charles Moore, Martin Newland, John Bryant and now Will Lewis – and all have given the obituaries desk their encouragement and support.

JAY ILIFF

FIRST WORLD WAR VETERAN

LEADING AIRCRAFTMAN
WILLIAM ROBERTS

Leading Aircraftman William Roberts (who died on April 30 2006, aged 105) joined the Royal Flying Corps as a fitter and rigger at 17 and transferred to the RAF on its formation in 1918.

Remaining in England throughout his service, he started going up in aircraft as a passenger when they were being tested, since this was considered easier than carrying ballast.

On his first flight he was strapped into a Maurice Farman pusher aircraft which turned over during its take-off run. The Belgian pilot dragged him out of the wreckage in case it caught fire; an hour later, the pilot took off in another plane, which crashed and killed him.

Roberts saw five planes crash but, undaunted, continued to fly. He was thrilled when the pilot of a BE2c looped the loop, and he also flew in some of the RAF's latest biplane fighters.

At one stage he was locked up for a few days for a minor misdemeanour but, on being released, was summoned to see his commanding officer, who told him that he had been made a corporal.

When the Royal Air Force was formed on April 1 1918, Roberts recalled that members of the RFC, who wore smocks, were looked down upon as commoners by the Royal Naval Air Service men, who wore collars and ties.

But he had made his mark as a fencer, and used to duel with an Olympic competitor, Sergeant-Major Storey. When he volunteered to be a physical training instructor at RAF Cranwell he passed out top of the list. At the end of the war, he was selected for pilot training, but elected to return to civilian life instead.

William Roberts was born on September 29 1900 at Hartlepool and educated locally. He then worked in the reading room of the *Northern Daily Mail*, earning five shillings and sixpence a week.

On the morning of December 16 1914 he was at work when German warships shelled the town, causing considerable damage and killing more than 80 people. A piece of shrapnel ricocheted off a Fry's chocolate sign next to Roberts as he was running for home. As he fled he passed a naked woman (the first he had ever seen) as she escaped from a damaged house.

It was when Roberts learned, as a 15-year-old school-boy, that his father had been killed by a German sniper while serving with the Royal Engineers that he decided to volunteer for military service.

Initially he tried to join the Durham Light Infantry, but was rejected due to his age and told to return later. Roberts next applied to join the Royal Flying Corps, and was sent to Laffin Plains at Farnborough, Hampshire, where the recruits lived under canvas near to the aircraft repair factory.

He was given the service number 81853, and was proud of still being able to quote it without hesitation until the end of his life.

On leaving the RAF Roberts took up an apprentice-ship on marine engines but was fired as soon as he had completed his indentures. Since there was virtually no work in the shipyards at Hartlepool at that time he rejoined the RAF and went on to become a leading aircraftman in the motor transport trade.

It was during this time that he briefly met T E Lawrence who, in the course of his strange post-war career, was trying to escape from his past by serving as an aircraftman. Roberts judged him "very, very quiet – an unassuming person".

On leaving the Air Force for the second time in 1926 Roberts decided that motor cars were the business of the future. After spotting a newspaper advertisement for mechanics he spent a few weeks with a private garage, then found a job with the Ribble Bus Company. Later he became foreman at the Halifax Corporation Bus Depot and in 1943 was appointed chief engineer with the Chesterfield Corporation Transport Department. He retired in 1967.

In later life Roberts enjoyed gardening, walking and painting in oils. But he was haunted by the tragic losses of "many good young men" who were killed in training whilst flying aircraft that were "not very good".

Alert until his death, he retained clear memories of his service, declaring that, in retrospect, the Great War had been "a lot of political bull".

William Roberts's wife died in 1980; they had two sons.

FIGHTER BOYS

SQUADRON LEADER PAT WELLS

Squadron Leader Pat Wells (who died on April 6 2002, aged 85) had the honour – as he came to consider it – of being shot down in flames over Kent by Adolf Galland, the German fighter ace; the two men became friends after the war.

The incident occurred on November 28 1940. Wells had already been shot down and wounded once, while fighting in the Battle of Britain: on September 7 he had been attacking a Heinkel 111 bomber (which he later claimed as a "probable") when his Hurricane was set alight by fire from Bf 109 fighters.

Wells baled out at 18,000ft; he had cannon shell splinters in his head, a hand, both legs and both arms. As he descended towards Canterbury, his flying boots fell off and he landed in his socks. (His boots were later returned to him by the police, but he was never reunited with his parachute, cigarettes and other personal items which had been, in the familiar wartime phrase, "liberated" by some soldiers on the scene.)

On November 11, having recovered and returned to the skies, Wells helped to destroy an He 59 floatplane. When he encountered Galland 17 days later, Wells became the German ace's 56th kill – a tally that had been started in the days of the Spanish Civil War.

November 28 was a bright autumn day. Wells was flying at an altitude of 23,000ft, and attempting to keep an eye on some 109s above him, when Galland attacked from below. Wells remembered taking evasive action until his controls were shot away.

Then his Hurricane caught fire. Wells observed tracers going over his left wing, and he heard bullets ricocheting off the back of his cockpit's armoured seat. He decided there was no point in baling out and exposing himself to enemy fire.

"So," he recalled, "I sat and fried."

There came a point, however, when Wells had no option but to try to get out. His first attempt to escape was unsuccessful – flames, smoke and lack of oxygen had dulled his senses, and his right foot was jammed beneath the instrument panel. Then his left foot got stuck.

Wells had known personally some very badly burned pilots, and took the decision "to go down with the aeroplane". Then, suddenly, he found himself hurled out of the cockpit. At that moment he was perilously close to the ground and, as he tumbled clear, the Hurricane's tail hit him, dislocating his left shoulder; using his right hand, he managed to pull his ripcord. He remembered later how the skin was peeling from his face and legs, and how his nerve ends were painful in the cold.

He also recalled that he smelled like roast pork – and that this seemed appropriate when he landed in an apple tree.

Wells was transferred from an emergency hospital at Leeds Castle, near Maidstone, to Ward 3, a hutted annexe to the Queen Victoria Hospital at East Grinstead in Sussex; this was where Archibald McIndoe, the plastic surgeon later knighted for his work, led the dedicated team which treated severely burned airmen. McIndoe's patients, who called him "the maestro", were known as his "guinea pigs"; they later formed the Guinea Pig Club, whose 60th anniversary dinner in 2001 was attended by Prince Philip.

Wells was an early "member", and was astonished by Ward 3's free and easy atmosphere – there was usually a barrel of beer on the go. Wells later recalled: "Initially, I thought I had been admitted to a lunatic asylum. The noise was unbelievable, with radio music blaring, patients shouting above the noise. In due course I became like the rest of them."

Patrick Hardy Vesey Wells was born on March 16 1917 in Johannesburg, South Africa. He was a scion of the Wells brewing family, and was educated at Bedford School; he later studied Mining Engineering at London University, and while there joined the university's air squadron. He was fortunate to be taught to fly by its adjutant, Flight Lieutenant John Grandy, who was later to become a Marshal of the RAF, Governor of Gibraltar and Constable of Windsor Castle.

Wells was commissioned into the RAFVR as a pilot officer in 1938. At the outbreak of war he received further training at RAF Cranwell and at No 5 Operational Training Unit at Aston Down, where he converted to the Hurricane. In June 1940, when Grandy was put in command of No 249 Squadron at Church Fenton, he remembered Wells, tracked down his former pupil, and welcomed him to the squadron.

After Wells had emerged from treatment under McIndoe, he returned to No 249 in time to embark in the carrier *Furious*, reaching Gibraltar on May 18 1941. The squadron's Hurricanes were transferred to the carrier *Ark Royal*, which was approaching the beleaguered island of Malta when the fighters were ordered to fly off.

The following day, about ten of the 21 Hurricanes were on the ground near the dispersal tent at Takali, on Malta, when they were attacked by Bf 109s. Two of the British planes were destroyed, while Wells was hit by a bullet in the right ankle as he rushed to his plane to get airborne. He sat in his cockpit until his Hurricane caught fire and his ammunition began to explode. Only then did he realise he had been hit.

By July 1941 Wells was fit for duty once more, and he took part in offensive sweeps over Sicily and attacks on enemy shipping. Shortly afterwards he was flown by Sunderland flying boat to Egypt, where Hurricane pilots were needed to support the Army in the Western Desert; he was posted to No 73 Squadron, and flew many low-level missions against Rommel's troops, armour and transport before Montgomery's 8th Army victory at El Alamein.

Wells was later posted in the rank of squadron leader as flight commander to No 255, a two-engine Bristol Beaufighter squadron providing night defence for the Tunisian campaign in north-west Africa, and later in Sicily and Italy.

In 1944 he was awarded the DSO. The citation pointed to his remarkable operational war record "in the face of numerous difficulties and setbacks". In the same year he was also mentioned in dispatches.

Wells was released from the service in 1946. For a time he lived in Kenya, where he met his wife Jess. After selling a Cessna aircraft to a farmer there, he decided he had the right gifts to be a salesman; he spent the remainder of his working life building up a business selling aircraft in southern Africa.

His wife predeceased him; they had a son, and a daughter who became a house matron at Gordonstoun.

WING COMMANDER
J G "SANDY" SANDERS

Wing Commander J G "Sandy" Sanders (who died on August 12 2002, aged 88) was an RAF fighter pilot credited with destroying at least 16 enemy aircraft, several of them during the Battle of Britain.

When fighter pilots' scores were assessed after the war, Sanders's tally was almost certainly underestimated – because he had lost his logbook and because of an absence of records during the confusion that surrounded the fall of France.

Sanders could not have had a more propitious start. After receiving a short service commission in November

1935 and completing his flying training, he was posted after a year to No 111 (Treble One) Squadron, which was equipped with Gloster Gauntlet biplane fighters.

Treble One was destined for a niche in RAF history as the first squadron to be re-equipped, in 1938, with the modern eight-gun monoplane Hawker Hurricane; it was in a Hurricane that the squadron's commander, "Downwind" Gillan, achieved the then unthinkable feat of averaging more than 408mph in a flight from Turnhouse (Edinburgh) to Northolt (London).

After Squadron Leader Gillan and one other officer, Sanders was only the third squadron pilot to fly the Hurricane; but his experience on the type was interrupted early in 1939 when he incurred the wrath of Harry Broadhurst, then Treble One's leader and later Air Chief Marshal Sir Harry Broadhurst.

Sanders, who was always very much his own man, disliked what he saw as Broadhurst's bragging about his aerobatic skills, particularly his roll off the top of a loop after take-off in a specially modified aircraft.

When Sanders executed brilliantly the same manoeuvre in an unmodified Gauntlet, Broadhurst ordered his arrest. Sanders was marched in front of his air officer commanding (AOC) and posted, in October 1939, from the prestigious Treble One to fly biplane Gloster Gladiators with No 615 (County of Surrey), an Auxiliary squadron.

The blow was softened by Sanders's appointment as a flight commander, and he very soon demonstrated that his skills and airmanship could to some extent compensate for the obsolescent biplane's performance.

As it happened, Winston Churchill was No 615's honorary air commodore. In November – when he was still First Lord of the Admiralty – he inspected the squadron, taking a special interest in the machine guns of Sanders's Gladiator.

As her husband stood in front of the aircraft, Mrs

Churchill climbed into the cockpit and was starting to toy with the aircraft's firing mechanism. Sanders, realising that the guns were cocked for instant take-off and combat, averted a tragedy that could have altered the course of history.

Sanders first fired his guns in anger during the "phoney war" of the winter of 1939-40. On December 29 he achieved the extraordinary feat, in a Gladiator, of damaging, possibly even destroying, an He 111 over the Franco-Belgian border. Hit by return fire, he crash-landed near Valenciennes, and was badly concussed.

When the Germans began their blitzkrieg towards the Channel on May 10 1940, 615 Squadron – recently re-equipped with Hurricanes – found itself being evacuated from one airfield to another; they occupied four different airfields in ten days. In one engagement, Sanders was forced down in his Hurricane near Béthune, and was obliged to make his escape from the advancing Germans by train. When the train was attacked he leapt out with his parachute on his back, then dumped it in a ditch and hitched a lift from a passing RAF truck to Abbeville, where he found an abandoned Blenheim light bomber which was overloaded with escaping groundcrew stowaways.

Although it was night, and he had never before flown a two-engined aircraft, Sanders took off in the plane and, at 3.15am, reached Northolt near London. Informed by a WAAF telephone operator that the station commander could not be woken until 8am, Sanders kicked up such a fuss that the next day he was marched in front of the AOC.

For the second time he was downgraded to Gladiators, but, after leading a flight of the biplanes from Manston, Kent, in operations over Dunkirk between May 23 and May 30, Sanders managed to engineer a return to 615.

James Gilbert Sanders was born at Richmond, Surrey, on June 19 1914. He was educated in Genoa, Italy, where his father, a wealthy archaeologist and dilettante, had settled. As a schoolboy, young Sanders developed such a dislike of Fascism that, aged only nine, he objected to singing the stirring slaves' chorus from Verdi's opera *Nabucco* with the school choir in front of Mussolini himself.

In his late teens, Sanders was arrested and charged after using newspaper pictures of Il Duce as lavatory paper. This incident convinced him that war was inevitable, and despite studying Marine Archaeology at an Italian university, he resolved to join the RAF.

In the early summer of 1940 Sanders resumed with 615, and was heavily involved in the Battle of Britain as it raged across the south of England. He was in his element as he encountered wave upon wave of enemy bombers and fighters attacking Biggin Hill and other No 11 Group airfields which had the responsibility of defending London.

Even now, Sanders managed to upset his station commander who, observing Sanders's Hurricane in a slow roll at the edge of the airfield, called him to account. Sanders, who had been testing the aircraft for a suspected problem, was maddened at being reprimanded at this critical time.

He told the group captain what he thought of him, and suggested that he might like to climb into a Hurricane and see some action. Not surprisingly, he was arrested and kept under guard for a night.

August 18 saw some of the heaviest fighting of the Battle of Britain, and Sanders was repeatedly scrambled. He destroyed two, and possibly more, enemy bombers. On one sortie he was climbing towards Biggin Hill when bombs from a Dornier 17 passed only a few feet from his Hurricane.

On the same sortie Sanders sighted a Ju 88 immediately in front of him. He aimed at the cockpit to kill the pilot and saw the bomber dive into woods and blow up at Ide Hill, near Chartwell, Churchill's home in Kent.

When, at the end of August, 615 was withdrawn to rest in Scotland, Sanders volunteered to stay on at Kenley, south of London, to help 253, the squadron's successor, settle in. This was because he had become smitten by a local girl, Joan Barley.

Staying put also gave him the opportunity to try some experimental night fighting; and this led, in the New Year of 1941, to service with No 255, which was forming as a night fighter squadron equipped with the turret-gunned Boulton Paul Defiant. In this aircraft he achieved three kills.

Towards the end of the year, he began a series of training appointments followed by station commands and a spell at SHAEF (Supreme Headquarters Allied Expeditionary Force), finishing his RAF career at Rangoon in charge of flying at Mingaladon airfield.

Sanders returned home in 1947. While he could have remained in the RAF, he opted to leave the service to join the Mayfair office of the insurance company Crown Life of Canada.

Meanwhile, he indulged his lifelong love of music; and he managed one of the most splendid family boxes at the Royal Albert Hall, together with adjoining boxes belonging to Caius College, Cambridge, and to Earl Spencer. Sanders was a frequent attender at the Proms.

He was awarded the DFC in 1940, and in the same year married Joan Barley. They had two sons, one of whom served in the RAF as a Jaguar aerobatic display pilot. The marriage was dissolved, and in 1949 Sanders married Josephine King-Farlow; they had a daughter.

AIR VICE-MARSHAL
EDWARD CREW

Air Vice-Marshal Edward Crew (who died on August 18 2002, aged 84) was an ace night fighter pilot and destroyer of V-1 flying bombs; after notching up at least 13 kills, he saved many lives on the ground by shooting down 21 "doodlebugs" over the Channel and the English countryside.

Joining No 604 (County of Middlesex), an Auxiliary Air Force Squadron, in July 1940, Crew began to learn his trade as a night fighter pilot; among those with whom he flew at this time was John "Cat's Eyes" Cunningham, who himself became one of the most famous night fighter pilots of the war.

It was a hard apprenticeship because Crew's Bristol Blenheim was equipped with early, and rudimentary, airborne radar, and much depended on the ability of his air gunner, Sergeant Gus Guthrie, to adapt to his new calling as a radar operator.

It was not until the following spring, when the squadron converted to two-engine Bristol Beaufighters, that the pair acquired a more suitable aircraft and sufficient expertise to dispatch five enemy bombers within a period of ten weeks.

This early run of success was speedily recognised with the award of the first of Crew's two DFCs. The citation stated: "This officer is a pilot of outstanding ability who has shown tenacity of purpose to engage the enemy, which culminated in the destruction of two enemy aircraft in one night."

Citations, by their very nature, are matter-of-fact, and do not capture the essence of their subjects. Others in the same squadron remembered Crew as a small, compact man who gave the impression of being larger than he was. He was seen as a patrician who hunted down his victims with a ferocity which was in marked contrast to his quietly spoken and always imperturbable manner.

From the end of July 1941, Guthrie – Crew's eyes in combat – was posted away, and Crew was joined by Sergeant Basil Duckett, with whom, in the spring of 1942, he achieved three further kills. Crew and Duckett made a brilliant team in which the radar operator's quiet persistence matched the pilot's natural hunting instincts.

In early May 1942 Duckett enabled Crew to shoot down two Dornier 17 bombers on successive nights. Returning from the first of these encounters, over Portland in Dorset, Crew arrived back at base with the Dornier's trailing aerial wrapped around his Beaufighter's starboard propeller.

The second encounter developed into a long, drawn-out chase as Crew stalked the Dornier well out to sea off the Isle of Wight. As the enemy pilot twisted and turned to evade his pursuer, Crew refused to be shaken off, despite the fact that his guns were out of ammunition and Duckett was struggling to reload.

Eventually, however, Crew's plane was able to deliver a burst which set the enemy bomber ablaze and slowed it down as its gunner continued to return fire. At this point, the Beaufighter overshot the enemy aircraft, but Crew managed to keep it in view while Duckett again reloaded.

Hunter and hunted continued to lose height until, at 2,000ft, Crew saw the enemy crash into the sea, raising a plume of smoke and steam.

Shortly afterwards Crew received a Bar to his DFC, the citation singling out his "readiness to fly in all weather, his skill and ability in dealing with the enemy at night and his great example to the squadron".

Edward Dixon Crew was born on December 24 1917 at Higham Ferrers, Northamptonshire. He was brought up by his step-father, Sir Kenneth Murchison, a Tory MP, and educated at Felsted School and Downing College, Cambridge, where, in 1939, he joined the University Air Squadron.

Following a sustained period of night operations with 604 Squadron, he was rested from October 1942 while commander of the Radio Development Flight; in March the following year he returned to operations in No 85, a Mosquito night fighter squadron.

In June 1943 Wing Commander Crew received command of No 96 Squadron, leading its Mosquitoes against night raiders until the summer of 1944; this was when Hitler launched his so-called "revenge weapons" against London and the south of England.

Chasing pilotless V-1s – or "chuff bombs", as Crew liked to call them – was by no means tame target practice. On June 25 he was on the tail of a V-1, travelling at high speed, when the force of the explosion as he shot it down split open his own aircraft's nose.

Crew held the Mosquito steady long enough for his radar navigator, Warrant Officer W R Croysdill, to bale out over land. Then, as the Mosquito became uncontrollable, Crew himself jumped, landing safely near Worthing.

Completing his Second World War operational career when 96 Squadron was disbanded in 1945, Crew was awarded the DSO. The citation emphasised his "great skill in devising tactics to meet the menace" of the flying bombs.

That year he received a permanent commission and attended the RAF Staff College, before being posted in 1948 to command No 45 Beaufighter Squadron in the Far East. Operational once again, Crew led his squadron effectively against Communist insurgents aiming to destabilise Malaya.

Harassing the jungle-based enemy in 100 night attacks, he consistently drove the terrorists into the hands of the security forces, for which he received a Bar to his DSO. The Air Ministry stated that Crew had displayed "an almost uncanny knack in locating the target and attacking it on the first run in".

From 1952 Crew served in Canada, where he commanded an operational training unit and introduced the Avro Canada CF100 all-weather fighter.

After two years there he returned to command the all-weather development squadron at the Central Flying Establishment, with particular emphasis on trials of the Javelin.

Later he commanded RAF Bruggen in Germany, before returning to the Far East in charge of the air task force in Borneo from 1965; his role here was dealing with the Indonesian Confrontation of the mid-1960s.

Subsequently Crew commanded the Central Reconnaissance Establishment; he also served at the Ministry of Defence as Director of Operations (air defence and overseas), and was Deputy Air Controller of National Air Traffic Services.

He retired as an air vice-marshal in 1973, when he joined the planning inspectorate of the Department of the Environment. From 1987 Crew enjoyed a quiet final retirement in the Cotswolds, where he played golf and served on the Cotswolds District Council from 1991 until 1995.

Crew was appointed CB in 1973 and elected a fellow of the Royal Aeronautical Society in 1972.

In 1945 he married Virginia Crew (née Martin), the widow of a cousin, George Crew, who had been killed while an RAF pilot early in the war. They had a son.

SQUADRON LEADER
DONALD "DIMSIE" STONES

Squadron Leader Donald "Dimsie" Stones (who died on October 22 2002, aged 81) was a fighter ace who survived continuous combat in the fall of France, the Battle of Britain, the Battle for Malta and the Burma campaign.

He was 19, and had not long joined his first operational squadron – No 32, equipped with Hurricanes at Biggin Hill in Kent – when he acquired the nickname with which he became stuck for life. It was in March 1940, while the squadron was detached to Gravesend; Stones had absent-mindedly stuffed a book into his greatcoat pocket before appearing for breakfast in the mess; his fellow pilots observed the title, *Dimsie goes to School* – a book for five-year-olds.

On another occasion, Stones was visiting the Hawker mess in the former flying club at Brooklands. Accepting a whisky mac from an avuncular character he took to be some unimportant old codger, he teased the man that he would never get a chance to fly a Hurricane. Taking Stones aside, his flight commander Mike Crossley exploded: "You bloody young fool!" Stones's "unimportant old codger" had been George Bulman, Hawker's chief test pilot who had flown the Hurricane on its maiden flight.

As he saw combat, however, Stones's cockiness began to transmute into an exuberant confidence bred of the success which brought him a DFC while he was still 19, then a Bar as well as the rank of squadron leader aged 21.

In May 1940, having moved to No 79, another Hurricane squadron, Stones was sent to France, where he claimed five victories, and one shared, inside a week. He was later shot down and returned to England to receive a DFC – only to be greeted by his mother with the words: "I hope you haven't got into bad habits in France at your age."

Shortly afterwards, on the eve of the Battle of Britain, his flight commander got wind that the young pilot officer was sexually innocent: "Can't have you killed as a virgin. I'll take you straight up to Jermyn Street and ask Rosa Lewis [proprietress of the racy Cavendish hotel in St James's] to see to your education."

Donald William Alfred Stones was born at Norwich on

June 19 1921, and educated at Ipswich Grammar School before joining the RAF on a short service commission in May 1939. He frustrated his parents' efforts to obtain him a place with an insurance company, and was sent to learn to fly at a de Havilland civilian flying school near Maidenhead in Berkshire.

Stones remained with No 79 Squadron throughout the Battle of Britain. On September 7 he was shot down by a Bf 109; with shrapnel wounds in one leg, he crash-landed at West Malling in Kent. But by September 29 he had resumed operations, and destroyed a He 111 bomber.

From Christmas 1940 he was rested as an instructor, before rejoining No 79 on May 26 1941; in July he moved on to serve with No 249 in defence of the beleaguered island of Malta, and was soon flying with the Malta Night Fighter Unit.

On the night of November 9-10 the engine in Stones's Hurricane failed after take-off, and he baled out at only 500ft above the airfield. After he was picked up by a gunner officer, the pair celebrated with a rare bottle of malt whisky. Then Stones called his dispersal hut to report; he was greeted with an instruction from the flight commander to get off the line, because Flight Lieutenant Stones had just been killed in a blazing Hurricane.

From January to April 1942 Stones was in temporary command of No 605 Squadron; he was then again rested as an instructor, this time in Egypt. Within a month, however, he was on his way to India to command No 155 Squadron, which was re-equipping with American Mohawk fighters at Peshawar. Here Stones discovered that, at 21, he was the youngest pilot in the squadron. At the end of October he led 155 to the front at Imphal, on the Indian border, and was preparing for an operation when, to his dismay, he was ordered to Madras, where an Army provost officer, with whom he had clashed over some piffling matter of red tape, had started court martial proceedings against him.

In the event Stones was severely reprimanded, and lost his command and squadron leader's rank, reverting to flight lieutenant, for using bad language to the provost officer – or the "jumped-up policeman", as Stones referred to him later.

Stones next joined the Hurricanes of No 67 Squadron, at Chittagong on the Arakan front, as a flight commander. On May 15 1943 he was wounded by ground fire while leading an attack on a landing ground at Kangaung, and this incident ended his operational career; he was posted as a test pilot to units in Bombay and Karachi. Having returned to Britain, where he was seconded as a test pilot to Vickers at its Weybridge works, Stones was watching a fellow officer fooling about with a detonator when it exploded, causing Stones to lose his left eye.

When Stones left the RAF in 1946, he had scored a tally of seven enemy aircraft destroyed; five officially credited as shared; three kills unconfirmed; and several probables. It was a fine war record to carry with him into the next phase of his career, which was with the Colonial Service.

Shortly after joining, he was asked whether he was an experienced shot. Stones replied that he was. "Birds or buck?" he was asked. "Neither," he replied. "Men."

Stones served in Kenya, Tanganyika and Malaya as a district officer and magistrate. On some mornings during the Malayan Emergency, before going into his office Stones would pilot a light aircraft to drop sacks of money on plantations, enabling the managers to make up pay packets. In the late 1950s, following Malaysian independence, he farmed for a while in the West Country before returning to Africa.

It was in Africa, in the 1960s, that he established an agency for British and European aviation companies. Acting as salesman and demonstrator, Stones managed to do business in the face of coup d'etats and other discouraging events. He did not return home until the mid-

1970s, when he gave up his flying licence.

Having retired to Hampshire, Stones kept busy by crewing for a yacht delivery syndicate. He also published two volumes of autobiography: *Bograt* (1990) and *Dimsie* (1991).

Stones married, first, Betty Thompson in 1945; they had a son. In 1952 he married Caroline Crawford, with whom he had two daughters and a son, Oliver, who served with the Army in the Falklands. He married his third wife, a Dutch woman, in 1965. His fourth wife was Beryl Thompson, whom he married in 1984.

JAMES SANDEMAN-ALLEN

James Sandeman-Allen (who died on May 21 2003, aged 83) was the top-scoring fighter pilot over Malaya and Singapore as they fell to the Japanese in February 1942, and was among the last of the handful of surviving Hurricane fighter pilots to get out of Singapore in time.

"Sandy", as he was known to his friends, always remained sad that, over the years, the feats of the "Few" in the Battle of Britain completely overshadowed the exploits – and the losses – of those who fought so valiantly against overwhelming odds in defence of Britain's colonies in the Far East.

An RAF Volunteer Reserve (RAFVR) sergeant pilot, Sandeman-Allen had become top scorer, with a tally of at least seven Japanese aircraft, when finally he took off under fire from enemy troops as they arrived to occupy his airfield in Singapore.

With the airfield under constant attack, Sandeman-Allen's difficulties had been compounded by the refusal of Malay and Chinese labourers to fill in the craters; as a result, groundcrew and fellow pilots had had to manhandle his Hurricane over the crater holes. There were also frustrations caused by red tape. On February 9, only days before the surrender of Singapore, Sandeman-Allen had returned from combat at low level only to be reprimanded for low flying during the afternoon siesta.

On February 14, when he finally left for Sumatra in the Dutch East Indies (now Indonesia), he had been in Singapore for less than a fortnight.

His escape to Sumatra followed an encounter over Singapore on February 7 1942 in which he had surprised three Japanese army bombers. He set one of the enemy aircraft on fire, killing its gunner, and managed to damage the other two before being driven off by Zero fighters.

Having reached Sumatra, from where increasingly feeble resistance continued for a time, Sandeman-Allen occupied himself strafing landing barges and advancing Japanese troops. By the time British resistance had petered out, he had destroyed two more Zeros. In a final engagement, Sandeman-Allen's Hurricane was riddled with cannon shells and bullets, and he was wounded in the head and in one leg; he was forced to land, and immediately requested a cup of tea.

Sandeman-Allen's hand was shaking so badly that, as he put it, "the cup stirred itself". But thus fortified, and disregarding his wounds, he took off once more. When the situation became hopeless, he was offered a seat in a Dutch KLM Lodestar airliner bound for Australia.

On boarding this aircraft, Sandeman-Allen was incensed to find that fleeing Dutch colonials had stuffed the cabin with personal effects. Drawing his revolver, he insisted that they removed their possessions to make room for wounded RAF personnel. The Lodestar finally took off from a road used as a makeshift runway, and safely made its way to Perth, Western Australia.

After his wounds had been treated, Sandeman-Allen sought to return to Britain, and was put in charge of a party of boisterous Australian trainee aircrew on the long voyage home. On his battledress he sported the ribbon of his DFM, which he had been awarded for his valour in the Far East, and this helped to reinforce his authority.

James Sandeman-Allen, the son of a Lloyd's under-writer, was born on November 15 1919 at Bromley, Kent, and educated at The King's School, Canterbury.

Although he went on to be awarded a cadetship at Sandhurst, he decided to resign before receiving a commission. He was then accepted for a commission in the RAFVR and for pilot training. At this point, however, the authorities apparently mislaid his papers, putting his training in doubt.

Although this was a disappointment, Sandeman-Allen enlisted as an AC2 (aircraftman second class) and, successfully defying all attempts to classify him as an air-gunner, he was accepted for a pilots' course. Training completed, he sailed for West Africa in the battleship *Prince of Wales* (later to be sunk off Malaya) and, having reached the RAF station at Takoradi, was ordered to fly a Hurricane across Africa to Khartoum, in the Sudan. At one refuelling and rest stop, he awoke to find a giraffe poking its head into the Hurricane's cockpit.

From Khartoum, Sandeman-Allen flew up to Cairo, where he chanced upon friends serving with No 32 Squadron. He successfully organised a posting to join them as they were ferried from Suez to the Far East in the aircraft carrier *Indomitable*. The prospect of his first deck take-off, en route to reinforce Singapore, was daunting; but Sandeman-Allen managed it, before going on to prove himself as a fighter pilot.

Following his return home, Sandeman-Allen had a short spell, in the spring of 1943, as a flight sergeant in No 56, a Typhoon fighter-bomber squadron, before moving to No 182 Squadron on his promotion to warrant officer.

On June 30 1943, as Sandeman-Allen attacked an enemy flak (anti-aircraft) train in France at low level, a Bofors shell exploded in the right side of his cockpit, shattering his leg and his right arm.

Contriving to fly with his left arm, while setting the rudder against his useless leg, Sandeman-Allen turned for home. He later recalled: "The ends of the bones in my arm grinding together started to give excruciating pain, and this stopped me from nodding off in the sunshine from the loss of blood.

"I spent the trip across the Channel trying with great difficulty to persuade myself that it was wiser to stay with the aircraft and fly home, rather than drop into the sea."

Fortunately, he was able with great difficulty to keep control of the Typhoon. As he arrived home, and careered along the runway at Tangmere, in Sussex, an ambulance and fire tender raced alongside his aircraft.

Two groundcrew were lifting Sandeman-Allen clear when his right flying boot fell off, spilling blood and causing one of his helpers to pass out and fall off the wing; the man thus joined him in the ambulance.

Six months later, although still on crutches, Sandeman-Allen resumed operations with his squadron. Rested after further combat, he was posted to qualify as an instructor, but the requirement to fly at higher altitudes aggravated his wounds, and he was referred to Archie McIndoe, the wartime consultant in plastic surgery to the RAF at the Queen Victoria Hospital at East Grinstead in Sussex.

Sandeman-Allen was fixed up and invalided from the service. He later qualified as a chartered accountant, going on to practise in the West Country.

Never forgetting what he owed to McIndoe, Sandeman-Allen became a member of the Guinea Pig Club, the association of burned and smashed-up airmen who were treated at East Grinstead during the Second World War.

Becoming treasurer and secretary and, effectively, chief executive, of the club following the death in 1994 of the founding chief Guinea Pig, Group Captain Tom Gleave, Sandeman-Allen managed the club's funds superbly: he enabled the club to donate large sums to the Blond-McIndoe Centre for Burns Research and the RAF Benevolent Fund, while retaining sufficient financial resources to continue to help Guinea Pigs in need. For this, and his charity work, he was appointed MBE.

Sandeman-Allen also devoted himself to charitable causes in the West Country, particularly the Abbeyfield Trust. He was a freemason, prominent in the Three Pillars Lodge, serving variously as treasurer and master. For relaxation he enjoyed golf.

Sandy Sandeman-Allen married, in 1943, Joan Burton; they had a son and a daughter.

AIR CHIEF MARSHAL
SIR KENNETH CROSS

Air Chief Marshal Sir Kenneth Cross (who died on June 18 2003, aged 91) survived the sinking of the aircraft carrier *Glorious* by the German battle-cruisers *Scharnhorst* and *Gneisenau* on June 8 1940.

Three weeks earlier, "Bing" Cross had led 18 Hawker Hurricane fighters of No 46 Squadron off *Glorious* to reinforce the already faltering Norwegian campaign. They were destined for Skaanland near Narvik, but the airstrip proved boggy. Cross damaged his propeller in landing, and another Hurricane was flung on its back.

He declared the strip unfit, and moved 50 miles north-east to Bardufoss, where the squadron launched a series of successful operations although, unknown to Cross, the decision to evacuate had already been taken.

At 3am on June 7, Cross spotted in the Arctic daylight four Heinkel 111 bombers beginning a shallow dive attack on their airfield. He damaged one himself, then the port tank on his Hurricane was blown to pieces and a bullet hit the side of the windscreen; but it missed Cross's head because he had failed to put on his harness and was crouched forward over the control column; he managed to glide back from a height of 4,000ft to the airfield.

Since *Glorious* was not equipped with arrester hooks for Hurricanes, Cross had sandbags placed on their tails when No 46 Squadron's ten remaining aircraft landed on the flight deck. Eventually all arrived safely, and Cross turned in at 4.30am after a warming mug of cocoa. He was awakened by the sounding of action stations.

Cross reached the flight deck as a shell tore a hole only 15ft away, and more landed around him as he made for the quarterdeck at the stern of the carrier. The hangars caught fire. "Bad luck your Hurricanes got it with the first salvo," shouted a passing Fleet Air Arm pilot over the din of the continuing crashes and explosions. Then the public address system packed up, and the word to abandon ship was passed from man to man.

Inflating his Mae West, Cross jumped overboard and swam to a Carley float, where he was joined by his New Zealand-born flight commander, Squadron Leader Pat Jameson, with a "Permission to come aboard, sir?" Soon they were joined by 35 other survivors. Attaching a shirt to an oar for a sail and a mast, they found that there was no food or water; then a naval warrant officer came up with a small tin of brown sugar. By June 11, after they had spent 70 hours exposed to the Arctic weather, a Norwegian fishing vessel picked up Cross, Jameson and the four other survivors. They were taken to the Faroes where they joined the destroyer *Veteran*.

Suffering from considerable pain in their feet, Cross and Jameson were landed at Rosyth a week later, and sent for treatment at the Gleneagles Hotel, which had been turned into a military hospital.

Kenneth Brian Boyd Cross was born on October 4 1911, at Portsmouth, where his father was a surveyor and estate agent. Young Bing was educated at Kingswood School, Bath, until his father fell on hard times and he had to leave at 16 to work at a local garage for ten shillings a week. In 1930 Cross was granted a short service commission in the RAF, and the next year he was posted as a pilot officer to No 25, an Armstrong Whitworth biplane fighter squadron stationed at Hawkinge, Kent.

After the squadron was re-equipped with the Hawker Fury, a biplane then considered the RAF's most modern fighter, Cross showed a talent for aerobatics which he demonstrated at the 1934 Hendon aerial pageant.

He was then selected for the prestigious Central Flying School course, where the pilots wore unorthodox breeches and light blue stockings. He played rugby for the RAF and Harlequins. After qualifying as an instructor he was next posted to No 5 Flying Training School at Sealand, near Chester.

In 1936 Cross was awarded a permanent commission and attached to the Cambridge University Air Squadron; he was reluctant to leave the easy tempo and golf there when he was later given an intelligence staff post at Fighter Command's 12 Group headquarters.

Eight weeks after the outbreak of war on September 3 1939, Cross was highly relieved to receive command of No 46, a 12 Group squadron at Digby, Yorkshire. Following a brief interlude leading ineffective night fighter sorties, guided solely by searchlight beams, he was sent to Norway.

By late August 1940, when the Battle of Britain was at its height, Cross was passed fit enough for light duty. Still wearing carpet slippers on his damaged feet he was posted as group controller to Fighter Command's 12 Group headquarters at Watnall, Nottinghamshire.

Passed fit to fly in November, Cross pulled strings with a former Harlequins and Hawkinge friend at the Air Ministry and was posted at the end of the year to Egypt, though he was uneasy about sailing in *Glorious*'s sister carrier *Furious*.

Moreover, he found himself with the onerous task of commanding 40 Hurricanes and their pilots, which were bound for Takoradi in West Africa, before making a 3,600-mile flight to Egypt.

After arriving in Cairo, Cross received command of No 252 Air Defence Wing at Alexandria, then was posted in the rank of group captain to command No 258 Wing, Desert Air Force, during the frustrating retreats and advances of the Crusader offensive in November 1941.

Amid these difficulties Cross had the encouragement of Fred Rosier, commander of No 263 Squadron, who liked to remark: "You know, a shave every morning makes all the difference between an orderly withdrawal and a disorderly rout."

Following the final advance from El Alamein, Cross, commanding No 242 Group, supported the First Army in Tunisia, then covered the Sicily landings and the Italian campaign. In the New Year of 1944 he returned home to staff appointments at the Air Ministry, including a spell as director of weapons and air defence operations.

When, in 1958, it was decided to pep up a decidedly moribund post-war Bomber Command with some legendary fighter boys' get-up-and-go, Cross received command of No 3 Group. This put him in charge of the group's new Valiant and Victor nuclear deterrent V-bombers.

The next year Cross became Bomber Command's commander-in-chief. It was an inspired appointment in which he established close relations with the leaders of the US Strategic Air Command.

During this period Cross, a man who always knew his own mind, insisted – with a ferocity that filled even the ante-room to his office with tension – that the Command would be the best in the Air Force. During the Cuban missile crisis of 1962 he brought his Vulcan and Victor crews to unprecedented and prolonged states of quick reaction alert.

The following year Cross moved over to the comparatively tranquil fiefdom of Transport Command, where he was commander-in-chief until his retirement in 1967.

Cross worked successively as director of the Suffolk and London branches of the British Red Cross Society, and was president of the RAF Rugby Union.

He was awarded the DFC in 1940 and DSO in 1943; and appointed CBE in 1945 and KCB in 1959. He also held the Norwegian War Cross, the US Legion of Merit, the French Croix de Guerre and Légion d'honneur and the Dutch Order of Orange Nassau.

His memoirs, *Straight and Level*, were published in 1993.

Towards the end of the war, Cross met Brenda Powell, a WAAF officer, when she was updating map positions in the Air Ministry war room; he married her within a month. She was murdered in 1991 at an antiques shop in Chelsea where she worked.

They had two sons and a daughter.

WING COMMANDER
PETER PARROTT

Wing Commander Peter Parrott (who died on August 27 2003, aged 83) won a DFC and Bar as a fighter pilot during the Second World War, when he was officially credited with six "kills"; he was later awarded an AFC as a test pilot on early jet fighters.

Parrott had joined 607 Squadron in France in January 1940, aged 20, to fly Gloster Gladiators. The squadron was soon re-equipped with Hurricanes, with Parrott ferrying the first one from Rouen to Vitry-en-Artois on April 8.

"I was the only pilot in the squadron who had flown a Hurricane and the most junior," he recalled. "So the squadron had only a bare four weeks with the Hurricane before we were embroiled in the most disorganised, chaotic week or ten days of action. Few, if any, of our pilots had sufficient experience on type to be classed as operational."

On a sortie on May 10, the day on which the blitzkrieg came to the Low Countries, Parrott claimed two Heinkel 111s destroyed and another two damaged. The next day he shared another. Two days later he was jumped by Bf 109s near Louvain and had his radio shot to pieces.

Back at base, the dashing-looking Parrott was one of several pilots who were snapped by a visiting photographer. After being sent home on leave he saw himself on an RAF recruitment poster, with the words: "Volunteer For Flying Duties"; to his embarrassment, the posters seemed to be plastered everywhere.

Two days after arriving back in England he received a telegram posting him to 145 Squadron, operating from Westhampnett. Over Arras on May 22, the day after the Germans reached Amiens on the Somme, Parrott damaged a Bf 110. On May 26 over Dunkirk, four days before the start of the evacuation, he damaged an He 111 but was hit by return fire. Heading home, his engine seized up as he crossed the coast, and he crash-landed in a field at Great Mongeham, near Deal.

Following the German victory in France, Parrott was soon in the thick of the action during the Battle of Britain. On July 18 he shared an He 111; on August 8 he claimed a Bf 109 and a Ju 87 destroyed; and on August 12 a Ju 88 destroyed. In September he was posted to 605 Squadron at Croydon and awarded the DFC.

Peter Lawrence Parrott was born at Aylesbury, Bucks, on June 28 1920 into a family of local solicitors. After Lord William's Grammar School, where he was a boarder, he joined the RAF on a short service commission in June 1938. He began his ab initio course at Hatfield, flying for the first time on his 18th birthday.

Posted to Shawbury on September 3, he trained as a fighter pilot on Hawker Hart and Audax biplanes. His first tour was at Catfoss, towing targets with the Hawker Henley. He then converted to Hurricanes at St Athan before joining 607 Squadron at the beginning of 1940.

After the Battle of Britain, Parrott continued flying with 605 Squadron, and on December 1, while acting as weaver, he was jumped by a Bf 109 and his Hurricane was damaged; he dived to 3,000ft and, fearing a fire, baled out at low level over East Hoathly.

He stayed with 605 Squadron until the summer of 1941, when he began a 12-month stint as a flying instructor, followed by a year-long tour at Hullavington with the RAF Handling Squadron, preparing pilots' notes for new aircraft types.

In July 1943 he joined 72 Squadron at Pachino, Sicily, as a supernumerary, and a week later he went to 111 Squadron, also at Pachino, as a flight commander. On September 4 he destroyed a Macchi 202.

From October 1943 to March 1944, Parrott commanded 43 Squadron at Capodichino, Naples. He returned to Italy six months later for a second tour in command of 72 Squadron. He was awarded a Bar to his DFC and served in Italy as a wing commander ops until his return to Britain in June 1946, when he began training as a test pilot.

After qualifying in 1948 at Farnborough, for the next two years he test-flew early versions of the Vampire and Meteor, as they were accepted into RAF service at Boscombe Down. The casualty rate among test pilots of the early jet fighters was high, but Parrott survived to earn his AFC in 1952.

There followed tours of duty at the Air Ministry, RAF Staff College, RAF Nicosia and RAF Geilenkirchen, and he completed his service in the RAF in 1965 in the rank of wing commander.

Thereafter Parrott worked for Autair and, after it was

taken over, for Court Line, initially flying commercial domestic routes in Britain and subsequently flying members of the Libyan royal family and government on tours of the Middle East.

During the Arab-Israeli war in 1967, Parrott arrived at the airport in Damascus by taxi to see his plane in the process of being destroyed by Israeli bombers. After seeking sanctuary at the British Embassy, he was co-opted into leading an overland convoy of British civilians fleeing the conflict to Turkey.

During the 1972 Arab-Israeli war, Parrott flew (at Gaddafi's behest) to Uganda to collect Idi Amin, whom he was to take to Khartoum, where Amin was supposedly going to act as the mediator in the conflict. On landing the Learjet at Entebbe, Parrott and his co-pilot found themselves arrested and interrogated as suspected mercenaries, before Amin realised who they were.

In 1973 Parrott returned to Britain to work as a training adviser until his retirement in 1983. After the Falklands conflict, he organised the sending of a telegram "From the Few to the Few", congratulating the Sea Harrier pilots on their part in the campaign. He was also instrumental in getting the statue of Lord Dowding erected outside St Clement Danes in the Strand. Whenever he signed a photograph, a donation went to the RAF Benevolent Fund.

Peter Parrott married, in 1948, Mary Dunning, who had served as a WAAF in Y service during the Second World War, listening to German transmissions at RAF Chicksands; they had a daughter and a son, who served in the Fleet Air Arm.

SQUADRON LEADER
"BUCK" CASSON

Squadron Leader "Buck" Casson (who died on October 8 2003, aged 88) escaped from France in May 1940 to fly Spitfires over south-eastern England during the Battle of Britain; later he was a flight commander in Wing Commander Douglas Bader's "Tangmere Wing" before being shot down over northern France in August 1941.

Casson was one of the original three trainee pilots to join the newly formed 616 (South Yorkshire) Auxiliary Air Force Squadron at Doncaster in early 1939. Training at weekends and during the annual summer camps, he qualified as a pilot in early 1940 before being sent to France as a reinforcement to 501 Squadron. But, before he could join them, the train on which he was travelling was bombed outside Amiens and he lost all his belongings. Casson managed to escape by boat back to England from Cherbourg.

After a brief spell flying Hurricanes with 79 Squadron at Biggin Hill, he rejoined 616 at Leconfield, Yorkshire, just as the Battle of Britain gathered momentum. At lunchtime on August 15, the fighter squadrons based in north-east England were scrambled to face the Luftwaffe's most concentrated attack against industrial targets in Scotland and the north of England.

Casson flew one of the 12 Spitfires which met the enemy as they crossed the Yorkshire coast. Within minutes, 616 Squadron had accounted for six of the unescorted bombers, with similar results achieved by other northern-based squadrons. A few days later 616 flew south to Kenley, where the squadron was involved in some of the fiercest fighting of the battle as part of Air Vice-Marshal Keith Park's No 11 Group.

Casson and his colleagues were scrambled three or four times each day and losses mounted; in a five-day period ten squadron pilots were killed or wounded. On August

30 Casson was credited with a probable and a damaged Heinkel 111. Two days later he claimed a Bf 109 fighter, followed by the destruction of a Dornier 17 bomber.

After suffering severe losses, the squadron was withdrawn to Kirton-in-Lindsey on September 4 with just seven of the original 21 pilots fit to fly. With barely 300 hours flying time, Casson was now a veteran; he remained with 616 to train the new crop of young pilots, and to fly patrols over coastal convoys and during the Luftwaffe's night blitz in December.

A steel buyer's son, Lionel Harwood Casson, always known as "Buck", was born at Sheffield on January 6 1915 and educated at Birkdale School and the King's School, Ely, before embarking on a career in the steel industry. Although working in a reserved occupation, he elected to remain with the Royal Auxiliary Air Force on the outbreak of war when he completed his pilot training.

Once 616 became fully operational again in early 1941, it was transferred and came under the command of the new wing leader, Douglas Bader, at Tangmere. The squadron boasted a glittering array of outstanding pilots, including "Johnnie" Johnson and "Cocky" Dundas. Viewed as a steadying and mature influence, Casson became a section leader. On May 5 he shared in the destruction of a Junkers 88, but was hit by return fire, and was forced to bale out over Chichester harbour.

Throughout the summer of 1941, the wing was heavily engaged over northern France escorting bombers and flying offensive sweeps, and it made regular contact with Adolf Galland's fighters. Casson destroyed a Bf 109 on June 22, claimed a "damaged" two days later and in July claimed two Bf 109s as probables. The squadron suffered heavy losses, and Casson soon found himself appointed to command B Flight.

On August 9 the "Bader" Wing took off for another sweep over France. During a hectic fight in which

German fighters surprised them from above, Bader was shot down, and the wing was forced to scatter. Casson had accounted for a Bf 109 when he went to the aid of a lone Spitfire, but before he could join up he was engaged by a German fighter. Cannon shells damaged his aircraft's engine, forcing him to crash near St Omer, where he was captured. Shortly after his arrival at Stalag Luft III at Sagan, it was announced that Casson had been awarded the DFC.

During his years in captivity Casson's outstanding talents as a draughtsman were put to good use by the camp's escape committee. Throughout his imprisonment he maintained a detailed and beautifully illustrated diary of events, which he was able to preserve during the "Long March" in the severe winter of 1945, when the PoWs were driven eastwards ahead of the advancing Soviet Army.

On returning home, Casson rejoined the steel industry in Sheffield. In June 1946 he was one of the first to volunteer for service when 616 Squadron was reformed at RAF Finningley. The squadron was initially equipped with Mosquito night fighters but it soon reverted to the day fighter role, flying Meteor F 4s before re-equipping with the F 8 version.

In January 1951 Casson was promoted to squadron leader and appointed to command 616 Squadron. His outstanding period in command culminated in the award of the Esher trophy, awarded annually to the most efficient Auxiliary Air Force squadron. Casson retired in 1954, when he was awarded the AFC for his service in command of 616. He was also the holder of the Air Efficiency Award with Bar.

He never forgot his South Yorkshire roots or those of his squadron, and his consideration and support of his pilots and, in particular, his groundcrew attracted great affection and loyalty. When the Squadron Association was reformed at Finningley in 1988, Casson was one of the first to join and he never missed a reunion until he became too ill to attend.

As a token of respect, the Meteor fighter at the gates of RAF Finningley was repainted with his personal markings as squadron commander. On the closure of the airfield the aircraft was moved to the Yorkshire Air Museum.

Casson and his wife "Dorfy" were ardent travellers, sometimes touring the Continent on a motor scooter. He was a gifted painter in watercolours, a keen golfer and an ardent supporter of his local church.

TIM VIGORS

Tim Vigors (who died on November 14 2003, aged 82) served as a fighter pilot in the Battle of Britain and in the Far East before embarking on a successful and flamboyant career as a bloodstock agent.

The scion of a long line of Anglo-Irish landowners, Vigors spent much of his youth in England; but he never lost his sense of Irishness, and had his country's tricolour painted on the nose of his Spitfire. Despite his evident heroism, he claimed never to have been "possessed of that uncaring patriotism which caused so many young Englishmen... unselfishly to lay down their lives for their country".

Timothy Ashmead Vigors was born at Hatfield, Hertfordshire, on March 22 1921. His father was originally a stockbroker, but the family had been landowners in Co Carlow for centuries, and Tim's grandfather was clearly something of a rake: when his wife caught him in bed with a maid, he attempted to excuse himself thus: "If one is going to appreciate Château Lafite, my dear, one must occasionally have a glass of vin ordinaire."

Tim was brought up near Melton Mowbray in

Leicestershire. Aged eight, he was hunting with the Mendip when his pony hit the top of a stone wall and turned a somersault: "Unfortunately, I had landed with my face on a jagged stone," he recalled. "Lots of blood. My mother jumped off her horse, threw me back on my pony with the words: 'On, on Tim!'"

After leaving Eton, Tim enrolled in January 1939 as a cadet at RAF Cranwell – his godmother, an air enthusiast, had taken him flying, and he had immediately caught the bug. In February 1940 he joined 222 Squadron at Duxford, flying Spitfires.

One of Vigors's engaging characteristics was his frankness about what it meant to be a raw young pilot during the Battle of Britain. He later reminisced about how, at 4am on May 29, he had bade farewell to his lurcher, Snipe, and then accompanied ten other pilots to receive instructions from their commander, Squadron Leader "Tubby" Mermagen, who told them that they were to head for Dunkirk.

"I walked over to my aircraft to make sure everything was in order. My mouth was dry and for the first time in my life I understood the meaning of the expression 'taste of fear'. I suddenly realised that the moment had arrived... Within an hour I could be battling for my life... Up until now it had all somehow been a game, like a Biggles book where the heroes always survived the battles and it was generally only the baddies who got the chop. I knew I had somehow to control this fear and not show it to my fellow pilots."

When he reached the coast of France, and came under fire from a Bf 109, his first reaction was "extreme fear which temporarily froze my ability to think. This was quickly replaced by an overwhelming desire for self-preservation". He survived the encounter, and the next day shot down a Bf 109, feeling the same satisfaction as on the occasion when, on the family estate at Clonmel, he had "pulled down a high-flying pigeon flashing across the evening sky with the wind up his tail". Two days later, also over Dunkirk, he shot down his first Heinkel 111.

On the night of June 19 1940 Vigors returned from a night out somewhat the worse for wear for drink, and retired to bed at his base at Kirton-in-Lindsey, Lincoln-shire. When a Tannoy message called for a volunteer to intercept German aircraft which had crossed the coast, Vigors took to the air wearing his scarlet pyjamas under a green silk dressing-gown. He shot down another Heinkel.

Flying from Hornchurch, Essex, 222 suffered heavy casualties during the summer of 1940, and Vigors was twice forced to crash land his damaged Spitfire. But his successes over the Thames Estuary mounted, and by the end of September he had destroyed at least six enemy aircraft with a further six probables. In October 1940 he was awarded the DFC.

On October 30 Vigors destroyed two Bf 109s over Kent, but any satisfaction was dissipated by the loss, in the same action, of his fellow pilot and close friend, Hilary Edridge. "A wave of misery swept over me," Vigors recalled. "I just couldn't get my mind to accept it... I started to cry."

Two months later he was posted to Singapore, joining 243 Squadron as a flight commander. After a year he took temporary command of 453 (RAAF) Squadron, and immediately became involved in one of the most distressing events of his RAF career.

On the afternoon of December 8 1941, the Royal Navy's Force Z – which included the battleships *Repulse* and *Prince of Wales* – sailed north from Singapore to provide support against possible Japanese landings at Singora. 453 had been designated the Fleet Defence Squadron, and Vigors had established radio procedures with *Prince of Wales*. Despite this, Admiral Phillips, the commander of Force Z, maintained radio silence and did not call for support. On hearing of Japanese landings at

Kuantan, Phillips changed his plan and, still maintaining radio silence, altered course. In the meantime, Japanese reconnaissance aircraft had located Force Z.

When an attack against the ships appeared imminent, Phillips broke radio silence on December 10, and Vigors finally got the order to scramble his 11 Buffaloes. But it was too late: when he arrived, *Repulse* had gone down, *Prince of Wales* was sinking, and there was no sign of Japanese aircraft. All Vigors could do was to fly over the survivors in the water and provide support for the rescuing destroyers. He always felt bitter about the failure of the naval forces to call for his assistance.

After this, Vigors led his squadron to northern Malaya. On December 13 1941 he had just landed at Butterworth when Japanese aircraft arrived to attack the airfield, and he ordered his six pilots to take off immediately to intercept the bombers. He attacked a large formation, and some reports claimed that Vigors hit three bombers in the melee. Eventually, his Buffalo was hit in the petrol tank and he was forced to bale out. Although repeatedly attacked by Japanese aircraft as he swung below his parachute, Vigors managed to land in the mountains near Penang.

His position was not promising – he was severely burned and a bullet had passed through his left thigh – but he was found by two Malays, who carried him down the mountain to safety.

After being evacuated to India, Vigors held a series of flying training appointments before assuming command of RAF Yelahanka, responsible for converting Hurricane pilots to the Thunderbolt ground-attack fighter. He finally returned to England in 1945, taking part in the flypast for the anniversary of the Battle of Britain on September 15. He retired from the RAF in November 1946 as a wing commander.

Vigors began civilian life by setting up a photographic agency in Ireland, but then joined the bloodstock auctioneers Goffs. In 1951 he left to start his own blood-stock agency, quickly establishing a reputation for flamboyance: when commuting between Ireland and America, he would hire a super-constellation from Aer Lingus, using the back half as his bedroom and the front as his office.

As one of the first people to foresee a future for private aviation, Vigors also set up, in the late 1950s, a firm specialising in private and executive aircraft. Based at Kidlington, near Oxford, he had the agency for Piper aircraft. When his firm was taken over by CSE Aviation, Vigors returned to the bloodstock business.

He was a considerable player in this market. In 1964 he broke a ten-year record for Newmarket's December sales when he bought Chandelier for 37,000 guineas. Two years later, again at Newmarket, he paid a record 31,000 guineas, on behalf of an international partnership, for a yearling colt by Charlottesville. He also bought Glad Rags and Fleet, who won the 1,000 Guineas in 1966 and 1967 respectively.

Shortly before the war, Vigors's father had returned to Ireland, in 1945 buying a farm in Co Tipperary called Coolmore, where he trained racehorses. After inheriting Coolmore, Tim Vigors moved there in 1968, and it was he who began building it into the famous stud farm which it is today. Among the stallions standing there were Rheingold (the Arc de Triomphe winner whom Vigors bought in 1973 for more than £1 million), Thatch, Home Guard and King's Emperor.

An old friend of Vincent O'Brien, in the mid-1970s Vigors sold two thirds of Coolmore to O'Brien and John Magnier, continuing to work in partnership with them and with Robert Sangster. Later, having sold his remaining interest to Magnier and O'Brien, Vigors went to live in Spain, although he continued to work in the bloodstock business. He returned to Newmarket in the early 1980s, remaining there until his death.

In 1990 Vigors became racing adviser to Cartier, and it was he who initiated the Cartier Racing Awards, given annually to mark the performances of individual race-horses.

Tim Vigors was an outstanding ukelele-player, and knew how to enjoy himself. When he was 72 he described his ideal night out as "a Lloyd Webber musical, dinner at San Lorenzo and a bop with the lovely wife at Annabel's". When he was working on his memoirs, he confided to a friend, "It's so embarrassing – I'm only 21 and I've got to page 530." His autobiography was eventually published posthumously as *Life's Too Short to Cry* in late 2006.

He married his first wife, Jan, with whom he had three daughters, in the North-West Frontier province of India in 1942. They divorced in 1968, and in the same year he married Atalanta Fairey, widow of the aircraft pioneer Richard Fairey; they had a son. In 1972 he married, thirdly, Heidi Bohlen, with whom he had two daughters. In 1982, in Las Vegas, he married his fourth wife, Diana Bryan.

GROUP CAPTAIN
JOHN PEEL

Group Captain John Peel (who died on January 7 2004, aged 92) was credited with firing the first shots of the Battle of Britain, in which he commanded a Hurricane fighter squadron.

Peel was already an experienced regular officer when, in July 1940, he was put in command of No 145 Squadron, based at Tangmere on the south coast. Shortly after his arrival, he shared in the destruction of a Dornier bomber.

Four days later he was leading his squadron against a

force of enemy bombers when his aircraft was hit by return fire. Despite serious damage to his Hurricane, he pursued an enemy bomber 25 miles off the coast and is believed to have destroyed it.

As he returned over the English Channel, Peel was forced to ditch south of Selsey Bill and was found five hours later, semi-conscious in the sea, by the Selsey lifeboat. The next morning he was again leading his squadron, and over the next few days shared in the destruction of two more German bombers.

On August 8 – the day which subsequently became acknowledged as the first of the Battle of Britain – Peel is said to have fired the opening shots. When the Germans mounted an attack on an important convoy, CW 9, Peel's squadron was scrambled. He shot down a Bf 109 and a Stuka before damaging a second of the dive-bombers. Many fighter squadrons came to the defence of CW 9, but only Peel's was engaged three times, and he led it on each occasion. One historian stated that: "Squadron Leader John Peel's Hurricane pilots had fought the fight of their lives."

After completing his final sortie, Peel discovered that he had to provide a pilot for night-readiness. Four of his young pilots had been lost during the day's fighting, so he detailed himself for the duty "to rest the youngsters".

Three days later he was wounded when enemy fighters damaged his Hurricane, forcing him to land on the Isle of Wight, where the men from a local gun battery pulled him from the wreckage.

On August 13 it was announced that Peel had been awarded the DFC. The citation stated that "his out-standing quality as a leader has raised the flying standard and morale of his squadron to the highest pitch".

The son of Colonel Basil Peel, DSO, of the Indian Army, John Ralph Alexander Peel was born on October 17 1911 at Boscombe, Hampshire, and educated at Clifton. At the RAF College at Cranwell he excelled at sport, and graduated as a pilot officer in July 1932, when he joined No 19 Squadron, flying Bulldog fighters at Duxford.

In January 1934 he was appointed to No 801 (Fleet Fighter) Squadron flying from the aircraft carrier *Furious*. He later joined the permanent staff of No 601 (County of London) R Aux AF Squadron as a flying instructor, before returning to Cranwell as the college adjutant.

In September 1937 Peel returned as an instructor to No 601 (known throughout the RAF as "the Millionaires' Mob") based at Biggin Hill. During Peel's time, the squadron's members included Max Aitken and Roger Bushell, who was later the mastermind of the "Great Escape" and was executed by the Gestapo. Peel was promoted squadron leader in 1940 and appointed to lead No 145 Squadron.

After his service during the Battle of Britain, Peel was appointed wing commander, and left 145 in January 1941 to become the first leader of the Kenley Wing, which was equipped initially with three Hurricane squadrons, and included the Poles of No 312.

Kenley was one of a number of wings, led by experienced fighter pilots, which were formed in early 1941 by Air Marshal Sholto Douglas, the C-in-C of Fighter Command; his plan was to send his squadrons on the offensive over northern France to engage the Luftwaffe fighters. In addition to providing escorts for bomber formations, the fighter squadrons also carried out sweeps against ground targets.

On April 7 Peel led his squadrons on a low-level machine-gun attack against Berck airfield, and he destroyed or damaged three German fighters as they prepared to take off. Throughout that summer he was in action over northern France.

On July 9 his wing was escorting Stirling bombers on a raid to Mazingarbe when the formation was attacked. Peel's Hurricane was badly damaged, and he was forced to ditch off the French coast and take to his dinghy. An air-sea rescue aircraft located him and directed an RAF high-speed launch, escorted by a Navy patrol boat, to the scene.

As the rescue launch came alongside, German fighters attacked it; the crew threw Peel a tin helmet and shouted that they would be back. Spitfires were called to provide cover, and they engaged the enemy fighters as Peel was snatched to safety. The next day he was once again leading his squadrons on another raid over France.

On leaving the wing on August 5, Peel was awarded the DSO.

In November 1941 he was appointed sector controller and wing leader at Debden; he was in the post for 14 months and was twice mentioned in dispatches. Promoted to group captain in January 1943, he became Deputy Director of Fighter Operations at the Air Ministry, where he remained for almost two years. After a tour in the personnel department of the Air Ministry, he was sent to the Central Fighter Establishment, where tactics were being devised for the new generation of fighters, including the first jets.

Peel was appointed the first post-war assistant commandant at the RAF College Cranwell in January 1947, but a year later he decided to leave the RAF to take up farming.

Initially, he farmed in Cambridgeshire before moving to Devon. In the early 1980s he retired to Wiltshire; he had always had a talent for art, and he now spent most of his time painting.

Some years after the war Peel had returned to Selsey to see the lifeboat crew which had rescued him in 1940, and he became a life-long supporter of the RNLI. He had a great love of the countryside, and in old age was ßstill taking long walks on Salisbury Plain.

John Peel married Barbara Hutchinson, the widow of Squadron Leader P Hutchinson, in 1942; the marriage was dissolved in 1964, and he married, secondly, Sue

Marsden, who died in 1998. From his first marriage he had a son and two daughters, and another daughter who pre-deceased him; from his second he had a stepson and three stepdaughters.

WING COMMANDER DAVID COX

Wing Commander David Cox (who died on January 20 2004, aged 83) was a young sergeant pilot flying Spitfires with the Bader Wing when he received a "rocket" from the legless wing commander after shooting down a German fighter.

Early in September 1940, Cox shot down a Messerschmitt 109 over Maidstone. His own Spitfire was badly damaged during the dogfight, and he just managed to limp home to Duxford. Cox recalled that Douglas Bader, who was waiting for him, "told me that my aircraft was a bloody mess, and when I pointed out that I had got a Messerschmitt, he told me that a one-for-one ratio was not so f★★★★★★ good."

Cox had joined No 19 Squadron at Duxford in May 1940, and he shared in the destruction of a Bf 110 fighter on August 19 while still wearing his pyjamas – he had been scrambled just as he was getting out of bed. A few days later he claimed another German fighter over Colchester. After his brush with Bader, he probably shot down a Dornier bomber before destroying another German fighter on September 15, his final success in the Battle of Britain.

On this occasion, he had become detached from his squadron, and joined up with what he thought were six Hurricanes. In fact they were Messerschmitts. As he tried to disengage, he shot down one of the enemy fighters before escaping.

Cox's part in the Battle ended on September 30, when German fighters jumped his formation. He went to the aid of a comrade, but both were shot down, and Cox was forced to bale out over Kent. With fragments of cannon shell in his leg, he spent the next three months recovering in hospital.

During the Battle, his squadron was part of 12 Group's "Big Wing", led by Bader. Bader's tactic of joining up three squadrons to attack German bomber formations was controversial at the time, and has aroused strong emotion ever since. Cox, who flew on many such sorties, always felt that "while the theory might have been good, in practice it did not work".

David George Samuel Richardson Cox was born on April 18 1920 at Southsea, Hampshire, and was educated at Bournemouth Collegiate School. Determined to be a fighter pilot, he volunteered for service with the RAF but was rejected on medical grounds. This spurred him to develop his strength, and he was finally accepted for service with the RAF Volunteer Reserve. He learned to fly in the evenings and during weekends at what is now Gatwick Airport. After being mobilised in September 1939, he completed his pilot training before being posted to No 19 Squadron as a sergeant pilot. Within weeks, he was fighting in the Battle of Britain.

Having recovered from his wounds, Cox returned to action in early 1941. He took part in the first big fighter sweeps over northern France, when the RAF used the same tactics as those employed by the Germans a year earlier to lure their adversaries into battle. During one engagement, on June 17, Cox destroyed a Bf 109 near St Omer, but his Spitfire was seriously damaged. Returning across the English Channel with his engine failing, he lost height, and just managed to reach Dungeness, crash-landing on the beach.

After a rest period as an instructor, during which time he was commissioned, Cox was posted in May 1942 to

No 72 Squadron as it left for Algeria to support Operation Torch, the Allied landings in north-west Africa. Cox proved to be one of the most successful fighter pilots in the campaign, flying 134 operational sorties in a five-month period. After destroying three aircraft, and probably two others, he was awarded the DFC.

Promoted to flight commander, Cox achieved further successes and, by the end of his tour of duty in April 1943, had been credited with eight aircraft destroyed and one shared, and had probably destroyed a further six in addition to damaging five others.

The citation for the Bar to his DFC drew attention to his "outstanding leadership, which has been responsible for a large part of the successes achieved by his squadron".

Cox returned to England and served at Fighter Command before assuming command of No 222 Squadron equipped with Spitfire IX aircraft. Flying patrols over the Normandy beach-head, he damaged a Focke-Wulf 190. For his work over this period, the French government awarded him the Croix de Guerre avec Palme.

A car crash shortly afterwards interrupted his operational career, but he returned in January 1945 to command No 1 Squadron, flying Spitfires on long-range bomber escort sorties.

Cox was promoted to wing commander in April 1945, when he left for Burma. He became wing commander (flying) of No 909 Wing, with two Spitfire squadrons operating in support of the 14th Army's advance to Rangoon, and remained in command until the last day of the war against Japan. He retired from the RAF in March 1946.

Cox became a trainee manager with the wholesale division of Macfisheries at Fleetwood, before transferring to Grimsby in 1950 as depot manager. In 1961 he became controller of eight depots around the country, and in 1967 he transferred to the retail division, becoming chief buyer of fresh and frozen fish to 350 retail units. He retired in 1980.

Cox retained his connections with the RAF, serving as chairman of two Air Training Corps squadrons in Lincolnshire and as president of the Grimsby branch of the RAF Association. He was an honorary member of the Officers' Mess at RAF Binbrook, near Grimsby, and always yearned to fly in the station's supersonic Lightning fighter.

Eventually he wrote to the Chief of the Air Staff, pointing out that the 40th anniversary of the Battle of Britain was approaching; and, at the age of 60, and on the day the RAF celebrated the anniversary, Cox flew in a two-seat Lightning.

Two years later he flew his final sortie in a fighter, having been invited to appear on the television show *Jim'll Fix It* to meet a wartime colleague. As a result of this, he flew from Manston, Kent, to Goodwood in a two-seat Spitfire flown by Nick Grace.

David Cox married, in 1939, Pat Thornhill, with whom he had two sons and a daughter.

GROUP CAPTAIN
TOM DALTON-MORGAN

Group Captain Tom Dalton-Morgan (who died on September 18 2004, aged 87) was one of the RAF's most distinguished Battle of Britain fighter pilots; he later achieved considerable success during the German night attacks on Glasgow before playing a prominent role in co-ordinating fighter operations for the D-Day landings.

Dalton-Morgan had virtually no experience as a fighter pilot when he was appointed a flight commander of No 43 Squadron – "The Fighting Cocks" – in June 1940. The squadron was flying Hurricanes from Tangmere, near Chichester, and together with others in No 11 Group, bore the brunt of the Luftwaffe attacks.

He quickly established himself as a fearless leader. On July 12 he shared in the destruction of a Heinkel bomber, but was forced to bale out the following day when he destroyed another and was then hit by crossfire. With no badges of rank in evidence – he was wearing pyjamas under his flying suit – he was "captured" by a bobby who placed him in the cells along with the German bomber crew he had just shot down.

Despite being slightly wounded, Dalton-Morgan was soon back in action, accounting for four more enemy aircraft in the next three weeks. In early September he shot down three Messerschmitt fighters. After one engagement he was wounded in the face and knee, and had to crash land. His DFC praised him for "displaying great courage when his behaviour in action has been an inspiration to his flight".

Despite his wounds, Dalton-Morgan returned to take command of the depleted squadron after the death of the CO, and took it to Northumberland to train replacement pilots.

A descendant of the buccaneer Sir Henry Morgan and the Cromwellian general Sir Thomas Morgan, Thomas Frederick Dalton-Morgan was born on March 23 1917 in Cardiff and educated at Taunton School. He joined the RAF on a short service commission in 1935, and trained as a pilot.

Following service with No 22 Squadron, flying the Wildebeeste torpedo bomber, he joined the training staff at the Air Ministry. In April 1940 he applied to return to flying, and was appointed to No 43.

After the Battle of Britain, Dalton-Morgan's primary task was to train new pilots for service with the squadrons in the south. He was also required to establish a night-fighting capability with the Hurricane. Few enemy night bombers fell victim to single-seat fighter pilots, but

Dalton-Morgan, hunting alone, destroyed no fewer than six.

Three of his victims went down in successive nights on May 6-7 1941, when the Luftwaffe embarked on a major offensive against the Clydesdale ports and Glasgow. On June 8 Dalton-Morgan achieved a remarkable interception when he shot down a Junkers bomber, having made initial contact by spotting its shadow on the moonlit sea. After two more successes at night, he was carrying out a practice interception on July 24 with a fellow pilot when he saw another Junkers.

Dalton-Morgan gave chase and intercepted it off May Island. Despite his engine failing and fumes filling the cockpit, he attacked the bomber three times. He had just watched it hit the sea when his engine stopped. As he was too low to bale out, he made a masterly landing on the water, but lost two front teeth when his face hit the gun sight. He clambered into his dinghy before being rescued by the Navy.

His station commander, Wing Commander H Eeles, commented: "I consider this to be a classic example of how a first-class fighter pilot can attack an enemy while his engine is failing, shoot it down, force land on the sea, and get away with it." Dalton-Morgan was awarded a Bar to his DFC. He scored another night victory on October 2, off Berwick-on-Tweed. Finally, in February 1942, after 18 months in command, the longest spell by any of No 43's wartime commanding officers, Dalton-Morgan was rested, having shot down at least 14 aircraft and damaged others.

After a spell as a fighter controller at Turnhouse, near Edinburgh, he returned to operations in late 1942 to become leader of the Ibsley Wing. Here he had eight fighter squadrons under him, with the task of mounting long-range offensive sorties over northern France and providing scouts for the tactical bomber squadrons. After damaging a Bf 109 in December, he shot down a Focke

Wulf 190 fighter and damaged another during a sweep over Brest. He was awarded the DSO in May 1943, which recorded his victories at the time as 17.

His experience of escort operations led to his being attached to the 4th Fighter Group of the US 8th Air Force, which was just beginning long-range bomber escort work. He flew more than 70 combat sorties with the group. Promoted group captain early in 1944, he served as operations officer with the 2nd Tactical Air Force.

For a period he worked on an air-to-ground fighter control system with Major John Profumo, whom he rated as the most capable and generous Army officer he had met.

Dalton-Morgan engaged in planning fighter and ground attack operations in support of the campaign in Normandy, then moved to the mainland with his organisation after the invasion. Years later Air Marshal Sir Fred Rosier, who had been his CO at the time, commented: "It would be impossible to overstate Tom Dalton-Morgan's importance and influence on the conduct of fighter operations for and beyond D-Day."

A month before the end of the war in Europe, Dalton-Morgan learned that his only brother, John, who also had the DFC, had been shot down and killed flying a Mosquito. Dalton-Morgan remained in Germany with 2nd Tactical Air Force after the war before attending the RAF Staff College, and becoming a senior instructor at the School of Land/Air Warfare. Later he commanded the Gutersloh Wing, flying Vampire jets, before taking command of RAF Wunsdorf.

On leaving the service in 1952, Dalton-Morgan joined the UK/Australian Joint Project, at Woomera, where he managed the weapons range for the next 30 years before retiring in Australia.

He made regular trips home to visit the missile testing range at Aberporth, to see his family and to attend service reunions. He was a vice-president of the Hawker Hurricane Society.

Dalton-Morgan was recognised as one of the RAF's finest fighter leaders. Slightly scarred by his wounds, he had the dashing good looks of the archetypal fighter pilot, and always attracted the greatest admiration from his air and groundcrews. In an article on leadership written after the war, one of Dalton-Morgan's former pilots wrote: "He had an awesome charisma; some sort of special aura seemed to surround him... he was a born leader."

Dalton-Morgan was appointed OBE in 1945 and mentioned in dispatches in 1946, the year President Harry Truman awarded him the US Bronze Star.

His first marriage, in 1939, ended in divorce. In 1952 he married Dee Yeomans. He had a son and a daughter from his first marriage and six children from his second.

GROUP CAPTAIN
MIKE STEPHENS

Group Captain Mike Stephens (who died on September 23 2004, aged 84) developed an outstanding reputation as a fighter pilot, earning a DSO and three DFCs during the fall of France, the Battle of Britain and the siege of Malta, and while serving with the Desert Air Force.

As a squadron commander, he was so generous that he attributed shared "kills" to his junior pilots whom he wished to encourage. Thus, his official score of 15 enemy aircraft destroyed would probably have been doubled if it included his shared as well as his unreported kills.

The exploit that led to the award of Stephens's immediate DSO occurred when he was leading No 80 Squadron's Hurricane fighter-bombers on December 9 1941 on a ground strafing attack on an enemy transport column in the Western Desert.

As he attacked, Stephens noticed that his fighter escort was involved in a dogfight above him. Climbing to assist, he evaded two fighters and had almost reached the escort when he saw a lone Hurricane diving with a Bf 109 on its tail. Stephens immediately turned in to engage the enemy fighter but, after opening fire, he came under attack from another Bf 109 on his tail.

Stephens's Hurricane was set on fire and he was wounded in both feet. As the starboard side of his cockpit was blown out, he decided to bale out. He was half way out of his cockpit when he glimpsed his assailant overshooting him. He regained his seat, and shot the Bf 109 down in flames.

Only then did he abandon the blazing Hurricane, beating out his burning clothes as he descended by parachute before landing within 300 yards of the barbed wire of the German front line. He started to hobble towards friendly lines when he was picked up by Polish troops who confirmed his victory and took him to Tobruk.

The son of an Army officer, Maurice Michael Stephens was born at Ranchi, India, on October 20 1919, and educated at the Xaverian Colleges at Clapham and Mayfield, Sussex. In 1936 he joined the Port of London Authority; he had little love for his job but represented the PLA at rugby, swimming and rowing. Two years later he was accepted by RAF Cranwell, for which he boxed and rowed.

As a newly-fledged pilot officer in 1940, Stephens joined No 3, a Hurricane fighter squadron based at Hawkinge, Kent. When Hitler launched the invasion of the Low Countries and France on May 10, the squadron was ordered across the Channel where, within ten days, Stephens destroyed at least eight aircraft, including two Ju 87 Stuka dive-bombers. Landing from his final sortie, he was told that the squadron had been given 30 minutes to evacuate the airfield.

His aircraft had lost six inches off one propeller blade,

enough to shake the engine to pieces if he tried to take off. The engineering officer decided he must burn the aircraft, but, not wishing to return by truck and ship, Stephens got the groundcrew to chop six inches off the other blade. He then took off and clawed his way into the air before staggering back to an airfield in England. On his return from France, he was awarded the DFC and Bar.

In July his flight was detached to the Shetland Islands, where it became the nucleus of a new squadron, No 232, which he commanded. On August 23 1940 Stephens shared in the squadron's first victory, an He 111 bomber shot down over Scapa Flow. He next volunteered for service in Greece, leaving aboard the aircraft carrier *Furious*. However, he was diverted to North Africa where he joined No 274 and then was sent to Turkey.

He remained for eight months, during which he flew operational patrols along the Bulgarian border. He twice intercepted Italian S-84 reconnaissance aircraft intruding across the border, and shot both down in a Turkish Hurricane, while wearing civilian clothes. After inspecting the wreckage of each, he sent samples of ammunition back to England in the diplomatic bag. These victories were not included in his official score.

He returned to the desert to command No 80 at the end of November. After recovering from his wounds, Stephens was rested in Kenya before returning to the Middle East, where he was briefly attached to the newly arrived 57th US Pursuit Group in Palestine, flying P40 Warhawks. He then volunteered to go to Malta, where he joined No 249 Squadron, equipped with the Spitfire Vc, and destroyed eight enemy aircraft while damaging others.

On October 12 Stephens was shot down and parachuted into the sea. When his dinghy failed to inflate automatically, he held one arm out of the water to prevent water getting into his watch – a recent present from his parents – whilst he tried to inflate the dinghy with the other; he was soon picked up by a rescue launch.

Three days after being given command of No 229 Squadron, he shot down a German bomber, but his Spitfire was badly hit. He survived by flying at very low level through the Grand Harbour barrage before crash-landing on Takali airfield. A little later he was awarded a second Bar to his DFC; the citation recorded: "This officer has greatly enhanced the gallant reputation he so worthily holds."

Stephens now sensed he was pushing his luck, confiding to his logbook: "Chased Ju 88 out to sea. Shot him down. Running fight on the way home with eight Me 109s. Shot one of these down, but thought it only a question of time before one of them got me. Guardian angel working overtime!" After being promoted to command the Hal Far fighter wing, he noted: "Home at last. Thank God!"

Stephens did an instructor's course at the Central Flying School at Hullavington, Wiltshire, then became chief flying instructor at No 3 Flying Instructor School. His operational war was over, and he celebrated VE Day in America, where he was a liaison officer with the USAAF.

He returned in September to attend the RAF Staff College, and in 1948 went back to Turkey as an instructor. Three years later he was posted to Supreme Headquarters Allied Powers Europe in Paris, and was the first RAF officer to join the newly-founded NATO. After a tour at Cranwell followed by one at Gutersloh in Germany, he had a spell in the Air Ministry where he was responsible for fighter operational requirements. He returned to SHAPE before retiring in 1960.

He joined the aero engines division of Rolls-Royce in Paris before becoming a consultant to Pilkingtons and Lucas. He retired to the south of France in 1980, returning to England in 1992.

Stephens was a keen fisherman, the highlight of his

year being the two weeks he spent on the rivers of Ireland or Scotland with his son. A great raconteur, he would regale his friends with stories of his career as a fighter pilot.

Mike Stephens married, in 1942, Violet May Paterson, always known as "Blue" because she was tagged at birth with a blue ribbon to distinguish her from her twin sister. They had a son and a daughter. Blue died in 2000.

GROUP CAPTAIN
FRANK CAREY

Group Captain Frank Carey (who died on December 6 2004, aged 92) was one of the highest scoring fighter pilots of the 1939-45 War; he earned 25 "kills" in the Battle of Britain and in Burma, as well as several shared victories.

Carey's career was all the more remarkable for the fact that he entered the RAF in 1927 as a 15-year-old apprentice, a "Halton brat". He was first employed as a groundcrew fitter and metal rigger before being selected in 1935 for a pilot's course. He was then posted as a sergeant pilot to No 43 Squadron, the "Fighting Cocks", whose aircraft he had previously serviced.

Demonstrating exceptional panache in the Hawker Fury biplane fighter, Carey was selected for the squadron's renowned aerobatics team. In early 1939 No 43 Squadron was re-equipped with the eight-gun Hurricane fighter at Tangmere, Sussex.

Carey opened his account at Acklington in Northumberland, when he shared in the destruction of several Heinkel shipping raiders during the cold winter of 1939-40. This was followed by a short spell at Wick defending the fleet at Scapa Flow before he was commissioned as a pilot officer and posted with No 3 Hurricane Squadron to Merville in France after the German invasion. "We patrolled the front line wherever it happened to be at the time," he recalled. "The Hun aircraft were all over the place. You just took off, and there they were."

On his sixth day of continuous combat, having bagged some 14 "kills", Carey was shot down. He had attacked a Dornier 17 bomber and was following it down as it fell to earth; the pilot was dead, but the surviving rear gunner pressed his trigger to set Carey's Hurricane alight, wounding him in the leg.

The fire went out, and Carey landed in a field between the Allied and enemy lines. After thumbing a lift on the back of a Belgian soldier's motorcycle, he joined a party of refugees until a British Army truck picked him up.

Eventually Carey arrived at a casualty clearing station in Dieppe, where he encountered the 16th Duke of Norfolk, a fellow patient who apologised that he was there only because of his gout. As the enemy closed in they were put on a hospital train, which was subsequently bombed. Carey remembered how he and the duke scampered to safety, before returning to help move the seriously wounded. Meanwhile, the engine-driver had uncoupled the engine and made off.

Carey and his fellow walking wounded pushed the carriages out of the danger area, then kept going until they reached the Atlantic coast at La Baule, where the Hermitage Hotel served as an officers' hospital; he was soon sent to the less salubrious RAF tented depot, near Nantes. In the second week of June, together with "three similar RAF derelicts", Carey located an abandoned Bristol Bombay. Obtaining fuel from the French Air Force, they filled it up and took off, with Carey manning the rear gun.

After landing at Hendon in north London Carey discovered that he had been listed "missing believed killed" and awarded a DFC and Bar to add to an earlier DFM. He returned to Tangmere just in time for the Battle of Britain.

The son of a builder, Frank Reginald Carey was born on May 7 1912 at Brixton, South London, where he led a gang in mock battles in the streets before being sent to Belvedere School, Haywards Heath.

Once, after several ships had been lost from a Channel convoy during the summer of 1940 Carey and five other Hurricane pilots of No 43 Squadron arrived on the scene to find enemy aircraft "stretched out in great lumps all the way from the Isle of Wight to Cherbourg. At the bottom were Ju 87 dive-bombers; above these Bf 109s in great oval sweeps, and above them Bf 110s. Three of us got up into them. It was absolutely ludicrous – three of us to take on that mob."

At one stage Carey found himself "hooked on to the tail of the last of an echelon of 109s and started firing away quite merrily. Then I had an awful wallop. It was an Me 110 with four cannons sitting just behind me. There was a big bang and there, in the wing, was a hole a man could have crawled through."

Carey was slightly wounded by an explosive bullet, then another 110 damaged his rudder; but he managed to return to Tangmere only to be fired at by its anti-aircraft guns. That he managed to land was, he said, "a great tribute to the Hurricane".

He had been in combat up to six times a day when, on August 18, the squadron's losses enabled him to lead No 43 for the first time in an attack on a mixed bunch of fighters and Ju 87 dive-bombers. "The fur was flying everywhere," he recalled. "Suddenly I was 'bullet stitched' right across the cockpit." Since Tangmere was under attack he turned away and found a likely field for a crash landing at Pulborough, Sussex, where his Hurricane turned upside down.

After a spell in hospital Carey instructed at No 52 Operational Training Unit (OTU), and served briefly as a flight commander in No 245, a Hurricane squadron at Aldergrove, Northern Ireland. In November 1941 he received command of No 135 Squadron, also Hurricanes, as it sailed for the Middle East. But with the outbreak of war in the Far East, No 135 was diverted to Rangoon in Burma where there was little hope of doing more than slightly delaying the Japanese jungle march on India. On February 27 1942 Carey was promoted wing commander to lead No 267 Wing, though it could seldom muster more than six serviceable Hurricanes. After destroying several Japanese aircraft he was forced to move to Magwe.

Shortly afterwards Carey, painfully aware that "the parlous state of our Hurricanes was showing" and that communications with Calcutta had broken down, attempted to reach the city in a broken down Tiger Moth. Having got as far as Akyab, he hitched a ride as a spare pilot in a Vickers Valencia transport and arrived in Calcutta, only to go down with malaria.

By then he had started to attract press attention in Britain as the RAF's cockney pilot. His recovery was aided when he was awarded a second Bar to his DFC and was charged with forming a defence wing for the city. As enemy raids increased Carey turned the Red Road, the main thoroughfare across the city, into a fighter runway. "One advantage," he recalled, "was that it was quite possible to sit in Firpo's, the city's fashionable restaurant, and take off within three to four minutes. I managed it on several occasions."

Early in 1943 Carey formed an air fighting training unit at Orissa, south-west of Calcutta, for pilots who were unfamiliar with conditions and Japanese tactics. So exuberant were his young pupils that Carey devised a ruse to reduce their drinking and high spirits to an acceptable level. He enrolled them in the Screecher Club, whose members were graded according to their sobriety and granted privileges to match.

In November 1944 he was posted to command No 73 OTU at Fayid, Egypt, in the rank of group captain. Having been awarded the AFC, Carey returned home as the war ended in 1945; he was granted a permanent commission and posted to teach tactics at a newly-formed Central Fighter Establishment at Tangmere.

After attending the Army Staff College he reverted to the rank of wing commander to lead No 135 Wing, 2nd Tactical Air Force in Germany, where he flew Tempests. Converting to jets, he moved to Gutersloh as wing commander, flying. A succession of staff appointments followed until 1958 when he resumed as a group captain and was appointed air adviser to the British High Commission in Australia.

Carey, who was awarded the US Silver Star and appointed CBE in 1960, left the RAF in 1962 and joined Rolls-Royce as its aero division representative in Australia, New Zealand and Fiji, retiring to Britain 12 years later. His biography, *Frank "Chota" Carey* was published in 2006.

Before the war Frank Carey married Kay Steele, with whom he had two daughters; after their divorce he married Kate Jones; and after her death he married, in 1993, Marigold Crewe-Read.

SQUADRON LEADER "CHIPS" CARPENTER

Squadron Leader "Chips" Carpenter (who died on February 11 2005, aged 83) accounted for at least eight enemy aircraft in the Battle of Britain and the siege of Malta.

Carpenter was already lucky to be alive when he joined No 222 Squadron in May 1940 aged 19. He was one of the few survivors of the Gladiator-equipped No 263 Squadron, which had fought during the ill-fated Norwegian campaign. As the Germans overran Norway, the squadron was ordered to fly to the aircraft carrier

Glorious, which was to sail for Scapa Flow. But he was not allocated one of the surviving aircraft, and made his way home in another ship as *Glorious* was sunk with the loss of most of his squadron's pilots.

He had just 50 hours on Spitfires when 222 was sent to Hornchurch and thrown into the Battle of Britain. In a hectic week, beginning on August 30, Carpenter shot down three enemy fighters, claimed another as a probable, and was himself shot down and forced to bale out. Finally, on September 3, he was hit by "friendly fire" and blown out of his Spitfire. He parachuted to safety, but was badly wounded and remained in hospital for six weeks.

After returning to 222, he captured the mood of a fighter pilot's life when he wrote to his mother on October 30: "More exciting events to report. We ran into 80 enemy fighters at 30,000ft and I dived down and had a good old blast at one of them, but before I had finished I was myself attacked by two Bf 109s and was absolutely peppered with cannon fire. The instrument panel broke up in front of me and the engine started thumping and vibrating when I thought it might shake the wings off.

"I managed to struggle back to the aerodrome after coming down through 3,000ft of thick cloud with no instruments. I managed with a bit of luck and then made an ordinary landing, but one wheel collapsed and I was stuck in the middle. There were over 300 holes in the fuselage, the wireless had been shot away and the aircraft looked like a sieve. Nothing more to tell you now. Will write again soon. Love John."

John Michael Vowles Carpenter was born on April 21 1921 at Rhos-on-Sea. After attending Clifton College, he joined the RAF in 1938 and trained as a pilot at the Civil Flying School, Redhill.

Soon after joining No 46 Squadron in April 1941, Carpenter and his fellow Hurricane pilots embarked on the aircraft carrier *Argus* and sailed for the Mediterranean. At Gibraltar they transferred to *Ark Royal* and, on

June 6, they took off from the carrier, arriving at Hal Far airfield on Malta as the re-numbered 126 Squadron.

Carpenter's first success over Malta was on June 30, when he led a section of six aircraft which intercepted Italian Macchi 200 fighters, one of which he shot down. Three weeks later, on August 20, he shot down a balloon during an attack on the seaplane base at Augusta, but his aircraft controls were badly damaged by anti-aircraft fire. Despite this, he flew his aircraft over 120 miles of water to Malta.

From September he was in constant action, leading his flight and accounting for another four aircraft, including a Junkers 88 bomber as it approached the island. After six months of intensive operations, he was awarded the DFC.

After a period instructing fighter pilots in South Africa, Carpenter returned to operations with the Desert Air Force, flying Spitfires with 145 and 92 Squadrons, before being promoted to squadron leader and taking command of No 72 Squadron in January 1944. Based at Lago in Italy, Carpenter led his squadron on bomber escort duties and provided fighter support and beach patrols during the landings at Anzio. He returned to England in May, and shortly afterwards was awarded a Bar to his DFC. He then tested Typhoon and Tempest fighters for Hawkers.

After the war, he was granted a permanent commission. He held numerous flying appointments on fighter squadrons before being appointed as the adjutant of No 601 (County of London) Auxiliary Squadron.

He commanded No 80 Squadron from 1951 to 1954, providing air defence for Hong Kong, initially with Spitfires and then with the powerful twin-engine Hornet. After serving at HQ Fighter Command, and an appointment as a fighter controller, he retired from the RAF in 1959 to operate hotels on Bermuda and in South Africa.

After his first wife, Gwendoline, died in 1974, he took

up sailing; he and his dog, Hardy, sailed to Poole, where he was reunited with a wartime friend, Becky, who had once worked at Chez Nina, the London nightclub beloved by RAF pilots. They married, and Becky ran a members' club, which she called the New Fitz, while "Chips" had a café near Poole. Becky died in 1989.

AIR COMMODORE
SIR ARCHIBALD WINSKILL

Air Commodore Sir Archibald Winskill (who died on August 9 2005, aged 88) flew Spitfires during the Battle of Britain before being shot down over northern France in the summer of 1941; with the aid of members of the French escape lines he evaded capture and returned to England after crossing the Pyrenees into Spain.

Later in his career, as a senior officer, he served as Captain of the Queen's Flight for 14 years.

During the summer of 1941, Winskill was the flight commander of No 41 Squadron, flying Spitfires as part of the Tangmere Wing. He was escorting a formation of Blenheims on August 14 to a target near Lille when two Messerschmitt 109 fighters attacked one of the bombers. He immediately went to its aid and engaged the enemy fighters, shooting one down.

The second scored hits on his Spitfire, which caught fire. He was forced to bale out, landing in a field close to his burning aircraft, and a French farmer immediately ushered him to a cornfield where he hid until nightfall. Eventually, the farmer's son took him to the farmhouse where he was fed.

Archie Winskill spent the next few days in a barn, the farmer's son visiting him each day with food. After two weeks in a "safe house", Winskill – dressed as a farm-worker – was passed to various houses by bicycle before being put on a train for Paris. Due to the necessary secrecy, he was not aware that he was being passed down the "Pat" Line, one of the most successful escape lines through occupied France. Two other evaders had joined him, and they were taken first to Marseilles and then to Aix-le-Thermes, at the foot of the Pyrenees.

On the night of October 3 they were passed to an Andorran guide who took them over the mountains. After an arduous climb, they reached Andorra before travelling to Barcelona, where the British consul-general arranged to send them to Gibraltar via Madrid. Three months after being shot down, Winskill arrived back in England.

Fifty-seven years later, Winskill returned to France to meet Felix Caron, the boy who had helped him to escape. He described it as "a very emotional moment as we chatted away like long-lost brothers". The Frenchman still had Winskill's flying helmet, discarded by him as he hid in the cornfield.

The son of an early motor car dealer, Archibald Little Winskill was born on January 24 1917 at Penrith, Cumberland, and educated at Penrith and Carlisle Grammar Schools. He was very interested in technical matters and once commented: "I was born with a screwdriver in my mouth, not a silver spoon." Inspired to fly after a five-shilling flight with the Cobham Flying Circus, he joined the RAFVR in April 1937 and trained as a pilot. He was mobilised in September 1939, commissioned in August 1940 and trained to fly Spitfires.

Shortly after joining No 603 Squadron in October 1940, Winskill achieved his first success when he shot down a Bf 109 over Dungeness. In November he shared in the destruction of a Heinkel bomber, and on November 23 he shot down two Italian CR 42 fighters. The following January he was appointed flight commander of No 41 Squadron and flew on offensive sweeps and bomber escort sorties over France. Shortly after his return from Gibraltar, he was awarded the DFC.

No longer allowed to fly over France, because of his knowledge of French escape routes, Winskill flew Spitfires in defence of the east Scottish ports. In November 1942 he was promoted to squadron leader and given command of No 232 Squadron, which was preparing to depart for North Africa. He was soon in action providing close support for the British 1st Army in Algeria and Tunisia.

On January 18 1943 he was shot down off the Tunisian coast and was forced to bale out into the sea. He managed to swim ashore behind enemy lines, and walked through the desert to rejoin his squadron. Winskill was one of very few men who evaded capture twice.

In April he shot down a Stuka bomber and shared in the destruction of a second. During May his squadron was primarily engaged in ground-strafing the retreating German army, and he destroyed two aircraft on the airfield at La Sebala. His final success came when he damaged a mammoth six-engine transport aircraft on the ground. His tour ended in June, when he was awarded a Bar to the DFC.

Winskill spent the rest of the war as chief instructor of the Fighting Wing at the Central Gunnery School at Catfoss, Yorkshire, before taking command of the school. He was granted a permanent commission in the RAF and served at the Air Ministry until 1947, when he went to Japan to command No 17 Squadron with the Occupation Forces.

In 1949 he was appointed air adviser to the Belgian Air Force for three years and formed their first Meteor Fighter Wing. As a group captain he commanded RAF Turnhouse before moving to Duxford.

After two years as Group Captain Operations at the headquarters of RAF Germany, Winskill was promoted to air commodore in 1963 and served as the air attaché in Paris before being appointed the RAF's Director of

Public Relations. He had been in the post for 18 months when he had to handle the press release following the crash of a Whirlwind helicopter of the Queen's Flight. Amongst those killed was the captain of the flight. On February 15 1968 Winskill was appointed as his replacement.

Winskill had the task of restoring both the morale of the flight and confidence in the helicopter as a suitable form of transport for the Royal Family. The arrival of the very reliable Wessex as a replacement did restore confidence – within a year members of the Royal Family were using helicopters again. Winskill's arrival also coincided with the introduction of the Andover aircraft.

In 1972 Winskill arranged for the body of the Duke of Windsor to be flown from France to Benson in Oxfordshire, where it lay in state in the station's church.

Winskill was a man of great charm and courtesy. He was a particular favourite of the Queen Mother, who was once heard to say: "It was for men like Sir Archie that made it worthwhile putting on my lipstick." He made annual visits to her summer residence at the Castle of Mey in Caithness. In 2000 he was taken by members of her staff round the island of Stroma in a high-speed rib during rough weather. He commented that it had been "as much fun as flying a Spitfire".

He enjoyed golf and tennis, and was still taking long walks and visiting the gymnasium until shortly before his death. He was also a keen bridge player.

Winskill was appointed CBE in 1960, CVO in 1973 and KCVO in 1980; he was appointed Extra Equerry to the Queen in 1968.

Archie Winskill married, in 1947, Christiane Bailleux, from the Pas de Calais. They had a daughter, and a son who pre-deceased him.

GROUP CAPTAIN
EDWARD "HAWKEYE" WELLS

Group Captain "Hawkeye" Wells (who died on November 4 2005, aged 88) was one of Fighter Command's outstanding pilots, credited with shooting down at least 12 enemy aircraft and probably destroying and damaging many others.

He began his brilliant fighting career during the Battle of Britain flying Spitfires with No 266 Squadron before transferring, in September 1940, to No 41, based at Hornchurch. He scored his first victory on October 17 when he shot down a Messerschmitt 109 fighter off the French coast. Twelve days later he probably destroyed a second and on November 2 he accounted for another Bf 109.

He was the first pilot to intercept an Italian Fiat CR 42 over England in November, shooting it down off Ordfordness on November 11. By the end of the year he had destroyed another enemy fighter. Wells had been a champion 12-bore shot during his schooldays in New Zealand, and his outstanding marksmanship earned him the nickname "Hawkeye".

In March 1941 he joined No 485 Squadron, the first all-New Zealand fighter squadron, scoring its first success on July 5 when he shot down a Bf 109 whilst escorting Stirling bombers over Lille. His successes mounted steadily, and in August he was awarded the DFC.

Almost all Wells's victims were fighters. He destroyed one on August 19, another a month later, two more on September 21 and probably destroyed another on October 2. In November, having completed 46 sorties over enemy territory, he was awarded a Bar to his DFC.

Wells was promoted to squadron leader and took command of No 485 in November. When the German battleships *Scharnhorst* and *Gneisenau* slipped out of Brest on February 12 1942, No 485 was one of the squadrons sent to attack the enemy fighters. Wells found no fighters to engage, and instead led an attack, through intense flak, on an E-boat, leaving the vessel sinking.

Wells shot down a Focke Wulf 190 over Abbeville on April 16, another on April 24 and damaged a third the following day. In early May he was promoted to wing commander and appointed to lead the Kenley Wing. He was awarded the DSO in July for "courage and inspiring leadership".

The son of a farmer, Edward Preston Wells was born on July 26 1917 at Cambridge, New Zealand. Known to family and friends as Bill, he was educated at the local high school before taking up farming. He joined the RNZAF in April 1939 and trained to be a pilot. In June 1940 he accompanied many of his fellow countrymen sailing for England in the passenger ship *Rangitata*.

In August 1942, after two years' continuous fighting, he was rested. Having taken part in the Battle of Britain, he had carried out 133 sweeps over enemy-occupied territory, probably more than any other pilot in Fighter Command. He was sent back to New Zealand, where he was offered an important post, but rejected it, preferring to return to Europe. He travelled back in March 1943 via the United States, where he visited aircraft factories and addressed the workers.

On his return he was sent to a course at the RAF Staff College, after which he again took over the Kenley Wing, which he led until November, when he went to HQ No 11 Group, responsible for fighter training. He found some of the work tedious and would regularly abscond to shoot mallard. These ventures did not endear him to his stuffy air commodore who, on one occasion, asked for the whereabouts of his training officer. Wells was finally tracked down and summoned; the air commodore was not amused when Wells offered him a brace of duck, which was turned down.

Wells returned to operations in March 1944 as leader of the Tangmere Wing, equipped with the latest mark of

Spitfire. He destroyed a Messerschmitt night fighter on the ground and led his wing on many sweeps over northern France during the build-up to D-Day. He later led the Detling and West Malling Wings before being rested in November 1944, when he went to the Central Fighter Establishment to command the Day Fighter Leaders' School.

Wells's amazing eyesight and superb shooting skills made him one of the RAF's outstanding pilots. Johnnie Johnson, the RAF's most successful fighter pilot during the Second World War, considered him the "complete wing leader and the finest shot and most accurate marksman in Fighter Command".

After the war Wells transferred to the RAF, serving in various appointments involved with fighter operations. In 1954 he took command of the air defence radar station at Bawdsey, on the Suffolk coast, where he was able to indulge his love of wildfowling. After serving with the Joint Planning Staff he retired from the RAF as a group captain in June 1960.

After a spell farming near Woodbridge, in 1975 Wells moved to Spain. He travelled around the world gathering species of sub-tropical fruits, many of which he grew commercially. He received many awards from the Spanish authorities for his fruit-growing and for his studies into fruit diseases.

From his boyhood in New Zealand, Wells had been deeply attached to the countryside. As well as being a fine shot, he was an expert fly-fisherman and could recognise any bird by sight or by its call. He was a modest and charming host with a great sense of humour.

In 1943 he married Mary de Booy, who three years earlier, aged 17, had escaped in a fishing boat with her parents and sister from Nazi-occupied Holland, landing on the east coast with no belongings. The de Booy family soon became involved with the Red Cross, and the two sisters were in demand for tea dances in London held for

Commonwealth members of the RAF. When an invitation was received by his squadron, Wells was detailed by his commanding officer to attend, thus meeting his future wife. She died in 2001. They had a son and a daughter.

WING COMMANDER
"BUNNY" CURRANT

Wing Commander "Bunny" Currant (who died on March 12 2006, aged 95) was twice awarded the DFC during the Battle of Britain, during which he was one of the RAF's most successful fighter pilots, credited with destroying at least 13 enemy aircraft.

Currant achieved his first success on August 15 1940, the day the Luftwaffe mounted its biggest raid against the north of England. In a co-ordinated attack, large formations of bombers attacked from Norway and Denmark and were intercepted by the few RAF fighter squadrons based in the north-east. Currant and his fellow pilots of No 605 Squadron scrambled in their Hurricanes and engaged the bombers off Newcastle. Currant shot down two Heinkel bombers and probably destroyed a third. The Luftwaffe's losses were so high that they never returned in force to the north.

No 605 was transferred to Croydon and fought throughout the most intense phase of the battle. On September 8 Currant damaged three bombers and shot one down over the airfield in full view of his groundcrew. He shared in the destruction of two more the following day. September 15 was the climax of the fighting, and during a morning scramble Currant shot down two Dornier bombers and damaged three others before his Hurricane was hit and he had to crash land. He was airborne again in the afternoon and shot down a Messerschmitt fighter.

By the end of September he had accounted for two more fighters and was awarded the DFC "for his great skill and courage in air combats in the defence of London". He celebrated the award by shooting down two more enemy fighters. The Battle of Britain officially ended on October 31, by which time Currant had added another to his score.

In December he destroyed a Messerschmitt Bf 109 over Dover and in the New Year was awarded a Bar to his DFC.

When Currant left 605 in January for a rest tour the squadron's diarist commented: "Bunny Currant had without doubt been one of the most successful pilots in the history of the squadron and whose leadership, wit and outstanding fighting spirit would be very sorely missed."

The son of a Luton hatter, Christopher Frederick Currant was born on December 14 1911 and educated at Rydal School. He joined the RAF in 1936 and trained as a pilot, when he gained the nickname "Bunny" which remained with him for the rest of his life.

After serving with No 46 and No 151 Squadrons flying biplane Gauntlet fighters, Currant converted to the Hurricane and joined No 605 (County of Warwick) Squadron in April 1940, when he was commissioned. He survived a mid-air collision before the squadron moved to Hawkinge in Kent to provide support for the beleaguered British Expeditionary Force.

Operating on his first patrol over France on May 22, he attacked three bombers over Arras. The engine of his Hurricane stopped and he prepared to bale out. Having stepped on to the wing he realised that the aircraft was still able to fly; so he climbed back into the cockpit and crash-landed in a field, breaking his nose. He made his way to Calais and eventually boarded a ship to return to England where he rejoined No 605 still carrying his parachute.

After the Battle of Britain Currant served as chief

flying instructor of a unit training fighter pilots. On August 14 1941 he began his second tour of operations in command of No 501 Squadron equipped with the Spitfire. Flying from Ibsley in the New Forest, he led many sorties escorting bombers over France and against shipping. On one occasion three German fighters attacked him and his aircraft was shot up. The instrument panel was destroyed and a bullet struck the back of his head – but Currant managed to escape at low level. In great pain he landed at a forward airfield, but his aircraft turned over on to its back due to the undercarriage tyres having been shot through. He was trapped in the petrol-soaked cockpit but was soon rescued from the wreckage. After a month in hospital, he returned to flying with fragments of shrapnel still in his head.

During September 1941 Currant played himself in the film *First of the Few*, which starred David Niven and Leslie Howard. Currant was cast as the squadron commander "Hunter Leader" and flew his Spitfire in the aerial sequences. In one shot he was shown firing his guns at a Heinkel bomber. The film was described as: "The epic of the Spitfire with pilots of Fighter Command." It was considered a great success.

Currant flew many sweeps over France during the spring of 1942 and in July he was promoted to wing commander to take charge of the three Spitfire squadrons that formed the Ibsley Wing. On July 7 he was awarded the DSO, being described as "a most courageous pilot and a brilliant leader". In August 1942 he moved to Zeals in Wiltshire to form and command No 122 Wing equipped with Spitfires, which came under the control of the new 2nd Tactical Air Force.

In April 1943 Currant added a Belgian Croix de Guerre to his British decorations. He led his wing during the D-Day landings in June 1944 before departing for a lecture tour in America. On his return, he crossed to France to join No 84 Group Control Centre working in the tactical air operations centre co-ordinating ground attack operations in support of the Army. He was twice mentioned in dispatches.

Currant remained in the RAF after the war and spent three years in Washington on the staff of the Joint Chiefs of Staff. After two years as the wing commander administration at the fighter airfield at Wattisham, and a year at the Ministry of Supply dealing with guided missiles, he left for Norway, where he joined the staff of the Royal Norwegian Air Force Staff College. At the end of his two-year appointment, the Norwegians asked him to remain for a further two years. On his departure in 1959 the Norwegian government awarded him the Order of St Olaf.

Currant retired from the RAF as a wing commander and joined Hunting Engineering in 1960, undertaking research and development work on weapons for the RAF. He finally retired in 1976.

He gave great support to local Air Training Corps squadrons and to the RAF Association. He was also a strong supporter of the Battle of Britain Memorial Trust. A keen sportsman, in addition to refereeing hockey matches, he umpired at a number of Wimbledon tennis championships. A passionate golfer, he claimed that he started to make his most significant improvement after he was 70.

"Bunny" Currant married, in 1942, Cynthia Brown. They had three sons and a daughter.

WING COMMANDER
JOHNNY CHECKETTS

Wing Commander Johnny Checketts (who died on April 21 2006, aged 94) was one of the band of New Zealanders who left their native land to gain considerable success as fighter pilots with the RAF during the Second World War.

Flying the latest version of the Spitfire with No 611 (West Lancashire) Squadron, Checketts had already gained some success against the formidable Focke Wulf 190 fighter when he was appointed in July 1943 to command No 485 (NZ) Squadron, also equipped with the Spitfire Mark IX and flying from Biggin Hill. Within two weeks of assuming command he had shot down four fighters and damaged two others during combat over northern France.

Over St Pol on August 9 he led a section of his squadron against eight Messerschmitt Bf 109s. He destroyed three of them and damaged another as it escaped. The other three New Zealand pilots in the section destroyed one each, and only one enemy fighter escaped unscathed. Following this action Checketts was awarded the DFC.

Over the next three weeks he destroyed three more FW 190s and probably a fourth. On September 6 his squadron provided high cover for a force of USAAF Marauders bombing marshalling yards at Cambrai. Twenty FW 190s attacked the Spitfires from above. Checketts shot one down but was then attacked by several others, who set his aircraft on fire. Burned and wounded in the legs and arms, he struggled to bale out and landed in a field full of French farm workers who immediately rushed to his aid. A boy took him on the back of his bicycle to a hiding place deep in a wood. Badly burned about the face and barely able to walk, he lost consciousness.

When he came to, a French farmer escorted him as they crawled through a cordon of Germans. He was taken to a safe house where he met another fighter pilot. Initially Checketts was unable to walk, but the farmer's wife nursed him back to health before members of the Resistance moved him between houses. With a group of

11 other evaders he was taken via Paris to the Brittany coast, where a lobster boat transferred them to a waiting Royal Navy launch, which brought them to Devon. He arrived back at Biggin Hill seven weeks after being shot down.

Checketts was rested from operations and posted to the Central Gunnery School as an instructor. Shortly afterwards, he was awarded the DSO.

John Milne Checketts was born on February 12 1912 at Invercargill on New Zealand's South Island. He was educated at Invercargill South School, and Southland Technical College, where he studied Engineering. He undertook an apprenticeship as a motor mechanic, developing a passion for motorcycles which never left him. As a youth he was a keen motorcycle scrambler in addition to being a fine shot.

Though he was anxious to fly when the war broke out, the RNZAF would not accept him until he had undertaken further education, and he finally entered the service in October 1940. After training as a pilot he sailed for England and, once he had completed further training on the Spitfire, he was commissioned and joined No 485 (NZ) Squadron. During the next six months he damaged at least three enemy aircraft, but would not submit claims.

On May 4 1942 an FW 190 hit Checketts's Spitfire and he was forced to bale out over the English Channel, having been wounded in the leg. He was rescued by an RAF air-sea rescue launch, commenting that the Channel "was bloody cold and I could never have survived the night". After completing a period as a gunnery instructor he joined No 611 at Biggin Hill and was soon made a flight commander. He damaged a number of enemy fighters but would still not make a positive claim. Finally, on May 30, he shot down an FW 190.

In later life Checketts commented on his first confirmed victory: "The pilot didn't bale out and it upset me considerably. He was somebody's boy with a mother and a father, but I also thought it could easily have been me. After that I didn't let it worry me because it was him or me." Within two weeks of this first success, he left to command No 485 Squadron.

Following his successful escape from the Germans in France and his rest tour as an instructor, Checketts returned to operations. After a brief period as the commanding officer of No 1 Squadron flying Typhoons he was promoted to wing commander in No 142 Spitfire Wing, based on the south coast. He led the wing during the Normandy landings in June 1944, when he damaged a Messerschmitt Bf 109. Within days, the wing was engaged against the new menace of the V-1 flying bomb, and Checketts shot down two of them in the first three days as they crossed Kent.

On August 1 he shot down another German fighter. His wing provided cover for the Arnhem airborne landings, when he damaged another Bf 109, his final success. He was credited with destroying at least 14 enemy fighters and sharing in the destruction of another in addition to the two flying bombs. He probably destroyed two other aircraft and damaged eight.

As well as his British decorations, he was awarded the US Silver Star and the Polish Cross of Valour.

In October 1944 Checketts had completed more than 400 operational sorties when he was made responsible for developing tactics at the Central Fighter Establishment. He returned to New Zealand in September 1945 and transferred to the RNZAF. Over the next few years he was based initially at Wigram before moving to Fiji to command the RNZAF base and No 5 (Flying Boat) Squadron. He returned to England to complete the RAF Staff College course before spending a year on the RAF staff in Germany.

On his return to New Zealand in April 1951 he commanded the Vampire jet fighter wing at Ohakea, then moved to a flying training school at Taieri, near Dunedin, where he also acted as the ADC to the Governor General, General Bernard Freyberg, VC. He finally retired from the RNZAF in March 1955.

Checketts established his own crop-spraying firm, using Tiger Moths and Piper Cubs, until demand dropped in 1958. He then became a salesman of agricultural chemicals until 1963. After working with the Otago Acclimatisation Society for a number of years he moved to Christchurch and joined the North Canterbury Acclimatisation Society, finally retiring in 1982. He took a great interest in conservation, and received a citation from the Nature Conservation Council for bringing the effects of water pollution to public awareness.

After his retirement he became involved with the RNZAF Museum at Wigram and helped restore Tiger Moth aircraft for display flying. An airworthy Spitfire in the New Zealand Alpine Fighter Collection carries his wartime markings, J-MC.

To those who knew him in later life Checketts was an unassuming man who never considered his war service as anything special. His experience evading the Germans in France left him with a deep affection for the French. He is the subject of a biography, *Johnny Checketts: The Road to Biggin Hill*.

He had two sons and a daughter.

WING COMMANDER
GEORGE "GRUMPY" UNWIN

Wing Commander George "Grumpy" Unwin (who died on June 28 2006, aged 93) was one of the most successful fighter pilots during the Battle of Britain and was twice awarded the DFM; he was one of only 60 men to receive the double award during the Second World War.

In August 1938 Unwin was a sergeant pilot serving on No 19 Squadron when it became the first to receive the Spitfire. He was one of the original RAF pilots to fly the new fighter and, in the early days, he flew regularly as Douglas Bader's wingman.

No 19 was heavily engaged during the Dunkirk crisis in May 1940. Although an experienced pilot by then, Unwin was not allocated an aircraft for the first sortie. He complained bitterly, and it was this that earned him his nickname, which remained with him for the rest of his life. He was in action the next day, however, and soon registered his first success. The squadron was in the thick of the intense fighting and, by the end of the evacuation he had claimed the destruction of five enemy aircraft, two of them unconfirmed.

Unwin flew throughout the Battle of Britain, mainly from Duxford. On August 16 his section of four aircraft attacked a large formation of fighters escorting bombers, and he shot down one fighter over Clacton.

Early September saw the introduction of the contro-versial Bader "Big Wing" employing three squadrons, including No 19. The wing flew its first offensive patrol on September 7. After attacking a fighter, Unwin became detached from the rest of his formation. Finding himself alone, he saw Hurricanes engaging a big formation of bombers and went to assist them. A large force of Messerschmitt Bf 109s immediately attacked him over Ramsgate, and he turned to engage them. He hit at least five and two were confirmed as destroyed.

On September 15, the height of the battle, Unwin and his section attacked a force of 30 Bf 109 fighters escorting a large formation of enemy bombers. He dived on one and shot down one of the escorts over London before climbing back to height, where he found two others flying alone. He shot down both. Two days later he was awarded an immediate DFM for "his great courage in shooting down ten enemy aircraft".

Over the next few weeks Unwin accounted for three more German fighters and he shared in the destruction of two others. He achieved his final success on November 28, when he was patrolling over a convoy. Early in December it was announced that Unwin had been awarded a Bar to his DFM.

The son of a Yorkshire miner, George Cecil Unwin was born on January 18 1913 at Bolton-on-Dearne. He was educated at the local grammar school, where he was a fine footballer (he later turned out for the RAF). Determined not to join his father in the mines, he answered an advertisement offering apprenticeships in the RAF; he joined as a boy clerk when he was 16 and trained at the air force's apprentice school at Ruislip.

After serving at Uxbridge for four years Unwin was selected for pilot training in 1935 and the following year he joined No 19, flying the biplane Gauntlet fighter. He served with the squadron for four years, and was one of the very few to fly in action throughout the Battle of Britain and survive unscathed. In December 1940 he was rested.

Initially, Unwin would not apply for a commission, since a senior flight sergeant earned a few more shillings than a junior officer. Once the rules were changed he relented, and was interviewed a number of times; but his background and passion for football did not impress the selection boards. A colleague tipped him off that an interest in horses would make a good impression, and for his next interview he decided to tell the panel of his knowledge and love of all things equine. The board accordingly recommended him for a commission – he had omitted to tell them that his experience was limited to the occasional meeting with the pit ponies at his father's coal mine. He was made a pilot officer in July 1941.

Unwin became a flying instructor, first at Cranwell and then at Montrose, where he remained until October

1943. He then converted to the Mosquito before joining No 613 Squadron in April 1944; he was based at Lasham and employed on night intruder operations. As D-Day dawned, No 613 roamed behind enemy lines attacking fuel supplies, airfields and road and rail links.

By October Unwin had flown more than 50 intruder operations, and he was sent to the Central Gunnery School as an instructor, remaining until June 1946. With the resurrection of the Royal Auxiliary Air Force, he joined No 608 (North Riding) Squadron as one of the regular RAF pilots training the squadron's weekend flyers.

Unwin was given command of No 84 Squadron in August 1949, flying the Brigand aircraft from RAF Habbaniya in Iraq. Within months No 84 was transferred to Singapore to provide ground support during the Malaya emergency.

The Brigand was not a popular aircraft, and the squadron suffered a number of losses. Unwin spotted that some were due to premature explosions in the Aden gun carried under the fuel tanks of the aircraft. He was critical of the Brigand's performance and was always prepared to display its weaknesses to higher authorities. Nevertheless, he led the squadron on more than 180 rocket and dive-bombing attacks against terrorist positions.

Not many commanding officers played football, but Unwin was a regular member of the squadron team until he broke a leg. He was invalided home and given a ground appointment as a wing commander. Shortly afterwards it was announced that he had been awarded the DSO, one of very few given to the RAF for operations during the Malayan campaign.

In 1955 Unwin returned to Singapore in charge of administration at the large RAF airfield at Tengah, where he still found time to fly the station's jet fighters. Three years later he returned to England to become the Permanent President of Courts Martial. He once commented: "I presided over 300 courts martial, and not one chap was found guilty of low flying." He retired from the RAF in 1961.

In retirement Unwin was the Controller of Spastics Appeals for the southern counties, but he never considered that to be work. A passionate golfer with a handicap of six, he lived within walking distance of the Ferndown Club, in Dorset, where he served for many years on numerous committees.

In earlier days he played seven days a week, once commenting: "I cut it down to five times in winter." He continued playing until he was 90, but visited the club two or three times a week until his death.

Small in stature, Unwin displayed all the characteristics for which Yorkshiremen are renowned: he was pugnacious, blunt, unafraid to speak out, and he had no time for wasters or for the unprofessional. One of his pilots said of him: "He was like a terrier, and an outstanding CO who always led from the front. He never failed to back you up if you were right."

George Unwin married Edna "Jimmie" Cornwell in 1939; she died in 2005.

WING COMMANDER "MOOSE" FUMERTON

Wing Commander "Moose" Fumerton (who died on July 10 2006, aged 93) fought in the Battle of Britain and then became Canada's most successful night fighter pilot of the Second World War, winning two DFCs.

With his inseparable observer and friend, Sergeant Pat Bing, Fumerton had already achieved successes over England and Egypt when he was sent to reinforce Malta at the height of the German onslaught in June 1942. He rapidly became the island's top-scoring night fighter pilot, claiming nine victories by the end of August.

Flying a Beaufighter with No 89 Squadron, he gained his first success over Malta on the night of June 24, when he shot down an Italian bomber before returning to re-fuel and re-arm. He was soon airborne again, and just before dawn destroyed a Junkers 88. Four nights later he accounted for two more; on July 1 he downed another, and the following night sent a sixth bomber crashing into the sea off Gozo; on July 28 he shot down another Ju 88.

On the night of August 10, Fumerton was scrambled to attack a force of incoming bombers but, shortly after take-off, both his engines failed, and he and Bing were forced to bale out. They spent a few hours in their dinghies ten miles north of the island before being rescued next morning by one of Malta's air-sea rescue launches.

As the crippled oil tanker *Ohio* approached the beleaguered island as part of Operation Pedestal on August 14, Fumerton destroyed one of a force of 15 Italian bombers heading for Malta.

A few days later he was flying over Sicily, seeking out enemy aircraft landing at night, when he caught one approaching an airfield and shot it down, his final success from Malta before returning to Egypt. For his remarkable achievements in such a short time he was awarded a Bar to his DFC.

Robert Carl Fumerton was born on March 21 1913 at Fort Coulonge, in western Quebec. He started out as a bush and timber worker, but contracted diphtheria and was told to rest. Instead he went to the North-West Territories and the Yukon, where he was surveying, mapping, prospecting and mining for gold over the next seven years.

In 1938 he obtained a licence as a bush pilot, and when war broke out he volunteered as a pilot with the Royal Canadian Air Force. After completing his training in Canada, Fumerton arrived in England in August 1940 with the first RCAF squadron, No 112, flying Lysanders.

Fighter Command was, however, desperate for pilots; so Fumerton volunteered to join No 32 Squadron, flying Hurricanes. From the moment his bulky figure was seen in a cockpit he was nicknamed "Moose".

After the Battle of Britain Fumerton moved to No 1 (RCAF) Squadron. In June 1941 he transferred to night fighting duties and joined the newly formed No 406 (RCAF) Squadron, based in Northumberland, where he teamed up with Bing.

On September 1 1941 he and Bing were on a practice flight when they were sent to intercept a raider approaching the coast. In the bright moonlight they identified a Ju 88. Fumerton closed to 50 yards and opened fire, setting the starboard engine of the enemy bomber ablaze. After a second attack, the aircraft broke up and crashed near Morpeth. It was the RCAF's first night success.

The duo spent most of the next day hacking out with wire cutters the big Iron Cross from the wing of their victim, which was hung in 406's crewroom. Six days later they intercepted another enemy bomber, and Fumerton fired two bursts, scoring hits, but the Heinkel 111 escaped into cloud. Shortly afterwards the two men were posted to Egypt to join No 89 Squadron in the defence of the Suez Canal.

On the night of March 2 1942 Fumerton was scrambled to intercept a hostile raider approaching Alexandria. After a very accurate pursuit controlled by Bing, he identified a Heinkel bomber and opened fire from 100 yards. The enemy gunner immediately returned fire and Fumerton was wounded in the leg. The gun sight and the starboard engine of his Beaufighter were put out of action, but Fumerton pressed home a second attack and set the enemy aircraft on fire, causing the German crew to bale out; they were later rescued from the sea.

By skilful flying and the use of radio beacons, Fumerton managed to reach an Egyptian airfield, where he discovered that he could not lower the aircraft's undercarriage. He made a successful wheels-up landing.

Four weeks after this success, he and Bing shot down two Heinkel bombers over Alexandria in the space of 15 minutes. Both men were awarded the DFC, and shortly afterwards they left for Malta.

By the end of 1942 Fumerton had been promoted to squadron leader and had left for Canada to take up training duties. But the following July he returned to England as a wing commander to assume command of No 406, now equipped with the Mosquito. Fumerton led it for almost a year, including during the run-up to D-Day, and left in July 1944.

He claimed a further victory on May 15 when he shot down a Junkers bomber over the English Channel. His final score was 14 destroyed and one damaged. On returning to Canada in August 1944, he took command of a Mosquito training unit and was awarded the AFC.

After leaving the RCAF in July 1945 Fumerton returned to mining. In 1948 he went to Hangkow to train Chinese pilots to fly the Mosquito and to organise the formation of three squadrons for General Chiang Kai-Chek's Nationalist Air Force. But when the Communists took over, he returned to Canada, where he became an estate agent.

Fumerton was a powerfully built man, well over six feet tall, who had excelled at ice hockey. Much of his outstanding success stemmed from his attitude to flying and his command of men in war, which can be attributed to the contempt for convention that the Canadian wilds breed in a man.

Moose Fumerton met his wife "Bobby" Reay, a flight controller at Dover, when they had an argument over the airwaves about the direction which she was giving him.

The couple married in 1946, and had four daughters and a son.

WING COMMANDER
BOBBY GIBBES

Wing Commander Bobby Gibbes (who died on April 11 2007, aged 90) was one of Australia's greatest and most colourful fighter pilots.

Gibbes displayed outstanding courage in battle, and was never afraid to buck authority. His exploits made him a household name, and on one occasion he was recommended for the Victoria Cross.

On December 21 1942 Gibbes was leading his squadron of Kittyhawk fighter-bombers on a strafing attack against an Italian airfield in the Western Desert. During the attack several aircraft were destroyed on the ground, two by Gibbes, but his formation came under heavy anti-aircraft fire. One of their number was shot down and a second was forced to crash land a few miles from the target.

Although his own aircraft had been hit by shrapnel, Gibbes went to the aid of his downed fellow pilot. With the rest of his formation providing cover, he landed and taxied his single-seat Kittyhawk across the rocky desert for a mile until stopped by a depression. He jettisoned the external fuel tank to reduce the weight of his aircraft before pacing out a take-off strip as his comrade evaded Italian troops and ran to meet him.

Gibbes ditched his own parachute to allow his friend to sit in the seat before climbing in after him and sitting on his lap. Then, as he took off, his undercarriage hit a small ridge, and he watched in horror as the port wheel fell off.

Escorted by his squadron pilots, Gibbes headed for his base. With fighters in short supply, he decided against a belly landing but came down on his one remaining wheel, thus causing minimal damage to the aircraft.

During the First World War such exploits had been recognised with a VC, and Gibbes was recommended for the supreme award. In the event he received an immediate DSO.

Robert Henry Maxwell Gibbes, always known as Bobby, was born on May 6 1916 at Balgowlah, New South Wales, and educated at All Saints College, Bathurst. Fascinated by flying, he joined the air cadets; having lied about his height, which was just below the stipulated minimum, he began pilot training in 1940. Since his ambition was to fly fighters, he deliberately failed his bomber training – and was fortunate to be transferred to fighters.

By June 1941 Gibbes was flying Tomahawk fighters with No 3 (RAAF) Squadron during the Syrian campaign. He achieved the first of his successes a few days after joining when he shot down a Vichy French fighter over Aleppo. In the Western Desert he proved to be a most aggressive pilot, attacking aircraft on the ground and in the air. He was promoted rapidly, and in February 1942 was appointed the squadron's commanding officer, a post he held longer than any other.

Once the squadron had re-equipped with the more capable Kittyhawk, Gibbes achieved more successes; but on May 26 he was shot down by return fire from a Junkers bomber and forced to bale out. He broke his leg on landing but six weeks later, with his leg still in plaster, he was back in action. Shortly afterwards he was awarded the DFC.

Three weeks after the daring rescue of his colleague, Gibbes was shot down for a second time after he had destroyed a Messerschmitt Bf 109. He crash-landed 180 miles behind enemy lines and, to fool the Germans, initially headed west. Three days later, after he had walked 50 miles, he was picked up by an advance Allied patrol, greeting them with the words: "G'day mate, got any water?"

Gibbes led his squadron throughout the Battle of El Alamein and the advance to Tunisia. Finally he was rested in April 1943, having undertaken 274 operations. He was awarded a Bar to his DFC. Gibbes was credited with destroying ten enemy aircraft and sharing in the destruction of two others, probably destroying a further five and damaging at least 16 more. In addition he destroyed at least two on the ground.

Having returned to Australia to fly Spitfires in the defence of Darwin, he suffered severe injuries and burns to his hands when his aircraft crashed on a training flight. He was nursed by "a little dark-haired popsy", whom he married a year later.

In spring 1945 Gibbes led No 80 Wing during the South-West Pacific campaign. But he and eight other senior fighter pilots became involved in the "Morotai Mutiny", when they resigned their commissions in protest at what they considered a move to sideline them from the main fighting theatre against the Japanese.

They were persuaded to withdraw their resignations, but Gibbes and two others were court-martialled for smuggling three bottles of whisky into their quarters; many considered this a trumped-up charge during a period of turmoil and split loyalties within the RAAF hierarchy.

After the war Gibbes established his own airline in Papua New Guinea, using war surplus aircraft, including three former Luftwaffe Junkers 52 transports, to develop links across the inaccessible highlands. After selling the business in 1958 he went into the coffee and tourist industries.

By the time he returned to Australia in 1975 he had established in the region vast coffee plantations and the biggest hotel chain in the Western Highlands. He was later awarded the Medal of the Order of Australia for his services in New Guinea.

Gibbes was in his sixties when he single-handedly sailed his 12.8-metre catamaran Billabong from England to Australia; on one occasion he escaped the attentions of pirates near Malaya by firing homemade petrol bombs from a modified signals pistol and faking a series of radio calls for assistance.

He was still flying in his eighties, when he built a miniature Cri Cri aerobatic aircraft in his living room – although he had to demolish a wall after miscalculating the wingspan. Gibbes flew the aircraft until the civil aviation authorities – much to his annoyance – grounded him when he was 85. In 1994 he published his memoirs, *You Live But Once*.

Bobby Gibbes married Jeannine Ince, with whom he had two daughters.

BOMBER BOYS

GROUP CAPTAIN
MIKE SHAW

Group Captain Mike Shaw (who died on January 31 2002, aged 81) survived more than 100 bombing, minelaying and torpedo-dropping missions in the Second World War, an actuarial improbability that led him, in later life, to the study and practice of spiritualism.

As he grew older, Shaw began to wonder why he had survived when so many of his comrades had lost their lives; he also found himself asking what had happened to them. His quest for answers led him to spiritualism and, subsequently, to healing and helping the sick, particularly those confronting cancer.

Shaw's exceptionally long operational career – he was one of the few bomber captains and squadron commanders to fly almost continuously throughout the war – opened unpromisingly as the pilot of an obsolete Vickers Vildebeest, a large biplane torpedo-bomber designed in 1928 and known to its crews as "The Pig".

After joining No 22, a Vildebeest squadron in the New Year of 1938, Shaw was based at Thorney Island in West Sussex. When war came his aircraft (maximum speed 124mph) was a sitting duck for enemy fighters.

Fortunately, the squadron began to be re-equipped in November 1939 with the two-engine, 265mph Bristol Beaufort torpedo-bomber, in which Shaw attacked enemy shipping in 1940 and 1941.

On one occasion he was banking his Beaufort over Den Helder on the Dutch coast at dawn when Tom Pickering, his sergeant air gunner, alerted him to "a large, fat, juicy-looking 15,000-ton ship tied up in the harbour". Shaw acknowledged: "Right lads, we'll have a go at that big one." The torpedo was made ready and, dropping the Beaufort to 60ft, Shaw had started his run-in when two flak ships opened fire.

The Beaufort's windscreen was shattered and bullets whistled through Pickering's turret before Shaw aborted the attack, hauling the aircraft into the clouds 1,000ft above. Shaw's eyes had filled with powdered glass from the windscreen, impairing his vision; cursing himself for not wearing goggles, he asked the crew for a pair, but no-one had brought any.

In a private memoir Shaw noted: "I uttered an instinctive prayer to God asking for protection and a safe return to base; and when my prayer was answered I think I voiced my gratitude. I suspect this was probably the first recognisable stirring of spiritual awareness within me."

After their plane had landed, Shaw's groundcrew told him how lucky he had been to get back; the oil tank was leaking, the aircraft was riddled with bullet-holes, and the port wheel punctured.

Shaw and his crew survived another crisis 24 hours after the Luftwaffe's devastation of Coventry on the night of November 15-16 1940. This event had prompted angry calls for retaliation, and an abortive attack was launched on an airfield at Abbeville, in the north of France.

As Shaw returned with an unspent bomb load, the port engine of his Beaufort caught fire. His fears that the plane would blow up were heightened when, as he prepared to land, he realised that his own airfield was under attack and the flarepath was unlit. With flames licking at one of his undelivered bombs, Shaw landed safely in the pitch dark. As he and his comrades ran for their lives, the fire crew saved the aircraft.

Michael John Apthorpe Shaw was born on April 12 1920. He was educated at Berkhamsted School, Hertfordshire, before joining the RAF on a short service commission in 1938.

Following his first operational tour he was rested (as a

flying and torpedo-bombing instructor) until June 1943, when he received command of No 221 Squadron. This was equipped with Vickers Wellington bombers and was stationed on Malta, from where it undertook night maritime reconnaissance and the bombing of ports in Italy.

After completing a second tour of 30 operations, Shaw returned home in February 1944 to an Air Ministry operational training staff post. On June 8 1944 – two days after the Allied landings in Normandy – he was posted to No 69, another Wellington squadron. In September, as Allied forces advanced into north-west Europe, the squadron moved from Northolt to Normandy, and Shaw took command.

Operating from French airfields behind Allied lines, Shaw's Wellingtons and air and groundcrews were particularly vulnerable to surprise enemy hit-and-run attacks. In one such attack Shaw had vacated his office only five minutes before enemy bullets tore through the walls; had he still been at his desk, he would certainly have been killed. Once again, Shaw wondered whether he had the benefit of some special protection.

When, in the New Year of 1945, Shaw was awarded the DSO, the citation emphasised the length of his operational career. Referring to his command of No 69 Squadron, the citation said he had undertaken reconnaissance by night with the utmost enthusiasm and skill; he had set a fine example and obtained outstanding results.

After VE Day Shaw received command of a Missing Research and Enquiry Service unit given the task of finding and identifying many thousands of missing airmen. After three years scouring Europe for information about more than 40,000 RAF personnel reported missing, he was posted home to command No 29, a de Havilland Mosquito night fighter squadron.

Fighter Command staff appointments followed until 1956, when he commanded No 72, a Gloster Meteor jet night fighter squadron, before returning to a further series of staff posts in Germany, at home, and in the Near East.

Shaw retired in 1975 and, after some initial scepticism, intensified his quest for spiritual knowledge. At one stage a medium assisted him in contacting comrades who had not survived the war.

He was in touch with a range of spiritual guides and healers, including Harry Edwards, Bruce Macmanaway and Brenda Johnston. In 1981 he set up a cancer support group at Tunbridge Wells, Kent, for sufferers seeking alternative ways to combat the disease.

Shaw married Tina Draghi in 1941. They had a son and three daughters.

AIR COMMODORE
BRIAN FROW

Air Commodore Brian Frow (who died on September 30 2002, aged 79) was awarded the DSO, and a DFC and Bar, for sustained operations over the most heavily defended targets in Germany and occupied Europe.

In the New Year of 1944 Frow was posted to No 7 Squadron in the Pathfinder Force. Shortly before his arrival at No 7's Oakington base, the squadron's Short Stirlings had been replaced by Lancasters. At the age of only 21, Frow was a flight commander in the rank of squadron leader, and he was soon given the added responsibility of acting on some raids as master bomber.

As such, he was provided with an additional navigator who was an expert in map reading and visual bombing at low level; he would help the squadron to identify and mark the target, while Frow's aircraft would endure heavy ground fire as he assessed the accuracy of the markers.

Frow would tell the main force bombers to wait until

he called them in to the target. When the first markers had been snuffed out by exploding bombs, he had to call in more aircraft to drop further target indicators.

As the bomber stream departed, the master bomber was required to make a final low level run to assess damage, and then to drop delayed fuse 1,000lb bombs to discourage enemy salvage operations.

On one such raid Frow was homeward bound over France when his rear gunner spotted a Ju 88 alongside him; it was stalking a fellow Lancaster. Frow reduced speed and, dropping behind the enemy night fighter, shot it down.

The Ju 88s usually operated in pairs, and a second night fighter attacked Frow's Lancaster from astern. It scored direct hits – but fortunately the mid-upper gunner managed to retaliate more effectively, and sent it blazing to the ground.

Even as this happened, Frow's Lancaster suffered a third attack. This enemy night fighter was also destroyed; but at that moment Frow's intercom failed, and the port aileron did not respond to an urgent attempt to take evasive action.

The aircraft, now over the moonlit sea, turned on its back, became unstable and lost height rapidly. Frow throttled back and continued to heave at the controls – and was much relieved to resume level flight when only 800ft above the water.

He took stock. Most main systems were not functioning correctly; the undercarriage could be lowered only manually; the brakes were defective; and one or more engines might seize up at any time. Even so, Frow reckoned that a controlled landing was possible, though the chances of fire were great because of fuel leaks in the tanks. He made his approach at Woodbridge, in Suffolk, and got away with it. The "Lanc", riddled with more than 100 bullet and cannon shell holes, was a write-off.

Brian George Frow was born on October 5 1922 at

Broadstairs, Kent, and educated at Dulwich College. As with so many adventure-seeking boys of the period, he was inspired to fly by the displays of Sir Alan Cobham's Flying Circus.

During school holidays he revelled in plane-spotting at Croydon Airport. Following membership of the Officers' Training Corps at Dulwich, Frow joined the Local Defence Volunteers in 1940 and at the age of 17 was placed in charge of a section of 20 men. At the same time he was articled to a solicitor. He enlisted in October 1940 and, having been commissioned as a pilot officer, was posted to No 144 in December 1941.

Frow was only 19 when, early in 1942, he was summoned by his station commander, the ebullient one-armed golfer Group Captain Gus Walker, and given temporary command of No 144 Squadron and its Handley Page Hampden two-engine bombers. He was responsible for 20 Hampden aircraft, 30 aircrew and 150 groundcrew as well as writing letters of condolence to the families of those who failed to return.

Shortly before, Frow had dropped a 2,000lb magnetic mine at low level in a daylight sortie against the battle-cruisers *Scharnhorst* and *Gneisenau* off the north coast of Germany.

When Frow's first attempt was aborted by anti-aircraft fire and Bf 109 fighters, his Hampden, weighed down by the mine, was badly damaged as it laboured towards protective cloud cover. Trying again, Frow released the mine and, while there could be no confirmation that he was responsible, *Scharnhorst* was damaged by a mine soon afterwards.

Having achieved this, his promotion was assured. After moving to No 408, a Royal Canadian Air Force Hampden squadron, he had just settled in when he took part in the first of "Bomber" Harris's three much-publicised 1,000 bomber raids over Germany.

On the night of May 30 1942, in a move which

foreshadowed the introduction of the Pathfinder Force in which Frow was to serve with distinction, 408 was sent on a mission to light up Cologne ahead of Bomber Command's main force.

Frow voluntarily extended his first tour of operations when Walker persuaded him to join No 61, a four-engine Avro Lancaster squadron in the embryo Lancaster force. However, in the New Year of 1943 Frow, already a bomber veteran at 20, was compelled to rest and become an operational training flying instructor.

In July and August 1944, in the aftermath of the D-Day landings in Normandy, Frow took part in what he described as a "grand crescendo" of attacks against V-1 flying bomb launch areas, marshalling yards, airfields, frontline positions and any installations supporting enemy units.

At the end of the year Frow flew for Transport Command in Australia and, following VJ Day in 1945, evacuated prisoners of war from South-East Asia to Australia. In 1946 he was appointed Staff Officer Administration No 300 Wing at Kai Tak, Hong Kong. Within days he was posted to Singapore, but swiftly moved on as a transport planning officer until November, when he joined No 48, another transport squadron, as a flight commander.

Offered a permanent commission, Frow abandoned plans to become a solicitor. He flew an Avro York transport home, and joined No 51 Squadron in Transport Command, then moved on to 511.

Frow flew the Avro Lincoln – a descendant of the Lancaster – on overseas trials before, in late 1948, becoming a Transport Command examiner.

When there was concern that planes in the Berlin airlift were ignoring certain regulations, he accompanied crews in and out of the city to check them out. Afterwards he reported that, yes, rules were being broken – but for very good reasons.

Much of the remainder of Frow's career centred on

transport operations. Home and overseas appointments included command at Bahrain in the Gulf in 1964. He also took jet fighter courses.

Finally, Frow served in Moscow as a defence attaché from 1972 until 1975, when he received command in Hong Kong. Retiring in 1977, he was responsible for the Falkland Islands Office in London until 1982, when he was appointed clerk to the Worshipful Company of Clockmakers.

Frow was awarded the DFC in 1943, a Bar in 1944, and a DSO in 1944.

In 1943 he married Anne Swancott, whom he had met at Streatham ice rink. They had four daughters.

PAUL HILTON

Paul Hilton (who died on October 6 2002, aged 80), was awarded the Conspicuous Gallantry Medal for his bravery when the bomber he was piloting was shot down over Germany in 1942; as a decoration for gallantry, the CGM is considered to be only just below a VC, and was rarely awarded to members of RAF Bomber Command.

Earlier that year Hilton had been posted to Linton-on-Ouse in Yorkshire, the base of No 35 Squadron and its Halifax bombers. On the night of June 2-3 1942, as a 20-year-old sergeant pilot, Hilton was on a raid in his Halifax when it was attacked by three enemy night fighters; his plane was badly damaged, with three engines put out of action. Hilton, as captain, gave the order to abandon the aircraft, and four of the five members of his aircrew jumped; Hilton then discovered that the fifth, his flight engineer, had remained put because his parachute was unserviceable.

In a remarkable act of bravery, Hilton surrendered his

own parachute to the flight engineer, "although he knew", as the citation for his CGM later noted, that "it meant almost certain death".

Hilton then had to attempt a forced landing. As his aircraft crashed and burst into flames, he was thrown clear; he was captured and sent to a prisoner-of-war camp. The citation concluded: "Sergeant Hilton displayed outstanding courage and coolness in the face of great danger. His complete disregard for his own safety in order to save the life of one of his crew showed a devotion to duty worthy of the highest praise."

Paul Hilton was born on March 24 1922 at Batu Gajah, in Malaya, where his father worked in the tin mining industry. Paul was sent to Brighton Grammar School; from there he went to Brighton Technical College before joining the RAF in September 1940.

After being shot down, Hilton spent the remainder of the war in captivity. Following his repatriation from Germany in May 1945, he joined de Havilland Aircraft as an apprentice. He went on to work as a stress engineer on the Chipmunk trainer, Venom and DH 110 jets, and the wings of the Comet.

He then set up his own company, P A Hilton Ltd, which designed and manufactured laboratory equipment for engineering students. Meanwhile, in his spare time Hilton became interested in making jet engines for the propulsion of helicopter rotors. He also designed and built a subsonic ram jet engine.

Hilton built his own development models, and was in the habit of testing his engines at night in a Land Rover on the Watford by-pass – a practice which astonished other motorists, and was apt to generate complaints about the noise. During this period, in the late 1950s, he lived in a caravan near Radlett, Hertfordshire, and carried out his work in a chicken shed.

He also developed two small-scale rocket test rigs, and went on to produce a combustion laboratory unit, a vapour compression mechanical heat pump, and a thermo-electric heat pump.

By 1967 Hilton had succeeded in selling his first ram jet to Imperial College, London. He also designed and built a test stand (a framework for accommodating teaching apparatus); it was very successful, and he began to export this and other engineering teaching aids around the world.

As his home and export business expanded, Hilton located his company at Horsebridge Mill, on the Test in Hampshire. In 1993, in recognition of his services to the teaching of engineering, he received an honorary doctorate from his alma mater, in its new incarnation as Brighton University.

Hilton married, in 1968, Gillian Thornton; they had a son and a daughter.

SQUADRON LEADER
KEN BROWN

Squadron Leader Ken Brown (who died on December 23 2002, aged 82) was awarded the Conspicuous Gallantry Medal – generally regarded as second only to the VC – after he captained a four-engined Lancaster bomber in the Dambusters raid in 1943.

The award recognised not only his exceptional leadership of a crew of six (all, like Brown himself at this time, sergeants), but also his superb airmanship at very low levels on the way into, and out of, Germany. Although his aircraft was badly shot up during the operation, Brown managed to bring it and his crew safely home.

Wing Commander Guy Gibson (who was awarded the VC after the raid) had built up No 617 Squadron to implement Bomber Command's audacious plan to launch Dr Barnes Wallis's bouncing bomb into the walls of the dams servicing the Ruhr Valley, Germany's industrial heartland.

The crews which flew on the mission were hand-picked, and then trained, by Gibson; and although later, on a visit to Canada, Gibson was careful to stress the value of the contribution to the raid made by Canadian aircrew, he was known to have had reservations about using them.

Indeed, after Gibson had dismissed one of four Canadian pilots in the squadron, Brown (himself Canadian) wondered how long he himself would last; he had already incurred Gibson's wrath on several occasions, and knew only too well that there was little future for those who failed to measure up to his exacting standards.

It was, therefore, in itself a tribute to Brown's flying skills that he was retained long enough to take off from Scampton, in Lincolnshire, at 12 minutes past midnight on May 17 1943.

His was one of the last of Gibson's force of 19 Lancasters and 133 aircrew to head for Germany and, at 2.50am, he saw Pilot Officer Warner Ottley's Lancaster crash, exploding on impact.

As a member of Gibson's reserve force, Brown was not briefed to attack the main targets, the Moehne and Eder dams. Thus when he spotted, from his altitude of only 150ft, three trains beneath him, he shot them up; in the process, his aircraft was hit by ground fire.

Shortly afterwards Brown received a call from base ordering him to attack a subsidiary target, the Sorpe dam. As it happened, this was concealed by a swirling mist; Brown had difficulty during his approach, both in avoiding a church spire and in getting right his line and height for his attack. He had to keep pulling his aircraft over the hills and returning for another attempt to release his bomb.

Brown made eight perilously low runs (at 60ft)

without finding his opportunity to attack. But, after dropping incendiaries to set alight the woods on either side of the lake, thus illuminating his target, he made his final run. At 3.20am he dropped his bomb and signalled "Goner". Brown reported that his weapon had fallen about ten feet from the earth dam, creating a spout of water 1,000ft high; but it had failed to cause breaches similar to those achieved in the concrete structures of the Moehne and Eder dams.

Having set course for home, Brown then decided to take a look at the Moehne, in which his flight engineer, Sergeant Baz Fearon, noted two large breaches. As the Lancaster approached the coast of Holland, dawn was beginning to break, and Fearon remembered that the ground fire was rising towards them "like scarlet beads". The aircraft was holed behind the wireless operator's seat, and the fuselage was riddled like a sieve on the starboard side where a shell had exploded, piercing the bomber's skin with shrapnel.

Flak pursued the Lancaster until it was out of range over the North Sea. Fearon, aware that Brown was by now exhausted, took over the controls and, although not trained as a pilot, flew the machine as far as Lincoln, before handing back control to Brown for the landing at 5.33am. Of the 19 aircraft which took off, only 11 managed to press home their attacks, and eight failed to return; 53 men were killed, and three were shot down to become prisoners of war.

Kenneth William Brown was born on August 20 1920 at Moose Jaw, Saskatchewan. He enlisted in the Royal Canadian Air Force in 1941 and, after getting his wings, was posted to No 44, a Lancaster bomber squadron, in February 1943. After surviving raids on such heavily-defended targets as Berlin and Essen, he joined No 617 in the spring of 1943.

A year later, by which time he had been commissioned, Brown was posted as an instructor to the

Lancaster Finishing School, and served with other RAF units until 1945, when he returned to Canada, soon to be followed by his English bride. After receiving a permanent commission in the RCAF, he completed his service at the Winter Experimental Establishment at Watson Lake and Churchill, flying a variety of aircraft ranging from the Lancaster and the Mosquito to Meteor and Vampire jets.

Brown also flew in Canada's first jet aerobatic team at Edmonton, Alberta, and, in 1949, bought a surplus Spitfire with a view to entering an air race.

In 1968 Brown left the RCAF with the rank of squadron leader, and joined the air section of Canada's Department of Transport. He spent 12 years there before retiring to British Columbia.

Ken Brown married Beryl Blackband in 1944. They had four sons and a daughter.

AIR MARSHAL
SIR IVOR BROOM

Air Marshal Sir Ivor Broom (who died on January 24 2003, aged 82) was awarded a DSO and three DFCs during his three tours of duty in some of the most hazardous bomber operations of the Second World War.

In May 1944 Broom joined No 571, a Mosquito XVI squadron of the Light Night Striking Force (LNSF), teaming up with his navigator (and namesake), Flight Lieutenant Tommy Broom. In their Mosquito – modified to carry a 4,000lb bomb – they were known to the press as "The Flying Brooms", and had the emblem of crossed broomsticks painted on the nose of the aircraft. Although the modified Mosquito was equipped with no guns or rockets, the Brooms made numerous raids over Berlin delivering their "cookies", as the 4,000-pounders were known.

In his reports, Broom barely troubled to mention the heavy flak and night fighters they encountered on these raids. After a particularly bad night, he recorded only "wizard trip" in his logbook; on another occasion, four 500lb bombs dropped accurately on a target in Hanover merited only a laconic "bang on". Ivor Broom also excelled at mine-laying, and his second DFC followed a neat low-level operation in which he dropped mines in the path of shipping in the Dortmund-Ems canal. It was an advantage in such pinpoint operations that Tommy Broom was an exceptional navigator; he had survived a crash-landing in Holland, then evaded capture and crossed the Pyrenees to Spain, before rejoining his unit six weeks later.

Searchlights were a perpetual problem which, over Berlin, coned the Brooms for as long as a quarter of an hour. After twisting, turning and diving to escape the glare, Ivor Broom once asked his disoriented navigator for a course to base. Tommy Broom replied: "Fly north with a dash of west, while I sort myself out." During this period the Flying Brooms lobbed a cookie up the mouth of a railway tunnel in Germany with two fighters on their tail, and Ivor Broom received a second Bar to his DFC.

In autumn 1944 he was promoted acting squadron leader in command of a flight in No 128 (another LNSF Mosquito squadron). A few months later he was appointed acting wing commander to lead No 163 Squadron. Tommy Broom, now DFC and Bar, joined him as squadron navigation officer.

The pair then led a series of brilliant offensive operations over Germany and occupied Europe. When the war in Europe ended on May 8 1945, the Flying Brooms had undertaken 58 missions (including 22 raids on Berlin). Ivor Broom was awarded a DSO, and Tommy a third DFC.

Ivor Gordon Broom was born at Cardiff on June 2 1920, and spent much of his childhood in the Rhondda, where his father was district manager for the Prudential Assurance Company and a Baptist preacher. Ivor was educated at the Boys' County School, Pontypridd, and grew up in a Christian home in which honesty, tolerance and fair play were encouraged. Temperance was also a virtue, and Broom rarely drank and never smoked – although this never prevented him from enjoying a party.

When he was 17 Broom passed the Civil Service exam and began work with the Inland Revenue. He learned to fly in 1940, while the Battle of Britain was being fought, and the next year was posted to No 114 Squadron; here he flew in Blenheim low-level daylight operations against Channel and North Sea shipping, and targets along the French and Dutch coasts as well as in Germany.

Broom's leadership qualities first surfaced in the early autumn of 1941 when, although still a sergeant, he was detailed to lead six Bristol Blenheim two-engine light bombers to Malta, en route to reinforce Singapore.

As the Blenheims touched down on the beleaguered Mediterranean island, Air Vice-Marshal Hugh Lloyd was quick to grab Broom and his aircraft in part replacement of his Blenheim losses, leaving the other five Blenheims to proceed to the Far East. But for this, Broom would have died or become a prisoner of war during the fall of Singapore. As it was, Lloyd retained him to fly with No 107 Squadron, whose Blenheims were incurring heavy losses attacking Axis shipping and targets in North Africa and Italy.

When 107 had lost all its officers, Lloyd told Broom: "Move into the officers' mess. We will sort the paperwork out later." Thus Broom became a pilot officer. The young, voluble and highly articulate "lad from the Rhondda" (as he was known) rapidly justified Lloyd's confidence, repeatedly pressing home low-level attacks on heavily escorted Axis shipping. On November 17 1941 he bombed and set ablaze a 4,000-ton ship in the Gulf of Sirte, and helped attack a destroyer. But the cost, as usual, was high: while Broom's skill and courage saw him through, two of a force of six Blenheims were lost. He had survived 43 sorties when, in January 1942, he returned home wearing the ribbon of his first DFC.

After his return from Malta, Broom took an instructor's course at the Central Flying School, then spent a year teaching novice Blenheim pilots how to attack at low level.

It was in May 1943 that Broom began his love affair with the de Havilland Mosquito, which was to figure so prominently in the remainder of his wartime operational career.

At first Broom remained an instructor, honing the skills of exceptional pilots creamed off by the Australian-born Air Vice-Marshal Don Bennett for his No 8 Path-finder Group. One night during this period Broom was landing with a Canadian pupil when the port engine failed at 400ft.

Broom recalled: "We had full flap down, and on a Mosquito with full flap there is no way you can go round again. I raised the undercarriage, and was going to let the aircraft settle on open countryside when the pupil suddenly said, 'We're going to crash' – and fully opened the throttle of the good engine." The Mosquito did crash, and the pupil was killed. Broom, who suffered a broken back, was flying again only four months later.

After VE Day, Broom was posted to Ceylon, but was spared further action by the Japanese surrender. He was sent to Singapore, where he dropped rank to squadron leader to command No 28, a Spitfire fighter squadron – although he had never flown the type before.

In 1948 he returned home, and dropped rank again in order to attend staff college as a flight lieutenant. When he passed out he resumed as a squadron leader, and learned to fly jets; in April 1953 he formed No 57, the third squadron to be equipped with English Electric Canberra jet bombers. Having moved on to the RAF

Flying College at Manby, in 1955 Broom piloted a specially-modified Canberra from Ottawa to London via the North Pole; this was the return trip on what was then a pioneering route over the Pole. Broom was then awarded the AFC.

In 1956 Broom was made responsible for the Bomber Command Development Unit at Wittering, where he led intensive trials on Valiants and Canberras of the nascent nuclear deterrent, V-Force.

In 1959 he moved into the Air Secretary's department until 1962, when he was appointed station commander at RAF Bruggen in Germany. Following a year at the Imperial Defence College, two years at the Ministry of Defence, and a spell as commandant of the Central Flying School, Broom took command in 1970 of No 11, the famous fighter group which had defended London and the south-east in 1940.

At this time he was concerned with the presence in the Iceland-Faroes gap of Soviet Bear (Tu 95) reconnaissance aircraft. To ensure that he was fully in control of every situation, he secured a radio to his golf bag; and one Saturday morning, he was summoned from the golf course at Stanmore, Middlesex, as two Soviet aircraft had appeared in the North Sea.

The Bears approached St Andrews (where the Open was in progress), but turned back some 15 miles from the coast; Broom continued his game.

In 1977 Broom concluded his RAF career as controller of National Air Traffic Services; but he maintained close links with the various veterans' organisations, in which he was a popular figure noted for his bonhomie. He was president of the Mosquito Aircrew Association from 1993, and a former president of the Pathfinder Association. He also worked energetically for the Royal Air Forces Association, the RAF Benevolent Fund, the Blenheim Society, the Aircrew Association and the Bomber Command Association. He was a member of the Civil Aviation Board (1974-77), and chairman of Farnborough Aerospace Development Corporation from 1985 to 1992.

He was appointed CB in 1972, and KCB in 1975.

In 1942 Ivor Broom married Jess Cooper, with whom he had two sons and a daughter.

LIEUTENANT-GENERAL
REG LANE

Lieutenant-General Reg Lane (who died on October 2 2003, aged 83) commanded the Royal Canadian Air Force's only Pathfinder squadron over some of the most heavily defended targets in Germany and occupied Europe.

Appointed to 405 (Vancouver) Squadron for his third bombing tour in the winter of 1943-44, he circled Berlin for up to 40 minutes at a time while directing a main force of more than 500 aircraft and while under constant attack from German night fighters.

Lane's long career as a bomber pilot began in October 1941 when he joined No 35 Squadron, with Squadron Leader Leonard Cheshire as his flight commander. The realities of the strategic bombing war were starkly illustrated on Lane's first operation, when he had to fly through storms and thick icy cloud to attack Berlin. In December he carried out two daylight attacks against the French port of Brest, where the German battlecruisers *Scharnhorst* and *Gneisenau* were sheltering.

In the first, he watched his squadron commander brought down in the sea by anti-aircraft fire; in the second, Lane's formation of six aircraft was severely damaged by German fighters.

His next encounter with the German fleet was on March 27 1942, when No 35 set off to attack the battleship *Tirpitz*, moored in a Norwegian fjord near Trondheim. Sea mines and incendiaries were to be dropped from very low level, but the combination of anti-aircraft fire and a smokescreen thwarted the attack. Lane returned after a nine-hour flight, but three other Halifax bombers were lost.

Another mast-height attack by moonlight was planned, but the German defences were ready, and Lane's aircraft was hit repeatedly as he attacked the battleship at 150ft. He was able to return safely; four Halifaxes were lost, including that of the future Pathfinder leader, Wing Commander Don Bennett, who managed to escape to Sweden.

On the night of May 30 1942 Bomber Command's new C-in-C, Air Marshal Arthur Harris, launched Operation Millennium, the first of his 1,000-bomber raids. Lane flew one of the 131 Halifaxes launched on Cologne by No 4 Group. Although the raid was considered a success, 41 bombers failed to return. Two nights later Lane took off on the second 1,000-bomber raid, on Essen.

By the end of June he had flown 23 operations, and was awarded the first of his two DFCs.

The son of a Yorkshireman who had emigrated to Canada after the First World War, Reginald John Lane was born at Victoria, British Columbia, on January 4 1920. He was educated at Victoria High School and worked for the Hudson Bay Company before joining the RCAF in September 1940.

The completion of his first tour of operations in the summer of 1942 coincided with the establishment of No 8 (Pathfinder) Group, for which No 35 was one of six squadrons selected.

Lane's first operation as a Pathfinder, charged with marking targets for the main bomber force, was as an illuminator on a raid over Kiel. Throughout the winter of 1942-43 he attacked targets in Berlin, Stuttgart, Munich, Milan and Turin.

During the early days of the Pathfinder Force, the new

and sensitive navigation and bombing equipment suffered numerous teething problems; but Lane retained his reputation for tenacity and courage in pressing on to mark the target. The final operation of his second tour, on April 16 1943, was almost his last. He had attacked the Skoda factory at Pilsen in Czechoslovakia when his Halifax was "coned" by searchlights and he had to dive to 1,000ft to escape heavy anti-aircraft fire over Frankfurt.

After 18 months of continuous bombing operations, Lane was awarded the DSO and returned to Canada, where he was selected to fly the first Canadian-built Lancaster, the "Ruhr Express", across the North Atlantic to England. The press reported that he had been selected "as much for his photogenic appearance as his brilliant piloting skills".

After being appointed group captain at 24, Lane flew his last operation, to Caen, just before D-Day, when he again acted as the master bomber; he was awarded a Bar to his DFC.

Staying on in the RCAF after the war, he assumed command of RCAF Edmonton, Alberta, and graduated from the Imperial Defence College in London.

In 1961 he was appointed the Air Officer Commanding Air Transport Command, then returned to Europe five years later to become Chief of Staff of the RCAF's No 1 Air Division Headquarters at Metz. This was when its division headquarters and operational squadrons were relocated from France to Germany, after de Gaulle invited NATO units to leave France. With the formation of the integrated Canadian Defence Force, Lane assumed the rank of major-general and, in August 1969, was appointed Deputy Commander of Mobile Command in Montreal.

Three years later he became Deputy Commander-in-Chief of the North American Air Defence Command (NORAD), based in Colorado, and was made an Officer of the American Legion of Merit.

In retirement he became a consultant to Systems Development Corporation, Santa Monica, before returning to his native Victoria.

From 1983 to 1991 he was a member of the Consultative Group on Disarmament and Arms Control of the Department of External Affairs, and in 1989 he was appointed director of the Canadian Institute for International Peace and Security.

As an honorary life vice-president he remained a strong supporter of his local branch of the Aircrew Association on Vancouver Island.

Reg Lane was also a patron of the Yorkshire Air Museum, home of the only surviving Halifax.

Lane married, in 1944, Barbara Andrews, from Harrogate, Yorkshire. They had two sons and two daughters.

AIR VICE-MARSHAL
TONY DUDGEON

Air Vice-Marshal Tony Dudgeon (who died on January 5 2004, aged 87) played a key role in a little-known but crucial air campaign that prevented the Germans gaining access to the Iraqi oil fields and a possible offensive from the east against the undefended Suez Canal.

When the rabidly anti-British Rashid Ali al Ghailani seized power in Iraq in April 1941, he immediately threatened the RAF's main staging post and training base at Habbaniya. Dudgeon had recently arrived to command B Flight of No 4 Flying Training School.

With virtually no operational aircraft available to defend the airfield, he and his colleagues set about converting their obsolete training aircraft to bombers; defying orders, Dudgeon equipped his own with a crude bomb release system.

Early in May the Iraqi army laid siege to the airfield,

and demanded its surrender. The flying school went to war, but by the end of the first day a quarter of the 39 pilots, and one third of the aircraft, were out of action. With a fellow squadron leader, Dudgeon both flew and personally controlled the bombing operations for five successive days as the airfield came under fire from Iraqi guns.

By the end, the survivors could barely stand for fatigue – but the enemy ground forces had withdrawn in disarray. By the close of the month the Germans had pulled out of Iraq, and the situation was saved. Dudgeon was mentioned in dispatches.

Later, Air Marshal Sir Arthur Tedder said that without the school's success the Germans might have got a foothold in Iraq, and that "our Middle East base could have been nipped out".

Antony Greville Dudgeon was born on December 6 1916 in Cairo, where his father was Professor of Psychiatry at a hospital. Tony was educated at Eton and the RAF College Cranwell, graduating as a pilot officer in December 1935. He joined No 11 Squadron at Risalpur on the North-West Frontier of India. In his single-engine biplane he flew many operations over hostile and mountainous country as the RAF policed the rebellious territory.

In 1940 he joined No 45 Squadron in Egypt as a flight commander. The long-awaited Italian invasion of Egypt began on September 13, and after initial successes they were driven back deep into Libya. In October Dudgeon was promoted to command another Blenheim squadron, No 55, based at the advanced landing ground at Fuka. He was constantly in action, leading his squadron in attacks against troop concentrations, ports and airfields in Libya. He flew 50 bombing operations in three months, and in February 1941 was awarded the DFC.

After a year in Iraq, Dudgeon was promoted to wing commander and sent on a rest tour to Cairo. He arrived at the headquarters of the recently formed 216 Group a week late, having taken unofficial leave in May 1941 to marry Phyl McFarlane, the daughter of his former commanding officer.

His new role was to establish the ferry and transport organisation, and he was an ideal choice. Following the closure of the Mediterranean, all aircraft reinforcements for the Middle East were shipped to Takoradi in the Gold Coast (now Ghana), where they were re-assembled and ferried 4,000 miles to Cairo. Once the Germans had retreated to Tunisia, it was possible to shorten the ferry route by transferring the western terminal to Casablanca. Dudgeon established his headquarters at Ras-el-Ma in French Morocco.

A man of great energy and enthusiasm, Dudgeon personally undertook some of the most difficult ferry flights. After returning a stranded Lancaster to England (his first flight in the four-engine bomber), he went back the next day with a new Wellington, in which he had had only 45 minutes experience.

Dudgeon took off in atrocious weather, and almost immediately the aircraft's electrics and all the instruments failed. The trainee navigator could not cope in the thick cloud, and, with no radio to assist with navigation bearings, Dudgeon flew the aircraft through the night without the aid of instruments or an automatic pilot, eventually landing in Morocco after a nine-hour flight.

When he was due to return to England in July 1943, his wife was eight months pregnant, and the rules required that she should remain in Cairo until three months after the birth before embarking on a six-week journey home by troopship. The ever-enterprising Dudgeon used his contacts to circumvent this problem, arranging to fly her himself to Casablanca in a Dakota, in which she sat in a wicker chair strapped to a cargo lashing point in the fuselage. From Morocco she was able to take an official flight to England, where their son was born a few days after her arrival.

Dudgeon then joined the recently-formed Transport Command, with which he played a key role in the planning and execution of the D-Day and Arnhem airborne operations. In order to better understand the role, he trained as a glider pilot.

When it became apparent that the dropping zones around Arnhem were being captured, with crucial supplies falling to the Germans, Dudgeon was ordered to take a small team by Jeep to establish a homing beacon and radio behind enemy lines, in order more precisely to direct the transport aircraft to the dropping zones. As he neared the area, he was saluted by a German army patrol that mistook his RAF uniform for the field-grey of the Wehrmacht. He returned the salute before making a hasty retreat.

After attending the RAF Staff College in 1946, Dudgeon spent three years flying and planning transport operations during the Malayan emergency. There was then a spell in the personnel department at the Air Ministry before he was promoted to group captain to command the RAF station at Benson. There he was given two responsibilities: to mastermind the ferrying of 400 Sabre fighters from America to Britain (Operation Becher's Brook, which was a resounding success); and secondly, to carry out a review of the terms and conditions under which airmen served.

Those who knew Dudgeon, and his unconventional approach to authority, expressed some surprise at his appointment to the second of these tasks. One sceptic was heard to ask: "Why Dudgeon? He has always thrown Queen's Regulations out of the window." To which the AOC replied, "Then open the window." Dudgeon devised many new initiatives, which were subsequently implemented across the RAF and are still in place today. For his work at Benson, he was appointed CBE.

After completing the Flying College course, Dudgeon was appointed to command RAF Bruggen, where he re-equipped his four fighter squadrons with the Hunter. Over the next two years he brought the wing up to full operational readiness, but then had the distressing experience of implementing its demise overnight following the savage cuts of the 1957 Defence Review.

On promotion to air commodore in 1960, Dudgeon was appointed AOC Air Cadets. After a tour as the Director of Flight Safety, he was appointed Chief of Staff to the British Defence Staff in Washington. He retired as an air vice-marshal in April 1968, and spent the next ten years as head of the Paris office of the management consultants McKinsey & Co.

In retirement Dudgeon fought tenaciously to have a battle honour awarded to No 4 FTS for its contribution to the Middle East war; but his proposal was rejected on the ground that the flying school was a non-operational unit. He always considered himself fortunate, and called the first instalment of his RAF memoirs *The Luck of the Devil* (1985). This was followed by *Wings Over North Africa* (1987), *The War That Never Was* (1991) and *Hidden Victory* (2000).

With his wife, who died in 1994, Tony Dudgeon had a son, who served as a wing commander in the RAF, and a daughter.

GROUP CAPTAIN
KENNETH HUBBARD

Group Captain Kenneth Hubbard (who died on January 21 2004, aged 83) was the pilot of an RAF Valiant bomber which dropped Britain's first live megaton thermo-nuclear weapon (the H-Bomb) in the South Pacific in 1957.

Hubbard had assumed command of No 49 Squadron, based at Wittering, in September 1956. The squadron was equipped with the Vickers Valiant bomber – the first of the RAF's V-bombers – and had been assigned the major role in Operation Grapple, the aim of which was to test the performance of thermo-nuclear weapons in the megaton range. The site chosen for the test – the largest joint service operation to be mounted since the end of the Second World War – was Malden Island, 400 miles south of Christmas Island in the South Pacific.

Specially-equipped Valiants were allocated for the task, and Hubbard supervised a concentrated training period for the four crews selected for the first phase of Grapple. Flying via Canada and the United States, he was the first to leave for Christmas Island, on March 3 1957; he was followed a few days later by the remaining three aircraft.

A further intensive period of trials and training took place to familiarise the crews with the target, and to allow the many scientists of the Armament and Weapons Research Establishment to set up the weapons range and establish the complex procedures and instrumentation for gathering crucial information.

Hubbard elected to carry out the first drop of the bomb. He flew his Valiant on a full dress rehearsal on May 11, using a conventional high-explosive bomb, when all the complex air and ground procedures were tested. At 9am on May 15 he took off for the first test, with a reserve aircraft following one minute later. The Valiant climbed to 45,000ft, and, after two practice runs, Hubbard was given clearance to drop the live H-Bomb. Fifty seconds after release, the bomb exploded at the pre-determined height of 8,000ft.

Hubbard had erected the anti-flash screens in the cockpit of his aircraft before turning away from the explosion. The drop was completely successful.

Over the next three weeks, two more bombs were dropped by other crews, before No 49 returned to

Wittering. Two days after they got back, it was announced that Hubbard and the other four members of his crew had been awarded the AFC.

During the following 15 months Hubbard returned to Christmas Island three times, when a further four weapons were dropped before Operation Grapple was concluded. Hubbard's Valiant bomber (XD 818) is on display at the RAF Museum at Hendon.

Hubbard held strong views about the importance of the H-Bomb tests, and the need for Britain to have a nuclear deterrent. He was not afraid to counter the arguments of the anti-nuclear lobby, and remained immensely proud of the part played by his squadron and of the effectiveness of the V-Force, which maintained a nuclear deterrent capability until the mid-1980s.

The son of a professional footballer, Kenneth Gilbert Hubbard was born on February 26 1920 at Norwich. He was educated at Norwich Technical College before joining the RAF in 1940 to train as a pilot. He was commissioned in May 1941 and spent the next two years as a flying instructor.

At the end of 1943 Hubbard left for the Middle East to train on the Wellington before joining No 70 Squadron, based at Foggia in southern Italy. For the next few months his squadron was heavily involved in bombing operations over northern Italy, Yugoslavia and Romania.

The squadron also bombed targets in support of the 5th and 8th Armies as they advanced on Rome after the fighting at Cassino. Hubbard attacked marshalling yards and bridges in the Po valley in a campaign to destroy the German lines of communications. He participated in a daring low-level attack on an important railway bridge in northern Italy, and was awarded the DFC.

By the end of the war Hubbard had been promoted to squadron leader, and commanded No 104 Squadron, based in Egypt with Lancasters. He then joined the flying staff of the Empire Armament School at RAF Manby, near Louth. Here he flew Lancaster and Lincoln bombers on long-range flights to South Africa and Canada. On the formation of the RAF Flying College, Hubbard joined the directing staff.

In April 1954 Hubbard assumed command of the RAF station at Shaibah in Iraq. Within three months he was faced with a potential crisis when the Persian authorities nationalised the Anglo-Iranian Oil Company's refinery at Abadan. With the possible need to evacuate British nationals, three fighter squadrons were detached to Shaibah, and 27 Hastings transport aircraft were positioned in the Canal Zone ready to deploy troops to the region.

Hubbard was heavily involved in developing contingency plans for an evacuation to his station that, in the event, were not necessary. For his work he was appointed OBE.

After a year as a student on the RAF Staff College course he was promoted to wing commander and appointed to No 49 Squadron. The spirit of the squadron was so strong following Operation Grapple that it was decided to form the Megaton Club; Hubbard was invited to be president, a post he held for more than 25 years.

In April 1959 Hubbard joined the staff of Bomber Command, being made responsible for developing operational requirements for the rapidly expanding V-Force. Promoted to group captain in 1961, he took command of the RAF airfield at El Adem in Libya, before returning to the V-Force in 1963 as commander of RAF Scampton, the home of three Vulcan squadrons. In 1965 he served at the headquarters of Transport Command, and retired from the RAF a year later.

Hubbard joined the board of the Hubbard-Reader Group, where he was responsible for marketing and sales until 1982. He retired to Blythburgh in Suffolk and gave many years service to the Air Training Corps in the county.

In retirement, Hubbard kept an aviary and a brood of chickens; but his particular love was dogs, and his faithful spaniel, Crusty, had been known to all his officers and airmen. He inaugurated an annual service for animals at his local church. His book, *Operation Grapple*, was published in 1984.

Ken Hubbard married, in 1946, Daphne Taylor, but the marriage was dissolved seven years later. In 1975 he married Daphne Grubbe, who pre-deceased him.

GROUP CAPTAIN
ROBERT McFARLANE

Group Captain Robert McFarlane (who died on May 19 2004, aged 89) was one of the few bomber pilots to locate the German battlecruisers *Scharnhorst* and *Gneisenau* during their high-speed dash up the English Channel; he later led a Lancaster bomber squadron at the height of the Battle of Berlin, when Bomber Command's losses were the heaviest of the war.

Scharnhorst and *Gneisenau*, protected by a fighter escort and accompanied by the cruiser *Prinz Eugen*, sailed from Brest under cover of darkness on February 12 1942. The very bad weather and low cloud provided ideal cover, and the German ships were not located until late morning when they were off Le Touquet. All available Royal Navy and RAF units were ordered to attack the ships before darkness. After a gallant, but unsuccessful, torpedo attack by Fleet Air Arm Swordfish, RAF bombers were sent in.

McFarlane was flying one of six recently delivered Avro Manchester bombers of No 83 Squadron, which had left Scampton that afternoon. Flying below the clouds at 500ft, he located the ships after a wide search but was immediately intercepted by enemy fighters in three separate attacks. The bomber's hydraulics were damaged, and the bomb doors could not be opened. Unaware of this, he successfully evaded the fighters and made his bombing run over the battlecruisers, which put up a fierce barrage of anti-aircraft fire in which his rear gunner was mortally wounded.

As the bomber became increasingly difficult to control, large holes appeared in the fuselage; the gun turrets were useless; smoke filled the cockpit and the elevator cables were so badly damaged that just one of seven strands of wire held them. Nevertheless McFarlane was able to crash land at Marham, Norfolk. He was awarded an immediate Bar to the DFC he had won eight weeks earlier.

Robert McFarlane was born in Glasgow on July 12 1914, the son of a steel mill manager. He was educated at Uddington Grammar School and the West of Scotland Commercial College, then worked as an organist and choirmaster in Glasgow before joining the RAF Volunteer Reserve in 1939.

In April 1941 he joined No 83 Squadron, which was equipped with the pre-war twin-engine Hampden bomber. His arrival on the squadron coincided with the start of a long period of concentrated attacks on naval targets, in particular the "residents" at the harbour at Brest – *Scharnhorst* and *Gneisenau*, known to bomber crews as "Salmon and Gluckstein". He also attacked the ports of Kiel, Hamburg and Bremen.

The Hampdens were also used extensively to drop mines in coastal waters and harbour entrances – operations described as "gardening". During these flights McFarlane also sought out other targets to attack after "sowing" his mines. He dropped bombs on searchlights on one occasion; on another, on a flak ship.

Returning from a "gardening" sortie in the Oslo area, he bombed a ship, setting it alight before returning to spray the decks with machine-gun fire. After 27 operations he was awarded the DFC.

McFarlane then had a rest tour as an instructor on heavy bombers before returning to operations in April 1943 in No 9 Squadron, equipped with the Lancaster. The Battle of the Ruhr had just begun, and he attacked many of the most heavily defended industrial targets, including Essen, Dortmund and Cologne.

Three months later he took command of No 50 Squadron, also flying Lancasters. By November, Air Marshal "Bomber" Harris had started his major offensive against Berlin – the longest bombing campaign against one target in the war. The RAF lost more than 600 aircraft.

The role of the bomber squadron commander during these intensive night operations was crucial. McFarlane flew on many of the raids to the most difficult targets and was a constant inspiration to his crews. In February 1944 he was awarded a DSO.

McFarlane was rested in March 1944 after completing more than 50 operations, and became the chief instructor at a bomber conversion unit before attending staff college. At the end of the war, by which time he had also been mentioned in dispatches four times, he was awarded a permanent commission.

In September 1945 he joined the staff at HQ Allied Command South-East Asia. He remained in the Far East for three years, during which time he also served in Hong Kong. After a tour of duty at HQ Bomber Command, McFarlane was appointed to RAF Bassingbourn, the home of No 231 Operational Conversion Unit, which had re-formed to train crews on the RAF's first jet bomber, the Canberra. McFarlane became the unit's first chief instructor.

Following a period as the Bomber Command Liaison Officer at Supreme Headquarters Allied Powers Europe (SHAPE), he was appointed to command RAF Wahn, near Cologne, the home of two RAF night fighter squadrons and a Canberra reconnaissance squadron. With their redeployment in the summer of 1957, he moved to command RAF Gutersloh, with four Canberra bomber squadrons.

McFarlane returned to Britain in 1958 and was deputy director of logistics planning at the Air Ministry, before retiring in June 1962.

McFarlane worked in the brewing industry in Edinburgh for several years before retiring to Surrey. In addition to his excellent musical skills, he was a highly accomplished photographer and artist.

He never forgot that his family's roots were on the MacRobert estate in Aberdeenshire. In 2002 he and his youngest son instituted the MacRobert Prize at RAF Cranwell in memory of Lady MacRobert's three sons who were killed flying in the RAF. The prize is awarded to the officer cadet who, in the opinion of his or her peers, has made the greatest contribution to the course.

Robert McFarlane married first, in 1944, Jane Weightman, an RAF doctor; she died in 1973. He married secondly, in 1979, Marjorie Lawrence. He had three sons from his first marriage.

WING COMMANDER
BASIL TEMPLEMAN-ROOKE

Wing Commander Basil Templeman-Rooke (who died on July 28 2004, aged 83) was a highly-decorated wartime bomber pilot and later helped to develop the Singapore Air Force.

Templeman-Rooke − known to all as "TR" − began his career as a sergeant bomber pilot in April 1943 with No 100 Squadron flying Lancasters from Waltham, near Grimsby. The Battle of the Ruhr had just begun, and he found himself attacking some of the most heavily defended targets in Germany's industrial heartland.

On an attack against Gelsenkirchen, he was over the target when his aircraft was hit by a heavy burst of flak. Two of the aircraft's four engines were put out of action, the rudders were seriously damaged and his gunner was killed. Templeman-Rooke managed to reach his base, where he made a crash landing; he found that the aircraft had been holed no fewer than 90 times.

After flying on the raid that devastated the city of Hamburg, Templeman-Rooke attacked Turin. Despite severe icing conditions that forced him to fly through the Alps rather than over them, he carried out a successful attack. Shortly afterwards he was awarded a DFC.

During this period, he discovered that empty beer bottles made a haunting screech as they fell through the air, and he made it a regular practice to drop them over the German countryside. It was one of the few episodes of his wartime career that this ever-modest man would be happy to relate.

Basil Arthur Templeman-Rooke was born at Wimbledon on June 13 1921. He joined the RAF in 1941 and trained as a pilot in Canada, before returning to England to convert to the Lancaster.

He began his second tour of bomber operations in May 1944 when he joined No 576 Squadron as a flight commander. Initially, the squadron was used to attack targets in France in preparation for the Allied landings in Normandy. The main strategic offensive against Germany was resumed in September.

Templeman-Rooke employed what he called his "unorthodox tactics" – returning from the target, he would dive to very low level to avoid the intense anti-aircraft fire and enemy night fighters. He was awarded a bar to his DFC for "pressing home his attacks with utmost determination and accuracy", and for displaying "outstanding leadership, sustained courage and initiative".

By early 1945 Bomber Command was attacking targets

in eastern Germany. After landing in the early hours of February 14 from the raid on Dresden, Templeman-Rooke was appointed to command No 170 Squadron, which operated from the nearby airfield at Hemswell.

On March 31 he attended the briefing for a daylight attack on Hamburg when the station commander began the brief by announcing that Templeman-Rooke had been awarded an immediate DSO. One observer commented: "This was a very popular award to a very fine, outstanding pilot and an excellent CO."

On April 25 Templeman-Rooke led 16 of his Lancasters on their last bombing mission of the war; the target was Hitler's Alpine retreat above Berchtesgaten. It was Templeman-Rooke's 64th operation over enemy-occupied territory.

His next operations were of a humanitarian nature. On April 29 he led one of the first sorties of Operation Manna, dropping food to the starving Dutch population in a large pocket of western Holland which was still in German hands. In this operation – popularly known among the aircrews as "Spam" – RAF bombers dropped 6,672 tons of food from very low altitude. In a field of tulips, the Dutch people had formed the words "THANK YOU RAF" out of the red and yellow blooms.

By the end of May, Templeman-Rooke was leading his squadron during Operation Exodus, the repatriation of British prisoners of war from an airport near Brussels. With 24 ex-prisoners crammed into the fuselage of each bomber, it was hardly luxury travel; but the PoWs did not mind, since some were seeing their homeland for the first time in years.

Templeman-Rooke also flew "Cook's Tours" over the shattered cities of the Ruhr in order to show the effects of air attacks to the ground personnel who had played such an important part in keeping the aircraft flying during the bombing operations.

Templeman-Rooke remained in the RAF after the

war. He specialised in maritime operations, flying the Lancaster on air-sea rescue and sea reconnaissance sorties from Northern Ireland with No 210 Squadron. In 1951 he was awarded the AFC.

After tours of duty in Malta, he commanded No 205 Squadron, flying the Shackleton from RAF Changi, Singapore. He retired from the RAF in 1971, when he joined the Singapore Air Defence Command (SADC) in the rank of major.

With the withdrawal of British forces from the Far East in September 1971, the recently established SADC assumed responsibility for the island's defence. Templeman-Rooke commanded the operations division at the former RAF Tengah, where Singapore's fledgling squadrons were forming with the Hawker Hunter fighter and Strikemaster ground-attack aircraft. After three years he returned to England.

In 1975 he was appointed general manager of the Chelmsford Golf Club at an anxious time, when its fortunes were at a low ebb. Thanks to Templeman-Rooke's planning and good management, the club recovered to thrive once again.

On Templeman-Rooke's retirement after 20 years, the club professional arranged a "flypast" with members pulling their golf trolleys in formation as the popular "TR" took the salute from the clubhouse steps.

He continued to enjoy his golf and the comradeship of the No 170 Squadron Association.

He never forgot his young aircrew who had lost their lives, and every year he made a point of attending the annual service of remembrance at the RAF memorial at Runnymede.

Basil Templeman-Rooke died a few weeks after his second wife, Joan. He had two daughters from his first marriage.

GROUP CAPTAIN
KEITH "SLIM" SOMERVILLE

Group Captain Keith "Slim" Somerville (who died on September 1 2004, aged 84) was an experienced bomber pilot when he became involved in the development, introduction and operational use of the "Oboe" blind-bombing system, used by Bomber Command's Pathfinder Force to achieve unparalleled accuracy.

After a successful tour flying 35 operations in Whitley bombers with No 10 Squadron, which earned him the DFC, Somerville joined the Wireless Development Unit (later No 109 Squadron) at Boscombe Down.

Intelligence and scientific officers had identified a radio beam from a transmitter near Cherbourg which was used by the Luftwaffe to guide their bombers to targets in England. Somerville and his colleagues had to gather intelligence about the beam before mounting a series of operations to fly down it and bomb the source. These missions provided valuable information for the scientists at the Telecommunications Research Establishment (TRE), who used it to develop a similar bombing aid.

This early work by TRE and the aircrew at Boscombe Down led to the development over the next two years of the highly accurate blind-bombing aid Oboe, so called because the radio tone heard by the aircrew was similar to that of the musical instrument. The system was based on the transmission of a radio beam from ground emitters located on the east coast and aimed at the target. Specially equipped Mosquitoes flew along the beam to the target before dropping markers and flares for the main bomber force.

Arriving at Boscombe Down in November 1940, Somerville joined a team of four pilots, headed by Squadron Leader Hal Bufton. They flew many sorties over Germany perfecting the system before it was considered ready for operations.

The son of a banker, Keith James Somerville was born on January 26 1920 at West Ewell, Surrey, and was educated at Dorking County School.

In 1938 he trained as a pilot at the Civil Flying School, Hamble, before joining the RAF at the end of the year. His colleagues called him "Slim" after a Hollywood actor of that period, and the nickname stuck for the rest of his life.

After completing his pilot training, Somerville joined No 10 Squadron at Leeming, Yorkshire, in 1940. With inadequate navigation aids and bombsights, results on the early bombing raids were poor, but they provided the crews with much valuable experience.

Flying a Mosquito, Somerville and his navigator took part in the first Oboe raid on December 20 1942. The attack achieved modest success but experience was gained and refinements to the system were incorporated. On March 5 1943 he piloted one of the five Mosquitoes to mark perfectly the Krupps factory at Essen – some of the markers were judged to have fallen as close as 75 yards.

In the words of Air Marshal "Bomber" Harris: "This was the precise moment when Bomber Command's main offensive began; the moment of the first major attack on an objective in Germany by means of Oboe."

After two years with 109 Somerville was awarded the AFC for his pioneering work in blind target marking and posted to the Pathfinder Force headquarters.

Although on a "rest" tour, Somerville was on the first Oboe-equipped Lancaster operation on July 11 1944, leading a formation to attack the flying bomb site at Gapennes. Somerville recalled that beam flying "needed great concentration to monitor the aircraft instruments and the sound of the dots and dashes [heard through the pilot's earphones], waiting for them to merge. Once they did, it was vital to hold the required heading, speed and height while the navigator listened for the radio signal which determined the moment to release the markers or the bomb." What is more, this had to be carried out under enemy fire.

Four days before this first Lancaster operation, an Oboe-equipped Mosquito had crashed in an area of fierce fighting near Caen. The top-secret equipment was salvaged and Somerville flew over in a Mosquito to prevent it falling into enemy hands.

In October 1944 Somerville returned to operations to command the second Oboe-equipped Mosquito squadron, No 105 at Bourn, near Cambridge. In March 1945 he was promoted to group captain when still four months short of his 25th birthday. During his period in command the crews on his squadron flew almost 2,000 sorties, and Somerville's own record of operations over enemy-held territory rose to 117.

In April 1945 the Oboe-Mosquitoes of 105 were sent to pinpoint precise locations in western Holland to allow the main bomber force to drop food supplies to the starving Dutch people as part of Operation Manna.

Together the Mosquito and Oboe were one of the technological successes of the Second World War – established as a result of the remarkable partnership between the scientists at TRE and the two Mosquito squadrons. The system depended utterly, though, on the ability of those who used it, and Somerville was one of the pilots at the forefront of the development. In March 1945 he was awarded the DSO.

In 1946 he was offered a permanent commission, but his hearing had been damaged by his wartime service and he was restricted to ground duties only. He decided to leave the RAF, and became a partner in a caravan manufacturing company, Travelmaster, based at Princes Risborough, which he managed for 22 years.

"Slim" Somerville married a former WAAF, Edith Gowing, in June 1947. They had met while serving at Bomber Command headquarters. They had two daughters.

FLIGHT LIEUTENANT
BOB KNIGHTS

Flight Lieutenant Bob Knights (who died on December 4 2004, aged 83) flew his Lancaster bomber of No 617 Squadron on the three major attacks against the *Tirpitz* that culminated in her sinking on November 12 1944.

With a firm foothold on the European continent, the Allies were anxious to deploy their naval forces to other theatres, but the threat posed by *Tirpitz* prevented this. Churchill pressed incessantly for the destruction of the "beast", as he called her.

Bomber Command and the Royal Navy had mounted many attacks against the battleship, and some damage had been inflicted; but the ship was still capable of making dangerous forays against the convoys to Russia.

In September 1944 Lancaster bombers of No 9 and 617 Squadrons were sent to attack the battleship with the 12,000lb Tallboy bomb and mines. *Tirpitz* was moored in Alten fjord in the extreme north of Norway, beyond the range of the Lancasters operating from Scotland, so the force flew to Yagodnik, near Archangel, on September 11.

Knights and his crew were accommodated on a houseboat, where bedbugs were their main companions. Four days later Wing Commander Willie Tait, the CO of 617, led the force to attack the battleship, but their efforts were thwarted by a dense smokescreen. Knights lost an engine over the target and returned to Yagodnik with his bomb still on board.

The Germans moved *Tirpitz* south to Tromso, which put her just within range of the airfields in northern Scotland, from where another attack was mounted on October 29. The bombers faced heavy anti-aircraft fire, but Knights was able to drop his bomb, which landed very close and rocked the battleship. He remained circling the target as other bombs fell around the ship. Reconnaissance photographs suggested that the battleship remained intact, but, unknown to the Allies, she had sustained sufficient damage to render her no longer a threat.

On November 12 the bomber force carried out their third attack, this time in perfect weather. Knights dropped his Tallboy, which was "a very near miss", then descended to low level and flew around the ship, which he saw roll over on to her side after three direct hits. Short of fuel, Knights landed at a small fighter airfield at Peterhead.

The crews of Nos 9 and 617 received a number of decorations, with Knights being awarded the DSO.

The son of a carpenter, Robert Edgar Knights was born on January 18 1921 at Fulham, London. He attended Fulham School for Boys, where he excelled at football. He played for the London Schoolboys' XI that won the schoolboys' cup at Stamford Bridge, Chelsea, in 1935. He volunteered for service as a pilot with the RAF and was called up in March 1941.

Knights was trained in America under the "Arnold Scheme". When flying over Florida, his instructor managed to get them lost and Knights was forced to bale out – a farmer thought he was a German. After returning to England to complete his training, he was forced to bale out again, badly injuring his hand, before his aircraft crashed through the roof of a barn. He was commissioned six months later.

In June 1943 Knights joined No 619 Squadron flying the Lancaster. Soon afterwards the Battle of Berlin began, and Knights made eight attacks against the "Big City"; Bomber Command's losses were particularly high. On another occasion he was en route to bomb Hamburg when one of his engines failed shortly after he reached the Dutch coast, and he would have been justified in turning back; but he pressed on and bombed the target successfully. Within six months he had completed his tour of 30 operations and was awarded the DFC.

Knights and his crew were due for a six-month rest,

but decided that they wanted to "do something more challenging". They volunteered for service with 617 (Dambusters) Squadron, and, after an interview with Leonard Cheshire, 617's CO, they were taken on.

Cheshire had developed low-level target-marking techniques with 617 and, with the arrival of Barnes Wallis's new Tallboy bomb, the squadron specialised in attacking pinpoint targets such as concrete U-boat and E-boat shelters, aero-engines works and the V-1 flying bomb sites.

During the lead-up to the Normandy invasion, Knights bombed tunnels, rail marshalling yards and bridges to block German reinforcement routes to the invasion area. The Tallboys, dropped with great accuracy on the target markers by Cheshire and his fellow marker crews, caused devastating damage. Once the Allies were firmly established in north-west Europe, 617 turned its attention to the *Tirpitz*.

After flying 67 bombing operations, Knights was rested, and in June 1945 he was seconded to BOAC to fly converted Lancasters on routes to the Middle East and Australia, which the airline was re-establishing. Knights left the RAF at the end of 1946 to join BOAC, and over the next few years flew the Argonaut and the Boeing Stratocruiser, the latter on the North Atlantic route. After a spell on the Britannia he converted to jets, and flew the inaugural VC 10 flight to Montreal in 1966. Later he flew the Boeing 747 and was one of the fleet's training captains. He retired from British Airways in 1976.

Knights gave strong support to RAF charities. He was president of the Guildford branch of the RAFA and a long-standing member of the Aircrew Association. He developed a keen interest in bell-ringing and became captain of the bell tower at St Peter and St Paul at Albury, near Guildford.

Bob Knights married, in 1947, a serving WAAF, Helen Maloney; they had two sons and a daughter.

FLIGHT LIEUTENANT
PAT O'HARA

Flight Lieutenant Pat O'Hara (who died on January 22 2005, aged 91) was a navigator in one of the most remarkable examples of combat between an RAF heavy bomber and German night fighters in the Second World War.

His Stirling bomber of No 214 Squadron attacked Bremen on the night of June 27-28 1942, and was hit by anti-aircraft fire over the target. With one of the engines ablaze, the aircraft set off for home on its remaining three. It was approaching the Zuider Zee when a German night fighter attacked from below, killing the rear gunner and damaging another engine.

A second fighter blew a large hole in the bomber's fuselage before one of the surviving gunners shot it down.

The front gunner had left his turret to render aid to the wounded wireless operator when the Australian captain, Sergeant Frank Griggs, warned him that two more fighters were attacking. Rushing back to his turret he found it would not rotate because it was jammed; with O'Hara holding his legs, the gunner was just able to lean forward and fire the guns. One of the fighters flew into the cone of fire and was destroyed.

When the other German aircraft attacked, the mid-upper gunner engaged it, but one of the two guns jammed. With the remaining gun he shot down the fighter. Another fighter was also beaten off.

The bomber had descended during this engagement, and the pilot was struggling to maintain control; the tailplane hit the sea and part of it was ripped away before he could climb to a safe height.

O'Hara showed great skill in guiding his aircraft to the airfield at Stradishall, in Suffolk, by map-reading and astro-navigation. But the three working engines had sustained damage and the undercarriage could not be lowered. Just before reaching the airfield, two more engines failed, and the pilot made a belly-landing after crashing through the boundary fence of the airfield.

The RAF described their night's work as "a memorable operation", and the six surviving crew members were awarded the DFM.

Arthur Patrick O'Hara was born on November 8 1913 at Bradford in West Yorkshire. After attending St Bede's School in his home town, he worked for a local potato merchant, then volunteered for the RAF at the end of 1940. Considered, at 27, too old to be a pilot, he was accepted for navigator training.

O'Hara joined No 214 Squadron at Stradishall and flew ten operations, including the first 1,000-bomber raid on Cologne. He attacked other targets in Germany before he and Griggs, his pilot, were commissioned and left to join No 109 Squadron, just as it was converting to the Mosquito and transferring to the Pathfinder Force.

No 109 was pioneering the new, and highly accurate, blind-bombing target-marking technique known as Oboe. Flying down a narrow radio beam directed towards the target by a ground-based emitter, the Mosquito dropped flares and markers over the target for the main bomber force. O'Hara and his pilot were one of the original six crews.

By early 1943 they had flown seven operations against heavily defended targets, and the early difficulties experienced with the unique system, developed by the scientists at the Telecommunications Research Establishment at Malvern, had been resolved.

Griggs and O'Hara were the first to drop a new type of target-marker when they spearheaded the attack on Dusseldorf on January 27 1943, flying at 27,000ft, where they were untroubled by the intense flak directed at the main bombers flying below them. O'Hara had soon flown more than 50 operations, the majority against targets in the Ruhr. He was awarded the DFC.

When his pilot returned to Australia, O'Hara flew a few sorties with another pilot whose navigator was ill. Just ten minutes before he was due to take off with this pilot for another attack against the Ruhr, the pilot's regular navigator announced that he was fit to fly and took O'Hara's place. The bomber was shot down over the target and the crew killed.

After a period as an instructor at the Mosquito Pathfinder Training Unit, O'Hara returned to 109 as one of the most experienced Oboe-Mosquito navigators.

He flew many daylight attacks against V1 sites, airfields and communications targets in the build up to D-Day. After completing almost 100 sorties over enemy-occupied territory, O'Hara was finally rested. In January 1945 he was awarded a Bar to his DFC.

O'Hara joined No 147 Squadron flying both passengers and freight in Dakotas between the UK and recently captured airfields on the Continent.

In September 1946 he was appointed a navigator in the King's Flight. When George VI and Queen Elizabeth made a royal tour of South Africa in the spring of 1947, O'Hara formed part of the crew of the No 3 aircraft carrying the Royal Household staff.

At the end of 1947 he left the RAF to become an air traffic controller with the Civil Aviation Authority. After appointments at Speke (Liverpool airport) and Ringway, Manchester, O'Hara became a radar consultant at the headquarters of the CAA in London. He finally retired in 1974.

Pat O'Hara's first wife, Emily, whom he married in 1937, died in 1978. In 1982 he married his second wife, Betty, who died in 1997. There were two daughters from his first marriage.

GROUP CAPTAIN
DUDLEY BURNSIDE

Group Captain Dudley Burnside (who died on September 20 2005, aged 93) flew bomber and transport operations over the North-West Frontier in the late 1930s and was decorated for gallantry; he went on to complete two tours of operations in Bomber Command, and later flew Sunderland flying boats during the Korean conflict.

Burnside arrived in India in 1937 and joined the Bomber-Transport Flight at Lahore, flying the antiquated biplane Valentia transport aircraft. He was soon in action against the dissident tribesmen of the region. This included night bombing against the villages and caves of the Fakir of Ipi, after leaflets had been dropped earlier during the day to warn the inhabitants to evacuate the area. He also carried out many bombing raids against the cave complexes on the Afghanistan border.

He transferred to No 31 Squadron in April 1939 and was appointed a flight commander. Throughout the remainder of the year he was continually engaged in operations against the Fakir's forces, and on one bombing operation destroyed the enemy's headquarters. In 1940 he was awarded the DFC.

In September 1940 the Army garrison at Chitral was relieved by air for the first time. Burnside and his pilots flew continually to effect a relief, taking a few days rather than the weeks involved in the previous overland operations. After taking off fully laden with troops and stores, the old Valentias had to circle for more than an hour before they had sufficient height to clear the 10,400ft Lawarai Pass.

Burnside and his fellow pilots flew reinforcements to Singapore in February 1941, and saw their first action at the end of March. A pro-German politician, Rashid Ali, seized power in Iraq, and Burnside led a flight of No 31's

Valentias from Karachi to Shaibah, near Basra, with Army reinforcements. He carried out many similar flights during April and May, and on one occasion was en route to Habbaniya when a fierce dust storm forced him to land, short of fuel, at a small airstrip. Within minutes he realised he was behind enemy lines; ground forces opened fire, wounding his gunner and damaging the aircraft. He immediately took off downwind and was able to escape, arriving at Habbaniya with virtually no fuel left.

Flying requisitioned Indian Airline Douglas DC2 transport aircraft, 31 Squadron moved to Burma in February 1942. Burnside was made a liaison officer with the American Volunteer Group (the Flying Tigers) before assuming command of the airfield at Akyab. Three weeks later he just managed to escape as the Japanese overran it.

After almost five years of operations in India, Afghanistan and Burma, Burnside returned to England, where he converted to the Wellington and joined Bomber Command.

Dudley Henderson Burnside was born on January 26 1912 at Woodford, Essex, and educated at King Edward VI School, Bury St Edmunds. Aged 17 he enlisted in the Territorial Army, serving as a private soldier with the 14th London Regiment for six years before joining the RAF in October 1935 to train as a pilot. After flying with No 58 Bomber Squadron for a year he was posted to India.

In November 1942 Burnside was promoted to wing commander and appointed to form and command a new Canadian Wellington squadron, No 427, based in north Yorkshire. He attacked many industrial targets during the so-called Battle of the Ruhr.

On the night of March 5 he was sent to bomb Essen, and his aircraft was hit by flak before reaching the target. The navigator, who was standing beside Burnside, was killed; the wireless operator had a foot blown off. The aircraft controls were damaged and fumes quickly filled the cockpit.

Burnside decided to press on, and he successfully bombed the target despite being illuminated by searchlights. On the return flight, night fighters attacked the Wellington, but Burnside's evasive action and the fire by his gunner shook them off. With limited control, he flew the badly-damaged bomber back to base, where he made an emergency landing at an airfield in Suffolk. For his outstanding airmanship and courage, he was awarded a Bar to his DFC. Two of his crew also received DFCs, and the wireless operator was awarded the Conspicuous Gallantry Medal.

Shortly after his squadron converted to the Halifax bomber, Burnside was attacked five times by different aircraft during a raid on München-Gladbach.

In May 1943 Metro-Goldwyn-Mayer adopted 427 Squadron and allowed the names of stars such as Lana Turner, Greer Garson and Joan Crawford to be displayed on the aircraft. In recognition of this association, 427 adopted the name "Lion Squadron", a title which persists to this day.

In September 1943 Burnside took command of RAF Woodbridge, Suffolk, one of three airfields on the east coast designed to allow crippled bombers to crash land immediately after crossing the coast on the airfield's extra-long and very wide runway. In one month alone, Burnside and his staff had to deal with 72 heavy bombers that had crash-landed. He was mentioned in dispatches.

In October 1944 Burnside volunteered to return to operations, and assumed command of No 195 Squadron, flying Lancaster bombers. He led it on many night and daylight bombing raids over Germany in the lead-up to VE Day. Returning from Gelsenkirchen, his Lancaster was badly damaged and set on fire, and he was forced to make an emergency landing on three engines at Brussels airport. He was awarded the DSO.

Burnside was granted a permanent commission in the RAF and served on the staff of No 38 Group before leaving for the Far East. After converting to the Sunderland flying boat he took command in early 1949 of the RAF base at Koggala in Ceylon, where his squadrons flew air-sea rescue and reconnaissance sorties over the Indian Ocean. On the closure of the base a year later, he took command of the Far East Flying Boat Wing at Seletar, in Singapore.

The wing's Sunderlands flew anti-terrorist patrols around Malaya before providing detachments at Iwakuni in Japan during the Korean War. Burnside commanded the units, which flew anti-shipping and coastal patrols off Korean waters. For his services with the wing during the conflict, he was appointed OBE.

After completing a familiarisation course on jet aircraft, Burnside assumed command of RAF Hemswell in Lincolnshire, the home of two Canberra bomber squadrons. The filming of *The Dambusters* took place during his time there. After two years he took up an appointment at the headquarters of the Allied Air Forces Central Europe at Fontainebleau. In 1959 he was the Deputy Director of Organisation at the Air Ministry, retiring from the RAF in 1962 with the rank of group captain.

Burnside was an excellent artist. He was a very early member of the Guild of Aviation Artists and exhibited for many years at its annual show. He specialised in oils, using a limited palette based on white and browns. Many of his subjects were drawn from his own flying career, but he also produced First World War aviation scenes. He was elected a vice-president of the guild.

He made numerous visits to Canada as a guest of his old squadron. Officiating at a change of command ceremony in 1995, he was made an honorary colonel of the Canadian Armed Forces.

Burnside was a keen sportsman, and represented the

RAF at squash in India; he also played hockey for his county. A quiet, unassuming man of great integrity and courtesy, he was deeply affected by the losses amongst his young bomber crews.

Dudley Burnside married first, in 1942, Denise Dixon; the marriage was dissolved in 1985, and the following year he married Joyce Waldren, who died in 2003. He had a son and a daughter from his first marriage, and a stepson and stepdaughter from his second.

GROUP CAPTAIN
KENNETH SMALES

Group Captain Kenneth Smales (who died on September 27 2005, aged 88) was serving as a bomber pilot when he escaped from France in 1940 by commandeering an abandoned aircraft and a motorcycle before boarding one of the last ships to leave Brest.

He returned to complete two tours of operations during the early campaigns mounted by Bomber Command, resulting in the award of the DSO and the DFC. In his post-war career he had two eventful appointments as an air attaché in Latin America.

Smales took command of No 44 Squadron in April 1942, shortly after it had been the first to be equipped with the Lancaster bomber, and at a time when it had suffered heavy losses – his predecessor had been lost on his first day in command. Morale was very low but, in the words of one of his officers, "he pulled it together by sheer example".

Although Smales had not previously flown the four-engine Lancaster, after a few familiarisation sorties he took off at the head of his squadron on the night of May 30 1942 to bomb Cologne on Operation Millennium, better known as "The First Thousand Bomber Raid". His squadron was due to be one of the last to arrive over the target, and he could see the flames when he was still 70 miles away.

As a wing commander, Smales was not expected to fly often, but that was not his style. He always flew with a scratch crew, often novices, a trait that endeared him to his men. He was once described by one of those who flew with him as "the antithesis of the Hollywood-style leader. His method was simple and effective. He only flew when an operation was known to be a stinker and he never had a regular crew. This was a special form of suicide, and he was undoubtedly the bravest man I ever flew with."

On a number of occasions Smales's bomber was damaged by anti-aircraft fire. On one operation, he had just taken off from his base in Lincolnshire to bomb a target in Italy when one of the engines of his Lancaster failed. Disdaining to turn back, he pressed on to his target, which could be reached only by flying over the Alps. His aircraft only just managed to clear the peaks, and Smales bombed the target successfully. He arrived back at his base after being airborne for more than ten hours. He was awarded the DSO.

On a trip to Berlin, his 50th over enemy-occupied territory, Smales was hit in the arm by shrapnel. Despite loss of blood, he remained at the controls for the four-hour return flight and landed the damaged bomber with one arm useless; an operation saved the arm, but he had to hand over command of No 44 to his deputy.

Throughout his tour in command of the squadron, Smales's calmness created a sense of confidence and, within a few months of his arrival, morale in 44 Squadron had recovered.

The son of an officer in the Durham Light Infantry who had been awarded the MC in the First World War, Kenneth Phillips Smales was born on January 7 1917 at Whitley Bay, Northumberland. He was educated at

Norbury College, and joined the RAF in 1937, training as a pilot.

Initially he served with No 37 (Bomber) Squadron. At the outbreak of war he was appointed ADC and personal pilot to Air Vice-Marshal Playfair, the Air Officer Commanding the newly-formed Advanced Air Striking Force sent to various airfields in northern France. During the "phoney war" Smales enjoyed the social opportunities to the full, and developed a love for the country that was to last all his life.

After the German blitzkrieg of May 10 1940, the AASF headquarters was constantly on the move. Smales was sent to an abandoned airfield near Rheims to recover some Hurricanes which had been left behind, but the light communications aircraft transporting him had to land after it was hit by machine-gun fire, injuring the pilot.

Smales, however, immediately grabbed the controls by leaning over the unconscious pilot and took off again. Despite two flat tyres and a major petrol leak, he managed to land at an Allied airfield. Smales and a comrade then commandeered another aircraft, which they flew to an airfield near Brest. There they took two motorcycles, on which they finally made it to the port, escaping in one of the last ships to leave.

Smales was appointed a flight commander of 44 Squadron, flying the outdated Hampden bomber. The primary targets of many of his 33 operations were ships and naval bases at Brest, Kiel and Wilhelmshaven, and casualties were high. In some attacks Smales adopted an individual technique of flying at very low level up the estuaries to gain surprise and to allow his gunners to engage the defences. On his return, the station commander – noting the salt and mud splashes on the aircraft – would comment: "I see you've been boating again."

Returning one night from a raid on Dusseldorf, Smales was circling his Lincolnshire airfield preparing to land when a German night fighter attacked his aircraft. As a stream of bullets hit the port engine he turned away steeply and escaped. The lights were extinguished on the airfield and Smales managed to land his badly-damaged bomber on one engine without the aid of any lighting. At the end of his tour he was awarded the DFC.

For a rest period Smales was appointed the chief instructor of the Hampden training unit, when he was mentioned in dispatches. After his tour in command of No 44, he served at Bomber Command and at the Air Ministry in the Directorate of Tactics.

In 1946 Smales was sent as the air attaché to Guatemala, where he experienced an attempted revolution. He also frustrated a Guatemalan plan to invade British Honduras – his prompt action after seeing a build-up of airborne troops and a practice amphibious landing resulted in the arrival of a Royal Navy warship, which landed a party of marines to guard the only airfield. The Guatemalan authorities learned of his actions, and he was transferred to Mexico City.

Smales helped to introduce into service the RAF's first jet bomber, the Canberra. In 1957 he was given command of the Flying Wing at RAF Wildenrath, in Germany, equipped with Canberras and Meteor reconnaissance aircraft. On promotion to group captain, he went on to command RAF Leeming with its Javelin night fighters.

In 1965 Smales was appointed air attaché in Buenos Aires. During his time there the President of Argentina was deposed twice, the second time by a military junta. After Smales had met the Air Force general of the junta, his car was fired on by mistake by two soldiers, and a bullet was later found embedded in the seat. Six months later he retired from the RAF to take up a senior appointment with the Road Transport Industry Training Board.

Though a keen and expert cricketer and squash player

in his youth, in retirement Smales concentrated on sailing, fly fishing and golf. He was a man to whom the sense of duty was paramount, and he often concealed his sensitivity beneath a cloak of formality. But his quick wit and sense of humour – in particular his sense of the ridiculous – made him an excellent companion.

Kenneth Smales married Eileen Kent in 1944. They had two sons and a daughter.

WING COMMANDER PETER WARD-HUNT

Wing Commander Peter Ward-Hunt (who died on December 7 2005, aged 89) took part in some of the most significant early wartime operations mounted by Bomber Command, which were a prelude to the large-scale strategic bomber offensive that followed.

On the night of May 15 1940, in retaliation for the German invasion of Holland and Belgium, the RAF was given political clearance to attack targets east of the River Rhine for the first time, and Ward-Hunt's Hampden was one of 99 bombers sent to bomb targets in the Ruhr. This was the first strategic bombing of German industry in the Second World War. But after three more raids against German targets, the Hampden crews were diverted to provide support for the British and French ground forces retreating towards Dunkirk. Over the next ten days Ward-Hunt flew 12 bombing operations against German troop communications and airfields.

With the fall of France, Ward-Hunt returned to attacks against German industry. On the night of August 25 he bombed Berlin, after the War Cabinet – following the Luftwaffe bombing of London during the Battle of Britain – had given approval for the first raid on the German capital. Three nights later he returned, and this was followed by an attack against Stettin on the Baltic coast. These raids of eight and nine hours duration – in obsolescent and cramped, unheated bombers with minimal navigation aids – were at the extreme range of the Hampden. After a third visit to Berlin, Ward-Hunt, having completed 32 operations, was awarded the DFC and rested.

The son of Captain W Ward-Hunt DSO, RN, Peter Ward-Hunt was born on December 6 1916 at Gibraltar. He was educated at the Imperial Service College, Windsor, and in July 1937 joined the RAF on a short service commission. He joined No 106 Squadron flying the Hampden, transferring to No 49 at the end of 1939.

After instructing pilots to fly the Hampden, Ward-Hunt returned to operations and joined No 207 Squadron flying the Manchester, a bomber with a notoriously poor record of serviceability with under-powered and unreliable engines. In order to reach bombing height, it was sometimes necessary to jettison some bombs on the way to the target.

At the end of September 1941 he was sent to drop sea mines in the Baltic. To reduce the range he positioned his aircraft at an airfield on the Norfolk coast, and, after five attempts were cancelled because of poor weather, he finally took off on the night of September 29. Over the Baltic Ward-Hunt was attacked by seven German fighters in a running battle that lasted almost 90 minutes, and he was forced to jettison his mine before escaping, finally landing in Norfolk with his fuel reserves almost exhausted. On return from an operation, he was in the habit of telephoning his wife to let her know of his safe arrival. After this demanding and exhausting flight, he was unable to reach a telephone and for several hours she feared the worst.

On March 3 1942 Ward-Hunt flew on another of Bomber Command's important operations, Air Marshal Arthur Harris's first attempt to fly a concentrated, precision attack against a single target. The Renault factory at Billancourt, near Paris, which was producing 18,000 lorries a year for the Germans, was selected for an attack by 235 bombers.

Ward-Hunt was forced to drop his bombs from 3,000ft with virtually every other bomber raining down their bombs from above him. The raid was considered a great success and was to prove the forerunner of the Command's tactics in the future.

By May 1942 Ward-Hunt was one of the most experienced pilots in Bomber Command, and he was selected to convert others to the Lancaster bomber, a four-engine descendant of the Manchester. On the night of May 30 1942 Harris launched the first of his Thousand Bomber raids. In order to generate 1,000 aircraft, he had to use instructor crews, and Ward-Hunt was ordered to fly a Manchester on the successful attack against Cologne.

After nine months as an instructor, Ward-Hunt was sent in February 1943 as a flight commander to No 106 Squadron, led by a colleague from his Hampden days, Wing Commander Guy Gibson, who a few months later would achieve fame as the leader of the Dambusters' raid. Ward-Hunt's fellow flight commander was John Searby, who went on to act as the master bomber on the raid against Peenemünde. They were a formidable trio.

Ward-Hunt arrived on the squadron just as the Battle of the Ruhr began, and over the next few weeks he attacked many of the most heavily defended targets in Germany, including Berlin, Essen, Nuremburg and Stuttgart. He also attacked Milan and the French Biscay ports, the operational bases of the U-boat force. By June 1943 he had completed 55 bombing operations and was awarded a second DFC.

On promotion to wing commander, Ward-Hunt became responsible for directing the bombing operations from Ludford Magna, a Lancaster airfield near Lincoln.

At the end of the war he was mentioned in dispatches.

He left the RAF in December 1945 and embarked on a career in air traffic control, serving for many years at Heathrow. He also had spells of duty at Benbecula, Hurn (near Bournemouth) and at Thurleigh, Bedford. He played a significant role in the design of some of the instrumentation of the Concorde flight simulator.

Ward-Hunt was a great rugby devotee and was still playing the game in his fifties. He was a founder-member of the Ellingham club at Ringwood and for many years served on the committee of Bedford RFC. He was a passionate gardener, and a skilled carpenter who was regularly asked to make bespoke rocking horses.

Peter Ward-Hunt married Erica Turtle in March 1940; she died in 2003. His eldest son predeceased him, and he had another son and a daughter.

GROUP CAPTAIN
DICK MAYDWELL

Group Captain Dick Maydwell (who died on January 8 2006, aged 92) commanded a wartime squadron of Marauder bombers that roamed the Mediterranean attacking ships and aircraft; as a pre-war big game hunter, he considered his flying operations to be a "Mediterranean safari with free accommodation, transport, guns and ammunition and the chance of a major trophy".

Commanding No 14 Squadron, based in Egypt, Maydwell flew operations against shipping in the Aegean and the eastern Mediterranean. On one occasion he was firing at barges north of Crete when German fighters attacked his aircraft. Taking evasive action at 100ft, he managed to escape, despite his aircraft being damaged and his gunners wounded.

In February 1943 he flew two mine-laying operations

in daylight to the Burgi Channel, north of Athens, a round trip of 1,650 miles. On the second occasion the weather was appalling, and the mountains surrounding the narrow channel made the operation particularly hazardous. He managed to drop his mines from a very low level – the splashes struck the underside of his aircraft. Intelligence later reported that two ships had been sunk and the channel blocked for a considerable time. Maydwell was awarded the DSO.

The aircrew of 14 Squadron included many South Africans, New Zealanders and Australians. The Aussies were renowned for their exuberance and irreverence towards authority and protocol, but Maydwell quickly recognised their fighting spirit and courage. His quiet authority, insistence on flying the most dangerous operations himself and his warm welcome to newcomers soon endeared him to his men, who called him "The Boffin"; he christened his aircraft Dominion Triumph, which was emblazoned on its nose.

After moving to Tunisia, Maydwell and his crews attacked shipping and aircraft on their long patrols off Italy, Sardinia and Corsica. Near Genoa, he intercepted a three-engine Italian transport aircraft and his gunners shot it down. Whilst supporting the Anzio landings, he came across a four-engine German transport plane and this too was shot down.

Maydwell's most remarkable action was on July 30, when he was patrolling to the north of Corsica. He saw a giant six-engine Me 323 transport aircraft, unescorted, flying low over the sea. He manoeuvred his Marauder to allow his gunners to open fire and three engines were set ablaze. The massive aircraft, described by Maydwell's navigator as looking like "a block of flats", crash-landed on the shore. The crew escaped unhurt and Maydwell held his fire.

On his final sortie in Dominion Triumph Maydwell attacked a Junkers 52 off La Spezia. His aircraft was hit by return fire, but the damage his gunners inflicted gave the German aircraft little chance of returning to base. The following day he was promoted, and he handed over command of No 14.

Wynne Somers Goodrich Maydwell was born on July 18 1913 at Bournemouth. Always known as Dick, he was educated at Malvern before entering Sandhurst as an officer cadet.

Commissioned into the Somerset Light Infantry in 1933, he served at Blackdown, where he commanded the anti-tank platoon. He learned to fly at Brooklands Flying Club before joining the 2nd Battalion at Poona, India, where he developed his love of game shooting and where, under licence, he shot a tigress and a panther. In May 1937 he volunteered for a four-year secondment to the RAF and trained as a pilot.

He joined No 53 (Army Co-operation) Squadron, flying Hector biplanes before the squadron was re-equipped with the Blenheim. He went to France in early September 1939, and was stationed near Epernay flying reconnaissance sorties. When the German blitzkrieg began in May 1940 he was on leave in England. On returning to France, he was unable to get back to No 53 and served as the adjutant of a Hurricane re-arming and refuelling unit at Rouen. He finally escaped from St Malo to Jersey.

Maydwell rejoined 53 Squadron and from July until the end of the year he bombed the Channel ports from Flushing to Lorient. By the end of 1940 he was the last surviving pilot from the pre-war squadron. He was awarded the DFC.

In March 1941 Maydwell left for the Middle East and commanded a small photographic survey unit flying Maryland aircraft. His photographs were used to produce maps of the strategic areas of Syria, Lebanon and Palestine that covered the anticipated area of a German advance through Turkey to the Suez Canal. In April 1942 he was posted to command No 14 Squadron, which was still operating the Blenheim for bombing airfields in Crete and Libya and attacking German re-supply columns in the Western Desert.

In August No 14 was withdrawn to the Canal Zone and re-equipped with the powerful B-26 Marauder bomber, one of only two RAF squadrons to fly the American aircraft. After early difficulties, when a number of aircraft were lost due to the failure of the fin and tailplane assembly, the fast and heavily-armed aircraft achieved great success under Maydwell's leadership.

Promoted to group captain, Maydwell took command of No 325 Wing at Trapani in western Sicily, flying convoy patrols and providing support for the Salerno landings. In early 1944 the wing moved to Naples, but Maydwell decided to return to operational flying. En route to the RAF headquarters to negotiate a flying appointment, his Jeep was hit by a train and he was severely injured. His right leg was severed above the knee and he spent the next 18 months recovering. He remained in the RAF, specialising in photography. After four years at the Air Ministry he moved to the Advanced Flying School at Driffield, where – despite his disability – he flew Vampire and Meteor jet fighters. In December 1954 he moved to HQ Western Command at Chester as the land/air warfare officer. He retired from the RAF in 1958.

Maydwell was an excellent shot, and after moving to Somerset he carried out the control of wood pigeon, shooting more than 10,000 in two years. He then turned to deer control, and over the next 38 years he shot 2,264 roe deer, the last when he was 87.

In 1982 Maydwell contacted Walter Honig, the German pilot of the Me 323 he had shot down over Corsica. They met at Honig's flying club at Baden, and Maydwell gave Honig a propeller tip from his aircraft, bearing the inscription, in German: "A memento of our meeting at Cape Corse, on 29 July 1943". They remained friends for the next 20 years.

After a brief wartime marriage, in 1949 Dick Maydwell married Sylvia Kent.

AIR COMMODORE
WILF BURNETT

Air Commodore Wilf Burnett (who died on November 26 2006, aged 91) led the first RAF V-bombers to drop bombs in anger during the attack on Almaza airfield at Suez.

As CO of No 148 Squadron, which provided five of the force of 25 Valiants, Burnett led his crews in training at 40,000ft; but on the night of the first attacks, on October 31 1956, they were ordered to make their drops from 30,000ft.

As the crews of 148 pressed on to Almaza they encountered a jet stream at 30,000ft as well as problems connected with their radar bombing system, which made the attack difficult. Burnett was the first to drop his 11 1,000lb bombs. But the raid was only partially successful.

When he returned to base on Malta, he protested at the order to bomb from an inappropriate height, and was cleared to attack from 40,000ft on subsequent raids. The following night he and his men attacked Fayid airfield. His bomb-aimer dropped an accurate flare, and, on a second approach, placed the bombs in the centre of the airfield. Three nights later Burnett bombed a barracks; the ceasefire soon followed. When the Valiants returned to England he was mentioned in dispatches.

Wilfred Jasper Burnett was born on November 8 1915 at Fredericton, New Brunswick. He was educated at Fort Francis High School, Ontario, and worked on a dairy farm while becoming a trooper in the New Brunswick Dragoons.

He learned to fly a ski-equipped Moth before working his passage to England to join the RAF in 1937. After gaining a short service commission, he trained to fly the Hampden bomber and joined No 49 Squadron as war broke out.

When German forces invaded Holland on May 15 1940, the RAF mounted its first bombing sortie east of the Rhine, and 99 bombers were sent to Dortmund. During this flight Burnett doubled his night flying experience and, passing near Rotterdam, which was still burning from the heavy German bombing, realised that the "phoney war" was over.

Over the next few weeks he attacked many targets in Germany and France and dropped mines in the Kattegat. After 32 operations he was awarded the DFC. Air Marshal "Bomber" Harris, his group commander, described him as "a fine type of bomber captain who does consistently excellent work".

Following a rest as a bombing instructor, Burnett became flight commander of the second RCAF bomber squadron, No 408, which was also equipped with out-dated Hampdens. While returning in bad weather from Hamburg in January 1942, his aircraft ran out of fuel after ten hours and crashed in the Yorkshire Dales. He was thrown clear and seriously injured, but his three crew were killed.

After a period as an air staff officer at HQ No 3 Group, Burnett volunteered to return to operations as commander of No 138 (Special Duties) Squadron, flying Halifaxes on clandestine sorties in support of SOE. He arrived shortly before D-Day and, although not required to fly often as a CO, regularly undertook missions to supply the Maquis, who were trying to stop German reinforcements reaching the Normandy beachhead. No 138 then made drops to the "Linge Group" of the

Norwegian Resistance. Burnett was awarded the DSO and Croix de Guerre avec Palme.

After the war he was seconded for a year to BOAC, for which he flew flying boats on the Far East route. On one occasion he had to divert to the Communist-held Hainan Island, where he found a fuel dump abandoned by the Americans. Using a felt hat to strain the contaminated fuel, he spent three days transferring it to the aircraft with a saucepan. He then served on the air staff in Jerusalem, when terrorist attacks were being made on RAF installations, before being posted to the RAF Mission in Greece during the civil war.

After two years as chief instructor at a pilot training school, Burnett commanded the Flying Wing at the RAF Flying College, Manby. He also carried out navigational flights to the North Pole. Once the airspeed indicator of his Hastings iced up, but a resourceful flight engineer rectified the problem; they proceeded to the Pole, where he dropped a miniature bottle of Scotch with a Union flag attached. In January 1956 he was awarded the AFC.

After Suez Burnett assumed command of the V-bomber base at Marham, Norfolk, before serving as air adviser to the British High Commission in New Delhi. His final appointment in the RAF before he retired proved to be one of his most demanding. In October 1966 he was appointed air officer, administration, at Air Headquarters, Aden.

Plans were being made for the withdrawal the following year, which was later described as one of the most successful military operations since the Second World War.

Despite the deteriorating internal security situation it was crucial that the essential services and infrastructure were maintained as the military presence was steadily withdrawn. It was also important that the run-down should be orderly, culminating in a secure and stable handover to the local authorities. A senior colleague commented that this required a steady hand and level head for the complex administrative planning, "and the ever-dependable Wilf Burnett provided just that".

Burnett described his RAF career as "the best a man could have". In addition to his decorations for gallantry, he was three times mentioned in dispatches. On leaving the service he was appointed secretary of the Unit Trust Association; in 1980 he was appointed OBE.

Burnett was an expert fly fisherman, maintaining a rod on the Itchen, which he fished until his 90th year. He was a fine woodworker, specialising in the old craft of Tunbridgeware, and was a keen photographer.

Wilf Burnett married, in 1939, "Joy" Wenham, with whom he had a son and a daughter.

AIR VICE-MARSHAL
JACK FURNER

Air Vice-Marshal Jack Furner (who died on New Year's Day 2007, aged 85) flew wartime operations with Bomber Command and took part in secret electronic counter-measure sorties on D-Day; in peacetime he made a major contribution to the development of the RAF's nuclear capability during the Cold War.

Furner was a specialist navigator when, in 1957, he was selected to command the operations wing at RAF Waddington, home of the first Vulcan V-bomber squadrons. With his expert knowledge of the aircraft's navigation and bombing systems, he provided support for the training of new crews as well as the development of its operational capability; and in 1958 he was the navigator of the Vulcan that broke the Ottawa to London record (in 5 hours 45 minutes).

With the rapid expansion of the V-Force, Furner was appointed to HQ Bomber Command to head the operational plans division, where he had the task of planning the action to be taken by Britain's 144 V-bombers and 60 Thor ballistic missiles in time of war. It was a job with "a strange air of unreality", he recalled afterwards.

As the Cuban missile crisis developed, the atmosphere in the Bomber Command operational bunker became tense, and Furner's immediate superior described him as "a tower of strength".

Derek Jack Furner was born at Southend on November 14 1921, and was educated at Westcliff High School, where he excelled at mathematics. After a brief period working for the Imperial Bank of India he was called up, and volunteered for flying duties as a navigator. He was sent to Canada under the British Commonwealth Air Training Plan.

In March 1943 Furner joined No 214 Squadron, flying the Stirling four-engine bomber. He flew 25 operations, including the major "firestorm" raids against Hamburg. On the night of August 17 his squadron was briefed to attack the scientific establishment at Peenemünde on the Baltic coast. Reconnaissance photographs had identified the site as the development centre for Hitler's terror weapons, the V-1 flying bomb and V-2 rocket. The raid successfully delayed their development, but 40 bombers failed to return.

When Furner and his crew completed their tour a few weeks later, they were one of only two crews to survive the six-month period. He was awarded the DFC.

After a brief rest Furner volunteered to return to operations as the navigation leader of his old squadron, which was re-equipping with the US B-17 Flying Fortress to operate in the secret world of electronic counter-measures. The squadron's role was to fly in support of the main bomber force and jam enemy radar and radio communications. On the night of the D-Day landings, Furner was airborne, jamming the enemy's early warning radar sites by dropping strips of tin foil. His aircraft was attacked and damaged by a German night fighter.

In early 1945 Furner transferred to Transport Command and was sent to India, where he flew Dakotas on re-supply operations in support of the advance in Burma. As the war ended he flew many sorties to Saigon and Bangkok to repatriate Allied PoWs, then remained in the Far East for a further two years flying VIPs and transport operations from Hong Kong and Singapore.

After a period as a navigation instructor he attended the RAF's specialist navigation course in 1950 before moving to Boscombe Down, where he was involved in the development of bombing and navigation aids, including the first Doppler equipment.

These became the core of most of the RAF's operational aircraft systems for the next three decades. He was awarded the AFC.

Furner spent two years on similar work with the USAF Weapons Guidance Laboratory, flying most of their strategic bombers before returning to complete the Flying College course and taking up his appointment at Waddington.

After three years in charge of the Nuclear Activities Branch at HQ SHAPE in Paris, Furner spent two years in the Ministry of Defence before taking command in 1968 of RAF Scampton, home of three Vulcan squadrons equipped with the Blue Steel stand-off weapon. He was the first navigator to command an operational flying station in peacetime.

In 1969 he took command of the Central Reconnaissance Establishment, then had two years as secretary to the Military Committee of NATO. At the end of this tour he was promoted to air vice-marshal, one of the first two navigators to reach the rank. He spent the last two years of his service as the Assistant Air Secretary with responsibility for the careers of the RAF's aircrew.

Furner worked for five years as general manager of his

brother's firm, Harlequin Wallcoverings, before finally retiring. But he continued to be busy in the last 20 years of his life. He was chairman of the Aries Association for specialist navigators, and administered the block of apartments in Eastbourne where he lived for many years. He was an active president of the Eastbourne Sinfonia.

In 1997 the Furners moved to Cromer, where they had met in 1944 when he was serving at nearby RAF Oulton. He became a stalwart of the Cromer Society and was in great demand to speak on a diverse range of subjects including space, computers, climate change and music.

Furner was elected a member of Mensa in 1989. He owned one of the first computers, and had almost completed his autobiography when he died.

Jack Furner was appointed OBE in 1959 and CBE in 1973.

He married, in 1948, Patricia Donnelly, with whom he had three sons.

FLIGHT LIEUTENANT
WALLACE McINTOSH

Flight Lieutenant Wallace McIntosh (who died on June 4 2007, aged 87) joined the RAF to escape acute poverty, and survived 55 bombing operations; by the end of the war he had shot down eight enemy aircraft and was recognised as Bomber Command's most successful air gunner.

On the night of June 7 1944 McIntosh was the rear gunner of a Lancaster with No 207 Squadron, which took off from Spilsby, Lincolnshire, to attack targets near Caen in Normandy. As the aircraft crossed the coast of France, a German Junkers 88 fighter attacked, forcing the pilot, Wing Commander John Grey, to take evasive action by "corkscrewing" under the direction of McIntosh and his fellow gunner, the Canadian Larry Sutherland.

The combined firepower of the two gunners set the Junkers ablaze and sent it spinning to the ground. A minute later a second Junkers closed in; there was an exchange of fire which ended in the German aircraft exploding.

The Lancaster crew pressed on to complete a successful attack on their target. On the return flight they were attacked by a Messerschmitt night fighter. Once again the two gunners opened up, and the enemy aircraft fell away on fire, crashing into the sea.

When news of this triple success reached the headquarters of Bomber Command, the C-in-C, Air Marshal Arthur Harris, telephoned RAF Spilsby and asked: "Who the hell were those guys?" A few days later McIntosh and Sutherland were awarded immediate DFCs and received a hand-written note of congratulation from Harris, a rare accolade.

Wallace McIntosh was born on March 27 1920 in a barn near Tarves, Aberdeenshire, during a blizzard. After a few days his teenage mother – an unmarried servant – gave him to her parents, who brought him up. As a result he was trailed around Aberdeenshire and Perthshire while his grandparents sought farm work. They were once reduced to living in a shed after his ailing grandfather was made redundant.

McIntosh did not learn about Christmas until he was seven, and never celebrated a birthday until he joined the RAF. But he could steal, kill and skin a sheep before he was 12; he could snare anything that could be cooked; and he could pull salmon from a river with the skill of a master poacher. He left school at 13 determined to escape the struggle to survive, and worked as a labourer and gamekeeper on several Perthshire estates.

Young Wallace recognised that the war offered an opportunity to escape poverty, and joined the RAF in

1939 as an airman. He volunteered for aircrew duties but was initially rejected and became a service policeman. On one occasion he tried to engage a low-flying German bomber with his rifle. After being accepted to train as an air gunner in March 1943 McIntosh joined 207 Squadron at Langar, near Nottingham, as the mid-upper gunner in a crew of seven.

On his ninth operation he shot down his first enemy fighter, and probably destroyed a second. He took part in the major raids against Hamburg in July 1943 and the raid on the rocket research centre at Peenemünde in August. He also flew on two "shuttle" raids, when targets in Italy were attacked by bombers which had to fly on to land in North Africa. After 32 operations, at a time when Bomber Command losses were at their highest, McIntosh was rested and awarded the DFM. Immensely proud of being commissioned in June 1943, he returned to No 207 the following February for a second tour of operations, flying as the rear gunner in the squadron commander's crew.

On the night of May 3 one of the four engines of his Lancaster caught fire on take-off, but Grey pressed on, flying at low level on three engines to the target at Mailly-le-Camp. They arrived to find most of the bomber force circling the target while German night fighters were starting to create havoc. Due to radio problems the instructions from the master bomber were not heard, and 28 of the 173 bombers were shot down. McIntosh's aircraft was attacked, and he shot down a Messerschmitt Bf 110.

In another raid over France, his Lancaster lost two engines after being attacked, and the crew prepared to bale out. As they flew lower they observed an American bomber in the water, and circled it to transmit its position until a third engine started to fail. Grey managed to make an emergency landing in Kent just as the third engine conked out.

After 55 operations McIntosh was rested again, and was awarded a Bar to his DFC, making him one of the most highly-decorated air gunners in Bomber Command.

After the war he remained in the RAF, dropping supplies from Dakotas to feed cattle in remote areas during the severe winter of 1947. He found it difficult to settle in a peacetime air force, however, and left the following year to work as an agricultural salesman in Aberdeenshire, where he met his wife Christina. McIntosh worked for Barclay, Ross and Hutchison in Montrose and Elgin. When the company was taken over by Elbar Farm Services he moved to its headquarters at Elgin as director of the ironmongery division.

On retiring in 1985 he completed a sponsored 2,000-mile tour of former bomber stations to raise money for two memorials to the aircrew of his squadron killed in action – 207 lost nearly 1,000 men during the war. He was a strong supporter of the Air Gunners' Association and of the 207 Squadron Association, regularly attending their annual reunions.

McIntosh had a great zest for life and was well-travelled. He always described his education as "faces and places", and actively encouraged his family to take every chance to see the world and never to pass up any opportunity that came their way.

His biography, *Gunning for the Enemy* by Mel Rolfe, was published in 2003, and two years later a painting depicting his Lancaster returning from a raid brought the public's attention to a very modest man whose family knew little of his achievements until late in his life.

Wallace McIntosh's wife Christina died in 1989; they had a son and two daughters.

DAREDEVILS

FLIGHT SERGEANT
ALFRED CARD

Flight Sergeant Alfred Card (who died on May 14 2002, aged 80) made 1,004 parachute jumps and was one of the pioneers of freefall parachuting in Britain; as an instructor with the RAF he trained more than 2,000 servicemen as well as agents who operated behind enemy lines.

He was also a founder member of the Edward Bear Club, whose members were accompanied by a teddy bear on every jump. The club originated when Card was training a party of officer cadets from Sandhurst; when an Army instructor produced a teddy, Card improvised a tiny parachute and harness. He then reported to the pilot: "Twenty troops and one teddy bear to drop."

Alfred Walter Card was born at Crewe into a family of master confectioners on October 21 1921. Aged 14 he left Edleston Road School to work at the Torkington hat factory; he also helped his father, who sold boiled sweets at street markets. In 1939 Card volunteered for the RAF. Three years later, when he was a physical training instructor, he ignored his father's advice ("Never volunteer for anything, Alfie") and applied for parachute training.

He later remembered being invited to jump or dive from the high board of a swimming pool at RAF Cosford, Staffordshire: "It looked the heck of a long way down. The sergeant called 'when you are ready' and, plucking up my courage, I fell off like a sack of spuds. Hitting the water with an almighty splash, I surfaced to see a group of grinning faces. The instructor said 'Okay, you'll do' — and that was my fitness test to become a parachutist."

Posted to RAF Wilmslow in Cheshire, Card found himself at the RAF's parachute training school at

Ringway airport, near Manchester, where Sergeant Taffy Evans, a cheerful Welshman, explained: "The course takes two weeks: one week in the hangar on basic, one week making two balloon and two aircraft jumps. Then, if successful, you become an instructor."

All went well and, after helping to train members of the Parachute Regiment, Card was posted in 1943 to Egypt, where he trained many of those who were dropped into Yugoslavia and Greece to fight behind enemy lines. He was a popular instructor, and no one was forced to jump; if a pupil refused, Card took the line: "It isn't everybody's cup of tea – and perhaps you have more sense than the rest of us." There would be no recriminations.

By 1956 Card had trained some 2,000 parachutists, and his contribution was recognised with the award of an AFM. Four years later, he achieved the rare distinction of being awarded a Bar.

In the early 1950s Card had joined the British Parachute Team, and in 1959 he became an early member of the British Parachute Association, which had been established to develop the activity as a sport.

He was also a founder member of the Oxford Parachute Club, one of the first such organisations. In 1960 he made a 62-second freefall jump from 12,000ft, then a rare feat.

Card was posted in 1961 to RAF Akrotiri, in Cyprus, to help train the Near East Air Force parachute medical team. In 1963 he was preparing to launch himself into a dropping zone there when an RAF doctor joked: "We should have a spot of first aid practice on the ground after we jump – why don't you break your leg for us, Alf?" On the way down, Card became tangled in another parachute; as a result his own collapsed and he landed awkwardly – duly breaking his leg. It was his first, and last, accident.

He was disappointed at not being offered a commission and, shortly after receiving a plaque in Cyprus commemorating his 1,000th jump, Card decided to seek early retirement; he became a postman at Crewe, later moving to the Civil Service as an executive officer.

Alfie Card married, in 1942, Ada Filer, whom he had met while on a bayonet fighting course at Dinas Powis in South Wales. They had two sons and a daughter.

NORMAN HOFFMAN

Norman Hoffman (who died on September 22 2003, aged 79) was a wrestler, a gymnast, an RAF physical training instructor and a champion skydiver; he was also one of the first parachutists to adopt the arms-out freefall method of descent and went on to invent a system for releasing weapons from a parachute which is still used by RAF paratroopers today.

The son of a stationmaster at Howth, Norman Hoffman was born on February 24 1924 in Dublin. As a youth he was very athletic and competed in more than 400 Greco-Roman wrestling bouts by the time he was 20.

In 1948, having recently married, Hoffman moved to Britain (against the wishes of his father, who had wanted him to become a fireman in Ireland) and joined the RAF. He soon volunteered to join a team of RAF skydivers and three weeks later found himself at the world championships in France. Although his team came last, Hoffman was hooked, and by the early 1960s (having become British champion in 1959) he was regarded as one of the best skydivers in Europe.

When Hoffman began parachuting it was commonly held that the skydiver should hold on to the ripcord during the descent. Hoffman, however, keen to perfect his technique, preferred to put both arms out like a bird in flight and reach for the cord when the time came to open the parachute. This freefall method is now standard practice.

He set a number of altitude records and his highest drop was from some 35,000ft, which was remarkable for its time as the planes and equipment were primitive and parachutists risked freezing to death at such heights. During his time in the RAF he also designed a mechanism to help paratroopers get hold of their weapons before they hit the ground.

In 1965 Hoffman was posted to Kenya where he helped to set up a parachute school for the Kenyan army. The following year, however, during an air display, his parachute failed to open and he fell 5,000ft to the ground, fracturing his spine in three places and breaking his sternum. Undeterred, he was jumping again five months later.

Hoffman returned to England in 1970. He was promoted to flight sergeant and spent a number of years testing parachuting equipment for the Joint Air Transport Establishment; but by 1979 the accident and the years of freefalling had taken their toll on his spine, and he was invalided out of the RAF.

After he retired Hoffman took up woodwork and made a number of items of furniture for friends and family. He continued to be an enthusiastic sportsman and at the age of 74, while on holiday in Florida, he raced on a jetski. Despite his athleticism, strength and reputation as a risk taker, in his private life he was the gentlest of men.

With his wife May, Norman Hoffman had two sons.

ADRIAN NICHOLAS

Adrian Nicholas (who died on September 17 2005 in a skydiving accident in Holland, aged 43) was not a man to let his own mortality get in the way of a good time;

known as "the man who can fly", he pushed the boundaries of "extreme" sports, pioneering new types of skydiving.

With curly fair hair and dashing good looks, Nicholas was an adventurer in the best British tradition of derring-do. He seemed to spend almost as much time in the air as on the ground, making more than 6,500 jumps in five years in 30 different countries. He baled out of a Russian jumbo jet on to the North Pole; jumped into a Dolgan Eskimo village in Siberia; made the first freefall flights through the Grand Canyon and over the Great Wall of China; and won numerous medals for extreme sports.

In 1998, wearing a webbed "Wingsuit", he set world records for the furthest unassisted human flight and for the longest freefall. Two years later he decided to test the theory that Leonardo da Vinci had designed the world's first working parachute.

In 1485 Leonardo had scribbled a simple sketch of a four-sided pyramid covered in linen. Alongside, he had written: "If a man is provided with a length of gummed linen cloth with a length of 12 yards on each side and 12 yards high, he can jump from any great height whatsoever without injury."

Defying expert predictions that it would not work, and with advice from Professor Martin Kemp of Oxford University, Nicholas and his Swedish girlfriend, Katarina Ollikainen, constructed a parachute according to Leonardo's design; and on June 25 2000 Nicholas launched himself from a hot air balloon 10,000ft over South Africa. Surrounded by two helicopters and two parachutists, he parachuted for five minutes as a black box recorder measured his descent, before cutting himself free of the contraption and releasing a conventional parachute.

Although aeronautical experts had predicted that it would tip over, fall apart or spin uncontrollably, Leonardo's parachute made such a smooth and slow descent that the two jumpers accompanying Nicholas had to brake twice to stay level with him. "It took one of the greatest minds who ever lived to design it," Nicholas observed, before adding modestly, "but it took 500 years to find a man with a brain small enough to actually go and fly it."

The son of a property developer, Adrian Nicholas was born on March 4 1962. As a boy he was always getting into scrapes, loved every kind of sport and was an avid reader of adventure stories in Boys' Own comics.

Nicholas was educated at Aldenham School, Elstree, and at a local sixth form college. He made his first parachute jump out of a plane aged 17 and went on to become a cave diver (a cave in Florida was named after him), skydiver, snowboarder, wrestler, jet pilot and rally driver before joining Capital Radio as the station's "Eye in the Sky" traffic and travel correspondent, working alongside Chris Tarrant.

He succeeded in raising what was once a prosaic element of Capital Radio's drive-time programming into an essential ingredient of its output. He even had his own fan club. "He's a madman," Chris Tarrant observed affectionately, "absolutely barking. He gave me a lift once from Charing Cross Road. I am never, ever getting into a car with that person again."

In 1994 Nicholas decided to concentrate on skydiving full-time after meeting Patrick de Gayardon, a pioneer of sky surfing. They became friends and dived together everywhere, Nicholas supporting his adventures by working as a photographer, selling television footage and lecturing company employees on how to overcome fears and phobias.

But in 1998 Nicholas watched in horror as de Gayardon plunged to his death trying to become the first man to fly. De Gayardon had been wearing a specially-adapted Wingsuit, with webbing between the arms and torso and between the legs; but a technical malfunction prevented him from opening either of his two parachutes towards the end of his flight.

Instead of giving up, Nicholas determined to carry on where his friend had left off, and on March 12 1999, after making further adaptations to de Gayardon's Wingsuit, Nicholas attempted to break two world records for time and distance.

He jumped over California from 35,850ft, wearing an oxygen mask, and nearly died in the attempt. "As I stepped out of the aeroplane, the exhaust valve in my oxygen mask froze solid," he recalled. "At 35,000ft the temperature is -120°C. It meant that, though I had taken in a breath of air, I couldn't breathe out. I couldn't take the mask off either because at that height I would have died."

By contorting his face, he was able to break the seal slightly, so that he could at least exhale; but he was not able to breathe properly for about four minutes. "The main thing I remember was feeling embarrassed that all these people were there and I was going to muck it all up and die." Despite nearly choking to death, Nicholas flew for four minutes 55 seconds and covered ten miles, establishing new world records for the longest sky dive and the furthest human flight. "I don't think of myself as a nutter but I believe I can fly," he said afterwards. "I'm a real life Peter Pan."

Nicholas featured in the IMAX film *Adrenalin Rush* and appeared on many television programmes, including *Tomorrow's World* and *Top Gear*. In 2000 BBC 1 screened a 50-minute documentary about his life, as part of its Extreme Lives series, called *Lord of the Skies*.

"I'll die skydiving," Nicholas predicted. "It will happen. We all die skydiving, eventually. But it will be worth it."

Adrian Nicholas had a daughter with his girlfriend, Katarina Ollikainen.

SQUADRON LEADER
RAY HANNA

Squadron Leader Ray Hanna (who died on December 1 2005, aged 77) was the leader of the RAF's Red Arrows aerobatic team in its early years, developing a level of expertise and panache in formation aerobatic flying that attracted universal acclaim and established "the Reds" as the world's premier team and star attraction at airshows worldwide.

During the 1950s and early 1960s, the RAF instructed various fighter squadrons to provide an official aerobatic team to participate in public events and provide welcome publicity.

The Hunters of the "Black Arrows" and the "Blue Diamonds" were extremely successful; but, with the loss of fighter squadrons due to budget constraints, it was a wasteful activity to withdraw a squadron from the front line each year. The Central Flying School was asked to provide an official team and, in 1965, the Red Arrows were formed at Little Rissington. Hanna was selected to join the team and within a year he became its leader.

He was the ideal candidate to lead a group of individualistic and brilliant fighter pilots. An outstanding and experienced fighter pilot himself, his determination, modest authority, skill and professionalism proved an inspiration to his nine colleagues.

After an intense period of practice, flying their highly manoeuvrable, all-red Gnat aircraft, the team's reputation for excellence on the airshow scene was soon established. In a very short time, the Red Arrows, together with the Battle of Britain Memorial Flight, had become the public face of the RAF.

Hanna led The Reds for four seasons, displaying at almost 100 events each year. Their appearances included a tour of the Middle East, for which the short range of the Gnat necessitated numerous stops en route before arriving in Amman to perform in front of King Hussein. This exposure to tens of thousands of new admirers immediately launched the Red Arrows on to the world stage.

Raynham George Hanna was born on August 28 1928 at Takapuna, New Zealand. He was educated at Auckland Grammar School before taking flying lessons on the Tiger Moth. In 1949 he worked his passage to England by ship to join the RAF.

Hanna gained his pilot's wings before the demise of the powerful piston-engine fighters such as the Tempest, Sea Fury and Beaufighter, and his opportunities to fly them proved to be the beginning of a love affair with these evocative fighters that was to last a lifetime. He joined No 79 Squadron in Germany, flying the Meteor jet in the fighter reconnaissance role, one of the most demanding for a single-seat pilot. This gave him the opportunity to indulge in authorised low flying, at which he excelled. Formation aerobatics was a routine for all fighter squadrons, and Hanna developed a passion for this type of flying.

His appointment to the Overseas Ferry Squadron provided him with the opportunity to fly a wide variety of jet fighters. He ferried the early Hunters from Britain to India and the Far East; this involved flying over Pakistan, where he was often intercepted by Pakistani fighters, enabling him to indulge in mock combat when fuel reserves allowed.

On one occasion Hanna was returning a Vampire fighter to Britain when the aircraft's only engine failed over India and he was unable to restart it. He eventually made a skilful crash-landing amongst a number of giant anthills close to a railway line. He waited for a passing train, which stopped for him; but the Indian guard refused to let him board since he was unable to pay the fare. Hanna finally offered his watch as payment; the guard scribbled out an IOU and allowed him to travel.

After qualifying as a flying instructor, Hanna became a member of the Meteor aerobatic team at the College of Air Warfare, and in 1965 was selected to join the Red Arrows team on its formation.

In 1971 he decided to leave the RAF to begin a new career in civil aviation. Initially he flew the Boeing 707 for Lloyd International Airways, followed by seven years with Cathay Pacific flying from Hong Kong. In 1979 he headed an international company operating executive Boeing 707s.

Shortly before leaving the RAF Hanna had been approached by Sir Adrian Swire, who had recently purchased a Spitfire IX. Swire invited him to fly and display the aircraft at a time when there were few of the wartime fighters flying regularly. This proved to be the beginning of a unique relationship between Hanna and MH 434 (the aircraft's serial number), an association which will be one of the lasting memories for Hanna's countless admirers.

In 1981, with his only son Mark, Hanna founded the Old Flying Machine Company, specialising in the restoration and operation of classic "warbirds" such as the Mustang, Spitfire and Kittyhawk. In addition to appearances at hundreds of airshows, Hanna and his son and their pilots were in regular demand by the film industry. Some of their flying sequences in the films *Empire of the Sun* (1987) and *Memphis Belle* (1990) were breathtaking in their skill and audacity. After seeing the former, Steven Spielberg insisted that Hanna and his pilots should provide the flying elements for his film *Saving Private Ryan* (1998). Hanna also featured in the 1988 television series *Piece of Cake*, a drama about an RAF fighter squadron.

Hanna regularly shipped some of the company's aircraft to his native New Zealand to participate in the Warbirds Over Wanaka airshow, recognised as the premier warbird flying event in the southern hemisphere. In later years he established a branch of his company in New Zealand.

In September 1999 Mark Hanna's death in Spain, whilst flying a restored Bf 109 fighter, was a devastating blow; but Ray Hanna vowed to continue their joint work, and he retained his passion for flying to the end; six weeks before his death he was practising formation aerobatics in Spitfire MH 434.

Hanna was never afraid to be blunt when the occasion demanded, but his intolerance of bureaucracy and all but the very highest standards was tempered by his modesty and warmth.

For his leadership of the Red Arrows, Hanna was awarded a Bar to the AFC he had received earlier. He also won numerous international awards, including the Britannia Trophy. In 2000 the Air League awarded him the Jeffrey Quill Medal for his "outstanding contribution to the development of air-mindedness in Britain's youth".

Ray Hanna married, in 1957, Eunice Rigby, with whom he also had a daughter.

SQUADRON LEADER
MICHAEL CASANO

Squadron Leader Michael Casano (who died on July 18 2006, aged 93) was one of the RAF's most colourful and dashing characters and took part in the fighting in Iraq and Syria in 1941 before joining Glubb Pasha in the Arab Legion.

Casano was commanding the RAF's No 2 Armoured Car Company, guarding airfields in the Western Desert, when he was ordered, on May 5 1941, to go immediately to the fort at Rutbah, 1,000 miles away on the main land route between Palestine and the large RAF airfield at Habbaniya, west of Baghdad.

Five days later he arrived to join HAB force, which had gathered to relieve Habbaniya, where the RAF flying training school had repulsed air and ground attacks led by the rabidly anti-British and pro-German Iraqi lawyer Rashid Ali.

On May 14 Casano's company was attached to Brigadier Joe Kingston's relief column, "Kingcol", whose task was to advance on Baghdad. Operating with the southern column during the move eastwards, he led his armoured cars to within 20 yards of enemy positions, although constrained by single-track and often flooded roads.

He came under continuous heavy fire, but progressed across the Fallujah Plain until he reached a canal 14 miles from Baghdad. The bridge had been demolished, and as his cars halted they came under intense machine-gun fire. Casano was forced to withdraw, but the following day was able to continue his advance when he once again came under heavy machine-gun and shell fire.

An armistice was declared on May 30, and Casano camped ten miles from Baghdad to carry out escort and patrolling duties. On June 20 he moved with his three cars for operations on the Syrian border. He was used as the advance guard, and the following day was spotted by Vichy French aircraft. For the next ten days he made repeated attempts to advance towards Palmyra, but each day encountered heavy opposition. During this period he carried out forward reconnaissance sorties and cut the telephone line on the main oil pipeline near Homs.

Casano finally withdrew to Amman on July 5, having been in constant action for more than two months. It was later announced that he had been awarded the MC. The citation recorded: "The successes of the 'HAB' force, both in Iraq and Syria, were largely due to this officer; he operated virtually alone, and his zeal and devotion to duty deserve the highest praise. He displayed the greatest gallantry."

Somerset de Chair, the intelligence officer of King-col, shared many experiences with Casano and wrote of him in his book *The Golden Carpet*: "His face was thin and sallow. He resembled Mephistopheles in every respect, with a thin pointed nose, arched black eyebrows and mocking dark eyes. After sharing every variety of adventure with him I see him now preparing for another campaign leaning forward in the lamplight as if he were the devil himself, and saying in a long drawn out whisper 'go the whole hog'."

Michael Peter Casano was born on June 7 1913 at Folkestone and educated at Dover College. He had always wanted to join the RAF, but failed the entrance examination to the RAF College, Cranwell; so he joined the East Kent Regiment as a private soldier. He purchased his release three years later and was given a short service commission in the RAF.

He trained as a pilot in Egypt, but crashed his Fury biplane, fracturing his skull. Assessed subsequently as "unlikely to become an effective service pilot", he was posted to No 2 Armoured Car Company in April 1936, serving in the Middle East.

After returning from Syria Casano and his company went back to the Western Desert, and he led them during the Battle of Alamein and the offensive that followed. On March 6 1943, while the company was at an advanced landing ground, German aircraft attacked his position; Casano was badly wounded and had to be evacuated to hospital. While recovering from his wounds he met Major-General Sir John Glubb (Glubb Pasha), who persuaded him to join the Arab Legion and take command of their armoured cars, a role he filled until the end of the war.

Casano was inseparable from his dog, Butch, who accompanied his master everywhere. On one occasion Casano entered Shepheard's Hotel in Cairo with Butch, to be told that dogs were not allowed. Casano responded:

"Well, you had better put him out then", and the two marched off to the bar. Butch was later killed by enemy fire – his demise made news in the *Egyptian Gazette.*

After the war Casano was granted a permanent commission in the administration branch and served in Germany, Malta and various units in England. He retired in 1958 and became a driving instructor.

With his striking profile, roguish appearance and adventurous attitude, Casano became something of a legend in the RAF; other units knew his company as "Cass's Boys".

His men found him an inspiring and courageous leader who led by example and never asked others to do what he was not prepared to do himself. On operations he would insist on taking his turn to "make a brew" for his men. At reunions many years later the respect and esteem in which he was held was clear – when he entered a room, every man would stand.

Michael Casano married, in 1943, Helen Czarnicka, an authoress and the daughter of a White Russian general. His wife, with whom he had a daughter, predeceased him.

SOE

SQUADRON LEADER
JOHN MOTT

Squadron Leader John Mott (who died on May 9 2002, aged 85) flew clandestine missions for the Special Operations Executive (SOE) after being shot down as a bomber pilot, evading capture and reaching home.

In the New Year of 1941 – before he exchanged bomber operations for SOE special duties – Mott, then a sergeant, was piloting a two-engine Armstrong Whitworth Whitley of No 78 Squadron when, after attacking the U-boat pens at Lorient on the French Atlantic coast, he was shot down over Brittany. Baling out of his burning bomber over Lanvallon, Mott was hidden by the Delavignes, a staunchly anti-Boche couple, at their home at Nantes for four months.

During this time he learned sufficient French from Tantine, his hostess, to be accepted as a local; he also assisted Resistance communications with London until he learned that a fellow airman, who knew his whereabouts, was being interrogated by the Gestapo. Fearing the worst, Mott walked into Spain in November and, as he put it, "thumbed a lift home from Gibraltar in an Australian Sunderland flying boat". Mott was debriefed and then posted to No 138, later 161, both special duties squadrons designated to SOE. Piloting a Westland Lysander, he began to fly agents and others in and out of occupied France.

On May 28 1942 Mott, by now a flight lieutenant, was forced to abandon his Lysander which had become bogged down in a field at Chateauroux. However, he had safely landed his passenger, a Belgian fighter pilot who, having been shot down and lost an eye, had volunteered to join the MI9 escape line which had helped him back to Britain.

The two men split up, Mott making his way to La Chartre, where he fell into the hands of the French police. It did not help that the town was strongly pro-Vichy. Mott was held in French prisons until he was passed on to Genoa, from where, following the Italian armistice in September 1943, he was put on a train to Austria. After cutting a hole in their cattle truck, Mott and some fellow officers escaped but encountered a band of Yugoslav partisans who mistook them for Germans; Mott was being forced to dig his own grave when a British liaison officer arrived and intervened.

The partisans were attacked by German troops and Mott, anxious to distance himself from the enemy, made his way back to Italy where, in February 1944, he was befriended by a Contessa Cancellucia and provided with forged papers.

In the company of a small group of others who were escaping, and who had pooled borrowed money, Mott put to sea aboard a German whaler which he dragged to the water with the help of some cows. Naming the boat *Pitch and Toss*, Mott and his friends reached advancing Allied troops at Porto San Giorgio, south of Monte Cassino, on March 19 1944.

Half-starved and seasick, Mott landed just as Mount Vesuvius was erupting. The first British officer to welcome and interrogate him was his younger brother Pip, whom he had not seen since 1937.

Arnold John Mott was born on May 12 1916 and educated at Christ's Hospital; it was here that his determination to fly was inspired by the sight of a Zeppelin overhead.

He joined the RAF Volunteer Reserve in 1938 and was mobilised on the outbreak of war, remaining in the regular service until 1959 when he retired and joined the Inland Revenue as a tax inspector.

After five years, and describing himself as a gamekeeper-turned-poacher, Mott joined the tax accountants Grant Thornton at Petersfield, Hampshire. As an active member of the RAF Escaping Society, he also devoted himself to the welfare of former Resistance people who had suffered at the hands of the Germans after helping him and others.

He remained especially close to the Delavigne family (Tantine and her husband Adrien had been arrested after Mott returned home: she survived torture in a concentration camp; Adrien died in captivity). Mott's wartime links and fondness for his Breton friends (and lobster) made the fishing village of Lesconil a second home; he and his family inherited the Delavignes' house.

Mott, who had been mentioned in dispatches, was appointed MBE in 1944 "for his great fortitude and determination to return to active duty".

John Mott married Barbara Phelps in 1945. They had three daughters and a son who served in the RAF until he was killed in a flying accident in his Phantom in 1980.

SQUADRON LEADER
JAMES "WAGGY" WAGLAND

Squadron Leader James Wagland (who died on April 2 2005, aged 91) was the senior navigator at RAF Tempsford, the home of the special duties squadrons flying clandestine operations for the Special Operations Executive (SOE) into occupied Europe; he became one of the RAF's most highly decorated navigators, honoured by four countries.

Pinpoint navigation was the key to success for the aircrews required to locate − after flying hundreds of miles − the lights from five or six torches in a farmer's field. This primitive arrangement marked the dropping or landing zone for delivering supplies or agents to enemy-occupied Europe.

The operations mounted by the two resident squadrons, Nos 138 and 161, ranged from Norway to the south of France, and Wagland was responsible for planning and co-ordinating the complex and dangerous routes and advising the aircrews.

He paid particular attention to the route-planning for the pilots who flew the single-engine Lysanders without the assistance of a navigator or of radar navigation aids. Relying entirely on map-reading, and flying during the periods of moonlight, the pilots used route "strip maps" on the long flights, which Wagland had helped to prepare. Not content with just fulfilling his crucial ground duties, he took part in many operations with both squadrons, sometimes flying long-range sorties in converted Halifax bombers to Poland and Norway, at other times flying in Hudsons and Lysanders to land in rough fields in France prepared, manned and guarded by members of the Resistance.

Wagland's early sorties to France in a Hudson were flown with Group Captain "Mouse" Fielden – also captain of the King's Flight. On one occasion they were taking two agents to a field south of Lyon when Fielden dived towards the ground because he thought he had seen a fighter. Wagland commented later: "This did not help navigation." They failed to make contact with the reception party and were forced to fly on to Maison Blanche in Algeria, where the Hudson was wrecked in a ground collision.

Wagland flew most of his sorties to France with the squadron commander, Wing Commander "Bob" Hodges (later Air Chief Marshal Sir Lewis Hodges). On the night of September 14/15 1943 they took eight "Joes", as their unidentified passengers were known, to a field near Cosne. Some of the return passengers failed to arrive on time and Hodges had to leave the engines running for fear that, if stopped, they might not restart. After ten anxious minutes he decided to take off with the four who had arrived, and asked if there were any volunteers for the spare seats. One young man stepped forward and came to England – they never discovered who he was.

A month later Hodges and Wagland, accompanied by a second Hudson, flew to a field near Lons-le-Saunier where Paul Rivière, of the French Resistance, had 18 passengers for England. Using the bends in the River Loire as a final navigation checkpoint, Wagland led the two Hudsons to the torchlit field. Hodges landed first and delivered his passengers, collected those for England and took off again after just three minutes on the ground. In 1948 the president of France, Vincent Auriol, came to London on a state visit, the first since the war. He asked if it would be possible to trace the crew who had brought him out of France on that flight five years earlier. Wagland and Hodges were later invested as Officers of the Légion d'honneur.

Wagland was always seeking ways to ease the navigation workload, particularly for the Lysander pilots who flew alone. The radar navigation aid "Gee" was fitted to an aircraft, and Hodges and Wagland set off for France with it; but the set interfered with the compass, and they had to return when they ran into foul weather over the Loire. The next night they flew the sortie without the Gee and delivered a Joe to a field south of Poitiers. There they picked up two passengers, including one of their own squadron pilots who had been forced to abandon his Lysander a month earlier when it became bogged down in a field.

On their return they found England shrouded in fog, and conditions rapidly deteriorated. Hodges and Wagland saw the runway at Tangmere at the last minute and were able to land. By the time two other Lysanders had returned, the weather had become even worse. Their agents did not have parachutes, so both pilots attempted to land; both aircraft crashed, and both pilots and two of the agents were killed. In September 1943 Wagland was awarded a Bar to an earlier DFC.

James Leslie William Wagland was born on November 4 1913 at West Ham, London. He attended Palmers School, in Essex, before joining his father in the banking world. Just before the outbreak of war he volunteered for flying duties in the RAF. After completing his training in August 1940, he joined No 78 Squadron at Dishforth, in Yorkshire, which was equipped with the pre-war Whitley bomber.

With the most rudimentary navigation aids, the Whitleys of No 78 bombed Berlin, and in November they attacked the Fiat works in Turin, a round trip of almost ten hours which included staggering over the Alps. The majority of Wagland's sorties were against industrial targets in Germany. After completing 30 operations he was awarded the DFC.

During his time with the Whitley force, Wagland's outstanding navigational ability had come to the attention of one of the squadron commanders, Charles Pickard, who later became the irrepressible leader of No 161 Squadron. In November 1942, after a short spell at HQ Bomber Command, Wagland found himself at Tempsford as the navigation leader working with Pickard. In charge of the map store of Wagland's navigation section was an attractive WAAF, whom he later married.

Throughout the war, Wagland sported a luxuriant moustache. Aircrew flying over enemy-occupied territory carried a series of photographs to be used on false identity papers if they were shot down. When it was pointed out to him that his RAF-style moustache would hinder his disguise, he said that, if necessary, he would shave it off. He was unable to explain how he would subsequently make use of the photographs.

Wagland was known for his conservative views. On one occasion he brought François Mitterrand, another future president of France, back to England. Years later he commented that perhaps this was the one flight on which he should have got lost.

Wagland remained at Tempsford until the end of the war. In October 1945 the Queen of the Netherlands awarded him the Dutch Flying Cross for his services to Holland. He was also awarded the Polish War Cross.

After the war, he returned to banking, joining the London branch of Martin's Bank as a foreign exchange dealer before becoming assistant manager. Following the takeover of Martin's by Barclays in 1969, he left to join the management team of the Manufacturers Hanover Bank in London, retiring in 1974.

A man of great modesty, Wagland rarely spoke of his wartime service, referring to his most dangerous sorties as "a bit tricky". He was a strong supporter of the Aircrew Association and the Tempsford Association, and continued to keep in touch with many of the Joes whom he had carried and with the members of the reception parties who manned the French fields used for his clandestine flights.

"Waggy" Wagland married his Tempsford WAAF, Molly Cleevely, in 1945. She died in 1999. They had a son and a daughter.

AIR CHIEF MARSHAL
SIR LEWIS HODGES

Air Chief Marshal Sir Lewis Hodges (who died on January 4 2007, aged 88) was one of the RAF's most highly decorated pilots; after an audacious escape from occupied France and an outstanding record flying clandestine operations in Europe and the Far East he went on to have a distinguished peacetime career.

Flying moonlit operations for the Special Operations Executive (SOE) Hodges landed his single-engine Lysander or the larger Hudson aircraft in remote French fields to deliver and pick up agents. He picked up two future presidents of the Republic (Auriol and Mitterrand), bringing them to England for meetings with General de Gaulle.

Unaware (for security reasons) of his passengers' identities at the time, Hodges was astonished when, in 1948, President Auriol appointed him a Companion of the Légion d'honneur; 40 years later President Mitterrand promoted him to be a Grand Officier of the Order.

Neither of these two sorties, nor the rest of his wartime operational career as a pilot and squadron commander, would have been possible had he not escaped from captivity after crash-landing his bomber in northern France in September 1940 and returned to his squadron the following June.

On the night of September 4 he was coming back from a raid on Stettin in his Hampden bomber of No 49 Squadron when he was forced to land in a field in Brittany. Together with his air gunner, who had not heard his order to bale out, he burned the aircraft before setting off to the south-east on foot.

Moving from farm to farm, the two men obtained civilian clothes to wear over their uniforms and eventually made their way to Marseilles in Vichy France, where they were arrested and imprisoned. Hodges escaped and stowed away on a French cargo ship, but was picked up in Oran and returned to Marseilles; he was then sent to the Vichy-controlled camp for British prisoners at St Hippolyte du Fort, near Nîmes, pending trial.

He escaped from the fort with a pass he had forged (using a potato to create the official-looking stamps), took a train to Perpignan and then a taxi to the Spanish border before crossing the Pyrenees. In Spain, however, he was arrested by customs officials and sent to the notorious concentration camp at Miranda del Ebro. Five weeks later a British Embassy official secured his release.

On June 13 1941 Hodges was repatriated from

Gibraltar and returned to his squadron. When asked what he had missed most whilst on the run for eight months, he responded without hesitation "my pyjamas". From that moment, he always wore them under his uniform when flying on operations.

He resumed night attacks over Germany until the following April, when he was awarded the DFC.

Lewis Macdonald Hodges (always known as Bob) was born on March 1 1918 at Richmond, Surrey, and educated at St Paul's School. On hearing that he had been selected for the RAF College at Cranwell, the High Master commented: "They seem to be taking anyone these days." On graduating in 1938 as a pilot officer Hodges joined No 78, a Wellesley bomber squadron, at Finningley, Yorkshire, before moving to No 49 in 1940.

He was talent-spotted for special duties by Wing Commander Charles Pickard, familiar as the Wellington pilot in the film *Target for Tonight* and later killed on the daring low-level raid against the Amiens jail. Pickard had just taken over No 161, one of two squadrons supporting SOE operations from Tempsford, Bedfordshire, and he selected Hodges as one of his two flight commanders piloting Halifax bombers used for dropping supplies and agents to resistance groups in Europe.

By May 1943 Hodges had been awarded a Bar to his DFC for "his extremely efficient and gallant conduct". He had also assumed command of 161, which had been re-equipped with the Lysander and Hudson, both small and manoeuvrable enough to land in fields and pick up passengers and vital packages. It was a lonely and exacting role, using moonlit rivers and lakes as navigation aids to find small fields lit by three or four hand-torches; and there was the ever-present risk of an enemy reception committee on the ground. By their very nature such operations were conducted in the deepest secrecy, and few in the RAF were aware of the squadron's activities.

Hodges made a point of having a few words with the

"Joes", as the agents were known, before they took off, many never to return. His calming influence, consideration and care for these gallant people was typical of him. He flew his last SOE operation to France in February 1944, and shortly afterwards was awarded the DSO.

Following a rest on the Bomber Command operations staff, in November 1944 Hodges was briefed to accompany Air Chief Marshal Sir Trafford Leigh-Mallory, the newly-appointed Air Commander-in-Chief, South-East Asia, as his personal staff officer. The posting was, however, cancelled at short notice, since Hodges wished to return to operational flying following the death in action in Burma of his younger brother; he was appointed to command 357, a special duties squadron supporting SOE's Force 136 in South-East Asia. Meanwhile, Leigh-Mallory's transport aircraft crashed in France en route to India; there were no survivors.

Equipped at Jessore, in India, with four-engine Liberators, twin-engine Dakotas and the small Lysander, No 357 supported Force 136 parties organising resistance among Shan, Karen and Kachin hillmen in Burma. Ranging further east, Hodges and his long-range Liberator crews flew sorties of up to 20 hours in dangerous monsoon conditions to assist the Force 136 teams and resistance groups in Thailand and Malaya. For his work in support of SOE, Hodges was awarded a Bar to the DSO.

Shortly after VJ Day in August 1945 he joined the directing staff at the staff college at Haifa, returning home in October 1946. He then attended the RAF Flying College and flew a Canberra PR7 in the London to New Zealand air race. Hodges was in the lead – having established a point-to-point record from London to Colombo – when his aircraft developed a fault and he was overtaken.

Following a series of staff appointments at the Air Ministry and Bomber Command, in March 1956 he took command of RAF Marham, where Valiant nuclear deterrent V-bombers were replacing the Canberra. As the year moved on Hodges was perplexed by an order to employ the remaining Canberras for stockpiling conventional 1,000lb bombs on Malta. All became clear in October, when he took a force of his Valiants to the island. As he later recalled: "It was only at the 11th hour that we discovered we were going to bomb the Egyptians."

Following an interlude as Assistant Commandant at the RAF College, Cranwell, Hodges became the Air Officer Administration of Air Forces in Aden. In 1964, after attending the Imperial Defence College, he was appointed a nuclear deputy at Supreme Headquarters Allied Powers Europe (SHAPE), returning the next year as Assistant Chief of Air Staff in the Ministry of Defence.

After serving as Commander-in-Chief of Air Support Command, Hodges was on the Air Board as Air Member for Personnel until 1973, when he was appointed Deputy C-in-C Allied Forces Central Europe and Air ADC to the Queen.

Hodges retired from the RAF in 1976, and became a director of Pilkington Bros (optical division). He was a governor of Bupa medical foundation from 1987, and from 1979 to 1986 served as chairman of governors of the RAF Benevolent Fund's Duke of Kent School. He was president of the RAF Association from 1981 to 1984 and served for many years on the council of the Friends' organisation of St Clement Danes, the RAF central church in London.

Hodges will long be remembered for his work directing the refurbishment and modernisation of the RAF Club in Piccadilly, which had become outdated and slow to adapt to the expectations of the modern-day officer, few of whom used what they perceived to be an old-fashioned establishment. Some of his measures were not popular at the time – every serving officer had to contribute a half-day's pay – but the transformation was remarkable, and the club's fortunes were dramatically improved. Hodges's portrait hangs in a prominent position in the club.

His experiences as an evader, and his contacts with the SOE and the French Resistance during his wartime service, left Hodges with a deep respect for those who risked so much and for the many who gave their lives. He was president of the RAF Escaping Society, a charity that provides assistance to former escape line "helpers" and their children.

Until the end of his life he maintained close links, and was in constant touch, with his wartime friends in France, Belgium and Holland.

He was appointed CBE in 1958, CB in 1963 and KCB in 1968.

Bob Hodges married, in 1950, Elisabeth Blackett; they had two sons.

FOREIGN FRIENDS

PRINCE EMANUEL GALITZINE

Prince Emanuel Galitzine (who died on December 23 2002, aged 84) was spirited out of Russia as an infant after the Revolution, and later became a Spitfire pilot, then a successful businessman in the aircraft industry.

A great-grandson of Emperor Paul I (a son of Catherine the Great), Prince Emanuel Vladimirovich Galitzine was born on May 28 1918 at Kislovodsk, a spa town in the Caucasus. Before the Revolution, his father had served as aide-de-camp to Grand Duke Nikolai Nikolaevich, head of all the Russian armies until 1916, and afterwards commander of the southern troops confronting Turkey. Emanuel's mother was a daughter of Duke George Alexander of Mecklenburg-Strelitz.

In 1919 conditions in the new Russia obliged the family to flee. They had packed their belongings in wicker laundry baskets, and were ready to leave when Emanuel's mother realised that she had mislaid her wedding ring. Deciding that this was a bad omen, they postponed their departure – later learning that the train on which they would have travelled had been attacked by the Bolsheviks, and every passenger killed.

In the event, the family (including Emanuel's two younger brothers) managed to embark on a Royal Navy ship in the Crimea, which took them to Constantinople. They made their way by train to Paris, home to many White Russian exiles.

Emanuel's father, Prince Vladimir Galitzine, preferred to settle in England, however, thinking that his sons would benefit from a public school education. Accordingly, they went to London, where Prince Vladimir opened a shop in Berkeley Square selling Russian objets d'art; Queen Mary was a regular customer. Emanuel was sent to Lancing and St Paul's, the school fees often being settled by the provision of family paintings (brought out from Russia) in lieu of cash.

After leaving school, Emanuel Galitzine worked briefly at Prudential. He then formed Curzon Films with a friend, Sasha, Count de Lasta, and soon became known for throwing glamorous parties. At one party – held on the banks of the Thames – Galitzine dived into the river and swam across, though dressed in white tie and tails.

On the outbreak of war he began to dream of flying with the RAF; but the Soviet attack on Finland in 1940 convinced him that he must first fight the Communists who had dispossessed his family. Having been accepted by the Finnish Air Force, he was just settling in when Mannerheim, the inspirational Finnish leader and an old friend of Galitzine's father, told Emanuel that his mother had been killed in the London Blitz.

As Mannerheim was on the point of having to side with the Germans through lack of Allied support, Galitzine accepted his offer to assist him to return home and, armed with a Finnish passport issued in the name of Graham, he sailed for Boston in the guise of an immigrant.

There the British consulate was unable to facilitate Galitzine's return to Britain, and he went to Canada, where he was again refused help. He therefore signed on as an ordinary seaman with a shipping line and reached Scotland, where he was promptly arrested on suspicion of being a spy.

Fortunately, Galitzine's father was at this time working for British Intelligence, and he swiftly satisfied the authorities; the way was now clear for Galitzine to be commissioned into the RAFVR and, following a period of operational training, he was posted in November 1941 to No 504, a Spitfire fighter squadron stationed at Ballyherbert, Northern Ireland.

In due course Galitzine was detached from his

squadron to experiment with a Spitfire which had been adapted for high altitude flying. The idea was to confront the Junkers 86 P, an extremely high-flying reconnaissance aircraft. In September 1942 Galitzine attacked one such aircraft, forcing it to jettison its bomb load and return to base. (Thirty years later Galitzine met the German pilot, Horst Goetz, who confirmed that his successful action had had a significant deterrent effect on the missions of the Junkers 86 Ps.) Returning to operational squadron service, Galitzine then fought with No 124, which was equipped with Spitfire VIIs prepared for high-altitude interceptions.

In this period Galitzine also flew with No 308, a Polish fighter squadron. He took part in Operation Rag, in which he spoke Russian cockpit chatter to dupe the enemy into thinking that a Soviet squadron was operating in the West. He also engaged in cross-Channel sweeps, during which he shot down a Focke Wulf 190 fighter.

After two years' continuous operational flying, Galitzine was rested as personal assistant to Air Vice-Marshal Sir William Dickson, subsequently a Chief of Air Staff but then commanding No 83, one of the groups preparing for the Normandy invasion. When Dickson was posted to Italy, Galitzine accompanied him, adding Italian to his already impressive list of languages. He then obtained a posting to No 72, a Spitfire squadron in No 324 Wing commanded by Group Captain Wilfred Duncan Smith, father of the former Conservative Party leader Iain Duncan Smith.

Receiving command of a flight as an acting squadron leader, Galitzine witnessed the advance beyond Monte Cassino and the liberation of Rome, before moving with his squadron to Calvi, on Corsica, to prepare for the invasion of the south of France.

After the war, Galitzine flew for Airline Services of India. He was in Calcutta when he encountered Boris

Lissanevich, a Russian who was running the 300 Club, where gin rummy games attracted the King of Nepal and a glittering array of Indian princes.

One day he had just landed passengers in Delhi when he was asked to fly to Bombay a passenger whom he described as "a dirty little man, who sat playing with his toenails, and four policemen". He was later told that the man had been Gandhi's assassin.

Galitzine returned to Britain in 1950, then had a spell in South America, before coming back to London to fly for British European Airways (BEA) until joining the Avro aircraft company. In this role he travelled widely, selling the Avro 748 passenger aircraft. On one occasion he was awaiting an audience with the king of Morocco, to whom he was hoping to sell a 748; frustrated by the tedium, he sent a message saying that he was a cousin of the British queen; he omitted to explain that he was actually a sixth cousin once removed, and it did the trick.

Some years later Galitzine was returning from a sales tour of the Far East via Moscow, where President Khrushchev had agreed to meet him; in the event, the Soviet leader failed to turn up, but he did send a gift, a cigarette case.

Such was Galitzine's success with Avro that he decided to launch his own aircraft sales business. He did particularly well in Peru, and decided to move there. While in Peru he represented the Isle of Wight aircraft builder, Britten Norman, and Aero Macchi. He was also appointed a director of Aero Condos of Peru.

In 1991 Galitzine returned to London and joined Air Foyle. Russia was now a regular business destination, and seven years later he attended the reburial and funeral service of the murdered tsar's family at St Petersburg.

Galitzine remained a cheerful extrovert until the end, and was never happier than when entertaining at parties, singing gypsy songs to the accompaniment of his guitar.

In 1942 he married his wife, Gwen, whom he had met in Northern Ireland. They had three sons.

JOE FOSS

Joe Foss (who died on New Year's Day 2003, aged 87) was one of the great American fighter aces of the Second World War, officially credited with shooting down 26 Japanese aircraft while serving in the Pacific; he later embarked on a successful career in public life, becoming Governor of South Dakota.

As a Marine Corps pilot during the war, Foss led a unit which became known as "Joe's Flying Circus"; including Foss's own tally, the unit of Grumman Wildcat naval fighters accounted for a total of 72 enemy aircraft.

When he received the Congressional Medal of Honor from President Roosevelt at the White House in 1943 for "aerial combat unsurpassed in this war", Foss was immediately hailed by the national media as "the American ace of aces". He was also awarded the American DFC, Bronze Star, Silver Star and Purple Heart.

Early in November 1942 Foss and his "Circus" played a major role in frustrating Japanese attempts to retake the island of Guadalcanal, which they wished to use as a staging post for attacking Australia, 1,600 miles to the south.

On one mission Foss was strafing Japanese ships 150 miles to the north of the island when fire from a Japanese fighter hit his Wildcat's engine. The bullets also shattered his canopy, narrowly missing his head. His engine failed, and Foss had to ditch. Having struggled to get free of his sinking aircraft, he floated in his lifejacket for five hours, circled by sharks.

Eventually he was rescued by members of a Roman Catholic mission who were paddling canoes from a nearby island, Malaita. They fed him on steak and eggs until – a fortnight later – he was picked up by a Catalina flying boat.

By the New Year of 1943 Foss's air strip, Henderson Field, had expanded into a substantial base, and had become an important target for the enemy. On January 15 a large force of Japanese bombers with escorting fighters made an attempt to destroy it.

Leading 12 Wildcats, Foss outwitted the enemy's attempts to lure his pilots into a scrap, which would have allowed the bombers to slip through and attack the base. He "stooged" in the vicinity, waiting for the Japanese force to start running out of fuel; eventually they were obliged to return to their bases on Bougainville and Munda, and Henderson Field never again became the target of a sustained attack.

After these actions Foss found himself lionised in the American press, and came to enjoy playing up to the image of a rugged, cigar-chomping war hero as he made personal appearances from coast to coast.

John Wayne was keen to portray him in a Hollywood film. As part of this project, Foss was offered $750,000 for his life story, but the deal fell through when he refused to countenance the inclusion of a fictional love story. Instead, he decided to concentrate on a career in politics and business.

Joseph Jacob Foss was born into a Norwegian-Scottish farming family at Sioux Falls, South Dakota, on April 17 1915. His fascination with flying began as a boy, when he saw Charles Lindbergh with his plane, Spirit of St Louis, at a local airfield. A joyride in a Ford Tri-Motor, and the spectacle of a Marines' aerobatic display, confirmed him in his ambitions – though his ability to fulfil them was delayed when his father was killed in an accident, and Foss had to help his mother and brother keep the family farm going during the Depression.

Yet he graduated in Business Administration at the

University of South Dakota, taking flying lessons until the Marine Corps offered him the chance to train as a pilot. He was awarded his wings in May 1941.

After demobilisation, Foss opened the Joe Foss Flying Service at Sioux Falls, offering charter flights and tuition in flying; he also set up a car dealership in Studebakers and Packards.

He found time to organise the South Dakota Air National Guard, himself commanding a squadron. Then, at the outbreak of the Korean War, the US Air Force appointed him a director of training with the rank of colonel. He was later promoted brigadier-general.

After the Korean War Foss was elected, as a Republican, to the South Dakota legislature, serving two terms before becoming State Governor in 1955. He served as governor for four years before failing in a bid to represent South Dakota in the House of Representatives in Washington. He was defeated by another distinguished war pilot, George McGovern.

Foss found some consolation, and considerable satisfaction, in his role as the first commissioner of the new American Football League as it battled to compete with the already-established National Football League. He was responsible for a number of innovations in the sport, including printing the players' names on their jerseys, and making both players and staff more readily available to the television networks.

Since boyhood Foss had enjoyed hunting and fishing, and between 1964 and 1967 he was the host of the ABC-TV programme *The American Sportsman*; thereafter, for seven years he appeared in a syndicated television series, *The Outdoorsman: Joe Foss*.

His interest in country pursuits – together with his prestige as a war hero – led to his appointment as head of the National Rifle Association from 1988 to 1990. He was uncompromising in his championship of the right of Americans to bear arms. *Time* magazine portrayed him on its cover wearing a Stetson and nursing a six-shooter, as he proclaimed: "I say all guns are good guns. There are no bad guns. I say the whole nation should be an armed nation – period."

Joe Foss was married twice. With his first wife, June, he had three children. His second wife, Donna "Didi" Wild was an activist with an organisation called Campus Crusade for Christ International – a cause to which Foss also gave his full support.

MAJOR-GENERAL
ALOIS SISKA

Major-General Alois Siska (who died on September 9 2003, aged 89) spent six days in an open dinghy in the North Sea before being captured on the Dutch coast and sent to Colditz Castle; but when he returned to Prague following two years' hospital treatment in England after the war he was not welcomed as a hero, but jailed and forced to do menial jobs.

On December 28 1941, "Lou" Siska – as he was known to fellow members of the RAF's all-Czech 311 Squadron – piloted a Wellington bomber in a raid on Wilhelmshaven docks on the German coast. He was turning for home after dropping his load when his port engine caught fire. Shortly afterwards the engine fell off, and the aircraft ditched.

Siska was knocked out as his head struck the instrument panel; but he was revived by the rising waters and managed to climb out on to the port wing. Although swept off by a wave, he hung on until he was rescued by four members of his crew who had scrambled aboard a dinghy; the rear gunner had gone down with the aircraft.

A floating mine narrowly passed them by; several ships in the night failed to respond to their signals. On New

Year's Day they sighted a seagull, indicating that land was close, and one of the crew suggested that they try to catch it in order to drink its blood; but they were too weak to make the effort.

After two of the crew had died and one had passed out, Siska and his front-gunner decided to end their lives with drugs from the medical box. But a cocktail of these mixed with sea-water did not have the required effect, and they then discovered that the dinghy was sinking. As they attempted to tip their two dead into the sea, the front-gunner sighted land. Later that day they were washed up on the Dutch coast and taken prisoner.

Siska's time in the dinghy had left him with frostbitten legs, and gangrene had set in. He was taken first to a naval hospital at Alkmaar, then to a military hospital in Amsterdam, where it was decided to amputate his legs. As he was placed on the operating table, Siska had a heart attack.

All thoughts of amputation were shelved. Alternative methods of saving his legs were attempted, and he responded in some measure to the treatment. Six months later, Siska was moved to Germany, where he was confined to several PoW camps until the Gestapo sent him to Prague in July 1944.

Since Czechoslovakia had been incorporated into the Reich, Siska was charged with espionage and high treason and sent to Colditz to await a court martial. He was lucky that the Gestapo was diverted by the July bomb plot against Hitler; the Red Cross also intervened, saying that Czechs in the RAF were British for the duration of the war.

Siska spent ten months in the fortress, but the day before the Americans arrived he was moved to another camp, where some 300 Allied soldiers wounded at Dunkirk were awaiting liberation.

A few days later, the 12 young German soldiers at this camp abandoned their guardroom to the prisoners. Seven more Germans arrived but, having been persuaded by the senior British medical officer that the war had virtually ended, they fled to a nearby forest to cook a meal; and when an American fighter strafed them they ran off.

Believing that the Germans' meal would be too good to waste, Siska went out to collect it. As he returned, 12 more Germans turned up, and were promptly made prisoners by Siska and his fellow inmates, who had found weapons abandoned in the guardroom.

The following day Siska hobbled out on his crutches with a white sheet to greet a column of American tanks. He was transferred to Brussels and then flown to RAF Manston on his 31st birthday, before being sent to Sir Archibald McIndoe's burns and plastic surgery unit at the Queen Victoria Hospital, East Grinstead. It took Siska two years to recover the partial use of his legs.

Alois Siska was born at Lutopecny, Moravia, on May 15 1914. After training as a commercial pilot, he did his national service with the Czech Air Force.

Following the German occupation of Czechoslovakia in March 1939, Siska sought anonymity working in an aircraft factory owned by the Bata shoe company before the Gestapo started looking for him. A plan to steal an aircraft was betrayed, so he fled through the Fascist puppet state of Slovakia to Hungary. There he was imprisoned and escaped from several jails before being confined in Budapest's Citadella. Again he got away, making his way through Yugoslavia to Beirut, where he joined the French Foreign Legion. But when it was realised that he was a pilot, he was sent to a newly-formed Czech air force unit in France.

After the French capitulated, Siska left the Merignac airfield near Bordeaux, and boarded a Danish cargo boat bound for England. Then, as a member of No 311 Squadron, he flew half a dozen missions to bomb harbour installations in the Channel ports before his capture.

After two years at the Queen Victoria Hospital, Siska

returned to Czechoslovakia. But the role of the Czech pilots who had served with the RAF was being played down. He was not allowed to return to England to complete his treatment, and when the Communists gained power in 1948 he was dismissed from the Czech Air Force, jailed, forced to do menial jobs and exiled from Prague.

Siska's wife, Vlasta Prochazkova, whom he had married in 1949, was prevented from finishing university, and the couple were sent to a collective farm in a remote country district. Now disabled and living on a tiny pension, which was periodically reduced, Siska was not allowed to work; but he taught himself to repair watches, wireless sets and, later, televisions.

In 1961 the family, which now included their daughter, was allowed to move nearer to Prague. Two years later Siska was called to East Berlin as a witness at the trial of the Nazi lawyer Hans Globke, who had been instrumental in charging him with treason in 1944; this drew attention throughout Europe to the plight of the Czech pilots, and led to an easing of their restrictions.

By 1966 Siska was working for the Czech civil airline as a fire and security inspector, and during the "Prague Spring" of 1968 he was reinstated in the Czech Air Force. The Russian invasion shortly afterwards, however, led to his second dismissal.

Siska was able to return to Prague only in 1989, shortly before the collapse of the Communist regime. At last he received proper recognition: in 2001 he was promoted to major-general, and a fighter squadron in the Czech Air Force was named after him.

A friendly and humorous man, Siska was, in his own opinion and that of his doctors, living on borrowed time after December 1941. He used it to the full. In his later years, he lectured to Czech schoolchildren about his wartime experiences, and was a regular attender at gatherings of the Guinea Pig Club, formed by the patients at East Grinstead. He died three weeks after making his first return visit to Colditz.

Alois Siska was awarded a full military funeral in Prague, with a flypast of army helicopters flying the Czech and British flags.

COLONEL
BOB MORGAN

Colonel Bob Morgan (who died on May 15 2004, aged 85) was the pilot of the B-17 Flying Fortress Memphis Belle, the first American bomber to survive 25 missions over occupied Europe during the Second World War and to return to the United States; a documentary was made about it in 1944, and a feature film in 1990.

In October 1942 Morgan and his crew were detailed to fly the bomber across the Atlantic to join the 91st Bomb Group (the Ragged Irregulars) of the USAAF Eighth Air Force. It was traditional for bombers to carry "nose art", and Morgan dedicated his aircraft to his fiancée at the time, Margaret Polk. A swim-suited pin-up representing the beautiful brunette was painted on each side of the aircraft's nose.

At that time the USAAF had little experience of strategic bombing, and elected to make daylight raids in large formations, initially without fighter escort. For the first three months most targets were in France and the Low Countries, allowing the crews to gain experience. On November 7 Memphis Belle was sent to attack the French U-boat port of Brest.

Early in 1943 the bombers turned to Germany, where the 91st suffered 80 per cent casualties. They flew their first mission over Germany on February 4, when they attacked Emden. Throughout that spring the bombers faced a dense barrage of anti-aircraft fire and attacks from fighters.

On one occasion Morgan experienced a new tactic, when the Luftwaffe dropped fragmentation bombs on to the tightly packed formation of Flying Fortresses. On another, his aircraft was badly damaged by a fighter, and he had to dive 5,000ft to extinguish a fire in its rear.

Morgan's crew had great faith in him, and in turn he established a close bond with them. Before each mission he would say: "If only one aircraft comes back today, it's going to be us."

There was an element of the buccaneer about Morgan. Returning from a sortie over France, he had to land at Exeter to rectify a faulty engine. With a party invitation for that night, he was determined to return to their airfield at Bassingbourn, near Royston, but the rogue engine refused to start.

He therefore told his crew that he would take off on three engines and allow the slipstream to turn the propeller and start the fourth. Apart from the engineer, the crew refused to go along with the idea. Morgan took off, the fourth engine started, and he landed back at Exeter to pick up the eight remaining crewmen. He arrived in time to keep his date.

By May 1943, when Memphis Belle was about to embark on its 25th mission, the Americans recognised the opportunity to gain much-needed publicity and support for the war effort. The film director William Wyler, who had joined the Air Force Film Unit, was told to produce a documentary. His cameramen flew with Memphis Belle, recording the sights and sounds of the crew's attack on the docks at Wilhelmshaven on May 17.

Also using combat film shot by cameramen in other bombers, Wyler produced a 45-minute colour documentary. In it a narrator described the ten-man crew as "simple average American boys doing a tough job". The film was highly acclaimed, and is still shown regularly as a true representation of the USAAF's bombing campaign.

A dramatisation, based on the original documentary,

was produced by Warner Brothers and released to cinemas in 1990. With Matthew Modine playing Morgan, it was a dramatised account of the 25th and final sortie of Memphis Belle, and was produced by Wyler's daughter Cathy. The flying shots were taken on location at the RAF airfield at Binbrook, near Grimsby. Visiting the set, Morgan and some of his crew were amused to see their screen characters; one crewman was heard to comment: "They seemed to have packed all our experiences of 25 missions into just one."

In June 1943 the 23-year-old Morgan and his crew were introduced to King George VI and Queen Elizabeth before taking their aircraft back to America, where they were welcomed as heroes. They embarked on an exhausting tour of 30 cities to boost morale and help sell war bonds. Morgan was awarded the DFC and the Air Medal with three clusters.

Robert Morgan was born on July 31 1918 at Asheville, in the North Carolina Blue Ridge Mountains where he lived most of his life. He attended the Wharton School of Finance at the University of Pennsylvania before volunteering for the Army Air Corps. Having gained his pilot's wings, he was commissioned as a second lieutenant five days after the Japanese attack on Pearl Harbor.

Following his tour of American cities in 1943, Morgan volunteered to return to operations. He converted to the B-29 Superfortress, and in October 1944 he deployed to the Far East in his new bomber, Dauntless Dotty, named after one of Margaret Polk's successors.

Having been appointed to command the 869th Squadron of the 497th Bomb Group, on November 24 1944 he led the first B-29 raid on Tokyo – the first such attack since General Doolittle's in 1942. He went on to complete 25 missions; then his general ordered him home "before your luck runs out".

After the war Morgan served with the USAF Reserve. He retired in 1965 as a colonel, but maintained his pilot's licence into his eighties. He worked in real estate, and maintained close links with his former crew members.

In October 1999 he was invited to fly in the USAF's B–1B strategic bomber. Subsequently, one was named Memphis Belle, and the appropriate nose art was painted on the aircraft.

Morgan's blend of swagger and humility won him many admirers during the war and afterwards. He was regularly asked to appear at air shows and aviation events, and he made many visits to Britain. In 1997 he was invited to the American Air Museum at Duxford when it was opened by the Queen.

Morgan did not marry Margaret Polk, but they remained close friends until her death in 1990. His first wife, Elizabeth, died in 1992, and later that year he married Linda Dickerson, herself a pilot of light aircraft. They were married at a ceremony held under the wing of Memphis Belle, with seven of his former crewmen in attendance and his co–pilot acting as best man.

AIR COMMODORE ROBBERT "BERGY" VAN ZINNICQ BERGMANN

Air Commodore Robbert van Zinnicq Bergmann (who died on June 14 2004, aged 87) escaped from the Netherlands during its occupation and became a Typhoon pilot with the RAF.

The rocket–firing Typhoons of Bergmann's squadron, No 181, were detailed for a special operation on November 4 1944, in which they were to attack the north wing of the Dutch Royal Family's summer palace, which was being used by the SS as a headquarters.

It was thought that some members of the Royal Household could be in residence in other parts of the palace – so extreme accuracy was essential. In the event, the attack was a complete success. Bergmann later commented: "We flattened the whole north tower and hardly anything else was damaged. When I met Queen Wilhelmina after the war she was impressed, but thought it a pity that the SS were not billeted in her palace in The Hague. She said it would have been a marvellous target and she was sorry that I did not attack it too, since she disliked it so much."

Earlier that day, Bergmann had flown on a precision attack against the headquarters, in Apeldoorn, of Germany's commissioner for the Netherlands, Arthur Seyss-Inquart. Bergmann's attack was so low that he returned with part of the front door in his aircraft's radiator.

The son of an advocate, Robbert Jacques Emile Marie van Zinnicq Bergmann was born on April 11 1917 at 's-Hertogenbosch. He was educated at the Roman Catholic school at Rolduc, in Limburg, before entering the Royal Military Academy at Breda, where he trained to be a cavalry officer.

Bergmann fought during the short war following the German invasion of the Netherlands, but was wounded on the third day and admitted to hospital with a broken leg. He joined a group of former cavalry officers planning an escape from Holland, but they were betrayed, and Bergmann went into hiding, first on a farm and then on a canal barge.

The barge took him to Liège, where he managed to join one of the escape lines through Belgium and France. After a long and dangerous journey, during which many "helpers" risked their lives to assist him and fellow escapers, he reached Perpignan before crossing the Pyrenees into Spain.

Bergmann was able to board a Dutch boat sailing from Barcelona to Lisbon, where his cousin, Joseph Luns (the future Dutch foreign minister and Secretary-General of

NATO) was working as a diplomat. Luns managed to get him a berth on a small coaster that took him to Gibraltar. He finally arrived in England in the summer of 1942, and joined the Dutch army. In September he volunteered as a pilot with the RAF.

After training in Canada, Bergmann joined No 181, part of No 124 Wing, shortly after D-Day; by this time the squadron was flying operations from hastily built airstrips in the fields of Normandy. The role of the Typhoons was to attack targets in support of the Army and to disrupt the road and rail transport system using rockets fired from low level. Once the Allied armies broke out of Normandy, Bergmann and his colleagues were constantly moving to new airfields in order to provide the essential close air support against the retreating Germans.

Shortly after arriving near Brussels in mid-September, Bergmann and his fellow pilots were sent to attack the anti-aircraft belt around Arnhem, in preparation for the airborne landings by the British 1st Airborne Division. On September 17, after he had fired his rockets, Bergmann's aircraft was badly damaged by flak, but he managed to make an emergency landing.

Five days later he returned to his homeland for the first time in three years. He landed at Eindhoven, where his squadron remained for the next four months. During this period Bergmann flew almost daily, attacking gun emplacements, tanks and convoys. With the aid of long-range fuel tanks, the Typhoons also ranged deeper into Germany, targeting the railway system – No 181 destroyed more than 60 locomotives, but losses to flak were heavy.

Hearing that his home town of 's-Hertogenbosch had been liberated on October 30, Bergmann obtained permission to visit and was able to surprise his parents with his unexpected arrival. He said later that "when I lay in my own bed for the first time in almost four years, I was unable to fall asleep".

During the latter days of the German offensive in the Ardennes in December, Bergmann's aircraft was hit by flak. He managed to get back to Eindhoven, where he made a crash landing. On New Year's Day 1945 he stood with his fellow pilots and watched as the Luftwaffe launched its last desperate attack against the Allied airfields, causing extensive damage and destroying many Typhoons.

In March 1945 Bergmann was appointed flight commander of another Typhoon squadron, No 182, with which he continued to attack road and rail communications.

By early May 182 was at Luneburg, and on May 4 Bergmann took off to lead an attack against a large concentration of aircraft on the airfield at Flensburg. After a successful operation, he received a radio message ordering him and his formation to return immediately; the war was over. Two days later he was summoned to his group headquarters, where Air Vice-Marshal Broadhurst decorated him with the DFC.

In June he transferred to the Dutch Air Force, and was immediately appointed air aide-de-camp to Queen Wilhelmina. In September he was awarded the Vliegerkruis (the Dutch DFC).

Bergmann played down his role in the war after visiting Belsen concentration camp. He commented: "What war really is I understood when I went to Belsen. I saw cartloads of bodies of those who had died just after liberation; that is something no pen can describe."

He remained on the active list of the Royal Netherlands Air Force, but for the next 25 years served Holland's three queens as Lord Chamberlain and Head of the Royal Household in addition to his aide-de-camp duties. He was also Master of the Royal Hunt, and spent much time preparing the estates for Prince Bernhard's shooting parties. Bergmann was himself an excellent shot, as well as a superb horseman, gaining international honours in showjumping.

After retiring in 1972 Bergmann maintained close links with the men of 124 Wing, arranging a large reunion in Holland in 1985 at which Prince Bernhard welcomed the veterans.

For his services to Holland he was appointed an Officer of the Order of the Orange Nassau with Swords, and a Commander of the House of Orange. The French government appointed him a Grand Officier of the Légion d'honneur.

"Bergy" van Zinnicq Bergmann was appointed an honorary KCVO by the Queen in 1958.

With his wife Caroline, whom he married in 1945, he had a son and two daughters.

———

MAJOR-GENERAL CHARLES SWEENEY

Major-General Charles Sweeney (who died on July 16 2004, aged 84) was the pilot of the B-29 Superfortress bomber that dropped the atomic bomb on Nagasaki in 1945, three days after the first bomb had hit Hiroshima.

In the early hours of August 9 Sweeney, commander of the 393rd Bomb Squadron of the 509th Composite Group, took off in his bomber (named Bock's Car) from Tinian in the Marianas Islands to drop his atom bomb, known as Fat Man, on the Japanese city of Kokura.

He encountered difficulties soon after take-off when a fuel transfer valve failed, and he was unable to use 600 gallons of fuel. He was due to rendezvous with two other B-29s but one failed to arrive on time, and Sweeney was forced to orbit for 40 minutes, wasting more precious fuel. He calculated that he could just complete the operation, and so decided to press on without the third aircraft.

Sweeney had been ordered not to drop the bomb if he

could not see the target. The weather reconnaissance aircraft flying ahead reported that the target would be visible, but by the time Sweeney arrived the city was obscured by cloud. After making three runs without sighting the target, and with anti-aircraft fire intensifying and Japanese fighters appearing on the scene, he diverted to the secondary target, Nagasaki.

On arrival, Sweeney's reserves were so critical that he had sufficient for just one attempt to drop the bomb. Flying at 30,000ft, his bombardier got a brief visual sighting through a break in the clouds and released Fat Man at 10.58am (Nagasaki time). The bomb exploded 45 seconds later at 1,500ft on the perimeter of the city above the Mitsubishi sports stadium, not far from the port's Catholic cathedral.

Sweeney broke radio silence to send a coded message announcing that Nagasaki had been bombed. It was the only bomb he dropped on an enemy target during the war.

The blast from the 22-kiloton bomb (the equivalent of 22,000 tons of TNT) was partly cushioned by the hilly terrain surrounding the city, and rivers and canals prevented the fires from spreading. Nevertheless, almost half the city was destroyed and some 70,000 people were killed.

Desperately short of fuel, Sweeney was forced to land at Okinawa, which had only recently been occupied by American troops. Since his arrival was unexpected and his radio calls went unanswered, he had to cut in front of other aircraft; and as his B-29 completed its landing run, one of the engines cut out through lack of fuel.

Even after the second atomic bomb attack, there was discord within the Japanese government between those in favour of surrender and those who urged continued resistance; but an attempted coup by militant extremists failed, and on August 14 Japan surrendered unconditionally.

In a break with tradition, Emperor Hirohito announced the surrender in a recorded radio message. Japan accepted the terms of the July 26 Potsdam Declaration calling for unconditional surrender, terms that the Japanese had previously rejected. This was the first time the Japanese people had ever heard their emperor's voice, and some Japanese officers committed suicide.

Charles W Sweeney was born on December 27 1919 at Lowell, Massachusetts, and came from a family of marines; three of his brothers served in the Marine Corps. After attending North Quincey High School, he studied at Purdue University, Indiana. He had an early passion for flying and interrupted his studies in April 1941 to join the US Army Air Corps.

Sweeney was one of the first pilots to fly the new four-engine B-29 Superfortress bomber, and worked as a test pilot at Jefferson Proving Grounds before moving to Eglin, Florida, as base operations officer.

In September 1944 he moved to Wendover, Utah, to train crews on the B-29. He joined the 509th Composite Group, commanded by Lieutenant-Colonel Paul Tibbets, on its formation in December 1944.

The group trained in great secrecy, and only Tibbets was aware of its ultimate mission; this was given the code name of "Silver Plate" – the military designation for the complicated effort of assembling and training more than 1,500 men to drop the first atomic bomb. By mid-July the necessary modifications to the bombs had been completed to the satisfaction of the scientists, and they were delivered late that month to Tinian, where technicians and scientists made the final adjustments required.

On August 6 Sweeney played a crucial role in the mission to drop the first atomic bomb on Hiroshima. Flying his aircraft, The Great Artiste, which had been modified to carry scientific instruments to collect data on the effects of the blast, he accompanied the Enola Gay, flown by Tibbets.

As America's first atomic bomb, Little Boy, was released from Enola Gay, Sweeney dropped a series of sensors that descended by parachute to collect scientific data.

With between 70,000 and 80,000 people killed and the city devastated, the effects of the bomb shocked the world. President Truman spoke of the "rain of ruin from the air" which the Japanese might expect if they did not surrender.

The Japanese did not surrender; and, to convince them that the United States had an arsenal of atomic weapons, a second raid was planned for August 11. A poor weather forecast, however, brought the operation forward by two days.

The second bomb, Fat Man, which was almost twice the size of Little Boy, did not arrive at Tinian until a few days before and complications arose during the preparation of the sensitive instrumentation and fusing circuits. The bomb was prepared just in time.

After the mission was over the 509th moved to its new home, Roswell, New Mexico. Because of its expertise with the atomic bombs, the unit became the core organisation for what would become the most powerful military force on earth at the time, the Strategic Air Command, created in 1946.

Sweeney was an outspoken defender of the bombings, often appearing on CNN and speaking at colleges and universities. He wrote a book *War's End: an Eyewitness Account of America's Last Atomic Mission*, to counter what he considered "cockamamie theories" that the bombings were unnecessary. He told his local paper in 1995: "I looked upon it as a duty. I just wanted the war to be over."

Sweeney remained in the USAF until 1976. At one stage he was the youngest brigadier-general in the service. Amongst many decorations, he was awarded the Silver Star and the Air Medal.

Bock's Car was restored and, in 1961, went on

permanent display at the Wright-Patterson Air Force Base near Dayton, Ohio.

After leaving the air force Sweeney went into business. He had three sons and seven daughters by his marriage, which was dissolved.

GENERAL
STANISLAW SKALSKI

General Stanislaw Skalski (who died in Warsaw on November 12 2004, aged 89) was Poland's most successful fighter pilot, credited with destroying at least 22 enemy aircraft and damaging others; he was decorated for gallantry four times by the British and six times by the Polish government in exile.

After escaping from Poland following the German occupation in September 1939, Skalski reached England and was commissioned in the RAF. He joined No 501 (County of Gloucester) Squadron at the height of the Battle of Britain in August 1940.

Flying Hurricanes from Gravesend, the squadron had seen much action, and Skalski soon claimed his first victory when he shot down a Heinkel on August 30. The next day he shot down a Bf 109 fighter and destroyed two more on September 2.

Three days later he took off to attack a large bomber force approaching Kent, and sent a Heinkel down in flames before attacking a Bf 109, causing the pilot to bale out. He then destroyed another Bf 109 over Canterbury.

As he turned away, Skalski was himself attacked and his Hurricane set on fire. He baled out and was admitted to Herne Bay hospital, where for six weeks he was treated for serious burns. Anxious to return to combat, he discharged himself at the end of October and returned to 501.

Stanislaw Skalski was born on October 27 1915 at the village of Kodyn, north of the Russian city of Odessa. After the Russian Revolution his father sent him and his mother to Zbaraz, near Lvov.

After attending school in Dubno, Stanislaw learnt to fly gliders in 1934, and the following year qualified on powered aircraft. He then decided to become a military pilot, and entered the cadet school at Deblin in 1936, graduating as an officer two years later.

Skalski was assigned to the 4th Air Regiment at Torun, where he joined No 142 Eskadra, the "Flying Ducks", to fly PZL fighters. Following the German invasion of Poland on September 1 1939, Skalski and his squadron were in action immediately. He claimed his first victory on the opening day, and by the fifth day he had destroyed four German bombers, to become the only Polish ace of the short campaign. As Polish resistance collapsed, the remnants of his squadron escaped to Romania. Skalski eventually made his way to the Mediterranean, where he boarded a boat for England, arriving in January 1940.

For his deeds during the Battle of Britain, Skalski was awarded Poland's highest decoration for gallantry, the Virtuti Militari. In March 1941 he was posted to No 306 (Torun) Polish squadron flying Spitfires, and that summer he was to claim another five victories over northern France.

Following these successes, he was invested with the Polish Cross of Valour, to which he would eventually add three bars, and in September he was awarded the DFC.

In March 1942 Skalski joined No 316 Squadron and soon accounted for a FW 190 fighter. He was promoted to squadron leader and given command of No 317 Squadron, which he led during the combined operations at Dieppe, during which his pilots destroyed seven German aircraft. He was awarded a Bar to his DFC.

In January 1943 Skalski became leader of the newly-created Polish Fighting Team (PFT) of volunteers.

Popularly known as "Skalski's Circus", it numbered 15 of the best Polish fighter pilots. They left for North Africa a month later when they were attached to No 145 Squadron. Flying the latest Spitfire Mk IX aircraft from Giarabub in the Western Desert, the team claimed its first victory on March 28 when Skalski and his wingman each shot down a Junkers 88 bomber.

Over the next few days Skalski shot down two Bf 109 fighters and damaged a third; and by May 13, when the German forces in Tunisia surrendered, his Polish pilots had destroyed 30 enemy aircraft.

In July Skalski took command of No 601 Squadron at Luqa, Malta, shortly before moving to Sicily. He was only the second Pole to be given command of an RAF squadron. Soon after receiving a second Bar to his DFC in October, he was promoted to be the wing leader of No 131 Polish Wing at Northolt, and in April 1944 he moved to command No 133 Wing, which had recently re-equipped with the Mustang. In May he was awarded a second Virtuti Militari.

Skalski led his three squadrons on long-range bomber escort missions, often as far as Hamburg. Then, with D-Day imminent, the squadrons began dive-bombing sorties against targets in northern France. On June 24 he chased two Bf 109s over Rouen, causing them to collide without his firing a shot. He ended the war as Poland's highest-scoring fighter pilot. In September his operational flying career was over and he was awarded the DSO. After spending six months in the United States he returned to become wing commander operations at HQ No 11 Group.

Although Skalski was offered a commission in the RAF, he decided to return to Poland in June 1947. Initially he served at the headquarters of the Soviet-dominated Polish Air Force, but, following the increasing tension between the Soviet Union and the western powers, he was arrested in June 1948 and charged with espionage and treason – a fate that befell many of his ex-RAF Polish colleagues. In 1949 he was condemned to death and spent the next six years awaiting execution. Eventually his sentence was commuted to life imprisonment, and he was finally released in 1956 after eight years in jail.

On his release Skalski was invited to return to the air force, an offer he accepted with some hesitation. He flew the Soviet-built MIG fighters, and in 1972 ended his distinguished career in the rank of general. He became the president of the Polish Aero Club before retiring to Warsaw, where he led a lonely life.

Skalski was remembered as a great individualist and man of action. One of his pilots described him as "an eagle in the air, he was a great commander and a brilliant leader and we would follow him to hell if necessary".

On the ground he could be stubborn, and he held strong opinions which did not always accord with those of his superiors; but his fighting qualities and courage were never in doubt.

He made numerous visits to England, and attended the unveiling in June 1994 of a memorial to 133 Wing at the site of their former airfield at Coolham in Sussex. In September 2000 he joined fellow veterans at the National Memorial to "The Few" at Capel le Ferne to commemorate the 60th anniversary of the Battle of Britain; he insisted on sitting with his surviving friends from 501 Squadron.

Stanislaw Skalski was unmarried.

PIERRE CLOSTERMANN

Pierre Clostermann (who died on March 22 2006, aged 85) was one of the leading French fighter aces flying with the RAF during the Second World War.

He flew 432 combat sorties and destroyed at least 18 aircraft in the air and on the ground. A charismatic and sometimes controversial figure, he wrote a classic account of his wartime experiences which is considered by many to be the finest aviation book to come out of the war.

Pierre Henri Clostermann, the son of a French diplomat, was born on February 28 1921 at Curitiba, in Brazil. When he was nine he was sent to be educated in Paris. After rejoining his parents in Brazil he obtained his private pilot's licence in November 1937.

When war broke out he wanted to enlist in the French Air Force, but was refused permission; so instead he left for the United States, where he studied aeronautical engineering at the Ryan Flying College in Los Angeles. His father opted to support Charles de Gaulle, and in April 1942 Pierre joined the Free French Air Force and travelled to England.

After completing his pilot training in early 1943, Clostermann joined No 341 "Alsace" Squadron at Biggin Hill, commanded by the French ace René Mouchotte. Flying the Spitfire Mk IX, he achieved his first success when he shot down two Focke Wulf 190s over northern France, soon following this with a third. On the day Mouchotte was shot down and killed Clostermann was flying as his wingman, and attracted some criticism from his wing commander for losing contact with his leader.

Clostermann was then posted to No 602 Squadron, and over the next ten months flew constantly on fighter sweeps, bomber escorts and dive-bombing and strafing attacks against the V-1 launch sites on the French coast. He achieved more successes in the air, almost all against fighters, but also against targets on the ground. On D-Day, June 6 1944, Clostermann flew two fighter sweeps over the Normandy beachhead, finding himself "astonished at the absence of the Luftwaffe".

Five days after the invasion he landed on a temporary airstrip in Normandy; he was one of the first French pilots to touch down on French soil, four years to the day after de Gaulle's famous radio address calling the French to resistance. Clostermann and two French colleagues had put on their best uniforms, but immediately regretted it when clouds of fine dust billowed up as their Spitfires landed; within seconds they resembled workers in a flour factory. Sixty years later, on June 6 2004, he was present when a road at Longues-sur-Mer, near the airstrip where he had landed, was named after him.

Once in Normandy Clostermann flew sweeps deeper into northern France, shooting down four fighters and probably destroying others. On July 2 1944, 602 Squadron was engaged in a fierce fight with Focke Wulf 190s over Caen, and Clostermann claimed two German fighters and damaged three others. A few days later he was awarded a DFC. Having flown far more than the accepted number of operations before taking a compulsory rest, he was mentally and physically exhausted, and was sent to the staff at the headquarters of the Free French Air Force.

In December Clostermann returned to operations, flying the RAF's most powerful fighter, the Tempest. He joined No 122 Wing in Holland, flying fighter sweeps and attacking motor transport and rail traffic over northern Germany. He also engaged enemy fighters whenever the opportunity arose, adding a further four to his total.

On March 24 1945 he was wounded in the leg by the intense German anti-aircraft fire that was a major feature of all the ground attack operations; he had to crash land his badly-damaged Tempest, but was back in action a week later as the flight commander of No 3 Squadron.

As the armies advanced, the Tempests roamed deeper into northern Germany, attacking any trains they found and shooting up aircraft on the ground. On May 3 Clostermann led a series of attacks against airfields and seaplane bases in the Kiel area. He strafed airfields and moorings, destroying several transport aircraft and flying boats. Shortly afterwards he was awarded a Bar to his DFC together with the American Silver Star, and French and Belgian decorations.

On May 12 Clostermann was leading a victory flypast over Bremerhaven when his aircraft collided with another. He baled out at very low level and his parachute opened seconds before he hit the ground. Clostermann was released from the service in August 1945 and returned to France.

After the war, he continued his career in aeronautical engineering, initially with the Societé Aubry et Cie in Paris. He later helped to found the Reims Aviation Company, acting as a representative for the American Cessna aircraft company, of which he later became a vice-president. He served on the boards of Air France and Renault.

In parallel to his business interests, Clostermann pursued a successful political career as a Gaullist, serving eight terms as a deputy in the French National Assembly before finally retiring in 1969. He also briefly re-enlisted in the French Air Force in 1956-57 to fly ground attack missions in Algeria. He retired as a colonel in the reserves.

Clostermann was no stranger to controversy. His final claim for the number of aircraft he destroyed has often been the subject of debate, but it is recognised that he achieved remarkable success. During the Falklands War in 1982 he praised Argentinian pilots for their actions and courage, and his perceived "betrayal" of the RAF attracted some antipathy in Britain. He also generated controversy in France for his vehement anti-war stance in the run-up to the Gulf War of 1991.

Clostermann's great passion was deep-sea fishing, an activity he indulged in throughout the world. He was a founding member and first president of the Big Game Fishing Club of France, and a representative of the International Game Fish Association from 1966 – he joined the association's board of trustees in 1977. He was a dedicated and effective spokesman for sportsmanlike angling and conservation policies.

Clostermann's wartime autobiography, *Le Grand Cirque* (The Big Show), which came out in 1948, was an immediate success. Marshal of the RAF Sir John Slessor described it as "a magnificent story, making one proud, not only of those French boys who fought so gallantly, but of the RAF in which they served". The book was subsequently translated into 50 languages and sold three million copies worldwide; it was reprinted in 2004.

Clostermann's book *Feu du Ciel* (Flames in the Sky), published in 1957, was also widely acclaimed; and he wrote extensively on fishing.

In addition to his British awards, Clostermann was awarded the Grand-Croix of the Légion d'honneur and appointed a Compagnon de la libération, France's highest awards for gallantry and service. He was also awarded the Croix de Guerre with no fewer than 19 palmes.

Pierre Clostermann was married with three sons.

MAJOR-GENERAL FRANTISEK PERINA

Major-General Frantisek Perina (who died on May 6 2006, aged 95) escaped from Czechoslovakia to become one of the leading fighter pilots with the French Air Force in 1940, and then joined the RAF; when the Second World War ended, he returned to his homeland but had to flee again when the Communists took power.

Perina arrived in France to serve in the foreign legion before joining the Armée de l'Air in December 1939 as a sergeant. He was assigned to the Escadre de Chasse 5, which was based near Rheims, flying the American-built Curtiss H-75 Hawk fighter.

When the Germans launched their attack on Belgium and France on May 10 1940, Perina and his commanding officer took off to attack a force of Dornier bombers. Co-ordinating their attacks, they shot down four enemy aircraft and had further successes in fierce fighting over the next few days.

On May 12 Perina shot down four Stuka dive-bombers in four minutes. Two fell behind the German lines, so he could be credited with only two destroyed and two probables. The French newspapers carried head-lines about his exploits, which earned him promotion. "Not bad," he commented. "From sergeant to lieutenant in five days."

With his squadron retreating towards the Swiss border, he shared in the destruction of three more bombers. On June 1 he took off with seven colleagues, and attacked 90 bombers which had a large fighter escort. He shot down one bomber, but could not confirm two others which fell inside Switzerland. He was then attacked by Messer-schmitts, and was downed with arm and leg wounds.

After a few days in hospital, Perina flew his Curtiss to Oran in Algeria, where he was decorated with the Légion d'honneur and the Croix de Guerre. He left for Casablanca and finally reached Gibraltar, where he joined other Czech, Polish and French airmen taking a cargo ship for England, where he arrived in September 1940 and joined the RAF.

The son of a farmer, Frantisek Perina was born on April 8 1911, near Brno in southern Moravia. On leaving school he became an apprentice machinist for three years. Then, stimulated by a visit to an airshow and by a recruiting advertisement, he joined the Czechoslovak Air Force in October 1929.

Three years later Perina attended the fighter school at Cheb in the Sudetenland, where he later joined the 36th Fighter Squadron. In 1937 he represented the air force at the Zurich International Air Show, where he met members of a large Luftwaffe contingent. Perina was placed third in the aerobatic competition and received awards in two other categories; he found himself at the prize-giving dinner next to Erhard Milch, second-in-command of the Luftwaffe.

On his return home he won a number of air-to-air and air-to-ground gunnery competitions and, following Hitler's occupation of the Sudetenland, became the chief pilot of the 52nd Fighter Squadron. On June 24 1939 he married Anna Klimesova, but two days later the Czechoslovak Air Force was disbanded, and he fled to Poland and then France. He had to leave his bride behind, and she was subsequently imprisoned by the Germans from 1942 to 1945.

After arriving in England, Perina joined No 312 (Czech) Squadron on its formation at Duxford, flying the Hurricane. Over the next few months he undertook many convoy patrols before the squadron went on to the offensive after re-equipping with the Spitfire. On June 3 1942 No 312 was involved in a major fight with Focke Wulf 190s over Cherbourg. Perina shot down one and damaged a second, but the squadron suffered losses.

In three years of continuous fighting he destroyed at least 12 aircraft, then was rested and sent to the Central Gunnery School. He served as gunnery leader at several fighter airfields, and was made an acting wing commander in March 1943. During the final year of the war he was at Fighter Command as an air intelligence officer.

Perina was awarded the Czechoslovak War Cross with three medals for bravery and two silver stars. In May 1945 he returned to his homeland to be reunited with his wife and to rejoin the new Czechoslovak Air Force as the commander of a gunnery school. But after the Communist take-over he was sacked, following a dispute with the head of the secret police, and once again escaped. Commandeering a sports aircraft, he left for Germany with his wife and a friend. Flying at tree top height to avoid detection, he had just crossed the German border when the aircraft ran out of fuel and belly-landed in a muddy field near Passau; his wife was injured but survived.

When Perina rejoined the RAF in May 1949, he was considered too old to fly squadron aircraft, and was commissioned in the administrative branch. He served for nine years, initially as a flight commander at a school of recruit training and later as the adjutant at the RAF School of Physical Education, first at Cosford and then at St Athan. As a member of the RAF Rifle Team he won numerous competitions and continued to fly light aircraft.

Perina and his wife then lived in Canada before moving to Los Angeles, where he worked for the Webber Aircraft Company. He supervised the plastics division as it fulfilled contracts for the manufacture of parts for the Boeing 747 and the seats for the Gemini space capsules. He retired to Nevada in 1979 but, after the fall of Communism in 1989, returned to Czechoslovakia. "The only roots I have are here and nowhere else," he said. "When I die, I want this piece of earth around me." He was given the Order of the White Lion by President Vaclav Havel in 1997, and three years later the honorary rank of major-general.

On Perina's 95th birthday the air force Chief of Staff presented him with a model of his Spitfire.

Frantisek Perina died only a few days after his wife, Anna, to whom he had been married for 66 years.

THE GIRLS

AIR COMMODORE
DAME FELICITY PEAKE

Air Commodore Dame Felicity Peake (who died on November 2 2002, aged 89) was appointed director of the Women's Auxiliary Air Force (WAAF) in 1946 at the age of 32; even in the context of accelerated promotions in the Second World War, she was astonishingly young for the post.

As Felicity Hanbury, it was her outstanding wartime service, her drive, unusual qualities of leadership and her rapport with the RAF's most senior officers which brought her this opportunity to lead the WAAF in the early years of peace. And her success was such that when, in 1949, the new Women's Royal Air Force (WRAF) was set up, she was appointed as its first director, remaining until her retirement in 1950.

Those familiar with Harry Saltzman's oft-televised feature film *Battle of Britain* (1969) will recall the poignant scenes in which Susannah York, as a junior officer, counts her dead WAAFs in the aftermath of a heavy attack on the fighter base at Biggin Hill in Kent. The part was inspired by Felicity Hanbury's experience on August 30 1940 when, aged 26 and serving at Biggin Hill as a section officer in charge of some 250 women, she survived an attack by German bombers.

Nine Ju 88s swung north to take "The Bump" – as RAF pilots knew Biggin – in a surprise attack. WAAF quarters were among the buildings hit, and an air raid shelter crammed with airmen was reduced to rubble. In all, 39 died.

Obeying orders, Felicity Hanbury had sheltered in a trench. She later recalled: "The vibration and blast were such that one felt that one's limbs must surely come apart." Then she had thought: "I had better go and see how the airwomen were getting on in their trenches." Scrambling over mounds of earth and around craters, she noticed a NAAFI girl lying on the ground and sought to help – until somebody shouted, "Don't bother, she's dead." It was the first dead person Felicity Hanbury had ever seen: "I remember thinking I must have a good look at her, as I might have to get used to this kind of thing."

Reaching the airwomen's trench, Felicity Hanbury surveyed the carnage and waited as casualties were dug out. On her way back across the airfield she noticed that somebody had covered the NAAFI girl with a blanket. She remembered: "Somehow this had a greater effect on me than when I had seen her the first time. It seemed so final, almost casual. I tried to put the picture out of my mind." Another scene she never forgot was a subsequent burial, when an air raid intervened and the padre jumped in with the coffin.

After the blitz on Biggin Hill, Felicity Hanbury was awarded what she believed was the first military MBE of the war.

Felicity Hanbury (later Peake) was born Felicity Hyde Watts on May 1 1913. Her father, Col Humphrey Watts, was a prosperous Manchester-based industrialist whose family's wealth derived from S & J Watts, a textile business founded in the city in 1798.

Felicity was educated at St Winifreds, Eastbourne, in Sussex, and at Les Grands Huguenots, Vaucresson, Seine et Oise, outside Paris. Brought up as a Christian Scientist, in later life she found she could not accept Mary Baker Eddy's teachings, and was baptised and confirmed in the Church of England. Subsequently she became a devoted supporter and benefactor of St Clement Danes, the RAF Central Church.

Shortly after her presentation at Court in 1933, Felicity was invited by an uncle to accompany him on a cruise ship bound for the West Indies. On board she met Jock

Hanbury, a member of the Truman, Hanbury and Buxton brewing family.

In the New Year of 1935 they were married at St Margaret's, Westminster, and honeymooned at Monte Carlo, spending much time at La Mortola, the Hanbury villa. When her husband took flying lessons, Felicity followed suit. Both obtained licences and enjoyed weekend trips to Le Touquet.

With war looming, her husband joined No 615 (County of Surrey) Squadron of the Auxiliary Air Force as a fighter pilot. With less than 25 hours solo flying experience, Felicity Hanbury was not accepted as a pilot by the Air Transport Auxiliary. Although disappointed, in April 1939 she volunteered to join No 9 ATS company of the RAF, becoming an aircraftwoman equipment assistant second class. On September 1 she was called up for active service and appointed company assistant – the equivalent of pilot officer, the RAF's most junior commissioned rank. Then, on October 3, Felicity Hanbury became one of the war's earliest widows when her husband crashed at Dorking, Surrey, while on a night-flying exercise.

In the New Year she qualified as a code and cipher officer but, sensing this might prove to be a dead end, she arranged to return to administrative duties. She was posted to Biggin Hill.

After the Battle of Britain, Felicity Hanbury joined the WAAF recruiting staff at the Air Ministry in January 1941. After touring in a van appealing to women through a loudspeaker to join, she was promoted flight officer and assigned to public relations duties. Tall, willowy and attractive, Felicity Hanbury had a way with the press. She had a talent for spotting a "story", and she also excelled at persuading crusty senior RAF staff officers to see the point of employing women in the service – and of giving them increasing responsibility.

She made a great success of making the WAAF case,

not least with Air Commodore Harald (later Sir Harald) Peake, who was then director of RAF public relations. She suggested that he take the PR for the WAAF under his wing. Ten years later, in 1952, they were to marry.

Meanwhile, Felicity Hanbury's duties brought her into contact with ever more senior "top brass". The lasting friendships forged in this period not only helped her rapid rise in the service, but also proved fruitful in post-war years – particularly whenever she needed to pull a string on behalf of the RAF Benevolent Fund or the Imperial War Museum.

Among those she lobbied on behalf of the WAAF were Sir Charles Portal, Chief of Air Staff, and his deputy Sir Wilfrid Freeman. Portal, indeed, used her as his "eyes and ears" about matters which might not normally filter through to him.

In 1943 Felicity Hanbury was posted as deputy WAAF admin staff officer at Bomber Command. She then moved on to command the WAAF officers' school at Bowness-on-Windermere as a wing officer.

The next year she was appointed senior WAAF staff officer responsible for the welfare of women radar opera-tors; and in 1945 she became senior WAAF staff officer to the Commander-in-Chief Mediterranean and Middle East Command in the rank of group officer (equivalent to group captain).

After commanding the WAAF and introducing and leading the WRAF, Felicity Hanbury retired from the service and joined the Truman, Hanbury and Buxton board as an executive director.

In 1952 her life was further transformed by marriage to Harald Peake. He was a director of Rolls-Royce, and chairman of Lloyds Bank and the Steel Company of Wales; he also owned a family colliery.

The Peakes bought Court Farm, a 17th-century manor at Tackley, near Woodstock in Oxfordshire, where they bred pedigree herds of Ayrshires and Jerseys. They had other homes in Mayfair and the south of France.

She devoted much time to the RAF Benevolent Fund, on whose council she had served since 1946. In 1963 Felicity Peake was appointed a Trustee of the Imperial War Museum, serving as chairman from 1986 to 1988. She also founded and presided over the museum's Friends' organisation.

In 1993 she published an autobiography, *Pure Chance*.

In 1949 she was appointed DBE. She was Honorary ADC to King George VI from 1949 to 1950.

Sir Harald Peake, with whom she had a son, died in 1978.

FAY GILLIS WELLS

Fay Gillis Wells (who died on December 2 2002, aged 94) led a charmed life as a dashing aviatrix and roving correspondent; in the 1930s she reported on Hollywood accompanied by her pet leopard, Snooks.

The daughter of a mining engineer, she was born Helen Fay Gillis on October 15 1908 at Minneapolis, Minnesota. Always fascinated by aeroplanes, she left the University of Michigan in her first year and made for New York, intent on taking flying lessons.

In September 1929 the biplane which her instructor was piloting broke up over Long Island, forcing Fay Gillis to parachute to safety. The episode earned her membership of the Caterpillar Club, open to those who had baled out of aircraft and been saved by silk parachutes.

Fay Gillis was not, as was widely reported, the first woman to win that distinction (Irene McFarland having parachuted to safety in Cincinnati in 1925), but the episode brought her widespread publicity – and a job as America's first saleswoman and demonstrator of aircraft.

Part of her role at Curtiss Flying Service (which she liked to say she had fallen into) was to convince women that flying was safe.

A month after her celebrated parachute jump, Fay Gillis earned her federal pilot's licence, whereupon she wrote to the 117 other American women who were licensed to fly, suggesting they meet on Long Island and form a club to foster camaraderie and promote opportunities for women in aviation. Ninety-nine responded, and that number was later adopted as the club's name. Amelia Earhart became its first president, Fay Gillis its secretary.

Fay Gillis then began working as a journalist, writing about aviation. She also designed and modelled pilot attire for women and acted as fashion editor of *Airwoman*, the magazine of the Ninety-Nines.

When her father was posted to Moscow in 1931, she followed to work as a stringer for the *New York Herald Tribune*, Associated Press and *The Sportsman Pilot*. She became the first American woman to fly a Soviet aeroplane and the first foreigner to fly a Soviet glider. In 1934 she covered the coronation of Emperor Pu Yi of Manchuria for the *New York Times*.

A year earlier, during Wiley Post's first solo round-the-world flight in the Winnie Mae, Fay Gillis had made all his refuelling arrangements in Russia. The grateful Post offered to take her with him in 1935 on a flight to Siberia by way of Alaska, but she turned him down in order to get married to the swashbuckling journalist Linton Wells. On the trip, Post and Fay Gillis's replacement, the comedian Will Rogers, were killed when they crashed on take-off in bad weather near Point Barrow, Alaska.

Fay Gillis and Linton Wells spent their honeymoon in Ethiopia, covering the war against Italy. He took the northern half of the country, she the south; her mysterious movements following the Italian invasion led the press in London to speculate that she was a spy. The

Wellses sometimes had front-page stories on the same day. During lulls in the action, she taught other foreign correspondents to knit.

On their return to America, Fay Gillis Wells bought a lioness, a cheetah and a leopard (Snooks), and lived for a time with them in her apartment in New York. The Wellses later moved to California where she covered the movie industry, always taking Snooks along with her to interviews.

In 1941 President Roosevelt asked the Wellses to investigate possible locations for a Jewish homeland in Africa, and they eventually recommended Angola.

After her son was born in 1946, Fay Gillis Wells succumbed for a time to the life of a housewife. While the family was living for four years on a houseboat in Florida, she began designing nautical furniture, and in 1961 she was granted a patent for a folding table for boats.

But in the 1960s she returned to journalism as a White House correspondent, to cover the Johnson, Nixon, Ford and Carter administrations. She travelled to Vietnam with Johnson and Nixon, and was one of three women reporters who went with Nixon on his historic trip to China and the Soviet Union in 1972.

Linton Wells died in 1976. He and Fay Wells had a son.

EVELYN "BOBBI" TROUT

Evelyn "Bobbi" Trout (who died on January 24 2003, aged 97) was the last surviving participant in the first women's transcontinental air race – the "Powder Puff Derby" of 1929 – and set several flight endurance records.

The term "Powder Puff" was singularly inappropriate in Bobbi Trout's case. A tomboy from childhood, she preferred oily engineering and mechanics to "sissy" cooking and sewing, and even persuaded her parents to buy a service station for her to run. As a teenager she acquired the nickname "Bobbi" after she adopted a severe bobbed hairdo.

Participants in the race, from Santa Monica to Cleveland, included Amelia Earhart, Florence "Pancho" Barnes and other great aviatrices of the day. Flying a Golden Eagle Chief, a high-wing monoplane, Bobbi Trout was forced to make two emergency landings and ran out of fuel five miles from Yuma. As she landed, the plane's wheels caught in the deep furrows of a ploughed field and the plane somersaulted, coming to rest upside down. On the way home from the race she was forced by bad weather to land in another field in Missouri. The plane got stuck in the mud and she had to abandon it there.

Evelyn Trout was born on January 7 1906 at Greenup, Illinois. At the age of 12 she saw her first aeroplane and immediately decided that she was going to learn to fly. In 1920 the family moved to Los Angeles where they bought a petrol station. Two years later one of her customers offered Bobbi her first ride in a plane, his Curtiss Jenny, and by 1928 she had saved enough money to pay for flying lessons. She began training in January 1928, flew solo for the first time four months later and received her pilot's licence two weeks after that. Later that year she got a $35-a-week job with R O Bone, demonstrating his new Golden Eagle monoplane. The same year she promoted (in the air) the birth of Mickey Mouse and met the aviator Charles Lindbergh who, she found, had a "very limp handshake".

On January 2 1929 she set the first of several women's endurance records, circling Van Nuys Airport for 12 hours and 11 minutes. Although Elinor Smith proceeded to beat her time by an hour a few weeks later, within a few days Bobbi Trout had gone on to set a new record of 17 hours 24 minutes, in the process becoming the first woman to log an all-night flight.

She recalled that she had become so bored during this flight that she fell asleep, waking up only when the plane went into a dive. One of the local papers marked her achievement with the headline: "Tomboy stays in air 17 hours to avoid washing dishes."

Four months later Bobbi Trout climbed into a new 90 horse-powered Golden Eagle Chief, ascended 15,200ft and shattered the altitude record for light-class aircraft. Also that year, teaming up with Elinor Smith, she set another endurance record of 42 hours $3^1/_2$ minutes, in the first all-woman in-flight refuelling operation.

Bobbi Trout had to lean out of the plane to catch bags of food, motor oil and a gasoline hose lowered from the refuelling plane. A previous attempt had to be aborted when the refuelling operation went wrong and she swallowed some gasoline, for which she needed hospital treatment.

In 1930 she became the fifth woman in America to earn a transport licence allowing her to fly for hire. The following year, with Edna May Cooper, she broke her own refuelling endurance record, staying in the air for 122 hours, 50 minutes.

During the Depression Bobbi Trout became a flying instructor and, along with her friend Pancho Barnes, formed the Women's Air Reserve, set up to transport emergency supplies at times of disaster. She also served in the American Civil Air Patrol.

When war came she went into business and invented a machine to sort unused rivets that were being scrapped by aircraft companies. She also developed de-burring equipment for smoothing the edges of machined metal.

In later life she became an estate agent in the Palm Springs area.

Bobbi Trout was an inspiration for many generations of women aviators. In 1994, when Eileen Collins became the first woman space shuttle commander, she took one of Bobbi Trout's record certificates with her – signed by Orville Wright.

Bobbi Trout's autobiography, *Just Plane Crazy*, was published in 1987.

She never married.

———

EDNA MORRIS

Edna Morris (who died on October 24 2004, aged 80) was one of the first three women – known as "the Flying Nightingales" – to fly into Normandy after D-Day; as a nursing orderly in the Women's Auxiliary Air Force (WAAF), she flew in the first RAF transport aircraft to evacuate the wounded from the French battlefields.

On the evening of June 5 1944 Edna Birkbeck, as she then was, was on duty at RAF Blakehill Farm, near Swindon, when the aircraft of her squadron, No 233, took off for Normandy. "Nobody mentioned an invasion, of course," she later recalled, "but everybody knew."

On June 12 the nurses were called together to be briefed on the invasion by an RAF medical officer. Corporal Lydia Alford, LACW Myra Roberts and LACW Edna Birkbeck were asked to remain behind at the end of the briefing when they were told that they would be on the first casualty evacuation flights from Normandy.

They were issued with parachutes and Mae West life jackets, which drew from one airman the comment, "Hey fellas, they're going in before we are". No Red Cross markings were allowed on the aircraft since they were transporting supplies.

Meanwhile in France, as soon as a foothold had been gained, the men of the Royal Engineer Airfield Construction Group had bulldozed a series of airstrips from the Normandy fields. The first was accepting RAF fighters the day after the landings, while the second, B2 at Bazenville near Bayeux, was re-arming and refuelling Spitfire and Typhoon fighters two days later.

With the construction of more airstrips – 20 in the first two months – there was sufficient capacity for transport aircraft to land with supplies. Since they would be empty for the return flight, casualties could be evacuated.

On D-Day+7 (June 13) three Dakotas of No 233 Squadron took off from Blakehill Farm and met an escort of Spitfires over Selsey Bill before heading for the B2 airstrip. On board each was a WAAF nursing orderly, one of them 20-year-old Edna Birkbeck. After four tons of supplies had been unloaded at B2, 14 stretcher cases and six sitting wounded were loaded on to the aircraft ready for an immediate return to England. The nurses had to deal with horrifying injuries. Many young men were missing limbs or had their faces burnt or blown away; treatment such as amputations, transfusions and colostomies had often been improvised in the field. But, as Edna Birkbeck later remarked, "you couldn't let it get to you".

Before the return flight she was driven along the beaches to see the battlefield, as British soldiers marching to the front exclaimed: "Blimey! Women!"

On landing back at Blakehill Farm a few hours later, the Dakota crews were met by 42 press correspondents representing many British, Canadian and American newspapers. They immediately dubbed the WAAFs "the Flying Nightingales", a name that was to remain with the air ambulance nurses for the rest of the campaign.

Edna Birkbeck was born in Northamptonshire on August 31 1924 and educated locally at Wellingborough. After leaving school she became a trainee nurse, and in February 1943 joined the WAAF as a nursing orderly "for excitement" and was trained at Morecambe and Sidmouth before moving to RAF Medmenham in Buckinghamshire. Shortly afterwards she responded to a call for volunteers for air ambulance duties, although she was not entirely sure what was involved.

Following training at Hendon she was posted to Blakehill Farm in February 1944 to be attached to No 233. During the period leading up to D-Day she and her two colleagues flew on training exercises with the squadron.

Four days after the first flight, Edna Birkbeck received a letter from Air Marshal Harold Whittingham offering her his congratulations on being one of the first three women to land in France at the opening of the Second Front.

The evacuations of June 13 were deemed a success and paved the way for the large-scale evacuation of wounded soldiers from France. By the end of June, 1,092 stretcher cases and 467 sitting wounded had been evacuated by 233's Dakotas. Edna Birkbeck flew a further 60 casualty evacuation operations from airfields in Belgium, Holland and Germany. Despite the severity of the injuries (and, on one occasion, a crash-landing after engine failure), none of her patients died on any of her flights, a fact of which she was justly proud. "They always wanted tea, those that could drink," she recalled. "We'd carry an industrial-sized urn. And they'd always want to know when we were over the coast. I'd tell them that and say: 'It won't be long before you're home'. And they'd cheer."

She was also on board one of the first aircraft to land at Copenhagen following the German surrender. After the victory in Europe, she continued to fly with 233 as the squadron returned repatriated PoWs to England.

During her time at Blakehill Farm Edna Birkbeck met Flight Sergeant Glyn Morris, a wireless operator/air gunner flying with 233. They married in March 1945 and six months later she left the WAAF. She remained, however, a strong supporter of the 233 Squadron Association and regularly attended annual reunions. She kept her war mementoes, including her log book and lapel pins.

After several years devoted to bringing up her three

daughters she was employed running the sports department of a shop in Gloucester. Glyn Morris died in 1987.

———

IRIS "FLUFF" BOWER

Iris "Fluff" Bower (who died on December 18 2005, aged 90) was one of two RAF nursing sisters to land on the Normandy beaches in June 1944 to establish a field hospital; later, following closely behind the advancing armies, she arrived outside Belsen concentration camp shortly after it was relieved and tended the desperate survivors.

On the night of June 11 1944, Iris Bower (then Iris Ogilvie, known to all as "Fluff") and her nursing colleague, Mollie Giles, boarded a tank-landing craft at Gosport along with 200 men and their tanks. Just before dawn she scrambled ashore on Juno beach near Courseulles-sur-Mer; only her Red Cross armband and diminutive frame marked her out from the men as she became the first woman to set foot on the D-Day landing beaches. When the beachmaster saw the two women in the dawn light he simply said "Good God!"

Her squadron leader was killed as he came ashore, and Iris Bower found herself plunged straight into the thick of the action, tending countless casualties amid chaos and enemy gunfire at a medical camp established a few miles inland at Creully. The sight of the two women was met with a great cheer from British soldiers. "Watch out Adolf, you've had it now," joked one of them.

Iris Bower was determined to look her best when she faced the Germans and commented: "I was not going to land in Normandy looking a sight."

She had put on her lipstick and carried a small waterproof bag she had made for her make-up. Once established ashore, she slept – as did her patients – in slit trenches, washed out of buckets and used a thunder box. Every morning, with shells flying overhead, she took care to apply her Elizabeth Arden lipstick before putting on her tin hat and battledress blouse.

Working out of a roughly-constructed field hospital, she tended to the 1,023 wounded soldiers treated in the first five days; she and Mollie Giles also escorted them to emergency landing strips from where RAF Dakotas flew them back to hospitals in England. She remembered some heartbreaking scenes, but realised that the sight of a pretty face and a smile were a great boost to the morale of the badly wounded.

She entered Caen three days after the city fell, noting that "the smell of death was everywhere". But her despair gradually gave way to elation as the liberated French came out to welcome them. The two nursing sisters were treated as stars by the British press, which ran headlines such as "Iris and Mollie shop in Bayeux". (In fact, they never went shopping, but it made rousing copy for the home front.)

Iris Bower was born Iris Jones on April 12 1915 at a hamlet near Cardigan, and was educated at Cardigan Grammar School. She had always wanted to be a nurse and moved to London to train at St Mary's Hospital, Paddington. After working at the East End Maternity Hospital she joined the Princess Mary's RAF Nursing Service as a staff nurse in April 1939.

On the night of July 19 1940 Iris was the duty sister at the RAF's hospital at St Athan near Barry when bombs hit the hutted hospital. She groped around amongst burst water-pipes in the darkness and helped guide the wounded to safety. For her conduct she was awarded the Royal Red Cross (2nd Class), which she received from the King a few months later.

Iris was bombed for a second time when she was serving at the RAF Officers' Hospital in the Palace Hotel at Torquay. Luftwaffe fighter-bombers had begun a campaign of "hit and run" tactics against the seaside hotels known to house RAF trainee aircrew and hospitals.

On the morning of Sunday October 25 1942 a direct hit on the east wing of the hotel killed 65 patients and nursing staff, including the VAD nurse to whom Iris had been speaking only seconds earlier. For the next 24 hours she was involved in the strenuous efforts to rescue the seriously injured patients, administering what aid she could. The following morning the hospital had to be evacuated to Wroughton, near Swindon.

In April 1942 Iris Bower had married Flight Lieutenant Donald Ogilvie, DFC, but he was killed on a daylight-bombing raid over Holland in June the next year. Later she recalled: "I was devastated. He had died for his country and I didn't care what happened to me. I knew I wanted to make some big contribution myself. I had a strong feeling that what we were taking part in was grand and noble."

She volunteered to join No 50 Mobile Field Hospital, in No 83 RAF Group, and was accepted as a senior sister. At the time she joined in August 1943 she was the only woman in the unit.

When the Allied armies advanced from the Normandy bridgehead, the Mobile Field Hospital followed closely in its wake. Iris Bower saw the liberation of Paris and tended the wounded after the Battle of Arnhem. Early in April she crossed the Rhine, and five weeks later reached an airfield on the outskirts of Belsen, four days after it had been liberated.

Some of the victims who were capable of travelling were brought to the airfield. She was stunned by their appearance and felt "very inadequate" as she and her nurses prepared them to be flown to hospitals in Belgium. She was deeply affected by what she saw, 50 years later remarking that "those moments with the

Belsen victims, on that patch of grass near the Dakotas, will stay in my memory all my life". For her work following D-Day Iris Bower was appointed MBE.

She remained in the RAF and served at hospitals in the Middle East, where she met her second husband, Major William Bower. They married in 1949, the year she retired with the equivalent rank of squadron leader.

Once her children had grown up, Iris Bower returned to the medical world, teaching psychiatric nursing at Harperbury Hospital, Hertfordshire. She finally retired at the age of 70.

During the events to commemorate the 50th anniversary of the D-Day landings she returned to Juno beach. She was one of the few to express the view that the Germans should be represented: "I think there should be forgiveness," she said. Ten years later, at the 60th anniversary, she recalled how proud she felt to have been involved; she also reflected that it was important that people knew about "the role the women played in the conflict".

Iris Bower's second husband died in 1977; they had a son and a daughter.

ELSPETH GREEN

Elspeth Green (who died on August 24 2006, aged 93) was one of three WAAFs awarded the Military Medal for their courageous conduct during the intensive bombing of RAF Biggin Hill at the height of the Battle of Britain.

In the last few days of August 1940 the Luftwaffe concentrated on knocking out the fighter airfields in the south-east of England; and Biggin Hill, one of the most important, suffered heavily.

During this period, when there were six raids in three days, the then Corporal Elspeth Henderson was on duty in the operations room, responsible for maintaining the vital contact between the airfield operations staff and the controllers at Fighter Command headquarters, Bentley Priory.

On August 30 nine Junkers 88 bombers delivered a devastating attack on the airfield. An air raid shelter was completely destroyed, and a number of WAAFs sheltering in an adjacent slit trench were amongst the 39 people killed. Others were entombed, and Elspeth Henderson was one of the first to help to dig them out.

After spending the night in makeshift quarters with her WAAF colleagues, she was back on duty the next day when the Luftwaffe attacked again. She maintained contact with Uxbridge despite the bombs bursting on the airfield. Later that afternoon the ops room took a direct hit, and she was knocked over by the blast; but she carried on with her work. "There was nothing much else we could do, anyway," she commented later.

Elspeth Henderson maintained contact with Uxbridge throughout the raid but, as fire broke out, the staff was ordered to take shelter. With her commanding officer and the rest of the staff, she hurriedly left the burning ops room through a broken window and threw herself to the ground as more bombs exploded. Her warrant officer shouted at her to move – she was leaning against an unexploded bomb.

Another WAAF, Sergeant Helen Turner, remained at her post in the adjacent emergency telephone exchange until she had to be dragged away to safety. Yet more attacks were aimed at Biggin Hill on the following day, but the squadrons remained operational and continued to take off from the badly-damaged runways.

Using hastily repaired telephone lines and signals equipment in a temporary operations room, Elspeth Henderson maintained contact with Fighter Command headquarters and the Observer Corps posts. Sporadic raids continued until September 7, when the Luftwaffe turned its attention to London.

On November 2 it was announced that Elspeth Henderson and two other WAAFs – Sergeants Helen Turner and Elizabeth Mortimer – had been awarded the Military Medal for their "courage and example of a high order". The commanding officer of Biggin Hill said: "These three girls have shown amazing pluck." Throughout the whole of the Second World War, there were only six awards of the Military Medal to members of the WAAF.

Elspeth Candlish Henderson was born on June 16 1913, the daughter of a Professor of Law at Edinburgh University. She was educated at St Denis School, Edinburgh, and Harrogate Ladies' College. On leaving school she travelled in Europe, becoming proficient in German and French.

During eight months' service with the VAD she was a driver and gained first aid qualifications. She joined the WAAF in January 1940. After two weeks training to be a plotter in the ops room of a fighter base, she was posted to Biggin Hill, one of Fighter Command's main sector airfields.

Elspeth Henderson was soon promoted to corporal, giving her the responsibility of supervising other WAAF plotters as they displayed the progress of incoming enemy bomber formations. Sometimes it was clear that the bombers were heading directly for Biggin Hill, but she and her colleagues remained at their posts plotting the progress of the attack.

Just before the announcement of her award she was commissioned as a section officer and trained in cipher duties. For the next five years she worked in this role on a number of bomber bases. She was posted to Egypt in August 1945 as a welfare officer and a year later left the service with the rank of squadron officer.

After leaving the WAAF she worked at the British Council and was later the secretary for the first

Edinburgh International Festival. After her marriage she devoted herself to her family and to voluntary work in Edinburgh. She was a strong supporter of the Aged Christian Friends Society of Scotland.

In July 1974 she returned to Biggin Hill, where a road in the RAF married quarters was named after her.

Elspeth Henderson married, in 1949, Alastair McWatt Green, who died in 1991. They had a son and a daughter.

CIVILIANS

CAPTAIN
RONALD BALLANTINE

Captain Ronald Ballantine (who died on October 30 2003, aged 90) was an Imperial Airways and BOAC pilot; on February 6 1952 he flew the new Queen Elizabeth home from Africa following the death of her father, King George VI.

Accompanied by Prince Philip, the then Princess Elizabeth had left London on January 31 on a Commonwealth tour, which was sup-posed to have lasted for five months. But, on the death of her father, she returned to London immediately in the BOAC Canadair Argonaut airliner which had brought her to Kenya a week earlier.

With Ballantine at the controls, the aircraft left Entebbe airport, Uganda, just before 9pm on February 6, and climbed to 16,500ft to fly across the Sahara on the 2,260-mile flight to RAF El Adem in Libya, arriving after a flight of nine and a half hours.

After the aircraft was refuelled, Captain R C Parker and his crew took over, and the Royal party arrived at London airport late on the following afternoon, 20 hours after leaving Entebbe.

In the Queen's Birthday Honours List in June 1952, both Ballantine and Parker were appointed MVO (Fourth Class).

Four years later, on January 27 1956, Ballantine and Parker shared the piloting duties for another Royal visit, flying the same aircraft, which was specially adapted for the flight to Nigeria. Parker flew the aircraft to Tripoli, Libya, where Ballantine was waiting to take command for the 2,000-mile flight to Lagos.

On the conclusion of the visit, Ballantine flew the

Queen to Kano for a brief visit on February 17, before departing later in the day on the overnight flight to Idris, where Parker was waiting to complete the flight to London.

Ronald George Ballantine was born at Plymouth on August 2 1913 and educated at Plymouth College. He studied Art in Plymouth and Paris but, like so many of his generation, his life changed after a five-shilling flight with Alan Cobham's Flying Circus.

He learned to fly privately, and by the time he was 21 he had obtained his commercial flying, navigation and wireless licences, enabling him to join Imperial Airways.

Initially Ballantine flew as a second officer in the open cockpit of a three-engine Argosy on the Croydon-Brussels-Cologne route; the 20 passengers were able to lounge in wicker chairs.

He then moved on to the stately four-engine HP 42 biplane airliner. With an almost complete lack of navigation aids, locating Croydon airport in poor weather depended on finding the twin towers of Crystal Palace, then setting a stopwatch and descending blind.

This potentially hazardous technique became unnecessary with the installation of a German-developed Lorenz blind-landing system, using a series of dots and dashes which merged when the aircraft was correctly lined up with the runway. (The Germans later developed the technique into a blind-bombing system for their attacks against Britain.)

Ballantine next flew on the Imperial Airways Empire routes to Africa and Asia, before being appointed to his first command at the age of 23; he was based in Hong Kong, flying the de Havilland DH 86.

During this period he carried out an aerial survey of the route to Bangkok via Hanoi, across the relatively unknown territories of Siam and Indo-China, and he established a 16-hour record for the Rangoon-Calcutta return journey in the DH 86 Delphinus.

Ballantine earned his nickname, "The Colonel", after General Chiang Kai Shek offered him a colonelcy in his nationalist air force – a post which the Englishman prudently declined.

Although he had joined the RAF Volunteer Reserve in 1939, Ballantine was retained to fly for BOAC, the successor to Imperial Airways. He flew Ensigns in the evacuation of France before being posted to Egypt, where he flew in support of operations in the Western Desert.

On one occasion an aircrew whose plane had crashed had to be rescued in a remote area of East Africa. The only available aircraft with the appropriate short landing and take-off capability was a pre-war DH 86 biplane; and, with a retired prospector recruited to act as navigator, Ballantine completed the rescue, which attracted a letter of congratulation from Air Marshal Tedder, the Air Officer Commanding.

On another occasion, when supplying fuel to the besieged garrison at Tobruk, he successfully landed his Hudson after the two preceding aircraft had been destroyed by enemy fire, only for the undercarriage to collapse as his Hudson hit a shell hole. Ballantine spent the night in a slit trench and, after his aircraft had been destroyed by shellfire, he managed to escape just before Tobruk fell.

Ballantine flew regularly on the London–Cairo route, staging through Lisbon, Lagos and Khartoum. Among his passengers during this period were General de Gaulle and General Patton. In 1943 Ballantine was awarded a King's Commendation for Valuable Services in the Air.

Shortly after the war he was seconded as chief pilot to the newly-formed Hong Kong Airways, flying Douglas DC 3 Dakotas to Canton and Shanghai until the Communist takeover. He returned with his family to England in 1949 to fly BOAC's new Canadair Argonaut airliners.

In 1951 a British athletics team toured Yugoslavia,

Greece and Turkey with Ballantine as pilot of the team's chartered aircraft. When the athletes were struck down by a stomach virus, he and his crew did much to assist them both on and off the athletics field, and the team won all three matches.

Ballantine was now regarded as the team's talisman. In August 1953 the British athletes faced their sternest post-war test when they met Germany in the stadium at Berlin. The British Amateur Athletics Board specifically asked for Ballantine, their "lucky pilot", to fly the chartered aircraft to Berlin, a request that was approved.

Shortly after the flight bringing the Queen back from Nigeria, Ballantine converted to the Bristol Britannia, before transferring to the Comet IV fleet. In 1963 he converted to the Vickers VC 10. When he retired in 1966, he had amassed 21,400 hours flying time during a career in which he had flown an estimated five million miles.

He then went to Singapore as director of flight operations for the company which subsequently became Singapore Airlines. He returned to England in 1971.

Ballantine was described by a colleague as "tall and debonair ...quintessentially English, and a genial man of great modesty and charm". During the war, following a spirited party with his fellow pilots, he had crashed his car; he never drove again.

Throughout his career at BOAC, Ballantine's uniform measurements never changed – perhaps a result of his fondness for tennis, at which he excelled, and which he played until his seventies.

The Guild of Air Pilots and Air Navigators awarded Ballantine the Master Air Pilot's Certificate in January 1954, and three months later he was elected an Upper Freeman. In May 1959 he was invited to take the Livery of the Guild and, for a number of years in the early 1960s, he sat on the Airline Pilots' and Navigators' Committee.

When based in Lagos in 1941, Ronald Ballantine met

Cherrie Whitby, who had worked at Bletchley Park and was travelling to Cairo to join the Y-service; they married 15 months later. They had two sons and a daughter.

CAPTAIN
IAN HARVEY

Captain Ian Harvey (who died on July 11 2004, aged 83) was awarded a George Medal for saving the lives of 27 passengers when he made a masterly landing after a bomb had exploded at the back of his airliner.

Harvey was the pilot of a British European Airways (BEA) Vickers Viking which took off from Northolt for a flight to Paris on April 13 1950. Over the English Channel there was a loud explosion in the rear of the aircraft, which the flight crew initially thought had been caused by a lightning strike. On investigation, the second pilot, Frank Miller, found the stewardess seriously injured; large holes had been torn in the rear fuselage of the aircraft.

The explosion had distorted the aircraft's fin and tail-plane assembly, rendering the rudder useless and damaging the elevators. As a result Harvey had only marginal control of the aeroplane, and he decided to return to Northolt to attempt a landing.

By this time night had fallen. Despite his efforts, and the assistance of his second pilot, he was unable to land the aircraft at the first attempt and was forced to over-shoot. For his second attempt Harvey decided to make a very long, low, flat approach, using the power of the engines to adjust his rate of descent; on this occasion he was successful.

Examination of the Viking revealed that an explosion had occurred in the rear lavatory; two large holes had been blown on either side of the fuselage, one measuring five feet by eight feet and the other only slightly smaller. The flying controls had also been severely damaged. Harvey's fellow pilots were full of admiration for the outstanding skill and airmanship that had undoubtedly saved the lives of his passengers and crew. It was also a testimony to the sturdy airframe of the Viking, a descendant of the Wellington bomber.

Five weeks after the incident it was announced that Harvey had been awarded the George Medal. The citation referred to his "extreme coolness" as he regained control of the aircraft. "It required all the strength of the pilot, coupled with superb skill, before the Viking was landed successfully without injury to any of the passengers. In the face of this very grave emergency, the action of Captain Harvey is worthy of the highest praise. The complete loss of the aircraft and all its company was avoided only as a result of his courage, high skill and presence of mind."

The report of the official inquiry confirmed that a bomb had caused the explosion, but no evidence of detonators or bomb fragments was found. The police investigation apparently failed to disclose either the motive for the attack or the person responsible. The material relating to the incident in the Public Records Office is not due for release for some years.

Ian Richard Harvey, the son of Lieutenant Herbert Harvey, of the Royal Scots, was born at Bristol on October 13 1920. After attending Cotham School, Bristol, he was employed as an engineer by the city council. In 1938 he joined the Territorial Army, enlisting in the Royal Artillery.

In early 1940 he accompanied his battery to France, and was heavily engaged in the fighting following the blitzkrieg. With a good command of French, he often acted as interpreter for his commanding officer.

On the fall of France, Harvey was evacuated from the beaches at Dunkirk. His mother, a senior officer in the St

John Ambulance Brigade, who had just rescued a German bomber crew from their crashed aircraft, did not hear of his survival for many days, and assumed that her son had been killed or captured.

Harvey transferred to the RAF in 1941 for aircrew duties. After completing his initial training, he went to the United States, where he joined, under the "Arnold Scheme", a pilot-training programme. He was awarded his pilot's wings and commissioned as a pilot officer before returning to England to convert to the Lancaster bomber. In June 1943 he joined No 106 Squadron, based near Newark.

Harvey began bombing operations over Germany in the summer of 1943 and flew continuously until the next spring. This period was the most intense of the strategic bombing offensive and saw the beginning of the so-called Battle of Berlin, when losses reached their height. Harvey and his crew were the first in No 106 for 18 months to complete a full tour of 30 operations.

On one occasion Harvey had just begun his bombing run to the target when his Lancaster was attacked by two night fighters. Displaying superb skill, he avoided the fighters and successfully bombed his target. On another occasion, when his aircraft was attacked by a Junkers 88 night fighter, he manoeuvred his heavy bomber so as to enable his two gunners to shoot down the enemy aircraft.

He was awarded a DFC for "his skill, courage and determination, which have been outstanding". The citation also highlighted the "coolness" that was to be so evident during his handling of the Viking incident six years later.

Harvey left the RAF in 1946 to join BEA. After flying the Viking and the Viscount, he converted to jet aircraft, and was a captain in BEA's Comet fleet. He then transferred to the Trident, and became a training captain at the time when simulators were being introduced. He retired in 1975.

Ian Harvey was twice married, and had a son by his first marriage and two stepdaughters from his second.

CAPTAIN
NORMAN TODD

Captain Norman Todd (who died on August 22 2004, aged 80) commanded the first commercial flight by a British Airways Concorde.

By January 1976 both British Airways and Air France were ready to start their respective Concorde services to the main destination of the United States, but the US Congress denied access to both airlines for environmental reasons. Anxious to start operations immediately, the French airline decided to launch its first supersonic flight from Paris to Rio de Janeiro via Dakar. British Airways chose the route to Bahrain, a sector they hoped would form an eventual route from London to Singapore and Australia.

At 11.40am on January 21 1976 the two Concorde aircraft took off simultaneously, to the second, in a set-piece move. Todd was at the controls of G-BOAA ("Alpha Alpha") with a flight crew of nine. Aboard the British Airways flight from Heathrow were 100 passengers, including government and airline officials, journalists and 30 fare-paying passengers. The aircraft flew over Paris and Venice to the Adriatic Sea, where Todd accelerated the aircraft to supersonic flight, achieving twice the speed of sound (Mach 2).

Air Commodore E M Donaldson, *The Daily Telegraph*'s air correspondent, was one of those aboard. He recorded: "One must sample it to believe it, for here I sit in a comfortable cabin in the calm air nearly 60,000ft up, hurtling along faster than the speed of a cannon shell, eating caviar and drinking exquisite Champagne that rests without a ripple on my table. This is history." The aircraft crossed Lebanon and Syria in six minutes before landing at Bahrain after a flight of three hours and 37 minutes.

The authorities in America finally gave Concorde a limited clearance to use Washington, and Todd took the first flight to Dulles Airport on May 24, flying G-BOAC, landing within minutes of his sister Concorde operated by Air France. Both flights had been completed in just under four hours.

On November 2 1976 Todd brought the Queen and Prince Philip home from Barbados at the end of their Silver Jubilee tour of Canada and the West Indies. This was a record-breaking flight which covered 4,200 statute miles to Heathrow in three hours 42 minutes at an average speed of 1,134mph. During the flight the Queen visited the cockpit and showed a keen interest as Todd explained the flight deck activities.

The son of a civil servant, Norman Victor Todd was born in London on June 14 1924. He was educated at University College School, Hampstead, and St Andrews University, where he read Languages. He joined the University Air Squadron, volunteering after a year for flying duties with the RAF. He trained as a pilot in South Africa, and was commissioned in December 1943 before converting to bombers. In September 1944 he joined No 355 Squadron, based at Salbani, near Calcutta, flying the four-engine Liberator heavy bomber.

His first operation was to bomb Japanese targets near Mandalay. Over the next few months he attacked land communications far behind the battle area, including the infamous Siam-Burma railway. He also attacked airfields, harbour installations and shipping; these often involved flights that exceeded 2,000 miles. On November 22 he attacked Huagang, on the Burma-Malaya border, a round trip of 2,300 miles – he was airborne for more than 14 hours, at that time the longest bombing flight of the war.

On July 10 1945 Todd took off to bomb the railway marshalling yards at Rajpuri in Siam. On the return flight one of his engines failed, and he had to make an emergency landing during which the undercarriage collapsed. It was his 42nd, and final, operation. He became an instructor on the Liberator before returning to England to train pilots at a Blind Approach Training Flight in Yorkshire. He left the RAF as a flight lieutenant in November 1946.

Todd joined BOAC at the end of 1946 and, after a brief period in converted Liberators, flew the elegant Lockheed Constellation on the North Atlantic route. After five years he transferred to the Boeing Stratocruiser fleet, becoming a training captain in 1957.

After a spell flying the long-range Britannia 312 turbo-prop airliner, he converted to jets in 1965 and formed part of the development flight for the introduction of the 163-seat VC10 airliner on the Atlantic and African routes. He was one of the first pilots to convert to the giant Boeing 747 when it entered service in 1971, and he eventually became the flight training manager for British Airways' 747 fleet.

In August 1973 Todd joined Brian Trubshaw, the United Kingdom's chief test pilot on the Anglo-French Concorde project, as the airline's captain appointed to assist in the flight test programme for the aircraft. Todd made his first flight in the supersonic airliner in August 1973.

He continued to fly the 747, but by 1975 he was fully involved in the development trials of the Concorde. He conducted the hot weather trials in Kuala Lumpur and various route-proving flights. During this period he established close friendships with the French test pilots and the Air France Concorde captains.

By the time Todd took the first fare-paying commercial flight to Bahrain in "Alpha Alpha", he had already flown more than 100,000 supersonic miles. He remained with the Concorde fleet as the flight training manager until he retired in 1979.

For his work with BOAC and British Airways, Todd was awarded a Queen's Commendation for Valuable Services in the Air in 1973. In 1977 the Royal Aero Club presented him with the Britannia Trophy for "the most meritorious performance in aviation during 1976".

After retiring from British Airways he became an aviation consultant specialising in advice on the piloting aspects of air disasters. He finally retired in 1984.

Norman Todd married, in 1946, Ruth Coates, with whom he had a son and daughter.

TEST PILOTS

GROUP CAPTAIN
JOHN "CAT'S EYES" CUNNINGHAM

Group Captain John "Cat's Eyes" Cunningham (who died on July 21 2002, aged 84) was a night fighter ace and later a consummate test pilot whose name guaranteed the reputation of British aviation.

After destroying at least 20 enemy aircraft, Cunningham piloted the maiden flight of the Comet, which became the world's first passenger jet airliner.

When the plane was involved in a series of dramatic crashes, Cunningham took a model off the production line, and tested it to the point of destruction. He then ushered its amended successors into both airline and service use.

The RAF's continuing employment of Nimrod, the Comet's maritime reconnaissance derivative, is a reminder of the debt owed to Cunningham for his lead in the exhaustive test programmes.

All this was far in the future when Cunningham, already a de Havilland junior test pilot and an Auxiliary Air Force weekend flier with No 604 (County of Middlesex) Squadron, was called up to full-time service shortly before the outbreak of war in 1939.

Equipped with the two-engine Bristol Blenheim, which had to search hopelessly for night raiders, Cunningham and his fellow pilots had little more to help them than training, eyesight and instinct.

"We didn't look on the so-called fighter version of the Blenheim as a very attractive aircraft," he recalled. "As we went off to war we thought 'We are not going to last long against the Me 109.'"

During the early stages of the Battle of Britain in 1940, Cunningham was relieved to be asked to experiment with a photo-electric bomb, devised to be dropped from above on heavy enemy bomber formations. When this project was abandoned, experimental airborne radar was beginning to become available for trial.

On the night of November 19 1940, Cunningham bagged his first Ju 88. After exchanging his make-do Blenheim for a two-engine Bristol Beaufighter he shot down a Heinkel 111 bomber over the Channel and another over Lyme Bay.

As Cunningham's score mounted the story was spread that his success owed much to a hearty consumption of carrots, which were said to sharpen his eyesight; and henceforth he was known as "Cat's Eyes".

The deception, which was aimed at the enemy, also helped Lord Woolton, the food minister, to get across the value of vegetables, particularly carrots, in the rationed wartime diet.

No allusion was made to the primary reason for Cunningham's success, the introduction of airborne radar and its operators; Jimmy Rawnsley, Cunningham's re-trained air-gunner, was one of the best.

Cunningham later mused: "It would have been easier had the carrots worked. In fact, it was a long, hard grind and very frustrating. It was a struggle to continue flying on instruments at night.

"The essential was teamwork – not just between pilot and radar operator. A night fighter crew was at the top of a pyramid, ground control radar and searchlights at the base, and up there an aircraft with two chaps in it. Unless they were competent and compatible all that great effort was wasted."

In mid-April 1941 Cunningham and Rawnsley des-troyed three enemy bombers in one night, and when Cunningham left 604 for a staff appointment, the squadron had shot down twice as many enemy aircraft as any other night fighter unit.

Cunningham returned to operations early in 1943,

when he received command of No 85, a Mosquito night fighter squadron. After adding several more kills to his score – including four fast FW 190 fighter bombers – Cunningham joined Fighter Command's No 11 Group headquarters as a group captain aged 26, still with a baby face and twinkling blue eyes.

John Cunningham was born on July 27 1917, the son of the company secretary of the Dunlop Rubber Company. At nine, he had a joyride in an Avro 504 biplane, and was immediately captivated by the idea of flying. His ambitions were further stimulated at Whitgift School by its proximity to Croydon airport. He then joined the de Havilland apprenticeship scheme.

This early association with de Havilland gave Cunningham a head start when, as the war ended, he opted to pass up the opportunity of a glittering peacetime career in the RAF and return to civil aviation.

Exchanging a group captain's brass hat for a test pilot's overalls, he took over flight development of the company's Goblin turbojet engine. Within a year the death, in a crash, of Geoffrey de Havilland, son of the company's founder Sir Geoffrey, cleared the way for Cunningham to become the company's chief test pilot.

He took over the major responsibility for investigating the characteristics of the single-seat DH 108's swept-wing design and also for obtaining basic data for the future DH 106 Comet and the naval fighter Sea Vixen.

Meanwhile, work had started on the Comet, and Cunningham, accompanying BOAC crews on five transatlantic flights and two round trips to Australia, also began to gain experience of the requirements of airline crews.

On July 27 1949, his 32nd birthday, he was conducting taxiing trials when, with no fuss, he made an unannounced 35-minute maiden flight. But within three years de Havilland began to pay the price of hastening the Comet into service. On October 26 1952, a BOAC

Comet taking off from Rome failed to become airborne; there were no casualties, but the aircraft was damaged beyond repair.

Although the pilot was blamed wrongly, Cunningham was not satisfied. But his exhaustive take-off tests proved fruitless; and the accident was repeated the following March when a Canadian Pacific Airlines Comet was destroyed at Karachi.

In each accident, as Cunningham was to discover, the nose had lifted too high too early, resulting in a great increase in drag. Following further tests, the leading edge of the wing was revised, along with Cunningham's advice on take-offs to pilots.

Despite a further take-off accident in May, when a BOAC Comet crashed shortly after leaving Calcutta in poor weather, all was fairly plain sailing until January 1954, when the first production Comet disintegrated at 35,000ft off Elba.

In April a similar break-up took place south of Naples over the volcanic island of Stromboli, and it was decided to test an entire Comet fuselage for fatigue in a water tank at the Royal Aircraft Establishment, Farnborough. Although Farnborough's findings centred on the fatal flaw of metal fatigue in a pressurised hull, the likelihood of potential disaster had arguably been heightened by design shortcuts and economies which had been made to ensure that the Comet became the world's first passenger jet.

Cunningham immediately busied himself with remedial action. He flew to Canada to bring back two RCAF Comet 1As; and after their fuselages were rebuilt took them home again.

In December 1955 Cunningham made a world tour, in which Comet III's performance was flawless. The next year President Eisenhower presented him with the Harmon Trophy, the highest American honour for services to aviation, in recognition of his contribution to jet transport.

Recognition at home came more slowly, and he was not elevated to the de Havilland board until 1958, when BOAC put Comet IV on to the London-New York route.

When, during this period, de Havilland became a division of Hawker Siddeley, Cunningham, always ready to get on with the job in hand, was not fazed. Sir Geoffrey de Havilland noted that Cunningham, a bachelor, was "test pilot, demonstration pilot and ambassador all in one and has made some sensational flights. He can do thousands of miles for many days and at the end of the flight can be charming, unruffled and apparently as fresh as ever when discussing points raised by a host of officials, pressmen and others."

While Trident, which was to become so successful with British European Airways and elsewhere, was on the way in 1960 and 1961, Cunningham remained busy testing Comet versions.

Eventually he was involved with Trident's initial trials and, with his colleagues, saw it through more than 1,800 hours of testing before the first Trident was certified airworthy in 1964.

Among Cunningham's greatest assets were his good relationships with overseas buyers and his talent for training foreign pilots. After delivering Tridents to Pakistan he became extremely busy with a substantial order for China.

From 1972 he began to deliver Tridents, one by one, to Kwangchow. Part of the deal was that he had to do a test flight with a Chinese crew on each aircraft from Kwangchow to Shanghai.

So far, other than a bale-out in 1939 from a Moth Minor, Cunningham had led a charmed life; but in 1975 he was piloting a DH 125 executive jet, conveying a party of Chinese visitors from the Hawker Siddeley airfield at Dunsfold to Hatfield, when his engines ingested a large flock of plovers.

Barely off the runway, Cunningham touched down at

some 130mph. The jet shot across a road and collided with a car (killing four passengers) before coming to rest in a field and catching fire.

Cunningham sustained two crushed vertebrae, but none of his own passengers was killed, and within a year he had resumed flying. Trident deliveries to China had three years to run and his Chinese customers asked him to see the contract out.

Cunningham remained chief test pilot after Hawker Siddeley had been merged into British Aerospace, where he was an executive director from 1978 until he retired in 1980.

With more time available, he enjoyed looking after the grounds of his home, not far from the former de Havilland airfield and factory in Hertfordshire, and devoted much time and effort to the nearby museum housing the prototype Mosquito and other historic de Havilland equipment and memorabilia.

He also supported fundraising efforts for a variety of organisations. These included the RAF Benevolent Fund, the de Havilland Flying Foundation, the Bedfordshire and Buckinghamshire Aircrew Association and 604 and 85 Squadron associations, of which he was president.

Additionally, Cunningham was a Liveryman of the Guild of Air Pilots and Air Navigators and much involved with the Battle of Britain Fighter Association and a staunch supporter of the RAF Club.

It was the more unfortunate that, following the collapse of Lloyds in 1988, he was faced with heavy financial commitments having been a Name in the organisation. Even though he re-mortgaged his property and was left with a much reduced income, he remained buoyant in the face of illness.

Cunningham was appointed OBE in 1951 and CBE in 1963. He was awarded the DSO in 1941 and Bars in 1942 and 1944; the DFC and Bar in 1941 and also the Air Efficiency Award (AE). He also held the Soviet Order of

Patriotic War 1st Class and the US Silver Star.

He was Deputy Lieutenant for Middlesex in 1948 and Greater London in 1965. He was awarded the Derry and Richards Memorial Medal in 1965, the Segrave Trophy in 1969 and the Air League Founders Medal in 1979.

AIR COMMODORE
CYRIL "CYCLOPS" BROWN

Air Commodore Cyril "Cyclops" Brown (who died on November 1 2003, aged 82) earned his nickname when he lost an eye during an encounter with a German bomber in the Second World War, but his disability did not deter him from pursuing a flying career that lasted for another 30 years.

Brown was serving with No 616 (South Yorkshire) Squadron when he was scrambled on May 25 1942 to intercept a German bomber approaching Leicester. Although he managed to achieve cannon strikes on a Dornier 217, his Spitfire was hit by return fire from the bomber's rear gunner. As the windscreen shattered, Brown was hit in the face by splinters, causing severe damage to his right eye.

He managed to struggle back to his airfield near Peterborough, where he landed safely before staggering to the control tower to report to his station commander, Group Captain Basil Embry; he explained that he had experienced "a bit of a problem" before collapsing. Brown was then placed on a stretcher but, as the party descended the stairs, he fell off and tumbled to the bottom. He later claimed that this was the most frightening aspect of the whole event.

Surgeons were unable to save Brown's eye, and after his wounds healed he was fitted with a clear blue false eye. The effect of a boisterous night out was that the colour no longer matched his remaining eye, in which case he would remove the false one, invite someone to "keep an eye on it", and place a black patch over the socket. Later he adopted the patch permanently.

Although medical staff wanted to ground him, Brown was able to display all his old piloting skills when he flew with Group Captain Embry, who immediately cleared him to return to operations as a fighter pilot.

Cyril Bob Brown was born on January 17 1921 and educated at Southend Grammar School. He joined the RAF Volunteer Reserve in 1939 as a sergeant, completing his pilot training in time to join the Hurricanes of 245 Squadron in the latter stages of the Battle of Britain.

Based in Orkney, his squadron flew patrols in protection of the Grand Fleet at Scapa Flow. He was commissioned in 1941 and joined No 616, flying patrols over the Midlands until he was wounded.

Once he had become fully fit again, Brown had a further spell on operations before joining the Aeroplane and Armament Experimental Establishment at Boscombe Down as a fighter weapons test pilot.

Since using the gun sights of fighters required binocular vision, he specialised in flying and testing the Typhoon and Tempest aircraft in the ground attack role. He commanded the Fixed Gun Firing Flight and became an expert in rocket-firing.

On one occasion Brown almost shot himself down when a rocket struck the ground, and the subsequent ricochet hit his Typhoon. After three years of test flying he was awarded the AFC.

After attending No 5 Course at the Empire Test Pilots' School, Brown returned to Boscombe Down to test fighter aircraft, including the new jets, before being appointed to command No 220 Squadron flying Shackleton maritime patrol aircraft from St Eval in Cornwall.

He resumed his test piloting career in 1956 when he

became a senior instructor at the Empire Test Pilots' School, which had relocated to Farnborough.

On one occasion he gathered together a one-armed colleague and another with a broken leg, and – with Brown sporting his eye patch at a jaunty angle – the trio hobbled arm-in-arm into the officers' mess bar to announce to the new students that they were the staff running the test pilots' course.

In 1958 Brown took command of D (Helicopter) Squadron at Boscombe Down. In August 1960 the new twin-rotor Bristol 192 helicopter, later known as the Belvedere, was due to fly to Idris, in Libya, for hot weather trials. He decided to use the transit flight to establish a long-distance helicopter record.

Setting off from Gatwick in the early hours of the morning, Brown and his crew arrived on Malta just over 12 hours later, after stopping twice to refuel en-route.

Promoted to group captain, Brown took command of the V-bomber airfield at Waddington, near Lincoln, in 1963. The three Vulcan squadrons he commanded formed part of Britain's strategic nuclear deterrent and were frequently tested to respond to no-notice dispersal and scramble exercises. He regularly flew the four-engine bomber, and his piloting skills were readily apparent; but, as one colleague recalled, Brown was never able to learn how to park his staff car without colliding with the steps.

It was during his appointment in command at Waddington that Brown learned that the last airworthy Lancaster was due to be retired to a museum. The engineers of one of his squadrons suggested that they should collect the bomber from Cranfield and fly it to Waddington, where they would maintain it in a flying condition. Brown was full of enthusiasm for the idea.

Although he incurred much displeasure from higher authority, the Lancaster was restored and subsequently became the flagship of the Battle of Britain Memorial Flight.

Brown was promoted to air commodore to take up the post of commandant at the Air Warfare College, where he continued to remain in flying practice.

After spending three years as the director of flight safety in London, he decided to retire in 1972 in order to pursue business interests and his passion for yachting. He became the managing director of Leigh Instruments, specialising in the development and manufacture of flight data recorders; his expertise as a test pilot and his knowledge of flight safety were invaluable.

Brown was a dedicated and skilful yachtsman who was never deterred by bad weather or heavy seas. He was appointed commodore of the RAF Yacht Club in 1972, and admiral of the club in 1992. During his period of office he was heavily involved in supporting the club's Tradeswind Round the World Rally, in which he himself sailed the first leg from Gibraltar to the Canary Islands.

He had a detailed knowledge of the battlefields of the Peninsula Wars, and a great love of the writings of Thomas Hardy – one of his greatest pleasures in later life was to take his granddaughters to Dorset, where he would introduce them to the countryside that inspired the author's works.

"Cyclops" Brown was appointed CBE in 1966. In early 2003 he was elected a fellow of the American Society of Experimental Test Pilots.

He married, in 1944, Brenda Elliott; they had a son, and a daughter who married one of his young Vulcan pilots.

DAVID MORGAN

David Morgan (who died on February 3 2004, aged 80) captured the public imagination with his exciting and extravagant displays at the Farnborough air shows during the 1950s.

Beneath these public demonstrations of dash and verve, however, Morgan was a dedicated and highly skilled test pilot of the new generation of jet fighters. He had already established his credentials as a first-class airman when he pulled off a remarkable crash-landing in the new supersonic fighter, the Supermarine Swift, in September 1951. It was the 13th flight of the prototype; Morgan had completed the test programme at high level, and was approaching to land at the company's Chilbolton airfield when the engine failed.

He was too low to eject, and was confronted with gently rising ground, a farm and overhead power lines. Morgan flew under the power lines and steered for the gap between the farm and a barn. It was too narrow, and his wing tip dismantled a brick-built lavatory – which was, fortunately, unoccupied at the time. He then completed a masterly wheels-up landing in a stubble field. Such skilful flying saved the aircraft (enabling it to fly again three months later), and also the Swift's development programme, which might have been set back for months.

As he climbed out of his largely undamaged jet, Morgan was met by the farmer's wife, who was not impressed: "Oh dear," she said. "We have been expecting something like this to happen." Back in the farmhouse, he met four farm workers looking unperturbed as they waited for their tea. They were grateful for the cigarettes Morgan offered, which they placed by their plates.

Morgan's unflappability was amply demonstrated the next day when he flew another Supermarine fighter to rehearse his aerobatic sequence for the imminent Farnborough air show.

David William Morgan was born on April 15 1923 at Heanor, Derbyshire. His family moved to north London, and he was educated at University College School, where his flair for precise technical description was demonstrated when he was commended for an account of "how to mend a puncture in 50 words".

Morgan volunteered for flying duties in the RAF in 1941, but was rejected on medical grounds, specifically because of his poor hearing, which he blamed on too much shooting at Bisley without ear protectors. Six months later the same doctor passed him as "exceptionally fit". After training at Cambridge and in South Africa, Morgan spent a period on air traffic duties at Woodhall Spa, the home of No 617 Dambusters Squadron, where he flew unofficially on attacks against the V-1 rocket sites. Because there was a surplus of pilots in the RAF, he transferred to the Fleet Air Arm in 1944, flying Seafire fighters from the aircraft carrier *Stalker* in the Indian Ocean.

After the war Morgan became a flying instructor, before completing No 7 Course at the Empire Test Pilots' School; he flew in a formation of Hawker Sea Fury fighters that broke the London to Malta speed record. In June 1950 he joined Vickers Supermarine as a test pilot.

Morgan test flew the Navy's Attacker jet fighter, which was also purchased by the Pakistan Air Force. While ferrying the prototype aircraft to Karachi, he was forced to land en route at Baghdad on one wheel; engineers quickly repaired the aircraft, and he was able to touch down at Karachi in time for the Independence Day flypast.

Morgan was one of the pilots who flew a Supermarine experimental swept-wing aircraft in David Lean's film *The Sound Barrier* (1952).

The Swift was an aircraft that had a number of significant shortcomings; and the Hawker Hunter, which was being developed at the same time, enjoyed a much better reputation. Morgan lost no opportunity to show the Swift in a better light, and, flying to an air display in Belgium at 667mph, he reached Brussels in the record time of 18 minutes.

In the event, the RAF chose the Hawker Hunter for its new fighter. But the Swift found its niche in a low-level, high-speed fighter reconnaissance role operating from RAF airfields in Germany. It performed very well, and Morgan always believed that the FR 4 version of the Swift was "the best that was available at the time to operate at really high speeds on the deck".

Morgan then became deeply involved in the development of the Navy's powerful and rugged Scimitar fighter-bomber. He was responsible for the weapons and engineering development of the aircraft, and carried out most of the test flights on the then-new toss-bombing Low Altitude Bombing System (LABS) manoeuvre.

He was then appointed the project pilot for the TSR 2's nav/attack system; but the Labour government cancelled the project before he could make his first flight. The aircraft's demise marked the end of Morgan's test flying, and he began a new career in marketing with the new British Aircraft Corporation. He combined his grasp of technical issues with an easy charm and a fine network of contacts as he sold military aircraft and missile systems (in particular, the Rapier air defence missile) to countries in the Far East.

In 1986 he was appointed MBE for his contribution to British aviation over 40 years.

Morgan's dashing good looks and outstanding flying skills epitomised the public's perception of a test pilot. It was said that the bars at the Farnborough air show emptied when he was flying, and many of his colleagues regarded him as the best display pilot of them all.

He continued on the air display circuit for some years, performing in the company-owned Spitfire in a "dogfight" with Bill Bedford, who flew a Hurricane. Morgan kept his flying licence, and only months before his death took his new wife Catherine up in a Russian-built Yak aerobatic aircraft. In 1988 he bought a farm on the edge of Dartmoor, where he indulged his love of animals.

David Morgan married Olivia Harvey in 1946. The marriage was dissolved, and, in 1965, he married Patricia Aldridge, who died in 2001. In 2002 he married his third wife Catherine. He had a son and two daughters from his first marriage, and a daughter from his second.

JOHNNY SQUIER

Johnny Squier (who died on January 30 2006, aged 85) pulled off what *The Daily Telegraph* described as "one of the most remarkable escapes from an aircraft" when he was forced to eject from his Lightning fighter in 1959.

A senior test pilot with the English Electric Company based at Warton, Lancashire, Squier took off in the prototype two-seat version of the supersonic Lightning on October 1. Flying eight miles high, he was in radio contact with ground control and was being tracked on radar when the operator saw the blip of his aircraft disappear from his screen 15 miles off Bees Head, Cumberland – a sailor saw an aircraft crash into the Irish Sea at the same time. A full-scale air and sea search was launched, but this was hampered by low cloud, very poor visibility and a 20ft swell.

Squier had been flying at more than 1,000mph when the aircraft suffered structural failure, and he was forced to abandon the Lightning; using the Martin Baker ejector seat, he was the first British pilot to eject at more than the speed of sound. He landed in the sea and scrambled aboard his dinghy to await rescue. But the air search, hampered by bad weather, failed to find him, and as night fell it was called off until first light. This too proved fruitless, and it was feared that he had not survived.

Squier's dinghy had drifted north and, after 30 hours, it came ashore near Garlieston, Wigtownshire. He was seen stumbling from the craft by the housekeeper of Galloway School, who immediately sought medical assistance. He was transferred to a hospital in Stranraer suffering from exposure and a compression fracture of the spine.

Inevitably, Squier became the centre of attraction for the RAF's doctors. He merely remarked: "I am all right except for earache and aching all over."

The Daily Telegraph commented that "his endurance after such an ordeal, during the long period of drifting in the water, was quite phenomenal. There is hope for mankind so long as it contains such men."

It took Squier a few months to recover fully, but by the following May he was cleared to fly again and he resumed his post as chief production test pilot.

John William Copous Squier was born on March 18 1920 at Chelmsford and educated by a private tutor, since his parents felt he was a delicate child. Anxious to prove them wrong, he drove the farm tractor as a boy, worked in the local garage and joined the RAF Volunteer Reserve in early 1939 to train as a pilot. With just three weeks experience flying the Spitfire, Squier was posted at the end of July 1940 to No 64 Squadron at Kenley, Surrey, at the height of the Battle of Britain. He was shot down on August 8, crash-landing and sustaining serious injuries to his face and arm. He was treated by Archie McIndoe, the pioneer of plastic surgery.

Within six months Squier returned to flying duties with No 64, and in March 1941 he began to specialise in test flying. He was later commissioned, and for the rest of the war served at numerous RAF units as a production test pilot. He left the service in August 1946 as a flight lieutenant and immediately joined the English Electric Aircraft Company.

Squier became the senior test pilot at English Electric's secondary airfield at Salmesbury, near Preston. He and his wife had bought a cottage on the edge of the airfield, and on one occasion he was forced to crash land a Vampire, which ended up in his back garden. From 1950 he was involved in the testing of the RAF's first jet bomber, the Canberra.

After the initial flights of the P1 supersonic fighter, later called the Lightning, Squier joined the test pilot team led by Roly Beaumont, remaining until 1968, when he joined the engineering development team of the British Aircraft Corporation, which had been formed by amalgamating a number of individual aircraft companies, including English Electric. Appropriately, Squier special-ised in cockpit escape systems.

Following his own escape in 1959 Squier had formed a close working relationship with James Martin, whose ejector seat had saved his life, and he worked on the design of escape systems for the TSR2, the revolutionary bomber that was later cancelled by a Labour government. He went on to work on the Anglo-French Jaguar fighter-bomber before retiring in December 1983.

In 1965 Squier was awarded the Queen's Commenda-tion for Valuable Services in the Air. He was unable to attend the investiture since he had made a commitment to deliver a West German Air Force Canberra to an airfield near Munich. Colleagues noted that the timing of the delivery flight coincided with the annual Munich *bierfest*.

Johnny Squier married Margaret "Lucky" Strike, a WAAF officer, in June 1944. She died in 1970, and he married, secondly, Joyce Young. There were two daughters from his first marriage.

———

WING COMMANDER
DICKIE MARTIN

Wing Commander Dickie Martin (who died on September 1 2006, aged 88) served with distinction as a fighter pilot over France and Tobruk; later he became one of Britain's foremost test pilots.

Within weeks of completing his training in August 1939, Martin was flying Hurricanes with No 73, one of two RAF fighter squadrons rushed to France a few days after war was declared. In what became known as the "phoney war", he flew patrols to intercept lone bombers and reconnaissance aircraft.

On November 8 he was scrambled to intercept a high-flying bomber, but his oxygen system failed and he fainted at 21,000ft. He recovered just in time to make a forced landing at an airfield in neutral Luxembourg, where he was interned. He was allowed out every day for exercise, and one foggy morning gradually widened his normal circuit before disappearing into the mist. When he returned on Boxing Day to his squadron, he was called the "Prisoner of Luxembourg".

As activity increased over northern France, Martin gained his first success on April 21 1940, when he probably destroyed a Messerschmitt Bf 110 fighter. Following the blitzkrieg on May 10, 73 Squadron was in constant action. Martin shared in the destruction of a Dornier bomber, and four days later attacked a formation of Stuka dive-bombers, shooting down two and probably a third.

Although still only a junior pilot officer, he returned to England as an instructor, and was awarded the DFC.

In early April 1941 Martin rejoined 73 at Tobruk just as Rommel launched his attack, and was immediately in action. He shared in the destruction of a reconnaissance aircraft, and shot down a Bf 109 on May 29. The following day he and six other pilots took off to intercept a raid by 60 aircraft. He was shot down during the fierce fight but, despite being wounded, was able to bale out.

After his recovery Martin was sent as a flight commander to No 250 Squadron, flying the Tomahawk. On the aircraft's operational debut he damaged a Bf 109, and two weeks later destroyed two Italian fighters. He was awarded a Bar to his DFC in August, and was also mentioned in dispatches.

Richard Frewen Martin was born on July 26 1918 at Bournemouth. He was educated at Cheltenham College and the RAF College, Cranwell, where he was awarded the prize for the best pilot in his entry.

After his time with No 250 in the desert, Martin instructed fighter pilots at RAF training schools at Khartoum and Aden before returning to England in 1943. A year later he converted to flying Dakota transport aircraft and left for India, where he joined No 52 Squadron. He was soon flying mail and supplies into Kunming, China, and, once the longer range Liberators had arrived on the squadron, he flew evacuation flights to Chungking. When the southerly advance into Burma began, resupply sorties to support the Fourteenth Army took on increasing importance.

At the end of the war Martin attended the Empire Test Pilots' School (ETPS) before becoming a flight commander with the Aerodynamic Research Flight at the Royal Aircraft Establishment, Farnborough. He tested the early experimental jets that led to the development of the Hunter, Swift and Sea Vixen fighter aircraft, for which he was awarded the AFC.

In 1949 Martin returned to the ETPS as an instructor for two years. After a staff appointment at the Air Ministry, he left the RAF in 1953 to become a test pilot at Gloster Aircraft Company, where he was appointed chief test pilot the following year. He joined the early testing programme of the delta-wing Javelin fighter, which had experienced control difficulties. In nearly 200 spins, Martin developed a technique for recovery.

Later a report appeared, strongly denied by the company, that the aircraft had serious defects at high speed. The following night Martin dived one over London, causing a sonic boom, which "just happened to be aimed at the Houses of Parliament". Thousands rushed into the streets where they claimed to have seen "blue flashes" and "meteorites". Martin suggested with a straight face that the noise was accidental – the result of his oxygen tube fouling the controls.

For almost seven years he tested every version of the Javelin and, by his perseverance, flying skill and management of the test programme, turned it into a successful aircraft which served on many night fighter squadrons. For his work at Glosters, Martin was appointed OBE.

In 1960 he joined AV Roe and tested Vulcan bombers, the Shackleton and the successful HS 748 airliner for a further seven years, being awarded a Queen's Commendation for Valuable Services in the Air. He then flew for various airlines before retiring from Monarch Airlines in 1984.

During his time at Glosters, Martin masterminded a project by the apprentices to restore to flying condition one of the company's pre-war Gladiator biplanes. This was presented to the Shuttleworth Trust, which Martin had joined in 1948, and for many years he flew the aircraft at air shows. He was a member of the executive committee, and gave 42 years service to the trust, displaying many of the vintage aircraft in the collection. He would often land his airliner full of holidaymakers at Luton Airport, then be found, shortly afterwards, flying one of the trust's First World War fighters at the nearby Old Warden airfield.

Martin amassed 19,000 flying hours, and flew 240 different types of aircraft. In 2003 he was elected an honorary fellow of the Society of Experimental Test Pilots.

A practical man, he once renovated one of his houses, which necessitated jacking up the main structure in order to re-lay the foundations – a task that did not daunt him.

Dickie Martin married, in 1961, Anne Gibson, with whom he had three daughters.

HUGH MEREWETHER

Hugh Merewether (who died on September 13 2006, aged 82) was one of the British test pilots who pioneered the vertical and short take-off and landing (VSTOL) techniques that led to the production of one of the RAF's most successful and enduring combat aircraft, the Harrier.

During 1957 the Bristol Aero Engine Company was developing a vectored thrust engine, later known as the Pegasus, which appeared to meet the emerging military need for a simple VSTOL tactical fighter capable of operating from unprepared areas. The Hawker Aircraft Company designed an aircraft, the experimental P 1127 powered by the Bristol engine, to test the new concept.

Merewether was the deputy chief test pilot at Hawker's airfield at Dunsfold when he joined the chief test pilot, Bill Bedford, in developing the techniques of vertical take-off in the P 1127.

Bedford made the first hovering flight in the prototype on October 21 1960, and three days later Merewether completed the second. Over the next two years the two pilots shared the experimental test flying task.

The P 1127 had its share of accidents. On October 30 1962 Merewether was flying at 3,000ft when the engine suffered a catastrophic failure and caught fire. Rather than eject, he decided to crash land at RAF Tangmere, thus allowing the engineers to investigate the failure fully. He was awarded a Queen's Commendation for Valuable Services in the Air; the Guild of Air Pilots and Navigators awarded him the Derry and Richards Memorial Medal (1963).

Over the next two years Merewether explored the characteristics and techniques of transition from vertical to conventional flight as well as short take-offs from various airfields and platforms. He also displayed the aircraft at the Farnborough and Paris air shows.

On March 19 1965 Merewether was diving through 28,000ft at very high speed when the aircraft's engine failed. He headed for the nearest airfield, at Thorney Island, but a layer of cloud obscured it. At 4,000ft a momentary gap in the cloud revealed the airfield, and he was able to continue the glide and make an emergency landing alongside the main runway. Shortly afterwards he was appointed OBE for "his great achievement in getting the aircraft back on the ground for examination, enabling the fault to be found and the elaborate trials to continue".

In 1967 Merewether was appointed Hawker's chief test pilot at Dunsfold. In addition to test flying, he helped convert military pilots to the P 1127's successor, the Kestrel, which was later developed as the Harrier.

The son of British parents, Hugh Christopher Henry Merewether was born in South Africa on May 20 1924. He was educated at the Diocesan College (Bishops) and read Engineering at the University of Cape Town. During the war he joined the South African Navy and, after secondment to the Royal Navy, trained as a pilot in the United States.

From 1948 to 1953 he worked under Dr Barnes Wallis as a junior technician in the research and development department at Vickers Armstrong, while completing an external degree with the University of London, obtaining first-class honours in 1952. He left Vickers in 1953 and spent a year as a freelance pilot ferrying aircraft to India and the Middle East.

Throughout this time Merewether flew with the RAF Volunteer Reserve, and in 1951 joined No 615 (County of Surrey) Squadron flying Meteor fighters from Biggin Hill. He was a member of the squadron's formation aerobatic team until he left the squadron in 1955. A year earlier he had gone as a test pilot to Hawker, where his former squadron commander, Neville Duke, was the chief test pilot.

Merewether was appointed deputy chief test pilot in 1956, and his aeronautical engineering interests led to a deep involvement in the development flying of the Hunter fighter.

He made detailed assessments of the aircraft's powered flying control systems – a technology that was in its infancy at the time – and he was responsible for the corrective actions which eventually made the system so reliable. He explored the aircraft's performance capabilities, including a comprehensive inverted spinning programme which became a standard exercise at the Empire Test Pilots' School for more than 30 years.

Merewether retired from test flying in 1970, and became an art dealer with a particular interest in maritime art. He purchased a 38ft Camper Nicholson yawl, Blue Idyll, which he sailed, with little previous experience, to Grenada, where he made it available for charter.

Over a period of six years he circumnavigated the globe, undertaking much of the journey alone. On the final leg, from Larnaca in Cyprus, a colleague from his Biggin Hill days joined him. After crossing the track of his outbound leg to complete his voyage, they decided to press on to the Azores.

On the return he suffered a major heart attack, but his colleague managed to reach Portugal, from where Merewether was invalided home. From 1998 he was cared for in a nursing home.

Merewether was the author of a book, *Prelude to the Harrier – P.1127*. He was elected a fellow of the Royal Aeronautical Society in 1994.

He was unmarried.

WING COMMANDER
WALTER GIBB

Wing Commander Walter Gibb (who died on October 4 2006, aged 87) was twice decorated for gallantry as a night fighter pilot before becoming a test pilot with the Bristol Aeroplane Company, flying the Brabazon and Britannia airliners; during the early 1950s he flew a modified Canberra bomber, twice breaking the altitude record for an aeroplane.

Gibb and his observer, F M Piper, took off from Filton, near Bristol, on May 4, 1953 in an English Electric Canberra powered by two Bristol Olympus engines. Climbing to the west, they reached an altitude of 63,668ft, more than 4,000ft higher than the previous record. The flight attracted worldwide attention and Duncan Sandys, the Minister for Supply, sent a telegram of congratulation in which he said: "To reach these truly Olympian heights is a triumph for the pilots, designers, research staff and workpeople of the Bristol Aeroplane Company and English Electric Company."

Flying the same Canberra, fitted with more powerful Olympus engines, Gibb made an attempt to break his record on August 29 1955. Again taking off from Filton, he climbed over the Bristol Channel towards Ireland and levelled off at 50,000ft in order to burn off fuel to lighten the aircraft before continuing his ascent. He turned east and finally reached a new record altitude of 65,876ft (nearly 12.5 miles high) over Bristol. Gibb, who was flying solo, observed: "The last 500ft took an awfully long time. It was the most difficult flying I have ever experienced."

The son of a Scottish mining engineer, Walter Frame Gibb was born near Port Talbot on March 26 1919. After Clifton College, he became an apprentice at the aero-engine division of the Bristol Aeroplane Company.

Having joined the RAF and trained as a pilot, Gibb

went to No 264 Squadron flying Mosquitoes on long-range fighter sorties over the Bay of Biscay in support of the anti-submarine aircraft patrolling the area. On March 22 1943 he shared in the destruction of a Junkers 88 bomber.

In low-level attacks against targets in northern France, Gibb damaged seven locomotives, and, during a later sortie, the formation he was leading destroyed two German fighters. In July he was awarded the DFC and appointed a flight commander with No 605 Squadron. On September 14 he led six Mosquitoes to provide support for eight Lancasters of No 617 (Dambuster) Squadron, which was due to make a daring low-level raid on the Dortmund-Ems Canal. But Gibb, flying ahead of the formation, reported very poor weather; the bombers turned back, although not before one of the veterans of the Dams Raid was lost.

The following night a further attempt was made. Gibb and his Mosquitoes went ahead and attacked the flak and searchlight positions near the canal. As the Lancasters prepared to bomb, three were shot down by anti-aircraft fire. When Gibb returned to base he learned that five of the eight, which included other survivors from the Dams Raid, had been lost.

Gibb went for a rest tour to the test squadron of the Central Flying School, where he flew many aircraft types and was assessed as an exceptional pilot. In September 1944 he was promoted to wing commander and given command of No 239 Squadron.

In a six-week period during February and March 1945 he was credited with shooting down five enemy aircraft during long-range night intruder sorties over Germany and France; and in May he was awarded the DSO. He left the RAF nine months later and returned to Bristols as a test pilot, becoming chief test pilot in 1955.

During the war the Bristol company had started to design a "super-bomber" with a range of 5,000 miles. The idea was abandoned, but it led to the huge airliner, the Brabazon, with its eight engines, twin-coupled and buried in the wings. On the morning of September 4 1949 more than 10,000 people gathered to watch the chief test pilot, Bill Pegg, and his co-pilot Gibb complete the taxi tests before taking off on the aircraft's maiden flight. As the crowds on the ground cheered, the story was transmitted around the globe in what was one of the first uses of live outside broadcasting after the war.

In an era devoid of good news, such was the value of this aircraft that the Queen was introduced to the crew and all the newspapers ran stories about the event. Some 250 reporters and photographers, television and newsreel staff were on hand, more than had ever before assembled in Bristol for a single event.

Apart from Pegg, Gibb was the only other pilot to fly the Brabazon. On his first flight in command (the aircraft's thirteenth) the airliner suffered a hydraulic failure, and Gibb was forced to land the aircraft without the flaps. Eventually the elegant Brabazon was scrapped as being uneconomical.

Gibb carried out a great deal of the test flying of the turbo-prop Britannia. On one flight he was checking the stalling characteristics of the aircraft. As he selected the flaps up, the big airliner rolled on to its back (unknown to Gibb, one of the flaps had failed to retract). After falling thousands of feet, he managed to regain control. Asked later what he had done, he replied: "I undid the last action I had made." By putting the flaps back down, he had restored the balance of the aircraft.

In March 1955 Gibb took a Britannia to Johannesburg with only one refuelling stop (at Khartoum), arriving in just under 19 hours, some two hours quicker than the Comet jet airliner.

Over the next few years Gibb demonstrated the Britannia on sales tours to many airlines, assisted in the training of their pilots and conducted many route-proving flights. In 1960 he retired from test flying to become head of service and technical support with the British Aircraft Corporation, which had absorbed Bristols. He held the post until 1978, when he became managing director, and later chairman, of British Aerospace Australia.

Gibb was modest about his many achievements. When asked in later life what had given him the greatest pleasure, he identified working as an apprentice on the Pegasus engine that powered the Wellesley aircraft which created a world long-distance record in November 1938.

A burly, imposing man, Gibb was a long-standing member of the Thornbury Sailing Club. He sailed regularly until he was 83, was twice the club's commodore and later its president.

Walter Gibb married, in 1944, Sylvia Reed, a flight officer in the operations room at RAF North Weald. They had three daughters.

ALEX HENSHAW

Alex Henshaw (who died on February 24 2007, aged 94) was an outstanding test pilot whose name will forever be associated with the Second World War's most famous aircraft, the Spitfire; between 1940 and 1945 he test flew some 2,360 individual Spitfires and Seafires (the naval version of the aircraft), amounting to more than ten per cent of the total built.

By 1939 Henshaw was already celebrated as a pilot, having won the King's Cup Air Race and broken the record for a flight to Cape Town and back. When war broke out he volunteered for service with the RAF but, while waiting for his application to be processed, was invited instead to join Vickers at Weybridge as a test pilot.

At first he was put into Wellingtons and the Walrus;

and, frustrated by the amount of administrative work, he was about to leave the company when he met Jeffrey Quill, the chief test pilot of Supermarine, who offered him a job. After test flying Spitfires at the company's Southampton factory, Henshaw moved in June 1940 to the Vickers Armstrong (Supermarine) factory at Castle Bromwich, near Birmingham, where he was soon appointed chief production test pilot for Spitfires and Lancasters.

It could be dangerous work. Henshaw suffered a number of engine failures, and on one occasion, while flying over a built-up area, he crash-landed between two rows of houses. The wings of his aircraft sheared off, and the engine and propeller finished up on someone's kitchen table. Henshaw – who sustained only minor injuries – was left sitting in the small cockpit section, which fortunately remained intact.

Only on one occasion was he forced to bale out, when the engine of his Spitfire exploded. Henshaw was thrown out of the aircraft by the blast and became entangled in his parachute, which was badly torn and held together by a single thread on its perimeter; the thread held, and he landed safely.

Castle Bromwich was not ideally suited to have an aerodrome; it was often blanketed by fog and a heavy industrial haze, closing the airfield for routine flying. With 320 Spitfires being produced each month, however, test flying had to continue, and Henshaw developed his own technique for landing: as he made his approach he would use the columns of condensation rising from some nearby cooling towers to locate the airfield and align him with the runway. No other pilot was authorised to fly in these conditions, and Henshaw sometimes tested 20 aircraft in a day.

Once he was asked to put on a show for the Lord Mayor of Birmingham's Spitfire Fund by flying at high speed above the city's main street. The civic dignitaries were furious when he inverted the aircraft, flying upside down below the top of the Council House.

Often he would be called upon to demonstrate the Spitfire to groups of visiting VIPs. After one virtuoso display Winston Churchill was so enthralled by his performance that he kept a special train waiting while they talked alone. Henshaw, for his part, considered Churchill "the greatest Englishman of all time, the man who saved the world".

Henshaw also tested other aircraft, including more than 300 Lancasters – he once famously barrel-rolled the big bomber, the only pilot to have pulled off this feat. But his great love remained the Spitfire, which he described as a "sheer dream".

For his services during the war Henshaw was appointed MBE. There were many who thought this a meagre reward for his contribution.

The son of a wealthy businessman, Alex Henshaw was born at Peterborough on November 7 1912 and educated at Lincoln Grammar School. As a boy he was fascinated by flying and by motorcycles, and with financial support from his father – who thought it safer to be in an aircraft than on a motorcycle – he learned to fly in 1932 at the Skegness and East Lincolnshire Aero Club. After his first solo his father gave him a de Havilland Gypsy Moth, and he made rapid progress as a pilot; the following year he felt competent to enter the King's Cup air race as one of the youngest-ever competitors.

The King's Cup was the most prestigious air race of the period and attracted enormous public interest. In 1934 Henshaw was invited to take part in his Miles Hawk Major. His prototype engine failed as he crossed the Irish Sea, and he was forced to ditch.

The next year he bought an Arrow Active, an aerobatic biplane. While he was performing an inverted loop, however, there was an explosion and the aircraft caught fire; Henshaw was forced to bale out, using the parachute he had been given on his birthday four weeks earlier.

In 1937 he won the inaugural London to Isle of Man air race in atrocious weather. Finally, in 1938, flying a Percival Mew Gull, he won the King's Cup at the age of 25, setting an average speed of 236.25mph, a record that stood until 1967.

Early in 1939 Henshaw made his record-breaking solo flight from England to Cape Town and back. In the spring of the previous year, accompanied by his father, he had surveyed possible routes down the eastern and western sides of Africa. On February 5 1939 he took off in the Mew Gull from Gravesend to fly the western route. The aircraft had nine hours' endurance, and his first stop was at Oran, in Algeria, before a 1,300-mile leg across the Sahara. Without navigation or radio aids, he made further stops in the Belgian Congo and Angola before reaching Cape Town, having flown 6,030 miles in just under 40 hours, a record.

After 28 hours in Cape Town, Henshaw set off on the return journey, following a similar route. Just after lunch on February 9 he landed at Gravesend, four days, ten hours and 16 minutes after his departure. Having completed one of the greatest ever solo long distance flights, he was on the verge of collapse, and had to be lifted from the tiny cockpit.

He had broken the homeward record, established in a twin-engine aircraft flown by two pilots, by seven hours, and the out-and-return time by almost 31 hours. Henshaw's epic flight was, however, overshadowed by the imminence of war and, unlike those pioneers who preceded him by a few years, he received no public recognition.

After the war Henshaw went to South Africa as a director of Miles Aircraft, but returned to England in 1948 and joined his family's farming and holiday business. He redeveloped six miles of Lincolnshire coastline which had been requisitioned during the war; the project included an 18-hole golf course. A residential estate at Sandilands bears the name Henshaw for the main avenue, while all the roads and streets are named for the various aircraft he flew.

In his youth he received a Royal Humane Society award for saving a boy from the River Witham, and in 1953 he was awarded the Queen's Commendation for Bravery following his rescue work during the great floods.

Henshaw remained in great demand at aviation functions to the end of his life. In his 90th year he gave a masterly presentation, without the aid of notes, at an event in London to commemorate 100 years of flight. During the evening Prince Philip invested him as a Companion of the Air League.

In the summer of 2005 he donated his papers, art collection, photographs and trophies to the RAF Museum, where he paid for a curator to catalogue and promote his collection, which reflects the "golden age" of flying. To mark the 70th anniversary of the first flight of the Spitfire, in March 2006, the 93-year-old Henshaw flew over Southampton in a two-seater Spitfire, taking the controls once airborne. His pilot commented that Henshaw could have landed the aircraft but for the prohibitive insurance conditions.

Henshaw was a tough-minded man, but was also an approachable and patient one who took a great interest in promoting "air-mindedness" in young people, for which the Air League awarded him the Jeffery Quill Medal in 1997.

The Royal Aeronautical Society elected him an honorary fellow in 2003. He was a vice-president of the Spitfire Memorial Defence Fellowship in Canberra, Australia.

He wrote three books about his experiences: *The Flight of the Mew Gull*; *Sigh for a Merlin*; and *Wings over the Great Divide*.

Alex Henshaw married, in 1940, Barbara, the widow of Count de Chateaubrun. They had a son. Barbara died in 1996.

————————

SQUADRON LEADER
NEVILLE DUKE

Squadron Leader Neville Duke (who died on April 7 2007, aged 85) had a remarkable record as a fighter pilot during the Second World War, being decorated six times for gallantry; he went on to become one of the world's foremost test pilots.

Duke was the chief test pilot of the Hawker Aircraft Company at a time when transonic and supersonic flight was at a highly experimental and extremely dangerous stage. He was one of a small group of men, some of whom would lose their lives, exploring the regions of the "sound barrier". On September 6 1952, at the Farnborough air show, he was to fly the supersonic Hawker Hunter jet fighter. He was scheduled to take off at the end of a display by the new de Havilland DH 110. As John Derry and his observer Alan Richards flew over the airfield at high speed, the DH 110 disintegrated, killing 28 spectators and the aircraft's crew.

Without hesitation Duke took off as soon as the runway was cleared. Although deeply saddened and shocked by the disaster and by the loss of his close friend Derry, Duke produced an immaculate display, ending with a sonic boom in salute to his dead friends. "My dear Duke," the Prime Minister wrote to him the next day, "it was characteristic of you to go up yesterday after the shocking accident. Accept my salute. Yours, in grief, Winston Churchill."

Neville Frederick Duke was born on January 11 1922 and attended Judd School, Tonbridge. Fascinated by flying as a small boy, he would save his pocket money for flights in joy-riding aeroplanes, including several from Sir Alan Cobham's Flying Circus. In 1939 he applied to join the Fleet Air Arm, but was turned down. He joined the RAF in June 1940.

After completing his flying training, Duke was commissioned and posted to Biggin Hill in April 1941 to join No 92 Squadron, flying Spitfires on sweeps over northern France. He scored his first victory in June when he shot down a Messerschmitt Bf 109, followed by his second a few weeks later. With 92 moving north and away from the action, in November Duke was posted to the Middle East, joining No 112 Squadron, equipped with the Tomahawk.

He soon discovered that the Tomahawk was far inferior to the Spitfire: in four sorties 14 of them were lost against the superior German fighters. In the space of six days, Duke was shot down twice and forced to crash land in the desert. His own score started to mount, however, and by the end of the year he had destroyed at least four aircraft and damaged others. The squadron re-equipped with the superior Kittyhawk, and, with eight confirmed victories, Duke was awarded a DFC.

After nine months as an instructor at a fighter school in Egypt, he returned to operations as a flight commander with his old squadron, No 92, which had arrived in the desert. After attacking a large force of fighters over Beurat, Tunisia, he shot down two of the enemy before his ammunition was exhausted; and a few days later he shot down a Stuka. He was awarded a Bar to his DFC.

In the space of three months fighting over Tunisia, Duke destroyed 12 enemy fighters and two bombers, and in March he was awarded an immediate DSO.

At the end of this hectic period he was promoted to squadron leader and returned to the fighter school as the chief instructor.

Although Duke found this job satisfying, he was

impatient to return to operations, and in February 1944 he was posted to command No 145 Squadron, based in Italy and flying the powerful Spitfire VIII.

Over the next few weeks Duke claimed five further victories and was awarded a second Bar to his DFC for "displaying the highest standard of skill, gallantry and determination".

On June 7, during a low-level strafing operation, the engine of his Spitfire was hit by anti-aircraft fire. Duke attempted to bale out, but his harness became snagged on the open cockpit. He kicked violently to free his parachute before pulling the ripcord, and seconds later landed in the middle of a lake, again almost losing his life as his parachute dragged him through the water. Italian partisans rescued him and gave him shelter until the arrival of American troops.

Duke returned to his squadron and achieved his final success on September 7, when he shot down two Bf 109s near Rimini. The AOC insisted that Duke ended his third tour after he had completed 486 operational sorties. He had destroyed 27 enemy aircraft, and probably three more, making him one of the RAF's two highest-scoring fighter pilots in the Mediterranean theatre. He was only 22.

In January 1945 Duke became a production test pilot at Hawkers, and a year later was selected to attend the fourth course at the Empire Test Pilots' School, where he flew a jet fighter for the first time. In June 1946 he was one of three pilots assigned to the RAF High Speed Flight. On one occasion he was flying his Meteor at its maximum speed at 120ft when one of the two engines failed. He managed to land safely. A few months later he was displaying a Meteor at an air display at Prague when he was presented with the Czech Military Cross for his wartime service.

Duke was posted to the Fighter Test Squadron at Boscombe Down and began research at high Mach numbers and altitudes up to 50,000ft in Meteors. He explored the extreme edges of the high-speed performance of the aircraft and the effect of compressibility at speeds approaching the speed of sound. For this pioneering work he was awarded an AFC.

Keen to continue test flying, Duke accepted an offer to join the Hawker Aircraft Corporation as a test pilot. He left the RAF in August 1948, but, anxious not to lose the camaraderie, joined the Royal Auxiliary Air Force, flying Spitfires and Meteors from Biggin Hill at weekends. He became CO of No 615 Squadron, whose honorary air commodore was Winston Churchill.

When Duke delivered a batch of Hawker Furies to the new Royal Pakistan Air Force he established records from London to Rome, to Cairo and to Karachi. By the end of 1949 Hawkers had developed a series of experimental jet fighters that led to the Seahawk naval fighter and another, the P 1067, which became the elegant and world-beating Hunter fighter, an aircraft with which the name Duke became synonymous. A year after his display at the 1952 Farnborough air show, on September 7 1953 he established a world airspeed record at sea level of 727.63mph flying an all-red Hunter (WB 188).

In August 1955 Duke was carrying out firing trials when the engine of his single-engine Hunter failed. By a brilliant piece of flying he managed to land the aircraft, a feat that earned him a Queen's Commendation for Valuable Services in the Air. Two days later, after an engine change, he collected the aircraft – but shortly after take-off experienced a serious loss of thrust and was forced to crash land at 200mph on the grass at RAF Thorney Island. He suffered serious back injuries, from which he never fully recovered, and in October 1956 he resigned from Hawkers.

For his contribution to the exploration of supersonic flight and his achievements at Hawkers, he was appointed OBE.

He took up freelance flying and consultancy work, then, in 1960, formed Duke Aviation and also became personal pilot to Sir George Dowty. After selling his company in 1982, Duke concentrated on test flying lighter aircraft and on consultancy, forming a fruitful and enduring relationship with Brooklands Aerospace Group. These activities he combined with his other great passion: sailing.

Duke received many national and international honours in addition to his gallantry medals. He was awarded the Royal Aero Club's Gold Medal, and in 1993 was elected a fellow of the Royal Aeronautical Society. In 2002 he received the Air League's Jeffrey Quill Medal. In the same year he was presented with the Award of Honour from the Guild of Air Pilots and Navigators for "his unique and incomparable record".

Duke's books included *Sound Barrier, Test Pilot, The Crowded Sky* and *The War Diaries of Neville Duke.*

In 2006 he attracted much attention in the national press when he sold his medals. He played down the popular notion that it was in order to pay for a hip operation for his devoted wife, much as she needed one. His main reasons for selling were the prohibitive costs of insuring them after being burgled three times, and his desire to keep the collection together.

Duke and his wife owned numerous light aircraft over the years and they regularly flew to air shows, air rallies and reunions at which their infectious enthusiasm was clear to all.

Neville Duke was a quiet, modest man, reluctant to talk about his achievements but always available to discuss other people's interests and aviation projects. He gave great support to the Tangmere Military Aviation Museum, of which he was the honorary president and where his record-breaking Hunter is on permanent display.

On the day of his death Duke and his wife, Gwen,

whom he married in 1947, were flying their aircraft when he suddenly felt unwell. He managed to land safely at Popham airfield, but then collapsed as he left the aircraft; he died later that evening.

MARITIME

AIR VICE-MARSHAL
DAVID McKINLEY

Air Vice-Marshal David McKinley (who died on April 23 2002, aged 88) flew President Roosevelt's personal envoy, Harry Hopkins, for a critical meeting with Stalin in Moscow shortly after the Germans invaded the Soviet Union.

When, in June 1941, Roosevelt required a first-hand report of the fighting in the Soviet Union and a personal assessment of Stalin, McKinley, one of RAF Coastal Command's more experienced flying boat captains, was selected to deliver Hopkins. Winston Churchill personally made the necessary arrangements on Roosevelt's behalf.

Walking with Hopkins on the lawn at Chequers, Churchill briefed him: "Tell him [Stalin] Britain has but one ambition today, but one desire – to crush Hitler. Tell him that he can depend on us. Goodbye – God bless you, Harry." It then fell to 28-year-old Flight Lieutenant McKinley to get Hopkins to Moscow.

Although McKinley had flown long-range patrols over the North Atlantic, he had not yet experienced the perilous flight round the North Cape of Norway to the Arctic port of Archangel.

Plotting his course from Invergordon in Scotland, McKinley reckoned that, fully loaded, his Catalina flying boat could manage only 135mph, and resolved to dive to sea level if attacked by fighters.

Fortunately, his worst fears were not realised. Keeping well away from the Norwegian coast, he avoided interception and, after more than 20 hours, landed Hopkins on the White Sea.

Since the Soviets were unable to fly Hopkins straight on to Moscow, the pair dined magnificently aboard an admiral's personal yacht. Hopkins later returned from his meetings in Moscow having endured some hair-raising flights with Russian pilots; he was mightily relieved to rejoin McKinley and his Catalina at Archangel.

Late on the afternoon of August 1 McKinley took off in a gathering storm with Hopkins, two other passengers and a large quantity of much-needed platinum aboard.

Forty-eight hours earlier, two British aircraft carriers had launched air strikes in the area, losing one third of the attacking Fleet Air Arm aircraft. McKinley had to look out not only for Germans, but also for rogue Russian attacks; and, despite issuing correct recognition signals, he was fired on along the Murman coast by destroyers he was certain were Russian.

But after 24 hours he put down safely in choppy seas at Scapa Flow, and made a hazardous transfer of Hopkins and his baggage to a launch.

An engineer's son, David Cecil McKinley was born on September 18 1913 at Ardmayle Cashal, Co Tipperary, and educated at Bishop Foy School, Waterford. He went to Trinity College, Dublin, where he abandoned Medicine to study Engineering.

McKinley worked briefly as a radio engineer with Ferranti, but he wanted to fly, and, on being told there were no pilot opportunities, he enlisted as a torpedo fitter in 1935. Soon afterwards he was remustered for pilot training and granted a short service commission.

Destined to become a maritime pilot, McKinley joined No 228, a Short Sunderland flying-boat general reconnaissance squadron, in late 1938; he served first at home, and then in the Mediterranean. As war came, the squadron returned to Pembroke Dock for convoy and anti-submarine patrols.

After a spell with No 210, another flying-boat squadron, McKinley joined the North Atlantic Ferry organisation and delivered American-built Catalina flying boats to the RAF.

Once, following a long and wearying haul from San Diego, California, McKinley thought he was over the Clyde when anti-aircraft fire awakened him to the uncomfortable fact that he was over the heavily-defended French Atlantic port of Brest.

McKinley was selected in 1942 for a specialist navigation course in Canada, and his skill in this field was soon recognised with his appointment as chief instructor at the RAF's central navigation school.

In 1944 his consummate flying and navigation skills on long hauls led to his selection to lead one of the most outstanding missions flown by the RAF up to that time. Captaining Aries One, a specially adapted Lancaster bomber, McKinley, in October and November, made the RAF's first full-length circumnavigation of the globe.

During this liaison and goodwill flight to New Zealand, Australia, New Guinea and the south-west Pacific, he faultlessly maintained an intricate and exacting schedule of visits. The return flight from Australia was made in 72 hours, which was regarded as a remarkable feat at the time since it almost halved the previous record.

On May 17 1945 McKinley captained the same aircraft on the RAF's first exploratory flight to the North Pole. By the time he and his crew of 11 returned to their starting point at Reykjavik, having been forced back by severe icing, he had personally flown 28 out of 30 and three quarter hours.

In the course of his extended polar expedition, on May 20 McKinley flew from the Labrador coast to the Boothia Peninsula, seeking the North Magnetic Pole. On May 26 he flew non-stop from White Horse, Yukon Territory, to his home base at Shawbury, Shropshire.

This mission took the Lancaster over the Magnetic North Pole and well into Arctic regions, a distance of 4,100 miles, and provided a practical demonstration of the possibility of exploiting polar air routes.

There followed appointments at the Air Ministry,

where his experience was useful in the selection and introduction of new weapons in the build-up of Britain's nuclear deterrent V-bomber force. McKinley also helped to draft operations orders which became of vital importance at the time of the Berlin airlift.

Postings to the Royal Aircraft Establishment, Farnborough, to the Imperial Defence College, and as Air Officer Commanding, Malta, and Deputy C-in-C (Air), Allied Forces, Mediterranean, prepared him for command, in 1962, at Christmas Island, Britain's nuclear test base in the Pacific. His final appointment was as senior air staff officer at Transport Command.

Often exposed to great danger, McKinley made light of it. He particularly enjoyed recalling the episode in which the four engines of a Short Stirling bomber failed, and he ordered all aboard to bale out – including the Belgian Astronomer Royal. McKinley landed the aircraft safely.

McKinley retired in 1968, and in 1984 went to live on Alderney in the Channel Islands.

He was appointed CBE in 1957 and CB in 1966. He was awarded the DFC in 1940, the AFC in 1944 and a Bar to it in 1945.

In 1940 he married Brenda Ridgway, with whom he had three sons.

WING COMMANDER
MICKY OGDEN

Wing Commander Micky Ogden (who died on October 21 2002, aged 99) put his pre-war experience as a pioneer "seat-of-the-pants" flier, instructor and test pilot to highly effective use as commander of a Beaufighter squadron involved in desert operations and attacks on Axis supply shipping in the Mediterranean.

Ogden's skills as a pilot came to wide public attention in 1934, when his first pupil pilot – Lady Blanche Scott Douglas, eldest daughter of the 9th Duke of Beaufort – invited him to accompany her as co-pilot on an adventurous flight to India, where she wished to visit her friend, the Maharajah of Cooch Behar.

The pair set off on November 20 1934 in Lady Blanche's new Miles M2 F Hawk Major. They followed the route of the historic London to Australia air race, taking them through France, Italy, Greece, Palestine, Cairo and Baghdad.

Continuing along the Persian coastline by way of Bushire, the couple encountered a severe sandstorm, but managed to climb above it. Then, half way to Bandar Abbas, their plane developed engine trouble, and they had to make a forced landing in the desert.

Lady Blanche, if not herself accident-prone, had already lost two husbands: the first, the 6th Earl of St Germans, died after a steeplechasing accident; her second, Captain George Scott Douglas, had died from injuries sustained during a polo match. Now Lady Blanche and Ogden were marooned in the wastes of Persia.

It was ten days before they were rescued by local tribesmen, after which they made serviceable the engine of their plane and took off for Karachi. Further misfortune, however, awaited them at Bandar Abbas where, on landing, the aircraft ran into a hole and tipped on to its nose. Although neither Ogden nor Lady Blanche was injured, the propeller was badly damaged.

Rather than incur the long delay waiting for a replacement propeller, the couple took a considerable risk: they decided to fly on to Jask, where a new propeller was brought in from Karachi aboard a KLM airliner. The remainder of their journey to India was uneventful.

Cecil Victor Ogden was born on July 10 1903 at Kasauli in India, where his father was an Indian Army schoolmaster. The young Ogden hated his Christian name; "Cecil" in the early years of the 20th century was considered in some circles to be effeminate – and throughout his life Ogden insisted on the more manly "Micky".

After attending Bishop's High School at Poona, he was sent to King Edward V Grammar School, Lichfield, and Gosport Secondary School in Hampshire. In 1922 he enlisted in the RAF, specialising in photography. He was posted from the Royal Aircraft Establishment, Farnborough, to photograph and to map operational areas on the North-West Frontier as a leading aircraftman.

When Ogden succumbed to malaria, his parents became alarmed and insisted on buying him out of the service for £45. Having returned to Britain, however, Ogden missed flying; in 1929 he was granted a short service commission as a pilot officer.

After being awarded his wings, in 1930 Ogden was posted to No 26, an Army Co-operation unit equipped with the Armstrong Whitworth Atlas and, the next year, he qualified at the Central Flying School as an instructor.

He excelled in this role until, in 1933, he was posted to No 16, also an Army Co-operation unit equipped with the Atlas and, later, the Hawker Audax. When his short service engagement expired in 1934, he joined the Bristol Aeroplane Company as a test pilot, and the Wessex Aero Club as a flying instructor. Lady Blanche Scott Douglas was his first pupil.

As rearmament brought a surge in orders for the Bristol company, Ogden was much involved with the development of the Blenheim light bomber, the Beaufort torpedo-bomber and the Beaufighter.

Vital though his civilian job was to the war effort, Ogden was determined to see some action. Resuming with the RAF, he was posted first to No 236 (a Beaufighter squadron covering the Bay of Biscay) and, in February 1942, to No 272 (whose Beaufighters were heavily engaged over Egypt, Libya and the Mediterranean).

Soon Ogden received command of this squadron which, on July 11 1942, intercepted a large formation of Ju 52s off the North African coast. The enemy transports were heavily escorted, and in the ensuing scrap Ogden and his crews accounted for at least 12 enemy aircraft destroyed or badly damaged; Ogden himself shot down one Ju 52.

He recalled later: "We were on patrol when we caught up with the Junkers. We followed in line astern, diving on them to attack. They were about 50ft above the sea. My victim went into the sea with a terrific splash, an engine on fire and the fuselage burning."

On another occasion, greatly outnumbered by enemy fighters while escorting Beaufort torpedo-bombers attacking a supply convoy, Ogden and his squadron were involved in an air battle in which the Beaufort losses were heavy; nonetheless, some of the vulnerable torpedo-droppers were able to press home their attacks.

One type of operation which Ogden did not enjoy was the strafing of enemy airfields, an activity which he regarded as suicidal. Ogden was very much his own man, and would remonstrate with his superiors about the wisdom of such operations. This is probably why he was never awarded a DFC – or even a DSO – for actions which, in other circumstances, might have merited such decorations.

In September 1942, when it was feared that the Germans might move on Persia, Ogden was posted to defend Teheran with a wing of Hawker Hurricanes. He later served as a wing commander in Malta and Algeria in preparation for the Allied landings in the south of France.

Ogden was released from the service in 1947 and, although he was invited to resume his career with Bristol, he opted to work in civil aviation. After serving as an operations officer with the Ministry of Aviation in London and Liverpool, in 1954 he moved to Wales as commandant of Cardiff airport, before becoming its director in 1965 when the airport was taken over by Glamorgan County Council. He retired in 1968 after he had planned the airport's future expansion.

Moving to West Moors in Dorset, Ogden spent 33 years in retirement. He married Betty Mansell in Algiers in 1943; she died in 2001. They had a son and a daughter.

GROUP CAPTAIN
ALAN ANDERSON

Group Captain Alan Anderson (who died on December 19 2002, aged 92) was an outstanding leader of low-level tactical missions and photographic reconnaissance operations; for his many exploits in the Second World War, he was awarded first the DFC, then a DSO and Bar.

The two DSOs recognised his leadership of No 268 Squadron's Mustang tactical reconnaissance fighters, and, later, No 35 Wing's 2, 4 and 268 Squadrons; his DFC, awarded in 1940, was for operational activities in the early stages of the war.

After patrolling the East Anglian coast in a trundling Lysander Army Co-operation high wing monoplane – which would have been a sitting duck in the sights of an enemy fighter – Anderson took part in an astonishing episode during the fall of France.

Leading a force of six Hector biplanes of No 613 Squadron on May 26 1940, he attacked enemy troops laying siege to remnants of the British Expeditionary Force trapped in the Citadel at Calais – this in an aircraft that was already obsolete, and had a maximum speed of only 170mph. Anderson exposed his Hector biplanes to both ground fire and the attentions of Bf 109 and 110 fighters, creating a scene reminiscent of a Royal Flying Corps operation from the First World War.

After receiving command of 268 Squadron, Anderson

was relieved in May 1941 to be re-equipped with American-built Tomahawk fighters, until the arrival of Mustangs in May 1942. He soon exploited his squadron's good fortune in having Mustangs, sweeping enemy shipping and positions along the Channel and the Dutch coast until August 1942, when 268 Squadron supported the ill-fated Dieppe raid. By the autumn, Anderson was ready to exploit the Mustang's long-range capabilities. In October he led four aircraft on the RAF's first daylight single-engined fighter escort and photographic reconnaissance sortie over Germany.

Shortly afterwards, he was photographing a bridge at very low level at Dordrecht in Holland when a cannon shell burst nine inches behind the armour-plating protecting his head. Although stunned and deafened, he completed his mission.

Alan Ford Anderson was born on November 21 1910 at Simla, while his father was serving with the Army in India, and was educated at Winchester. Following a cadetship at the Royal Military Academy, Woolwich, he was commissioned into the Royal Artillery in 1931, joining the Royal Warwickshire Regiment in the same year.

But the young subaltern was ambitious to fly. In 1934 he obtained a welcome secondment to the RAF, and was posted to No 13 Squadron at Netheravon and Old Sarum in Wiltshire. After serving in Palestine and Egypt, he moved to No 2 Squadron, flying Westland Lysander Army Co-operation sorties in France until the end of December, when he received command of No 613 Squadron.

In the New Year of 1940, Anderson was temporarily detached from normal duties when he volunteered to ferry a Lysander to Finland for operations against the Russians. But he had to make a forced landing in Norway, and the mission was aborted.

Shortly before completing his hectic period of

command of 268 Squadron in March 1943, Anderson was awarded his first DSO, before beginning a succession of staff appointments. There followed command of No 35 Wing whose Mustangs, in early autumn 1944, gave vigorous support to the Allied advance in north-west Europe.

Anderson's prowess as a leader was further reflected, in 1945, in the citation for the Bar to his DSO; after paying tribute to his "great drive and outstanding devotion to duty", it continued: "Much of the great success of the squadrons under his command can be attributed to this officer's brilliant leadership and tactical ability."

No sooner had hostilities ceased in Europe than Anderson suffered the blow of having to "fly a desk" (as he put it) at the Air Ministry department dealing with accident prevention. After three years pushing paper, he was relieved to resume operational command, joining No 342 Wing of Tempest fighter-bombers in the Middle East.

Anderson returned home in 1950 to command RAF Linton-on-Ouse, moving after two years to fighter staff duties at Supreme Headquarters Allied Powers Europe (SHAPE). Further appointments followed at No 61 Group, Western Sector headquarters, and at a maintenance unit until, in 1957, he retired in the rank of group captain and took over the Channel House hotel at Minehead, Somerset.

After seven years as a hotelier, he opted for growing tomatoes commercially in Somerset until 1971, when he finally retired to Minorca; he lived there for more than 20 years before returning to Britain.

Anderson was appointed to the Order of Orange in 1947. He married, in 1935, Geraldine Tyrell, with whom he had three sons. In 1944 he married, secondly, Brenda Scott, with whom he had a son and a daughter.

AIR COMMODORE
E W "BILL" TACON

Air Commodore "Bill" Tacon (who died on September 9 2003, aged 85) was one of the most decorated pilots in RAF Coastal Command before becoming captain of the King's Flight.

Tacon's most outstanding wartime successes took place in 1944, after he converted to Beaufighters, joined No 236 Squadron, and rapidly began to demonstrate dead-eyed accuracy with his front guns and rockets. On June 23 he attacked four R-boats entering Boulogne harbour; although his aircraft was badly hit and his navigator killed, R 79 was sunk, earning Tacon a Bar to the DFC he had won in 1940.

Tacon, who was based at Davidstow Moor, was soon involved in helping the Navy destroy the remaining Kriegsmarine vessels off western France. In the first of these attacks, at Les Sables d'Olonne, nine Beaufighters sank a German Jupiter escort ship with armour-piercing rockets weighing just 25lbs, using a procedure devised by Tacon and the armaments officer at North Coates.

They had calculated that, in a 25-degree dive from 1,500ft at 230 knots, the pilot should always score hits if he closed to a distance of about 800 yards. While not popular with all aircrews – for it involved flying steadily at the target whilst ignoring the return fire – the method worked. The Jupiter vanished under a hail of cannon fire, with no loss to the attackers.

The second attack was equally successful. On August 8, 15 Beaufighters of 404 Squadron and nine of 236 Squadron, led by Tacon, set off on another armed sweep, working with the naval squadron Force 26. In the shallow Bay of Bourgneuf, they found four M-class mine-sweepers. Flak rose to meet them and one Beaufighter exploded but, as the remaining Beaufighters left, all four vessels were ablaze.

By now the strike wings' attacks, combined with those of Bomber Command and the Navy, had all but destroyed the remains of Marinegruppekommando West. The surviving U-boats had departed for Norway and the Germans were scuttling many of their damaged surface vessels. Two important warships remained afloat, however: the destroyer Z 24 and the torpedo boat T 24, which had survived the thwarted attack on the western flank of the Allied invasion forces.

Still well-armed, the two ships were thought to be at Le Verdon on the southern tip of the mouth of the Gironde estuary. On August 15 the naval Force 27 had damaged T 24 near La Pallice, but the German warships were in the shelter of coastal batteries, so an air attack was needed.

This was the last big strike required of the Davidstow Moor wing. Tacon was to lead ten Beaufighters from 236 Squadron and ten from 404, all armed with cannon and 25lb rockets. Taking off at 4.15pm, they were scheduled to attack near the limit of their range, with the prospect of returning in darkness.

Two Beaufighters of 404 Squadron turned back en route with mechanical trouble, but the remaining 18 aircraft made their landfall and turned north to the Gironde estuary. Spotting the two warships in the harbour of Le Verdon, Tacon called: "Keep down low, everyone. We'll head to the estuary first and fly along it for our climb. Then straight out to sea after the attack."

Tacon hoped to take the enemy by surprise, but the two vessels had steam up by the time the Beaufighters dived, and the flak was the most intense the crews had ever experienced. Nevertheless, every Beaufighter followed Tacon's leadership in one of the most dangerous attacks made by a strike wing. Several 25lb warheads penetrated T 24 below the waterline, causing an uncontrollable rush of sea-water into the hull, The warship sank almost immediately.

Z 24 received numerous hits above and below the waterline. Her starboard engine was disabled but she remained afloat, and there was time to tow her the short distance to a quay at Le Verdon, where she was made fast alongside the harbour railway station. Frantic efforts to patch the underwater holes were to no avail; five minutes before midnight she capsized and sank.

Although none of the Beaufighters was shot down, 15 were damaged. They were a long way from home, with darkness ahead. Tacon's "Call in, anyone in trouble" elicited several responses. After instructing one of the crippled aircraft to ditch near the naval force (the crew was picked up after ten hours), Tacon led five Beaufighters to Vannes aerodrome, planning to leave three of the damaged aircraft, before returning to England in the remaining two.

One of the aircraft crash-landed, however, and there was no alternative but to leave the two crew there and hope that medical help would arrive before long. With Davidstow Moor closed due to fog, the remaining Beaufighters were redirected to alternative landing strips in the south-west. Their fuel was almost exhausted, and one landed just as its engines cut out. Tacon eventually landed at Portreath, six hours after take-off. He was awarded a Bar to his DFC.

The destruction of the two German warships caused much excitement in the Admiralty. Some naval officers were incredulous; others were alarmed that such powerful destroyers could be defeated by the tiny 25lb warheads. Tacon took command of 236 Squadron the day after the attack on the Gironde, and the detachment returned to North Coates. He continued to fly with the same determination until September 12 1944, when he led 40 Beaufighters from North Coates and Langham against a convoy assembling in Den Helder harbour.

Diving down against a hail of fire from the ships and the harbour, his Beaufighter was badly hit in the wing and fuel tank. Tacon fired his rockets for the last time, before his aircraft was hit in the fuselage. Ammunition in the cannon boxes caught fire and exploded. His navigator cried out and Tacon turned round to see him lying dead on the floor. He began to climb, tugging on the lanyard of his bottom escape hatch, but this remained closed.

As flames licked around him, burning his face and helmet, he almost gave up hope. When his Beaufighter was hit for the third time, Tacon could see the gun post firing at him and decided to take the gunners with him. He rolled the Beaufighter on its back and dived straight at the post. His last recollection was of the airspeed indicator showing 360 knots. Then there was a violent explosion and he floated through the air, pulling his ripcord just in time.

He landed on the island of Texel, so badly burned around the eyes that he could barely see. He was soon taken prisoner by German soldiers, who bundled him roughly aboard a boat which took him to Den Helder. On arrival, he was surrounded by a group of sailors and kicked violently before being marched off to the local jail.

After medical treatment, he was taken to Dulag Luft, near Frankfurt, and then to Stalag Luft I near Barth on the Baltic coast. He was eventually released by the Russians and quietly made his way back to North Coates. In his absence he had been awarded the DSO.

Ernest William Tacon was born into a farming family on December 16 1917 at Napier on the North Island of New Zealand. He was educated at St Patrick's, Wellington, where he played for the 1st XI and 1st XV. He later played club rugby as a scrum-half.

He joined the RNZAF in July 1938, and transferred to the RAF in May 1939 under an arrangement whereby New Zealand supplied six trained pilots each year. He joined No 233 Squadron at Leuchars, initially flying Ansons but switching to Hudsons on the outbreak of war.

For the next year and a half he was engaged in a mixture of anti-submarine work, escorting naval vessels during the Norwegian campaign, and bombing airfields. He was intercepted by German fighters on nine occasions, shooting down two of his adversaries. He was awarded the DFC in May 1940 and completed his tour in January 1941.

He flew a Flying Fortress from Portland, Oregon, to Prestwick, introduced the Hudson to the newly-formed No 407 (RCAF) Squadron at North Coates and was responsible for converting No 59 Squadron at Thorney Island from Blenheims to Hudsons. He was awarded the AFC. Tacon was then sent to Nova Scotia to open up a new operational training unit, and next, after a return to New Zealand, on to Fiji as commanding officer of No 4 Squadron, equipped with Hudsons, earning a Bar to his AFC. Back in Britain, he converted to Beaufighters and joined No 236 Squadron in May 1944.

Tacon transferred permanently to the RAF in 1946 and was appointed officer commanding The King's Flight at RAF Benson. Over the next three years he flew the King's plane all over the world, including the tour of South Africa with the Princesses Elizabeth and Margaret on board. He was appointed MVO (4th Class, later LVO) in 1947.

There followed overseas tours as OC Flying Wing, Fayid, Egypt (Canal Zone) from 1951 to 1953, and as station commander, RAF Nicosia, Cyprus, from 1955 to 1958, when he was appointed CBE. In 1960 he became lecturer at the School of Land/Air Warfare, at Old Sarum, and in 1961 commander of the Royal Air Force, Persian Gulf.

Returning to England in 1963, he served as commandant, Central Fighter Establishment for two years, and then air commodore, Tactics, HQ Fighter Command Bentley Priory. His final tour was as AOC Military Air Traffic Operations from 1968 to 1971.

On retirement from the RAF in 1970, he returned to New Zealand with his family, where he ran the Intellectually Handicapped Children's Society (IHC) and then fulfilled a management role with Air New Zealand before full retirement.

After the death of his first wife, Clare McKee, with whom he had two daughters and a son, Bill Tacon married, secondly, in 1960, Bernadine Leamy; they had three sons.

GROUP CAPTAIN
"BILL" SISE

Group Captain "Bill" Sise (who died on December 23 2003, aged 86) was regarded as Coastal Command's leading "ship-buster"; his reputation as a torpedo-bomber was formidable, and he ended the war with a DSO and Bar, and a DFC and Bar.

In late 1942 Sise was appointed flight commander of No 254 Squadron, which specialised in dropping torpedoes. The squadron, flying Beaufighters as part of Coastal Command's first "strike wing", attacked important convoys transporting raw materials from Scandinavia to the Dutch port of Rotterdam.

Its first major attack, on November 20, was against a southbound convoy off the Hook of Holland. Twenty-five Beaufighters took off, with Sise leading the torpedo-carrying flight of nine aircraft. But an expected fighter escort failed to appear, and Sise's formation was repeatedly attacked by German fighters. His own aircraft was badly damaged, although he managed to reach home to make a crash landing near Frinton-on-Sea, Essex. He was awarded the DFC.

After this reverse, the wing started intensive training in new tactics. Then, on April 20 1943, 21 Beaufighters went into action once again. As the anti-flak force attacked the strong convoy escort with cannons, Sise led the torpedo-bombers at low level against a large Norwegian ore-carrier. Three torpedoes were thought to have hit the ship, and it was later confirmed that the 5,000-ton vessel had sunk, and that others had been badly damaged.

Nine days after this initial success, Sise led an attack on a convoy off the Friesian Islands during which a large merchant vessel was badly damaged. To deter the low-flying torpedo-bombers, ships in the convoy flew balloons on 400ft lines; Sise's formation still made its way successfully through them.

On May 1, 11 Beaufighters took off to attack a German cruiser off the Norwegian coast. But before Sise could get his aircraft into position to attack, German fighters struck, and the Beaufighters had to jettison their torpedoes to fight their way home; three failed to return.

Losses among the Beaufighter strike wings were some of the heaviest in the RAF, and Sise was rested in June 1943 after 18 months. A few weeks later he was awarded the DSO for "leading attacks against enemy shipping during which no less than seven large merchant vessels have been destroyed. He has pressed home his attacks undaunted by any danger or opposition".

Gage Darwent Sise, always known as Bill, was born on January 22 1917 at Dunedin, New Zealand. After being educated at Otago Boys' High School and Otago University, he trained as an accountant, and joined the RNZAF as an aircrafthand on the outbreak of war.

He was selected for pilot training, commissioned in May 1940 and posted to No 254 Squadron in England, operating the fighter version of the Blenheim.

Sise flew many routine patrols in support of convoys, in addition to escorting light bomber formations attacking enemy shipping off Norway. But on March 28 1942

No 254 launched six aircraft in daylight to support "Secret Force Chariot", the withdrawal of the survivors of the daring commando raid on St Nazaire.

In searching for survivors, Sise's aircraft was badly damaged by anti-aircraft fire and he was forced to crash land in Cornwall.

Shortly afterwards the squadron was re-equipped with the rugged and powerful Beaufighter. Sise was promoted to squadron leader, and 254 moved to Lincolnshire as part of the new North Coates Wing.

After becoming the chief flying instructor of a torpedo training unit near Stranraer, Sise was given command of No 248 Squadron, which had recently been re-equipped with rocket and cannon-firing Mosquitoes at Portreath, Cornwall.

He led numerous attacks against shipping between Brest and Bordeaux, including a devastating strike from mast-height against minesweepers in the Gironde estuary, during which the canopy of his Mosquito was shattered by anti-aircraft fire. He was awarded a Bar to his DFC.

In September 248 moved to Scotland to become one of the three squadrons of the Banff Strike Wing. As its most experienced squadron commander, Sise led many of the attacks, almost all against convoys in the Norwegian fjords. Leading two squadrons in an attack against a convoy in Floro harbour, an engine of his Mosquito was set on fire by flak; but he pressed home his attack before returning 400 miles across the North Sea on one engine.

Throughout the winter of 1944-45, Sise continued to lead the Mosquitoes against shipping sheltering under high precipices, making steep dives in the face of intense opposition.

In one sortie at Nordgulen Fjord, 36 Mosquitoes attacked a convoy; almost all the ships were hit by rockets and cannon fire, and two were left burning furiously.

At the end of February Sise was finally rested, having completed more than 150 operations. The citation for the

Bar to his DSO described him as "a brilliant leader whose great gallantry and personal example and untiring efforts have done much to raise his squadrons to the highest standard of fighting efficiency".

After the war Sise was offered a permanent commission in the RAF as a squadron leader. He specialised in fighter operations, holding appointments at Biggin Hill and Waterbeach before assuming command of No 64 Squadron at Duxford, flying Hunter aircraft.

On promotion to group captain in 1958, he commanded the fighter station at Church Fenton, in Yorkshire. When the Hunter and Javelin squadrons were transferred to Leconfield, near Beverley, Sise assumed command until June 1960, when he took up a three-year appointment at HQ Far East Air Force in Singapore. He returned to the headquarters of Fighter Command in September 1963, and retired from the RAF in January 1967.

Sise then returned to New Zealand, where he lived at Dunedin and became the chief executive of Wilson Neil, which specialised in exporting venison and game. He finally retired in 1981 to Wanaka, South Island, where he enjoyed trout fishing and speedboating.

While serving at Portreath in 1944, he met Section Officer Mary Hollingworth Crear. They married in 1945 and had a son. Mary died in 1987.

AIR VICE-MARSHAL
JOHN STACEY

Air Vice-Marshal John Stacey (who died on Christmas Day 2003, aged 83) led a brilliantly executed raid to lay mines in the entrance to Singapore harbour in March 1945; it was the first raid there for three years, and involved a round trip from Ceylon of 3,460 miles, one of the RAF's longest bombing raids in the Second World War.

After five months as the flight commander of No 160 Squadron, Stacey took command in November 1944 when he was ordered to convert it to a mine-laying role. Flying the long-range four-engine Liberator bomber from a hastily prepared airfield hacked out of the jungle in Ceylon, the squadron perfected techniques for dropping mines from 200ft at night on targets up to 1,200 miles away in Malaya, Thailand and Sumatra.

Led by Stacey, 160 took on its first mine-laying operation in January 1945, when three aircraft flew to Penang harbour, an area swarming with Japanese fighters. After dropping his mines, Stacey climbed to reveal his aircraft on the enemy radar, flying on a north-west course to give the impression that he was making for India. After a short time, he descended to sea level and turned for Ceylon. All the Liberators returned safely.

On March 26 1945 Stacey led a force of eight Liberators to attack Singapore harbour. To increase the range of the aircraft, extra fuel tanks were fitted; in order to reduce weight, two of the gun turrets, the oxygen equipment and the armour plating were removed – together with the Elsan chemical lavatories.

Flying at sea level on the outbound leg, the aircraft flew down the Malacca Straits before climbing to 500ft to drop their mines. To save fuel on the return journey, they were forced to fly a direct route, which involved climbing over the mountains of Sumatra and through severe electrical storms. After a flight of more than 21 hours, the eight bombers touched down at Minneriya in Ceylon. Stacey was awarded an immediate DSO.

John Nichol Stacey was born on September 14 1920 in Cardiff, but spent most of his childhood in Croydon, where he attended Whitgift Middle School. Always keen on aircraft, he spent many hours at Croydon airport; but after leaving school he chose to join the Merchant Navy as an apprentice.

He spent time at sea, but missed playing cricket and rugby. On shore-leave he met a friend who could not hide his delight at having just been accepted by the RAF. Stacey promptly went to the recruiting office and volunteered, and was accepted for a short service commission.

Having joined up in July 1938, Stacey specialised in flying boats during his pilot training. Shortly after the outbreak of war he was attached to No 240 Squadron, equipped with the biplane Saro London flying boat and based on the Shetland Islands. He flew on anti-submarine and convoy patrols in northern waters before moving to Stranraer, where he became an instructor.

In September 1941 Stacey joined No 202 Squadron at Gibraltar, flying Catalinas on patrols in the Mediterranean and the eastern Atlantic. Despite being only 21, he was already a veteran of many patrols when he was appointed a flight commander of No 205 Squadron in July 1942.

The squadron was reforming at Koggala, in Ceylon, and it soon began anti-shipping and anti-invasion patrols, interspersed with air-sea rescue missions. On August 26 Stacey took off to search for survivors of a ship sunk by an enemy submarine. He located three lifeboats with 60 survivors and dropped supplies to them. He then circled overhead for ten hours until relieved by another aircraft.

In December 1942, three Catalinas were sent to carry out a reconnaissance and bombing operation against airfields and harbours in northern Sumatra. Stacey flew one of the aircraft, reaching the targets at Sabang at midnight on December 20. After carrying out a reconnaissance of the airfield, Stacey climbed to start his bombing attack against harbour installations.

Despite intense anti-aircraft fire, he successfully dropped his four 250lb bombs before returning to Ceylon. He was awarded a DFC.

During 1943 Stacey flew many patrols over the Indian

Ocean, often operating from Madagascar and Mauritius, before taking command of the flying-boat training unit at Mombasa. In February 1944 he was seconded to the Royal Navy for special duties, in particular the hunt for the German submarine mother ship *Charlotte Schliemann*.

Ten Catalinas were gathered at Mauritius for the task, but warnings of a severe cyclone prompted the local air officer commanding to order Stacey to evacuate the flying boats. Stacey, mindful of his extensive experience of operating in severe weather in the Shetland Islands, refused to obey – and was threatened with a court martial if any aircraft were damaged.

Stacey alerted his commander-in-chief to his actions, and was relieved when the chief signalled the AOC: "I appointed Stacey for this task and have complete confidence in his judgement." The cyclone passed without incident, and in an outstanding joint operation, the submarine mother ship was later sunk.

After his long and arduous tour as the commanding officer of No 160 Squadron, Stacey was rested from operations and sent to HQ 222 Group in Ceylon to co-ordinate the special operations flown in support of the clandestine organisations in South-East Asia.

At the end of the war, he was granted a permanent commission. As well as being awarded the DSO and DFC, he was three times mentioned in dispatches.

After a tour as assistant air attaché in Washington, where he met his future wife, Stacey attended the RAF Staff College and the RAF Flying College. He then converted to jet aircraft before taking up the appointment of wing commander flying at Binbrook, where the first Canberra medium bomber squadrons had recently formed.

In April 1960, Stacey was seconded to the embryonic Royal Malayan Air Force as the Chief of Staff. Pilots and groundcrews were recruited from all races, and included some former RAF personnel. Stacey was a genial, ever popular man, and his sensitivity was greatly appreciated; on his departure two years later he was invested with one of Malaya's highest orders, the Johan Mangku Negara (JMN).

He returned to the RAF in 1963 to take command of the large Canberra base at Laarbruch, on the Dutch-German border, before becoming Group Captain Plans at the RAF Staff College, Bracknell, where he reformed and updated the syllabus.

On promotion to air commodore, he was appointed AOC Air Cadets, a post for which he was ideally suited, and one that gave him great pleasure. At the end of this tour he was appointed CBE.

His final appointment was as the Air Officer Administration, Support Command. He retired to Kent in 1975.

Stacey was a member of the Tunbridge Wells Health Authority. He served three terms as a governor of Bedgebury School, until he was made a vice-president for life in 1999.

He was a keen golfer and sailor.

John Stacey married, in 1950, Veronica Sutherland Rudd-Clarke. They had two daughters.

WING COMMANDER
DOUGLAS WILSON

Wing Commander Douglas Wilson (who died on June 6 2004, aged 87) won a DSO, a DFC and an AFC as a photographic reconnaissance Spitfire pilot, test pilot and bomber squadron commander during the Second World War.

Wilson was one of the small group of pilots at the RAF's Photographic Development Unit (PDU), an unconventional body formed to take photographs of Germany and surrounding countries during the so-called "phoney war". The aircraft used included a small number of specially equipped Spitfires capable of flying at very high level.

In April 1940 Wilson was appointed to command a small flight which provided the British Expeditionary Force with photographs of German Army movements. Following the German thrust through Belgium on May 10, the Spitfires operated at maximum effort until after the evacuation from Dunkirk. Retreating to Poitiers, and finally to an airfield near La Rochelle, Wilson and his handful of pilots flew until mid-June photographing the German advance across the river Seine.

With the Germans poised to capture their airfield, the Spitfires departed for England, leaving all the unit's ground equipment and vehicles to be destroyed. Wilson commandeered an abandoned Fairey Battle bomber and supervised repairs to the wing using a piece of a tree trunk and some fabric before cramming six airmen in the back of the three-seat aircraft and taking off for Heston, where they arrived after a four-hour flight.

Stationed at Wick in Scotland, Wilson flew long-range photographic reconnaissance sorties for which the squadron's single-engine aircraft were stripped of their guns and armour plating, allowing them to fly above 30,000ft. With extra fuel tanks, Wilson and his pilots flew five-hour sorties to the Baltic and Norway in their unheated cockpits and without navigation aids to bring back valuable photographs of the activities of the German Navy. For this crucial and dangerous work, he was awarded the DFC and mentioned in dispatches.

Louis Douglas Wilson was born on March 31 1917 at Vigo, Spain, where his father was the head of station for Eastern Telegraph. With his father re-assigned every few years, Wilson was educated in Lisbon and Alexandria before returning to England, by which time he was fluent in Spanish, Arabic and Portuguese.

He was then sent to King's School, Bruton, and the

RAF College at Cranwell, where he was awarded the Groves Memorial Prize for the best pilot in his entry. In January 1937 he joined No 40 Squadron flying the Hind and later Battle and Blenheim bombers. The day before war broke out, Wilson flew one of 16 Battles to an airfield near Rheims as part of the Advance Air Striking Force. Six days later he led six aircraft on the squadron's first war sortie, a reconnaissance of the Metz area. There was little activity over the coming weeks, and the squadron was withdrawn to England to re-equip with the Blenheim, but Wilson soon found himself appointed to the PDU.

In January 1941 Wilson was loaned for six months to Vickers Armstrong as a test pilot. During two years at Farnborough he flew more than 100 different types of aircraft, including Britain's first jet, the Gloster E28/39, as well as captured Luftwaffe aircraft.

Some of Wilson's work was extremely hazardous. In 1942 the scientists at Farnborough were trying to develop a system which would allow low-flying bombers to cut the wires of barrage balloons. To obtain data, Wilson had to make a series of flights in a specially modified Hurricane, a task which involved flying the aircraft into the wires of tethered balloons. On one occasion the wire jammed his controls, and he had great difficulty bringing the aircraft out of a spin. He recovered at 1,000ft, and landed with a length of wire trailing behind his aircraft.

On November 30 1942 he took off from Exeter in his Hurricane for a further test. As a special precaution, his cockpit was reinforced to reduce the risk of decapitation, but the heavy structure gave him a very limited view, and he failed to spot two German fighters which were on a tip-and-run raid over Devon. Their cannon shells thudded into the Hurricane, severely damaging the aircraft's controls. Wilson tried to bale out, but could not open the heavy canopy; after several attempts he managed to land, then discovered that most of the rear of the aircraft had been shot away.

Early models of the four-engine Halifax bomber suffered control problems resulting in many accidents with heavy loss of life. A test crew from Farnborough endeavouring to identify the problem was killed when the aircraft crashed. Immediately afterwards, Wilson took an engineer on a test flight for a further attempt to obtain data. As the heavy bomber began a turn, it rolled violently and entered a vertical dive. With great difficulty, Wilson managed to regain control before landing the aircraft safely. A major modification to the aircraft's two fins eventually solved the problem. Wilson was awarded the AFC.

After spending six months briefing pilots in the United States on RAF flight testing methods, Wilson was given command of No 102 Squadron equipped with modified Halifax bombers, and led his squadron on many raids over Germany.

On four separate occasions his aircraft was damaged by anti-aircraft fire. While leading a raid to Scholven in October 1944 his aircraft was badly damaged as he started his bombing run. But he continued to fly straight and level over the target until the bombs had been dropped. The citation for his DSO described him as "a squadron commander of outstanding quality".

Wilson was deeply affected by the loss of his young crews. He insisted on writing personal letters to the next of kin of all the aircrew posted missing, often remaining at his desk for hours after he had returned from an operation.

After the war he had appointments in Iraq and the Far East, and commanded Nos 9 and 49 Squadrons when they were converting from the Lancaster to the Lincoln.

After a series of appointments at the Air Ministry, Wilson served in Germany before flying fighters as the chief instructor at the Central Gunnery School and taking a two-year appointment on the operations staff of the Second Allied Tactical Air Force in Germany.

He retired in 1959, when he joined the export department of the aero-engine division of Rolls-Royce. He finally retired to Hampshire in 1973.

Douglas Wilson married Valerie Roche in 1940. The marriage was dissolved in 1953, and in the same year he married Eileen Farrell. He had twin daughters and a son from his first marriage.

AIR COMMODORE LEONARD BIRCHALL

Air Commodore Leonard Birchall (who died on September 11 2004 at Kingston, Ontario, aged 89) became known as "the Saviour of Ceylon" after he spotted the Japanese Fleet approaching the island, which was the base for the Royal Navy's Eastern Fleet in 1942; as he radioed the position of the enemy force, his flying boat was shot down in flames.

Admiral Sir James Somerville had taken up command as C-in-C, East Indies Fleet, two days before being alerted by intelligence sources to the probability of a Japanese attack on Ceylon on April 1 1942. Fearful of another "Pearl Harbor", Somerville dispersed some of his forces, and ordered air patrols to search for the enemy fleet.

Birchall and his crew, who were part of No 413 (RCAF) Squadron, had arrived in Ceylon only 48 hours earlier, and were immediately sent into action. After two days of fruitless searching, their Catalina took off early on April 4 and, eight hours later, sighted the Japanese force 350 miles south-east of Ceylon, steaming towards the island.

Realising that he had found the Japanese strike force,

Birchall closed to observe that the fleet included five aircraft carriers. Almost immediately his lumbering flying boat was attacked by 18 fighters. A sighting message was hastily coded and transmitted to base before cannon fire destroyed the Catalina's radio. The aircraft was then set on fire and as Birchall came down in the sea the tail broke off.

Two of the crew were seriously injured and went down with the aircraft. As the survivors swam away from the burning fuel, the radio operator was killed by machine-gun fire. All six of the survivors had been wounded, three seriously, by the time they were picked up by the destroyer *Isokaza*.

Birchall's signal was garbled on arrival in Ceylon, and requests for amplification went unanswered; it gave the clear impression, however, that invasion was imminent. The defences were alerted and 48 ships, including the aircraft carrier *Hermes*, sailed from Colombo and Trincomalee. And when the first Japanese air attack came, the following morning, the defences were on full alert. The British suffered considerable losses, but the Japanese fleet retreated; Ceylon suffered no further attacks.

Although *The Daily Telegraph* reported at the time that there was talk of erecting a memorial to Birchall, it was not until the end of the war that he learnt of his award of a DFC for his unique mission. At a formal dinner in Washington in 1947, Winston Churchill declared that Birchall's courage in helping to foil the Japanese invasion was "one of the most important single contributions to Allied victory".

Leonard Joseph Birchall was born on July 6 1915 at St Catharine's, Ontario. After serving in the Royal Canadian Corps of Signals, he joined the RCAF to train as a pilot in 1937 before specialising in maritime reconnaissance. Following the outbreak of war, he flew convoy and anti-submarine patrols from Nova Scotia. Early in 1942 he joined No 413 Squadron in the Shetland Islands, flying patrols over the North Sea. Following the Japanese advances in South-East Asia, 413 was ordered to Ceylon to provide a reconnaissance force.

On board *Isokaza*, Birchall was singled out as the senior officer, and beaten by his captors in an effort to find out if a radio message had been sent. He steadfastly denied sending any, resisting all attempts to extract information.

The crew were put in a damp lock-up with room for only the three most badly wounded to lie down. After three days they were transferred to the carrier *Akagi*, flagship of the Japanese commander Admiral Nagumo, before being landed at Yokohama, where the injured received medical attention.

Birchall and his crew were eventually taken to a new camp in the mountains near Yokohama, where 250 Commonwealth prisoners from Hong Kong and 75 Americans from the Philippines soon joined them. These men had been so badly let down by their officers in previous camps that they proved extremely troublesome, but Birchall quickly instituted a strict code of discipline. He endeared himself to the PoWs when he struck a Japanese guard, who was insisting that a badly-wounded American should join a working party. Birchall was severely beaten and placed in solitary confinement.

For most of his time in captivity, Birchall kept detailed diaries of camp life, recording deaths and maltreatment by Japanese guards. He completed 22 diaries, which were kept hidden. "If they are found," he told a friend at the time, "I am for the chop."

In early 1944 he was moved to another camp, where ailing men were forced to work in the docks until they collapsed. In protest, Birchall ordered the men to stop working and sit down. Although the guards beat him with clubs and rifle butts, the PoWs did as Birchall commanded until the sick were excused from work. He was then taken to a "discipline camp", beaten senseless and left without food and water for days.

In June 1945 Birchall and 200 prisoners were sent to a camp near Mount Fuji. When three men died of malnutrition, he organised "stealing teams" to raid nearby farms for fresh vegetables; no more deaths were recorded. Finally, on August 27, American troops arrived to take over the camp. After his release, Birchall stopped off in Manila, where he left eight of his diaries with instructions on how to find the remaining 14, which were wrapped in oilcloth and buried at one of the camps.

Birchall was appointed OBE in 1946, the citation recording that "he continually displayed the utmost concern for the welfare of fellow prisoners with complete disregard for his own safety. His consistent gallantry and glowing devotion to his men were in keeping with the finest traditions of the service". His own flight engineer, Brian Catlin, who spent much of the time with him as a PoW, echoed the feelings of many when he said: "There are many alive today who would not have survived without Birchall."

In 1950 President Truman appointed Birchall an officer of the Legion of Merit, saying: "His exploits became legendary throughout Japan and brought renewed faith and strength to many hundreds of ill and disheartened prisoners."

Birchall was a member of the American prosecuting team at the war crimes trials held in Japan, at which his diaries were used in evidence by the prosecution. He later joined the Canadian NATO delegation in Paris. After commanding a fighter base he was promoted air commodore. He was commandant of the Royal Military College at Kingston, Ontario, and finally retired in 1967 rather then be associated with the unification of the armed forces.

While acting as a Canadian observer during Sri Lanka's general election of 1994, he was struck by the poverty of its hospitals. At his own expense, he arranged for eight tons of medical supplies to be sent to the country. He also organised visits to the war cemeteries in Sri Lanka and a memorial at No 413's wartime base. One veteran commented: "Birch is still looking after his men."

Birchall was appointed a member of the Order of Canada in 1999. He was one of only two recipients of a fifth clasp to the Canadian Decoration; the other was Queen Elizabeth the Queen Mother.

Leonard Birchall was twice widowed before marrying his third wife, Kay. He had two daughters and a son from his first marriage.

FLIGHT LIEUTENANT CHARLES CORDER

Flight Lieutenant Charles Corder (who died on May 31 2005, aged 87) was the navigator of a Beaufighter that managed to return to base against all the odds after it had been severely damaged by a Luftwaffe fighter; both he and his pilot were decorated, Corder receiving the Conspicuous Gallantry Medal, one of only 113 awarded to airmen.

Corder was the long-serving navigator of the Free French pilot Max Guedj, DFC, who adopted the *nom de guerre* Lieutenant Maurice to safeguard his Jewish family, who remained in France. On the morning of March 10 1943 they took off for a patrol over the Bay of Biscay, their 71st operation together. When they encountered a Junkers 88 long-range fighter, Guedj attacked, and sent it crashing into the sea. But return fire from the German fighter's gunner severely damaged the aircraft.

Guedj was wounded during the attack and the inter-communication in the aircraft was put out of action. With the situation appearing hopeless, Corder crawled forward to assist the pilot before returning to his seat, where he obtained radio bearings and gave Guedj a course to steer for their base in Cornwall, 180 miles away. One of the two engines failed, and Guedj had to fly a few feet above the sea. Corder once more crawled forward to assist him, having managed to repair the intercommunication system.

Just before they reached the English coast, the second engine caught fire, which spread to the cockpit. Corder transmitted an SOS and fired distress cartridges to attract the attention of those ashore. As they approached Cornwall, it was clear that the aircraft had either to ditch in the heavy seas or clear the cliffs. As Corder guided Guedj to the cliffs' lowest point, observers on the ground were convinced that the aircraft would crash; but Guedj managed to clear the cliffs by a few feet before making an emergency landing as the second engine finally failed. Corder's navigation had been so accurate that they managed to crash land on their own airfield at Predannack.

The incident attracted a great deal of press interest. Guedj told one reporter: "It would have been impossible without my navigator; he was really the key man on board the most hair-raising adventure we have lived through." For their actions in recovering the aircraft, Guedj was the first French airman to receive the DSO. The long citation for Corder's CGM remarked on how he had "calmly continued his duties, showing great navigational skill and teamwork and doing everything within his power to assist his pilot". It concluded: "In the face of an appalling situation, this airman displayed courage in keeping with the highest traditions of the RAF." Both men were also awarded the Croix de Guerre avec Palme.

Charles Clayton Corder was born on July 29 1917 at West Thurrock, Essex. He was educated at Palmer's Grammar School before joining Lloyds Bank. In May 1940 he enlisted in the RAF, but poor eyesight prevented him from training as a pilot. Instead he became a navigator and was posted to No 248 Squadron, where he teamed up with Guedj, a partnership that would last for almost two years.

Corder had already flown many patrols off Norway and over the Bay of Biscay when 248 was sent to Malta to provide escort for the supply convoys to the beleaguered island. During this period, Corder and Guedj were sent to search for a missing Canadian pilot. They located a dinghy and dropped survival aids and rations. After circling for 30 minutes, they watched as an enemy seaplane arrived on the scene.

Deciding to allow the aircraft to rescue the survivor, they repeatedly dived over the dinghy to mark its position. The seaplane landed and completed the rescue, with German fighters arriving on the scene to provide an escort. In the event, there were two men in the dinghy, the crew of an Italian Air Force bomber. Twenty-nine years later, Corder received a letter from Generale Antonio Cumbat thanking him for saving his life. In his letter he commented that, when rescued, the seaplane pilot had said: "You should thank the Junkers 88 for saving your life" – the enemy seaplane and its escorting fighters had mistaken the Beaufighter for a German aircraft. The two former enemies became good friends.

After a rest tour, Corder was commissioned and joined No 404 Squadron, completing many more anti-shipping patrols. He was deeply saddened to learn that his pilot Guedj had been killed leading a Mosquito strike against Norwegian shipping in January 1945.

After being discharged from the RAF the next year, Corder returned to Lloyds Bank in London with responsibilities for the bank's premises, and qualified as a chartered surveyor.

Corder was, until the last 15 years of his life, a dedicated pipe smoker; and on his retirement from Lloyds, he was presented with a wastepaper basket fitted with a tap, in recognition of the many small fires he had started with his pipes and as a precaution for his retirement. On national no-smoking days he would line up his many pipes and smoke from each one.

He was a staunch supporter of the Royal British Legion and Probus. He was also an accomplished carpenter.

Charles Corder married his childhood sweetheart, Irene Feal, in 1941; she died in 2003. They had a son (Maurice, named in memory of his French pilot) and a daughter.

WING COMMANDER
PETER CUNDY

Wing Commander Peter Cundy (who died on August 4 2005, aged 88) was one of the RAF's leading anti-submarine pilots.

He had already seen much action in the Bay of Biscay when, in July 1943, he sighted a surfaced U-boat which he attacked and sank with depth charges and a new bomb, known as the Hedgehog.

Cundy and his crew had taken off during the morning of July 3 1943 in their 224 Squadron Liberator from St Eval in Cornwall to patrol in the south of the Bay of Biscay, which had become the centre of the RAF's campaign against the U-boat menace.

Among the weapons on board was an adapted Royal Navy Hedgehog bomb, which had not yet been used from an aircraft. Flying as an observer was Lieutenant-Colonel Farrant, a weapons expert, who went along to see the effect of the weapon should a target be found. He was briefed that his chances of seeing any action were slim, since the great majority of Coastal Command's crews never sighted an enemy submarine.

But a submarine was contacted on the aircraft's radar,

and Cundy sighted a U-boat on the surface several miles ahead. With his gunners opening fire with their cannon, he dived to attack and dropped the Hedgehog over the submarine. He immediately turned for a second attack despite his aircraft suffering serious damage from withering return fire from the U-boat. Cundy dropped four depth charges, which straddled the submarine.

The enemy started to take evasive action, so Cundy made a further attack as the submarine settled low in the water. As he circled the area after his third attack, the Liberator crew saw that the U-boat had disappeared and men were in the water. Farrant offered to throw his life jacket to them; but the Liberator crew persuaded him that he might need it if the damage to their aircraft prevented them from returning to base. Cundy nursed his aircraft back to St Eval on three engines; there was also damage to the fuel tanks and the aircraft's tail, but he was able to make a safe landing. Shortly afterwards it was confirmed that he had sunk U-628, which had recently left Brest on its fourth cruise. He was awarded the DSO.

One of twin sons of a brewer, Peter John Cundy was born on October 3 1916 at Bognor and educated at Eastbourne College. He was commissioned into the 9th Battalion, Middlesex Regiment, in July 1937 and three years later transferred to an anti-aircraft battery of the Royal Artillery. He was seconded to the RAF in August and trained as a pilot, then joined No 53 Squadron to fly Blenheims in Coastal Command attacking the U-boat bases along the French Atlantic coast, including Brest.

In 1941 Cundy joined No 120 Squadron, which was re-forming with the new long-range American-built Liberator. On January 11 1942 he was on patrol in the Bay of Biscay when he saw a twin-engine seaplane. He manoeuvred his heavy aircraft so that his gunners could bring effective fire to bear; the enemy escaped into cloud with one of its engines on fire.

Shortly after this engagement U-373 was sighted

refuelling alongside a large tanker. Cundy immediately attacked both craft with depth charges and cannon fire. The submarine dived, leaving a large patch of oil on the surface; Cundy then attacked the tanker with cannon fire. A second enemy seaplane arrived on the scene, and the Liberator's gunners opened fire, driving it away with smoke pouring from it. After this eventful patrol, Cundy was awarded an immediate DFC.

In May 1942 he and his crew were detached to America with their aircraft "Dumbo" and were involved in the development of a new air-to-surface radar. They returned with Dumbo, joining No 224 Squadron in October, to continue the war against the U-boats.

On February 26 1943 Cundy was on patrol in the Bay of Biscay when they spotted U-437 on the surface. The U-boat immediately crash-dived as Cundy dropped a stick of depth charges, without any visible effect. The Liberator continued its patrol. Shortly afterwards, Cundy saw a second submarine and attacked with his remaining depth charges.

The crew soon saw the submarine's bows appear almost vertically, and she sank below the surface. All the depth charges had been used, and Cundy and his crew were amazed to see the U-boat surface and sail away 20 minutes later; U-508 had been damaged and was forced to return to Lorient.

In November, after three years of constant operations, Cundy was rested and served at the headquarters of Coastal Command on operations and armament duties. During this period he flew many sorties testing and evaluating the Leigh-Light, a powerful searchlight carried on the wing of an anti-submarine aircraft. For this work he was awarded the AFC, and in September 1945 he was transferred to the RAF and granted a permanent commission. He flew Dakota transport aircraft before training as a flying instructor.

Afterwards, with the Air Training Wing in Rhodesia,

Cundy returned to the maritime world as an instructor at No 236 Operational Conversion Unit, equipped with a version of the Lancaster bomber. In May 1951 he assumed command of No 210 Squadron operating the Lancaster in the maritime reconnaissance role from Ballykelly in Northern Ireland. During his period in command, the squadron won the prestigious Aird Whyte Trophy.

From 1952 Cundy spent three years as the senior air staff officer in Gibraltar before taking up an appointment on the joint planning staffs at the Air Ministry. He was then attached to the Pacific Fleet of the US Navy for three years, returning in January 1960 to be the RAF staff officer to the Commander-in-Chief, Home Fleet. He retired from the RAF in 1963.

Cundy became a personnel manager for the market research company AGB before taking up property management. In 1995 he was invited by the surviving crew members of U-373 to go to Bavaria as guest of honour at their annual reunion. He formed firm friendships with his former adversaries and attended every reunion for ten years, making his final visit just two months before his death.

Cundy retired to East Anglia, where he enjoyed fishing and shooting.

Peter Cundy, in 1945, married Section Officer Sheila Frost, WAAF, with whom he had three sons and a daughter. Sheila died six days before her husband.

ESCAPERS AND EVADERS

WING COMMANDER
NORMAN MACKIE

Wing Commander Norman Mackie (who died on New Year's Day 2003, aged 80) evaded capture after being shot down over France, then made a remarkable escape through Europe to return to his squadron, with which he resumed his career as a bomber captain in Air Vice-Marshal Don Bennett's Pathfinder Force.

On the night of March 11-12 1943, while flying as captain of a four-engine Avro Lancaster, Mackie was setting out on what would be his 51st operation. As it happened, his was the last aircraft of No 83 Squadron to take off from RAF Wyton because of a delay caused by the fact that the helmets of two of his crew members had been found to be unserviceable.

The outward flight was uneventful and, though he made up some time, he was still one of the last aircraft to reach the target at Stuttgart, where he dropped his target indicators and bombs.

After turning for home, Mackie observed that his engines were running somewhat roughly. But all was well until, over France, his Lancaster was attacked from below by a two-engine Bf 110 night fighter, and the starboard inner engine caught fire.

Mackie dived from 16,000ft to 11,000, but the fighter followed, scoring further hits. Mackie then plunged to 6,000ft in an attempt to extinguish the flames streaming from a full petrol tank. But even at 2,500ft the fire continued to rage, and Mackie ordered the crew to bale out.

Meanwhile, he remained aboard, fighting to retain control, until the Lancaster went into a shallow dive. Mackie threw himself out, head first, at only 1,500ft, landing in a tree near St Dizier. Although he injured a thigh getting down from the tree, Mackie found himself otherwise in good shape. He buried his parachute, harness and Mae West, and walked until he was stopped by a German soldier who locked him in a lean-to shed.

Mackie forced the lock, emerged from his makeshift prison and continued his journey, gratefully accepting the aid and refreshment offered by French farmers. Finally, he encountered what were known as "escape and evasion helpers" who provided him with a boiler suit to cover his uniform before assisting him to cross the frontier into Switzerland. It was a moonless night as Mackie crossed into neutral territory, but he identified the lights of Geneva in the distance and walked towards them until he was able to hop aboard a tram; a considerate conductor told him where to alight for the British Consulate.

In the event, Mackie never reached it: a gendarme stopped him in the street outside, and marched him off to prison and interrogation by a Swiss Air Force officer who then dispatched him to Berne, where he was welcomed at the British Embassy by Air Commodore Freddie West, who had won the VC with the Royal Flying Corps in the First World War and was serving as an air attaché.

West lodged Mackie in the Hotel d'Angleterre with a group of evaders and escaped prisoners of war; but, rather than attempting to facilitate Mackie's repatriation, West put him to work in his office at the embassy.

This did not appeal to Mackie, who was anxious to rejoin his squadron, and West eventually consented; but when he came up with an unreliable scheme for two Dutch airmen to fly Mackie out in a light civilian club aircraft, Mackie refused. Finally, in the face of Mackie's frustration, West approved his request to leave Switzerland with Captain Jeff Morphew, a South African pilot who had escaped from Italy after being shot down in the Western Desert.

Having travelled through France, in early December

1943 the two men reached Perpignan, where they smuggled themselves on to a goods train. After what seemed like an interminable period of shunting, they abandoned the train at Port-Bou, only to walk straight into two Spanish policemen who were in conversation with two German soldiers.

The Germans took no notice, and walked off; but the Spaniards were more curious, and arrested Mackie and Morphew, placing them in Figuras prison until they were handed over to the Spanish Air Force. Eventually they were released into the custody of the British Embassy in Madrid. The next stop was Gibraltar, where they got a flight home.

Norman Alexander John Buist Mackie was born on December 22 1922 at Ootacamund, where his father was a major in the Indian Army, and was educated at Taunton School, at which he became head boy.

Mackie enlisted in the RAF in 1940. Having gained his wings and been commissioned as a pilot officer, he was posted in May 1941 to No 83 Squadron, which was led by Wing Commander Roderick Learoyd, who had won the VC while serving with Bomber Command.

Mackie piloted two-engine Handley Page Hampdens and Avro Manchesters, and survived numerous sorties over the heavily-defended industrial centres of Germany. He was awarded the DFC before graduating to the Lancaster in which he was shot down.

Following his escape and his return to 83 Squadron, Mackie enhanced his reputation in further sorties, and was awarded a Bar to his DFC, the commendation recalling his exploits in France and paying tribute to his "utmost courage and unfailing determination to make every sortie successful".

Mackie had been promoted squadron leader, and was a flight commander when, while flying as second-in-command of No 571 Squadron, he was awarded the DSO. This came after an exceedingly hazardous operation in which he led a formation of Lancasters in a daylight attack on Duisburg, one of the most heavily defended targets in the industrial Ruhr.

Despite encountering heavy and accurate flak, Mackie kept his formation together and ensured an accurate attack. Noting that he always elected to take part in the most difficult operations, his commanding officer's commendation added that he had completed no fewer than 92 sorties in three tours of operations.

Opting for a peacetime career in the RAF, Mackie served routinely at home and in Germany in a mixture of flying and desk jobs. He was appointed, in 1950, as flight commander in No 12 Squadron, which was equipped with Avro Lincolns (derived from the Lancaster); and, in 1954, he was given command of No 69 Squadron's English Electric Canberra reconnaissance jets in Germany.

In 1958 this photo-recce experience led to an appointment with Intelligence in Washington, where he was involved in the secret flights of the U2 and in other high-altitude Cold War reconnaissance operations.

Mackie concluded his career in a series of flying and administrative posts, retiring in 1967. He then became bursar at Highgate School, and later worked as a personnel administrator in the City.

He retained his links with the RAF through the Pathfinders' Association and the RAF Escaping Society. He also made occasional visits to France to meet members of the families who had helped him evade capture; he also managed to trace the remains of his crashed Lancaster.

Norman Mackie married, in 1958, Thelma Vallis. They had a daughter.

WING COMMANDER
"TAFFY" HIGGINSON

Wing Commander "Taffy" Higginson (who died on February 12 2003, aged 89) had already downed at least 15 enemy aircraft when, on June 17 1941, he was shot down over France and baled out of his burning Hurricane fighter.

After fighting throughout the Battle of Britain in the preceding summer and autumn and being awarded the DFM, he was determined to evade capture and return to No 56 Squadron.

Higginson was escorting bombers raiding Lille when his Hurricane was hit, though he was never sure whether anti-aircraft fire or an enemy fighter pilot was responsible. In the explosion his left boot was torn off and his trousers shredded. Worse, the control column snapped at the base, making it impossible to control the aircraft and forcing him to bale out. He landed in a wood, to be confronted by a German officer and sergeant in a motorcycle combination.

Higginson was seized and placed in the sidecar – but at that moment his captors were distracted by a low-flying Bf 109. Higginson, seizing the handlebars, tipped the motorcycle and sidecar over and ran off. He got himself to Lille, where he met Paul Cole, a Dunkirk survivor, who took him to Abbeville; there the Abbé Carpentier, a local priest, provided him with false identity papers.

Cole then escorted Higginson to Paris, where he lodged in a brothel until going on by train to Tours and St Martin-le-Beau. But there they were questioned by a pair of German soldiers.

Not satisfied with Cole's explanation that Higginson was an idiot seeking work, the Germans insisted on looking inside his valise. Fortunately, its contents were smothered in chocolate which had melted in the summer heat. When Cole opened his own bag they failed to discover a pistol and incriminating papers which had been rolled up in dirty laundry, and the pair were sent on their way.

After entering Vichy France, Higginson reached Marseilles, where he was welcomed by Georges Rodocanochi, a Greek doctor, and his wife Fanny, who ran a safe house for Pat O'Leary's MI 9 escape line.

It shocked Higginson, who was acutely aware of the debt he owed Cole, when he heard later that his companion, far from being the Army captain he claimed, was a sergeant who had absconded with mess funds, and, among his many betrayals, had informed on Carpentier, who was later executed.

Higginson caught a train to Perpignan where, impatient at being kept waiting, he teamed up with an Australian corporal and persuaded a Catalan guide to start them on their way to Spain. But they were stopped by gendarmes and Higginson, incensed by their attitude, struck one of them. But for this, he might have been released. As it was, he was imprisoned for six months for having false papers.

On March 5 1942 he was about to be freed when he was detained in reprisal for a raid on the Renault factory at Billancourt. Twelve days later he was placed in Fort de la Revere above Monte Carlo, where he decided to assume the name Captain Bennett, since he believed the Germans particularly disliked airmen. At this stage MI 9 in London urged O'Leary to make every effort to get Higginson out, in view of his exceptional record as a fighter pilot.

Using a Polish priest called Father Myrda as a go-between, O'Leary smuggled a hacksaw blade into the prison. On the night of August 6 Higginson and four others – under cover of a noisy concert – dropped through a coal shute and into a moat and some sewage. Evading his pursuers, Higginson reached Cap d'Ail, where he found he had mislaid his ID card. Despite this setback, he managed to reach a safe house in Monte Carlo. There tea was brought in by Eva Trenchard, a spinster who had run the principality's Scottish Tea House since 1924.

In due course Father Myrda provided Higginson with a cassock, and accompanied him to Marseilles. On September 17 Higginson made for Canet Plage, a beach resort, where he was picked up from a dinghy by *Tarana*, a Polish trawler employed on clandestine missions as a Q Ship. A week later he was put aboard the destroyer *Minna* and landed at Gibraltar, whence he was flown home by the RAF.

Frederick William Higginson was born at Swansea on February 17 1913. He joined the RAF as an apprentice in 1929 and in 1932 was posted as a fitter-airgunner to No 7 Squadron. Higginson was accepted for pilot training in 1935 and the next year joined No 19, a Gloster Gauntlet biplane fighter squadron, moving almost immediately with C Flight to form No 66, another Gauntlet squadron.

A useful rugby player, Higginson was selected to play for the RAF, which helped to bring him to the notice of his superiors. He moved on in 1937 to No 56, a Gloster Gladiator biplane squadron which was re-equipped shortly afterwards with the new Hawker Hurricane monoplane fighter.

Promoted flight sergeant in 1940, he fought over France as it fell, then found himself in the thick of the fighting over south-east England and London during the Battle of Britain. When awarded the DFM on July 27 1940, 16 days after the battle began, he was praised for having already destroyed at least five enemy aircraft. The citation emphasised that despite being an "airman pilot" he led a section of 56 Squadron during all operations, "his determination in the face of the enemy and his cool and courageous leadership" being an example to his squadron.

As the battle wore on Higginson continued to build his score until he reached a total of at least 15 – taking into account shared victories and probables; by this time he had exchanged his sergeant's stripes for the thin blue ring of a pilot officer.

Almost 60 years afterwards Higginson met Hans Mellangrau, a Luftwaffe fighter pilot whom he had shot down over the Thames Estuary. "I saw this Messerschmitt coming towards me and suddenly we were face to face," Higginson recalled. "After he hit my Hurricane's engine with incendiary bullets I shot him down and he crash-landed in a field. By this time his incendiaries had set my engine on fire and I actually crash-landed alongside him."

Following his evasion of capture and escape from prison in France, Higginson rejoined 56 Squadron in October 1942. By this time it had exchanged its beloved Hurricanes for Hawker Typhoons, much more advanced in speed, performance and firepower than their predecessors.

In the New Year of 1943 his further success, particularly in sweeps over France – often leading the squadron – was recognised with the award of the DFC. The citation stated: "He has now destroyed at least 12 enemy aircraft and throughout has displayed great skill and courage in combat with the enemy."

After a stint with No 83 Group's communications squadron Higginson was posted in 1946 to the headquarters of Fighter Command's No 11 Group. He concluded his war on attachment to Napiers, the engineering business.

In 1948 the Air Ministry sent him to the RAF Staff College at Bracknell, and in 1951 to the Army Staff College at Camberley.

Higginson was promoted wing commander and from 1952 served on the operational requirements staff, taking a helicopter course at the same time. In 1956 he retired and joined Bristol Aircraft as its military liaison officer.

After two years British Aerospace appointed him sales and service director in the guided weapons division. In 1963 his success in opening up overseas markets for guided weapons, particularly Bloodhound, was recognised with an OBE.

Meanwhile, Higginson had met the businessman Abdullah Alireza, who had established an engineering, construction and oil business in Kuwait and wished to open a London office.

In 1964 Higginson launched Rezayat Services for Alireza, building a substantial business for the Kuwaiti's European company.

In 1969 he bought Pen-y-Coed, a 250-acre farm in his native Wales, with a large 17th century house. He had not farmed before, but "bought some books and set about reading everything I could on the subject".

Higginson married, in 1937, Sian Jenkins, who died in 2002; they had four sons.

FLIGHT LIEUTENANT
TONY BETHELL

Flight Lieutenant Tony Bethell (who died on February 17 2004, aged 81) was one of the 76 air force officers to break out of Stalag Luft III during "The Great Escape" on the night of March 24 1944.

Two hundred men were supposed to slip through "Harry" tunnel, which ran for 365ft, 28ft below the surface; but the 77th was spotted by a guard at around 5am, and the alarm sounded. Bethell was posted to "Leicester Square", the second halfway house along the tunnel. He was to pull 20 men through until relieved by escaper number 65, and then lie in the woods to wait for nine more.

But after pulling out 12 men, Bethell had to sit in his

cramped underground space for 45 minutes, which made him feel that he was condemned to a permanent coffin; finally, the next man arrived and explained that someone had got stuck and had to be pulled back while the tunnel was patched up.

Shortly after Bethell's group had assembled outside the wire, they heard a shot, signalling that the escape had been discovered. They split into pairs, and Bethell went off with "Cookie" Long, hoping to cross the Czech border, about 40 miles away.

Snow and flooding forced them to change their minds and they headed toward Frankfurt, with the idea of hopping on a freight train and escaping to Sweden. They walked along a railway line, slept in a barn at night then resumed their journey at daybreak.

At Benau, however, they were captured, and taken to a Gestapo prison at Gorlitz. Long was taken away and shot – one of 50 recaptured escapers executed on Hitler's orders. Only three of the PoWs reached England – two Norwegians and a Dutchman, all RAF pilots.

The son of a colonial administrator, Richard Anthony Bethell was born on April 9 1922 at Dar es Salaam, Tanganyika. Tony and his brother lived for some years in Gibraltar, where their father was state treasurer, then returned home after his death.

Tony was educated at Sherborne, where he became head boy. Early in the war there was an air raid on the school, and he was nearly expelled for being outside the shelter at the time.

Joining the RAF in February 1941 he was sent to America for pilot training and was then posted to a training unit at Hawarden, before joining No 268 Squadron.

Bethell spent much time flying "rhubarbs", or low level sweeps. On November 26 1942, during an operation over Holland, he shot down a Bf 109 and a Junkers 52 transport aircraft. These were the squadron's first successes, and the first of hundreds to fall to Mustangs during the war.

Eleven days later Bethell took off at 9.15am and was flying with three other Mustangs when they were met by flak at the Dutch coast. His aircraft was damaged and then hit again 20ft above the ground; after crash-landing at around 10am, he was soon in German hands. Bethell was transferred to an Amsterdam jail and then Stalag Luft III.

As the Russians approached the camp in January 1945, Bethell and the other PoWs were marched from Sagan, near the Oder river, to Lubeck, where they arrived three days before the war ended.

With the return of peace, Bethell went into business in Africa, joining the trading company Gellatly Hankey to serve at Khartoum and Addis Ababa; but he became bored and rejoined the RAF as a flight lieutenant in 1949.

After a series of specialist courses, he was a navigator instructor, then personal assistant to Air Chief Marshal Sir George Pirie.

On returning to Britain in 1953 he was posted to No 145 Squadron at Celle, flying Vampires, before becoming a flight commander on No 16 Squadron, also operating Vampires from Celle, an airfield close to the East German border. He finally retired from the RAF in June 1955 and went to live in Canada.

Bethell settled down happily across the Atlantic, where he was employed in the brokerage business in Montreal for many years, and then worked for Elican, a Belgian company. He later moved into money management.

He often returned to England, and attended several reunions of Great Escape veterans. But he was no fan of the film *The Great Escape*, which he felt should have been made in black and white.

On retiring in the early 1990s he and his second wife Lorna moved to a farm at Caledon, north of Toronto, where he spent much time on a John Deere tractor, cutting fallow hayfields.

Tony Bethell had two sons and two daughters from his first marriage and three stepchildren from his second. Another son died in 2003.

———

WING COMMANDER
NICKY BARR

Wing Commander Nicky Barr (who died on June 12 2006, aged 90) was one of Australia's most successful wartime fighter pilots, credited with destroying at least 12 enemy aircraft.

Shot down three times, on the third occasion he was badly wounded and was taken prisoner by the Italians. He then escaped three times, and remained behind enemy lines for more than a year conducting clandestine operations with the partisans and special forces.

On January 11 1942 Barr was flying a Kittyhawk fighter with No 3 (RAAF) Squadron escorting bombers over El Alamein. When enemy fighters appeared on the scene Barr attacked, shooting one down.

He then observed one of his fellow pilots being forced down by two enemy aircraft and he immediately engaged them, dispatching one. Minutes later Barr saw his colleague waving to him from the ground, and, as he was preparing to land in the desert to rescue him, two Messerschmitt Bf 109 fighters attacked.

Although the undercarriage of his aircraft was not fully retracted, Barr engaged his attackers, only to find that his guns had jammed. He quickly rectified the fault and shot down one of the Bf 109s before two more appeared. When they attacked he was wounded and forced to crash land.

While on the ground Barr was again wounded by enemy fire, but still managed to make his way through enemy lines. He reached Allied territory after walking through the desert for three days, bringing with him valuable intelligence on the dispositions of enemy tanks and defences. He was awarded an immediate DFC.

Andrew William Barr, always known as Nicky, was born on December 10 1915 at Wellington, New Zealand, but he grew up in Australia. He was educated at Swinburne Technical College, in Victoria, where he excelled as a sportsman. But it was at rugby that he made his greatest mark, playing as hooker for Victoria and Australia.

Barr was selected for the Australian team to tour England. But shortly after their arrival war was declared, and he immediately returned to Australia to train as a pilot. Commissioned as a pilot officer in November 1940, he joined No 23 Squadron, flying Wirraway aircraft patrolling the coasts of Queensland. After demanding to see some action, he was sent to join No 3 (RAAF), a squadron that developed a reputation as one of the most aggressive and outstanding fighter squadrons of the Desert Air Force.

Initially flying the Tomahawk, Barr achieved his first success on December 12 1941, and this was quickly followed by four more before his encounter with German fighters over El Alamein. His philosophy in combat was simple: "The Tomahawk and Kittyhawk were not considered by us to be top fighter aircraft. I decided early on that any deficiency either type had could be offset by unbridled aggression. I had done some boxing, and had beaten better opponents by simply going for them, and I decided to use this tactic in the air. It paid off."

After recovering from his wounds, Barr returned to combat and immediately destroyed an Italian fighter near Tobruk. He was made a flight commander, but on May 27 1942 the engine of his Kittyhawk overheated and he had to land in the desert. He took off the covers to repair the engine, having already prepared a rough strip for take-off. Then he heard enemy tanks approaching and, despite the malfunctioning engine, he took off without replacing the engine covers and reached base after being missing for four hours. The next day he was promoted to squadron leader. It was just six months since he had joined as a junior pilot officer.

On May 30 Barr went to the aid of his wingman, who was being attacked by fighters. Flying at only 50ft, his aircraft was hit by ground fire and he was forced to crash land. On this occasion he returned after spending two days in the desert.

In June he accounted for another Bf 109, his twelfth confirmed victory, in addition to having damaged at least five others. During the fierce fighting around Tobruk on June 16, Barr flew six sorties during the day in support of the retreating ground forces engaged against Rommel's panzers. Ten days later he was escorting bombers when he suffered engine trouble, and was then attacked by two Bf 109s. Badly wounded, he baled out of his burning fighter.

After 84 sorties, in which he was 3 (RAAF) Squadron's top-scoring pilot of the war, Barr became a prisoner of the Italians, and nothing was heard of him for three months – he had been put in hospital in Tobruk before being moved to Italy. Once his survival had been confirmed, it was announced that he had been awarded a Bar to his DFC.

Barr spent five months recovering in a hospital at Bergamo, in northern Italy. As soon as he felt fit enough he escaped, getting as far as the Swiss border, where he was apprehended by a customs official; Barr knocked him unconscious, but was soon captured. After a court martial, in which a Swiss border guard spoke in his defence, he was given 90 days' solitary confinement in the notorious Garvi jail, near Genoa.

Following the Italian capitulation in September 1943 the Germans started to transport all Allied PoWs to Germany. Barr jumped from a moving train and travelled south to join the Italian partisans. He helped other escaped prisoners to make their way towards the Allied forces, but after two months he was recaptured by the Germans and badly beaten up.

He escaped for a third time, and, with the help of Italian farmers, eventually joined an Allied special operations group collecting intelligence and conducting sabotage operations.

Finally, in March 1944, Barr escorted ten other prisoners through the German lines and met up with the advancing armies. For his gallantry in organising escape routes and on clandestine operations against the Italian Fascists and Germans, he was awarded the MC.

Barr arrived in England in April 1944, and two days after D-Day he landed on Omaha Beach in charge of an air support control unit. Despite being grounded, he managed to fly Typhoons on a number of rocket-firing operations against German forces in Normandy. In late 1944 he returned to Australia as chief instructor, fighter operations, and then flew fighters in Papua New Guinea and Celebes in support of Australian ground forces.

After leaving the RAAF in 1946 Barr was involved in the development of the Murray Valley Basin in Victoria; he later joined the oil seed industry, becoming chief executive of Meggitt Ltd. He was the Australian representative on, and chairman of, the International Oil Seed Group. In 1983 he was appointed OBE for his services to the industry.

Barr earned a reputation amongst allies and enemy alike for his acts of bravery, his selflessness, dogged determination and his infectious sense of humour. He was an ardent supporter of the RAF Escaping Society, and regularly returned to Italy to meet the Italian farmers and peasants who had aided him.

Nicky Barr married his wife Dot in 1941; they had two sons.

INDUSTRIALISTS & ENGINEERS

SIR GEORGE EDWARDS

Sir George Edwards (who died on March 2 2003, aged 94) was an outstanding aircraft designer and engineer whose timely conception of the four-engined Viscount turbo-prop airliner bridged the gap between piston-engined and pure jet aircraft; he was also an important figure in the development of Concorde.

Edwards began his career as an engineer, but was to become a consummate salesman and businessman. His persuasive presentational and organisational skills went a long way towards preserving and building the British aircraft industry in the two difficult decades which followed the end of the Second World War.

Edwards was the least pompous of industrialists. He would exchange his work-day tweed "ratting suit" (as he used to call it) and his family saloon car for a smart pinstripe and a Bentley only when occasion demanded. Indeed, he was suspicious of the atmosphere of the boardroom, relishing the fact that he had "knocked the skin off my knuckles" in the engineering workshop before earning a reputation at the drawing board.

He disdained paperwork, and would return long-winded memoranda with a crisp "OK" or "Must we?" initialled "GRE" – the name by which he was known throughout the industry.

George Robert Edwards was born on July 9 1908 at Chingford, Essex. His mother died two weeks after his birth, and he was brought up by an aunt; his father worked for Burroughs Wellcome. George won a scholarship to South-West Essex Technical College at Walthamstow, where he showed a talent for mathematics. Moving on to the West Ham Municipal College, he learned to be a practical engineer, then took a BSc in

Engineering from London University.

After first working in engineering workshops, Edwards joined Vickers Armstrong at Weybridge in 1935, starting in the design and drawing office. When war broke out he was promoted to the post of experimental works manager; one of his first tasks was to design an aerial minesweeping system for the Wellingtons of Coastal Command. Edwards had come to the notice of Lord Beaverbrook, then Minister for Aircraft Production, who put him to work developing aircraft types for the war effort.

From 1935 Edwards worked under the company's long-serving chief designer Rex Pierson, who was his mentor and whom he succeeded in 1945.

Edwards often liked to accompany the crews carrying out test flights of new aircraft, and, in 1946, he obtained a pilot's licence; this enabled him to pilot the company's products and to fly himself between factory airfields in a twin-engined executive Beagle.

Edwards's contribution to the development of post-war civil and military aviation is evident from the list of aircraft on which he worked at Vickers: he was responsible for the Viking (an airliner developed from the Wellington bomber); the Valetta and the Varsity (military variants of the Viking); the Viscount; and the Valiant, the first of the RAF's three nuclear deterrent V-bomber types.

If one aircraft had to be selected as Edwards's memorial, it would have to be the Viscount. Appearing in 1948, it was not only the world's first turbo-prop airliner to operate passenger services, it was also the first British airliner to make significant headway in the American domestic airline market. Edwards pulled off the astonishing feat of selling a total of 445 Viscounts to British European Airways and 37 other airlines.

In the Valiant, which appeared in 1951, Edwards provided Bomber Command with its first aircraft capable of carrying a nuclear weapon. It was used for nuclear trials, including Wing Commander Ken Hubbard's dropping of Britain's first H-bomb off Christmas Island in 1957.

Throughout his career, Edwards accompanied his painstaking care when undertaking a design with a favourite pronouncement: "If you drop a clanger, people are going to get killed." It was therefore very much in character that, when Jimmy James, a BEA Viking captain, reported freezing water pouring through windows and ruining his uniform, Edwards was mortified, and did not rest until the fault was rectified.

Appointed managing director of Vickers Armstrong (Aircraft) in 1953, and of the British Aircraft Corporation, as the company became, in 1955, Edwards remained responsible for overall technical direction of his successor to the Viscount, the Vanguard. Unfortunately, this large, four-engined turbo-prop was marketed just when the pure jet was superseding propeller-driven aircraft.

It was inevitable that Edwards should experience setbacks and disappointments in a business which is subject to the whims of politicians and which he called "the ulcer industry". Probably none hit him harder than the cancellation of the supersonic TSR 2 in early 1965; despite its highly encouraging performance, there was a feeling in the government of the day that manned aircraft were becoming obsolete. Edwards did, however, counter this setback by taking the company into the design and building of guided weapons.

Another big disappointment – a decision described by Edwards as "the biggest blunder of all" – was the cancellation, in 1955, of the world's first trans-Atlantic big jet transport, the V 1000, for RAF Transport Command, and its civil version, the VC 7. Edwards was convinced the type would have upstaged both the DC 8 and Boeing 707, which were not to appear until the end of the decade.

Against these setbacks, successes included not only the Viscount; there was also the VC 10; and the Anglo-French Concorde, the world's first supersonic civil airliner. Without Edwards's patience and perseverance when dealing with politicians and with his counterparts across the Channel, it is doubtful if the Concorde project would have survived.

A vital element was Edwards's rapport during the early stages of the project with Sud Aviation's General André Puget, a former Free French bomber pilot. This relationship was illustrated by the way in which Concorde acquired the 'e' on the end of its name. The name had been suggested by a Cambridge under-graduate, the son of one of BAC's publicity team. When someone remarked that it would be more attractive to the eye with the addition of an 'e', Edwards immediately replied: "Agreed. It will also give pleasure to André."

Edwards's appointment to the Order of Merit in 1971 acknowledged his overall contribution to British aviation, but more particularly it marked his participation in the development of Concorde.

Edwards also initiated, in the early 1960s, the development of the BAC 111 short-haul jet airliner, the first passenger aircraft in regular service to have automatic landing. In the military arena, he was responsible for the Anglo-French Jaguar; and the Anglo-German-Italian Panavia multi-role reconnaissance aircraft, which became the Tornado.

In 1966 the Saudi Arabians ordered an entire defence system from BAC. It was the most important contract the company had ever received, and kept the factories busy until Edwards's retirement from the chairmanship in 1975, when he was 67.

Edwards's decision to retire in that year was coincidental with, but not caused by, the mooted creation of the nationalised British Aerospace. (This actually came to pass two years later, with the merging of BAC with Hawker

Siddeley Aviation, Hawker Siddeley Dynamics and Scottish Aviation, Edwards having made it clear that he was not a candidate to lead BAE.)

A few days after the Queen's Speech in October 1974, which had announced the forthcoming public ownership of the aircraft industry, Edwards had written from his holiday accommodation in Cornwall to the Secretary of State, Tony Benn: "Whatever views I might have about the desirability of nationalising BAC, this letter is to say that I am determined to do what I can to make the industry in its new form a success." He continued to maintain a low profile over the matter, and was equally non-committal when, in 1981, the Conservatives denationalised much of the industry.

Edwards was appointed MBE in 1945; CBE in 1952; and elected a fellow of the Royal Society in 1968. He was knighted in 1957.

After retiring, Edwards devoted himself to his other interests, including the Royal Aeronautical Society, of which he had been elected a fellow in 1947, president in 1957, and an honorary fellow in 1960.

Cricket was a lifelong passion. Turning out at Guildford in the 1930s, with Alec Bedser bowling at the other end, Edwards had dismissed Sir Learie Constantine for 11 runs, and in 1979 he was elected president of Surrey County Cricket Club.

He was pro-chancellor of Surrey University from 1964 to 1979. In 1981 he was appointed a Deputy Lieutenant of the county.

Edwards received many academic honours, including honorary degrees from Southampton, Salford, City, Stirling, London and Bristol universities and Cranfield Institute of Technology.

He was awarded the George Taylor Gold Medal (1948); the British Gold Medal for Aeronautics (1952); the Daniel Guggenheim Medal (1959); and the Royal Medal of the Royal Society (1974). He published many papers, and lectured in both Britain and America.

Among his hobbies were painting and sailing. He enjoyed music, and he designed and built hi-fi equipment which he installed at home.

He married, in 1935, Marjorie Annie "Dinah" Thurgood; she died in 1994. They had a daughter.

SIR FREDERICK PAGE

Sir Frederick Page (who died on May 29 2005, aged 88) was chairman of the aircraft division of British Aerospace and one of Britain's most distinguished aeronautical engineers, having played a part in the design and development of military aircraft from the Canberra and the Lightning to the Jaguar, the Tornado and the Euro-fighter.

After a starred First at Cambridge and an apprentice-ship at the Hawker Aircraft Co during the Second World War, Freddie Page joined the aircraft division of English Electric at Preston in 1945 as "chief stressman". There, under the chief engineer W E W Petter, he was a member of the team which created the first British jet bomber, the Canberra. Though the overall concept was Petter's, much of the radical thinking underlying it was Page's, driven by painstaking scientific analysis.

The prototype flew in May 1949; Page became assistant chief designer in that year and succeeded Petter as chief engineer in 1950. The Canberra − of which 1,352 were eventually built − saw service with 15 air forces around the world over the next 50 years.

Page's next project was the P1 prototype, the first British aircraft to achieve supersonic speeds in level flight. This led to the development of the Lightning fighter, which went into service with the RAF in 1960. In its advanced form, to the envy of American engineers of the era, the Lightning achieved supersonic climbing speeds and exceeded Mach 2 in level flight. It was another export success – notably to Saudi Arabia, where Page forged relationships which were the foundation of a substantial flow of contracts for BAC and British Aerospace in later years.

Page had been appointed chief executive of the aircraft division of English Electric Aviation in 1959. In 1960, at the instigation of the air minister, Duncan Sandys, the company became part of a tripartite merger with Vickers Armstrong and Bristol Aeroplane to form the British Aircraft Corporation, which had the contract to build a new supersonic strike-reconnaissance aircraft, the ill-fated TSR2.

It was Page's old mentor at Hawker, Sir Sidney Camm, who said: "All modern aircraft have four dimensions: span, length, height and politics. TSR2 simply got the first three right." Despite Page's best efforts as the project's chief engineer, and his willingness when necessary to face down ministers and officials with irrefutable logic, the TSR2 was mired in problems. By 1965 its estimated cost had tripled to £750 million, and its first delivery date had slipped by at least two years; under pressure to find budget cuts, the Labour defence minister, Denis Healey, announced TSR2's cancellation.

At the same time, however, an agreement was signed with the French government to produce an advanced naval attack aircraft, the Jaguar, in a joint venture between BAC and Bréguet Aviation. Page was co-chairman of the Jaguar joint venture company, Sepecat, and was also later chairman of Panavia, a company formed with Fiat and Messerschmitt to develop the Tornado fighter.

From 1967 he was chairman of the military aircraft division of BAC, and from 1972 he was also chairman of the commercial aircraft side – in which capacity he performed the official handover of the last Concorde built for British Airways. When BAC became part of the nationalised British Aerospace in 1977, Page joined the board and was chairman of the aircraft group until 1982.

A recipient of both the British Gold Medal for Aeronautics (1962) and the Gold Medal of the Royal Aeronautical Society (1974), he commanded universal respect in his industry and was particularly revered by the younger engineers whose careers he encouraged. His final involvement in the military field was to oversee early project studies for what emerged as the Eurofighter joint venture.

Frederick William Page was born at Wimbledon on February 20 1917, the son of a chauffeur who was killed while serving in the First World War. Freddie was brought up by his mother in very modest circumstances but won scholarships first to Rutlish School, Merton, and then to St Catherine's College, Cambridge, where he achieved the rare distinction of a double starred First in the Mechanical Science tripos.

Having known since his teens that he wanted to design aircraft, he began his career in 1938 in the Hawker works at Kingston-upon-Thames, where he trained under Sidney Camm, the designer of the Hurricane fighter bomber. Page worked on the Hurricane Mk II and the Typhoon and Tempest before moving to English Electric at the end of the war.

He was appointed CBE in 1961 and knighted in 1979. He was a fellow of the Royal Society and of the Royal Aeronautical Society.

After retiring from the board of British Aerospace in 1983, Page devoted himself to gardening, latterly at Christchurch in Dorset, where he also enjoyed listening to classical music and taking long walks on the seafront.

Frederick Page married, in 1940, Kathleen Edith de Courcy, who died in 1993. They had a daughter and three sons, of whom the eldest son, Gordon, followed his father into the aerospace industry and became chairman of the aircraft systems maker Cobham plc.

SIR PETER MASEFIELD

Sir Peter Masefield (who died on February 14 2006, aged 91) was one of the leading figures in Britain's post-war aviation industry, playing an important role at British European Airways (BEA) and in the development of the Britannia aircraft; from 1965 to 1971 he was chairman of the British Airports Authority.

Masefield was that rare phenomenon, a journalist who succeeded in business. In 1939 he was contributing freelance reports of Royal Aeronautical Society lectures to *The Aeroplane*, whose editor C G Grey appointed him technical editor. Although he wrote highly readable accounts of the activities of characters such as Geoffrey de Havilland and Frederick Handley Page, Masefield was also enough of a scientist to meet the requirements of his job description. Moreover, he already held a pilot's licence.

When he was taken on by Grey, Masefield was earning £3 10s a week working in the drawing office and wind-tunnel of Fairey Aviation, and he leapt at the offer of £7 10s a week and the opportunity to broaden his horizons.

Peter Gordon Masefield was born on March 19 1914, at Trentham, Staffs, the son of a doctor. He was educated at Westminster, Chillon College in Switzerland and Jesus College, Cambridge. While reading for an Engineering degree, he spent the long vacations helping to overhaul Argosies and the first HP 42 in the Imperial Airways workshops at Croydon. This 1s-a-week holiday task was the happy realisation of a dream which had been born when, aged 13, he had been "bitten", as he put it, "by a mad aeroplane" while listening to a lecture by Handley Page at the Royal Aeronautical Society.

The air show at Olympia in 1929 fanned his enthusiasm. And in the same year he was thrilled to meet the pilot of an Armstrong Whitworth Siskin which had beat up Heston airfield; this was Wing Commander

Sholto Douglas, a former 1914-18 Royal Flying Corps squadron commander, who 20 years later – as Marshal of the RAF Lord Douglas of Kirtleside and chairman of BEA – would employ Masefield as his chief executive.

By the outbreak of war in September 1939, Masefield was well placed to make use of his developing talents and contacts as an aviation jounalist. He was appointed air correspondent of *The Sunday Times* and war correspondent with the RAF, initially with the Advanced Air Striking Force in France. Between 1939 and 1943 he flew on operations; and after the Americans entered the war he accompanied Eighth Air Force daylight B-17 Fortress sorties as either a co-pilot or an air gunner, as well as in his role as a reporter. He also edited an official aircraft recognition journal for Lord Beaverbrook's Ministry for Aircraft Production.

Before Masefield was 30, Beaverbrook (by now Lord Privy Seal) had appointed him his personal aeronautical adviser and secretary of a War Cabinet committee planning for post-war civil air transport. In mid-war, the committee's deliberations on airline and airport requirements struck Masefield as a supreme act of faith – not least on the occasion when, as a V1 flying bomb cut out overhead, he and Beaverbrook dived for cover under the committee table.

Beaverbrook's patronage opened doors, and at one point Masefield was offered a safe Conservative seat. But he had no interest in a political career, later noting: "That extraordinary posture so beloved of politicians of sitting on the fence with both ears to the ground did not seem to me to be likely to be elegant. My first love was aviation and I wanted to be faithful."

Instead, when the war ended Masefield was appointed Britain's first ever civil air attaché in Washington. In 1946 he arranged, and was a signatory in Bermuda to, the first Anglo-American agreement on the future of air transport. Afterwards he negotiated the purchase by

BOAC of six C-69 Lockheed Constellations from the US Air Transport Command.

Masefield returned home as director-general of long-term planning and projects at the Ministry of Civil Aviation. Even though ambitious projects such as the Bristol Brabazon and the ten-engine Saunders-Roe Princess flying boat proved costly failures, it was valuable experience for his later career in commercial aviation.

From 1949 Masefield and Lord Douglas worked together for seven years, developing BEA from a small, newly-formed airline operating with makeshift wartime conversions into a substantial and profitable carrier of world stature. Masefield provided the airline with a new fleet, beginning with 20 elegant Airspeed Ambassadors, operated as Elizabethans, the best twin-engine transport of its day, and also the more numerous Vickers Vikings.

Following BEA's move from Northolt to Heathrow, Masefield introduced the turbo-prop Viscount, which set the airline on the road to profitability. In 1953 he entered a BEA Viscount in the air race from London to Christchurch, New Zealand. Determined not to miss the fun, he flew as team manager and employed John Profumo MP, deputy minister of civil aviation, as steward; the Viscount's time was 40 hours and 43 minutes, earning it second place in the transport handicap class.

Yet for all Masefield's success with BEA, he did not always have an easy time. Frequently at odds with the airline's Whitehall paymasters, he had to fight off attempts at control by Lord Pakenham (later Lord Longford) and his Ministry of Civil Aviation.

By 1955, therefore, Masefield was ready to accept the post of managing director of Bristol Aircraft, with the principal task of bringing the turbo-prop Britannia into production and airline service ahead of jets. (Before this appointment had been announced, he was asked to succeed Sir Miles Thomas as chairman of BOAC, but felt obliged to decline the offer.)

In the event, Masefield flourished at Bristol, which was involved not only in airframe and engine manufacture, but also in building helicopters, guided weapons and cars. He made frequent business trips between Bristol and London piloting a personal de Havilland Chipmunk which he modified with a bubble canopy, spat wheels and ejector exhausts, adding 20mph to its 119mph cruising speed.

On a visit to America to sell the Britannia, Masefield spent "a fascinating week" with Howard Hughes, who insisted on flying the aircraft with bare feet, claiming that he got a better feel of it through his toes. Hughes was impressed, and asked for 30 aircraft for TWA. Unfortunately, Bristol's capacity was unable to meet Hughes's demand for one a week from May 1957. In all, during Masefield's period in charge 85 Britannias were built – 60 for BOAC and 25 for RAF Transport Command.

Meanwhile, in 1960 Pressed Steel invited him to launch a new light aeroplane manufacturing company to fill the gap made by de Havilland's moving out of light aircraft and being absorbed by Hawker Siddeley. Hence, the next year Masefield was appointed managing director, later chairman, of British Executives and General Aviation, soon to be sensibly contracted as Beagle Aircraft.

Following the success of his souped-up Chipmunk – which, in 1962, he flew into third place in the King's Cup air race – Masefield was in his element. He relished developments such as the Beagle-Auster Husky, Airedale and Bulldog trainer until he left in 1970.

Since 1965 Masefield had coupled Beagle with the chairmanship of the new British Airports Authority, established by the Labour government to take over responsibility for the country's airports from the Ministry of Aviation.

Under Masefield, runways were extended, new terminals built, management was streamlined. Heathrow was successfully expanded, and by the end of Masefield's period in charge the BAA was making a profit.

He was knighted in 1972.

In 1975 he returned to airlines as a director, later deputy chairman (1978-87), of British Caledonian, remaining until 1988.

Throughout the 1970s and 1980s Masefield served on many boards, councils and committees. Yet he still found time, between 1980 and 1982, to serve as a trouble-shooting chairman and chief executive of London Transport.

As Masefield wound down his business career, he continued to be involved in a range of voluntary activities, and he wrote articles on aviation, transport management and the 1914-1918 war.

As a member of the wartime committee on peacetime aviation, he had examined the feasibility of reintroducing airship passenger transport, and this led to an enduring interest in the R101 disaster near Paris in October 1930, when 48 people – including Lord Thomson, Secretary of State for Air, and Major-General Sir Sefton Brancker, Director of Civil Aviation – lost their lives. In 1982 Masefield published a book about the disaster, *To Ride the Storm*.

Masefield had been president of the Brooklands Museum Trust since 1993. He was also a liveryman of the Guild of Air Pilots and Air Navigators. He was a fellow of the Royal Aeronautical Society and its president in 1959-60.

He married, in 1936, Patricia Doreen Rooney, with whom he had three sons and a daughter; one of his sons, Sir Charles Masefield, became the president of BAE Systems.

STANLEY HILLER JNR

Stanley Hiller Jnr (who died on April 20 2006, aged 81) was recognised worldwide as one of the pioneers of helicopter design and manufacture.

Still a teenager when he started his own company, Hiller designed and flew his first helicopter in 1944; he soon became a major force in US Army aviation, and his helicopters played a significant role during the Korean conflict of the early 1950s.

Even as a young boy Hiller had shown an amazing aptitude as an innovative designer. The son of an aviation pioneer who had first flown in 1910, Stanley Hiller was born in San Francisco on November 13 1924. His playground was his father's workshop, and he was only eight when he removed the motor from a discarded washing-machine and attached it to the chassis of a buggy he had built himself; he would then drive the buggy round the local neighbourhood. Sitting on his father's lap, he learned to fly when he was ten, and he soon started to make and fly model aircraft.

His first major enterprise was the building of a model racing car powered by a small petrol engine. The "Hiller Comet" went into production, using an innovative die-casting process he had developed at his father's workshop. By his 17th birthday, Stanley had founded Hiller Industries, and was producing the Comet at the rate of 350 a month, making a profit of $100,000. Within a year he had a million-dollar business manufacturing parts for Second World War combat aircraft.

After attending school at Berkeley, Stanley entered the University of California, but left after a year to concentrate on his business. He had been interested in helicopters since the age of 15, and had read about Igor Sikorsky's experiments with rotary wing aircraft, noting that the early vehicles were compromised by elaborate ways of compensating for inherent instability. "I have ideas about how to correct that," Hiller told his father, who suggested he put the ideas into some hardware.

The teenager's idea was a co-axial rotor design, which would avoid elaborate tail rotors and gears that controlled the inherent yaw of Sikorsky's single-rotor models. Initially, the concept seemed to work; a model co-axial helicopter was dropped from his father's ninth-storey office window, as Stanley's schoolmates cheered on the ground below.

With the support of his father, Hiller decided to devote his entire effort to helicopter development, and in 1942 he founded Hiller Aircraft Company, which subsequently became Hiller Helicopters. The war effort resulted in shortages of materials and equipment that delayed production. He and his staff had to scrounge or manufacture almost all their components, and the power plant was a critical item that no small firm could manufacture or afford. His approach to the War Production Board, claiming that his helicopter was worth promoting, resulted in their providing him with a small reciprocating engine.

Hiller designed and constructed the XH-44 (Experimental Hiller) helicopter in 1944. It was the first co-axial helicopter in America, and the first anywhere to fly with all-metal blades. In addition to serving as company president and chief engineer, Hiller – still a teenager and without any prior helicopter experience – flew as chief test pilot. He received the Fawcett Award for his "major contribution to the advancement of aviation".

By the time Hiller was 24 he had built a single-rotor UH-4 helicopter; this was the forerunner of his successful Hiller 360, which received its civil certification in October 1948. The stability of the 360 resulted in its use as a medical evacuation vehicle in the French Indo-China war in 1949, and it became the first light helicopter adapted for such a task.

When the Korean conflict broke out in 1950, the US

Army finally responded to Hiller's earlier pleas to create a light utility helicopter for their use. He personally directed the sales efforts that resulted in his firm producing hundreds of military helicopters based on his UH-12, primarily for medical evacuation; the machines later became familiar in the television series *M*A*S*H*. Civil models flew for police departments, herded cattle, and battled James Bond in spectacular scenes in *From Russia with Love*. Many British Army pilots were trained on his helicopters in the 1950s and 1960s.

Not content with becoming a leading manufacturer of light helicopters, Hiller kept his company at the forefront of rotary-wing and vertical take-off and landing technology.

He encouraged creativity, which included the development of rotary tip propulsion using a ramjet in his Hornet project. He also designed, for the US Navy, a one-man Rotorcycle, which could be parachuted behind enemy lines and assembled in nine minutes by its recipient on the ground; it could then take off and fly with all the speed, height and hovering capability of a helicopter.

In 1956 Hiller developed and tested a high-speed vertical take-off transport aircraft, proving that the idea of a tilting wing-engine approach to high speed vertical flight was feasible. The Hiller company created aircraft so fantastic that they could have been from the world of science fiction, but they did what they were supposed to do.

In 1964 the company merged with Fairchild, but the loss of a crucial contract at the time of the Vietnam War prompted Hiller to leave the aviation industry, and he embarked on a new and successful career as a venture capitalist. Hiller was a vocal critic of American corporate practices which undermined the vitality of companies – asset-stripping; excessive payouts to executives not matched by performance; and the "feudal" system of corporate governance residing with a few individuals at the top. He believed in motivating all employees, enabling them to contribute and perform for the common good.

Hiller retired when he was 70 and devoted his energies to creating the Hiller Aviation Museum at San Carlos, near San Francisco's International Airport, as an institute of education and research to encourage future generations to learn about aviation. He was adamant that the museum was about the future of aviation and not about him. He enjoyed visiting unannounced and chatting with visitors without declaring his identity.

In 2002 Hiller was awarded the National Air and Space Museum Trophy for Lifetime Achievement by the Smithsonian Institute. In the same year he was awarded the San Francisco Aeronautical Medal of Achievement, and in 2003 he received the Helicopter Foundation International Heritage Award.

Stanley Hiller married, in 1944, Carolyn "Kiki" Balsdon, whom he had met at university and with whom he had two sons and a daughter.

GROUP CAPTAIN
THE 9TH EARL OF ILCHESTER

Group Captain the 9th Earl of Ilchester (who died on July 2 2006, aged 86) started his 40-year career in the RAF as a 15-year-old apprentice and rose to become one of the service's leading nuclear weapons engineers before taking his seat in the House of Lords, where he later sat on the Science and Technology Select Committee.

Ilchester was one of "Trenchard's Brats", training as an apprentice at RAF Halton, where he graduated as an armaments tradesman. Sixteen years later, as a squadron leader, he specialised in the development of nuclear weapons when he was appointed to the Directorate of Air Armament Engineering. After two years he moved to the headquarters of Bomber Command to take a leading role in the introduction into service of the RAF's Thor inter-continental ballistic missile, which was developed in the United States. With a range of 2,000 miles, the missiles were sited on 15 RAF airfields to be an effective strategic nuclear deterrent.

Ilchester worked on the Thor programme for six years before leaving for Australia, where he was involved in the nuclear weapons programme at Woomera testing range. He later pointed out that "these were not missiles, they were projectiles, for they projected our power, influence, and desire for peace around the world, to all those who understood and valued the sanctity of human life – and they don't miss." On his return to England he was an armaments officer on the nuclear V-bomber base at RAF Finningley in Yorkshire.

Promoted to wing commander, he served in the officer and aircrew selection centre at Biggin Hill, involved in recruiting the RAF's future officers. In 1969 he was at the Ministry of Technology where, as a group captain, he was the assistant director of air weapons development, working at the centre of nuclear weapon policy and procurement. Three years later he fulfilled a central role in the Polaris engineering programme. He retired from the RAF in 1976, having held every rank from aircraft apprentice to group captain.

The son of Walter Angelo Fox-Strangways, an accomplished linguist who worked in the consular service, Maurice Vivian de Trouffreville Fox-Strangways was born on All Fool's Day 1920 at Tewfik, Egypt. He was sent to boarding school when he was five years old, going on to Kingsbridge School, where he showed himself a fine cricketer.

When he joined the RAF in January 1936 he was one of 700 apprentices in No 33 Entry, of whom only 400 lived to see their 25th birthday. The RAF became "his family" and he devoted much of the rest of his life to the service and its associated charities.

After completing his apprenticeship Fox-Strangways was posted to RAF Brize Norton. One evening in August 1940 it was his turn to take a bath when the air raid siren sounded. Disobeying orders, he remained in the cast iron tub. A bomb demolished the adjacent building and he soon found himself out of the bath and some distance from his barrack block. Naked, he fled for the nearest air raid shelter, which happened to be reserved for the WAAFs. As he appeared at the entrance a tall, attractive girl shouted "he's mine" – a year later she became his wife.

Fox-Strangways spent most of the war on armaments duties in India and the Far East, returning to England in 1946 as a warrant officer. Shortly after his return he was commissioned in the technical branch, where he specialised in maritime armaments, before spending the next few years at RAF Negombo in Ceylon and at RAF Kai Tak, Hong Kong. On his return in 1955 he started his long association with nuclear armaments.

He succeeded as the 9th Earl of Ilchester, a title created in 1756, on the death of his father in 1970. On his retirement from the RAF in 1976, he took up his seat in the House of Lords, where he sat as a crossbencher. Never a man to rush things, he waited until he understood all the intricate customs of the House before he finally stood up to make his maiden speech on February 27 1980.

He elected to speak on the Finniston report, a government enquiry into the health of the country's engineering industry and manufacturing base. He sat down after 17 minutes to warm congratulations. He became a very active member of the House, with an exemplary attendance record. In addition to the select committee, he was a member of the all-party groups for defence, energy and engineering development.

After 23 years of service he left the House of Lords in 1999 following the reforms introduced by the Labour government. Ilchester refused many entreaties to join the ballot for a place among the 92 hereditary peers created in the Weatherill Amendment, modestly declaring: "There are many better candidates than me."

Ilchester led a very active commercial life. He was a director of the Nottingham Building Society, serving as vice-chairman for two years. He worked tirelessly for the Biggin Hill News Group and assisted in its sale to the Tindall Group. For 19 years he was vice-chairman of the Biggin Hill Airport Consultative Committee.

He devoted a great deal of his time to the RAF Association at Biggin Hill and was south-east area president for many years. When he stepped down at the age of 83, he was presented with an inscribed dish "for over 60 years of service to the RAF and RAFA, greatly admired and sadly missed". He had a particularly strong affection for No 2427 (Biggin Hill) Air Training Corps Squadron, serving as its president until his death.

He took great interest in the young cadets' achievements and rarely turned down an invitation to attend their open days and prize-giving ceremonies.

Ilchester was president of the Society of Engineers and was later appointed a patron. After his election as a fellow of the Institute of Nuclear Engineers he served as its president from 1982 to 1984. He was a freeman of the Guild of Air Pilots and Navigators.

A man of natural sartorial elegance, Ilchester could appear reserved and shy, but he simply saved his views for the occasions when he had something significant to say. A colleague described him as: "the very embodiment of his family motto; *Faire Sans Dire* – deeds not words". Polite, modest, utterly dependable and calm, he had a dry wit and was very generous with his time and energy. He enjoyed the arts and had a wide taste in music.

Lord Ilchester married Diana Simpson in 1941, when they obtained a 24-hour pass before having to return to duty.

There were no children, and his nephew, Robin Maurice Fox-Strangways, succeeded him as the 10th Earl.

SIR ARTHUR MARSHALL

Sir Arthur Marshall (who died on March 16 2007, aged 103) developed a modest 1920s car hire and garage business into Marshall of Cambridge, the internationally renowned aerospace engineering company.

Combining his entrepreneurial flair and his engineering and flying skills with his father's belief that, after the First World War, there would be a sound future for aviation, Marshall placed the company in pole position to profit from rearmament and wartime contracts in the 1930s and 1940s.

At the same time he devised a revolutionary procedure for the rapid training of pilots and their flying instructors; during the Second World War the Marshall Flying Schools trained more than 20,000 pilots and instructors for the RAF, and its methods continue to be used by the RAF to this day.

The 1939-45 war also saw the beginnings of Marshall's aircraft repair organisation. During the conflict the company repaired more than 5,000 aircraft, Marshall often test flying the repaired aircraft himself. After the war he built huge servicing hangars at Cambridge and constructed a runway capable of accepting the largest aircraft – the only such runway in Britain built without public funding.

Recession did not inhibit the steady growth of Marshall's company. Among many initiatives, he contracted to design and build Concorde's distinctive droop nose and he established at Cambridge a thriving technical centre for the RAF's Hercules and TriStar fleets.

In support of his aviation activities Marshall established a commercial vehicle and bus-building facility with a peak production of 140 a week. At one time he supplied more than 80 per cent of Britain's military thin-skinned vehicles and buses.

Meanwhile he further expanded the company's garage group to 20 depots throughout the south-east, selling a wide range of cars and commercial vehicles. Remarkably, every Marshall initiative – including the provision of an airport for Cambridge at no cost to the community – was self-financed.

The eldest of eight children, Arthur Gregory George Marshall was born on December 4 1903 at Cambridge. His father, David, had begun as a 14-year-old kitchen boy at Trinity College before becoming steward of the Pitt Club and going on to start a car hire service with two chauffeur-driven limousines.

Arthur was six when his father launched the Brunswick Motor Car Company in a former stable. In 1914, however, fearing that Brunswick sounded too German, David Marshall renamed the business Marshall's Garage. During the First World War he also organised Army and munitions factory canteens.

When the war ended Arthur's early interest in aviation was further stimulated when his father bought, for £5, a surplus Handley Page bomber; it was installed in the grounds of the family's Cambridge home, which was re-named Aviation Hall.

In 1919 Arthur and his father were taken up for their first flight (the fare was 10 shillings each). After circling Brighton pier in a Fairey 111A seaplane they were convinced they knew where the firm's future lay.

But first Marshall senior had to restore the garage business, neglected during the war years, while his son progressed from Tonbridge School to Jesus College, Cambridge, where he shone as an athletics Blue (he was selected as a reserve for the British team for the 1,600 metres at the Paris Olympics in 1924).

After graduating with a First in Engineering, Arthur Marshall joined the family business in 1926 and qualified as a pilot at the Norwich and Norfolk Flying Club. Shortly afterwards he bought a de Havilland Gipsy Moth for £740, housing it at home in a paddock hangar opening on to a private landing ground at Fen Ditton.

He began to fly his father to race meetings, to obtain orders for aeroplanes and to teach the purchasers to fly. In October 1929 the landing ground became the company's first aerodrome and the base of its flying training school. Marshall was to be made a master instructor by the Guild of Air Pilots in 1931 after completing only 70 hours, and his pupils would include the future test pilots Bill Humble and H G Barrington.

In 1930 Marshall met Rosemary Dimsdale, a blue-stocking granddaughter of the 6th Lord Dimsdale. He taught her to fly, and after they married in 1931 they toured Switzerland and Italy on a flying honeymoon in Marshall's Puss Moth.

In 1932 they flew to the south of France on the first of a series of annual holidays which lasted until the eve of war. The garage business began to make shell covers, converted Austin 12s into armoured cars and equipped Tiger Moth trainers with bomb racks to be used in the event of an invasion. Once the threat of invasion had receded Marshall concentrated on the company's two flying schools; before long Marshall of Cambridge accommodated the largest of the Elementary Flying Training Schools.

Meanwhile, Marshall's Aircraft Repair Organisation grew until it was handling a wide range of military aircraft, including Flying Fortresses, Mosquitoes,

Typhoons and Hamilcar gliders as well as battle-weary
Spitfires and Hurricanes.

Although he became chairman and joint managing
director in 1942, Marshall kept his hand in as an instructor and continued to fly, despite increased executive
burdens following his father's death in that year.

The immediate post-war problem was to restore the
company's pre-war, bread-and-butter motor business,
and this preoccupied Marshall until 1948, when the
Berlin Airlift required the rapid servicing of a variety of
RAF aircraft. Thereafter, as the RAF re-equipped with
jets, the aircraft engineering floodgates opened.

Marshall collected contracts throughout the aircraft
industry, and from the 1950s his workshops were busy
with Venoms, Vampires, Canberras, Valiants and the civil
Viscount. At the same time his Cambridge aerodrome
was a centre for flying training, including that of the
Cambridge University Air Squadron.

In the 1960s, amid government pressures to rationalise
the aircraft industry and the cancellation of the TSR2
advanced swing-wing aircraft (in which project the
company was involved), Marshall kept the business afloat.

And then came his great break. Hearing of RAF
interest in Lockheed's Hercules C-130 transport aircraft,
he was contracted to open a Hercules technical centre.
From 1964 Marshalls provided design, repair and modification facilities for the world's celebrated air transport
workhorse and other Lockheed products.

In the early 1970s Marshall diversified into space
artefacts and specialised containers to hold sophisticated
equipment, including black boxes; always keen to
encourage youth training, he supported Air Training
Corps adventure schemes. Marshall himself remained
youthful and adventurous, and in 1978, at the age of
75, he upgraded his pilot's licence so that he was licensed
to fly the company's new Citation 2 communications
aircraft.

In September 1980 the Ministry of Defence placed a moratorium on all defence contracts. A saddened Marshall ordered redundancies; then, in 1982, he had to expand once again to meet the needs of the Falklands campaign.

Winning a contract to provide the Hercules with air-to-air refuelling, he put a rejuvenated design office to work. Contracts were again falling off when TriStar transport-tanker conversions saved the day, and Marshall rapidly expanded the design office.

In 1989 he handed over the reins as chairman and chief executive to his elder son, Michael, accepting that, at 83, it was time to step aside; to the end he had continued to work seven days a week. Saying goodbye, Marshall thanked his sisters Margery and Violet for their services as directors and wished Michael and his colleagues "the best of Marshall luck". In 1994 he published *The Marshall Story – a century of wheels and wings.*

Arthur Marshall was appointed OBE in 1948 and knighted in 1974. In 1990 he was awarded the Order of El Istiqual First Class by King Hussein of Jordan. He was a Deputy Lieutenant for Cambridgeshire in 1968 and High Sheriff for Cambridgeshire and the Isle of Ely in 1969-70. He was elected companion of the Royal Aeronautical Society in 1980 and an honorary fellow of Jesus College, Cambridge, in 1990.

With his wife Rosemary, who died in 1988, he had two sons and a daughter.

GEORGE CROSS WINNERS

AIR VICE-MARSHAL
SIR LAURENCE SINCLAIR

Air Vice-Marshal Sir Laurence Sinclair, GC (who died on May 14 2002, aged 93) was awarded the George Cross for rescuing an airman from a blazing bomber.

On the night of September 30 1940, at the RAF Station at Wattisham, Suffolk, Wing Commander Sinclair was sitting in the officers' mess when the officer in charge of night flying telephoned for some help. As Sinclair got to the flare path, the next bomber was taking off. When it reached a height of about 150ft, the starboard engine cut out and the plane skewed to the right, crashing in flames almost on top of the control tower.

Sinclair ran to his car and drove down the flare path. He was halfway down when the first of the plane's 250lb bombs detonated with a shattering explosion. As he reached the aircraft, a second bomb went off. The aircraft was burning fiercely.

Sinclair saw that the fuselage had been blown open and that the air gunner was lying close to it. He dashed into the flames and, grabbing the man's arm, dragged him clear. He and the station doctor, unaided, managed to get him into the ambulance.

The citation declared: "Undeterred, and knowing that two more bombs were in the aircraft, Wing Commander Sinclair pressed on and, dashing into the fire, he succeeded in dragging the air gunner to a safe distance. Unfortunately, the rescued air gunner has since died of his injuries." Reflecting on that night some 50 years later, Sinclair recalled his sense of shame that only the doctor had stayed to help him and that, in this, their first taste of war, so many had been found wanting.

Laurence Frank Sinclair, always known as Laurie, was

born on June 13 1908 at Frinton in Essex. He was educated at the Imperial Service College (later amalgamated with Haileybury) before going to the RAF College, Cranwell, where he took part in all the sports and whipped in with the pack of beagles.

His first posting was to Farnborough, but in March 1930 he sailed for India. Disembarking at Karachi with two colleagues, he sent a telegram to Ambala, saying: "Heath, Barrow and Sinclair arriving Tuesday midnight." At Ambala, the three were met by a furious adjutant demanding to know why they had sent such a ridiculous message. The telegram in his hand read: "Heart, Broken and Sincere arriving midnight."

Ambala had once been a large cavalry station. The officers' mess and bungalows dated from the Indian Mutiny, and the old polo ground had been turned into an airfield. While Sinclair, in his Bristol Fighter, was struggling to get over the mountains of the Hindu Kush, the tribesmen used to stand on their roof tops and shoot at him with their black powder rifles. In his spare time, be enjoyed shooting duck and snipe, as well as pig-sticking.

In July 1932 Sinclair was posted to No 5 Training School at Sealand, in Cheshire, before moving to the Special Reserve Squadron at Filton, near Bristol. In 1935 he was promoted to flight lieutenant and sent to Hendon as a flying instructor. The following year he returned to India and Ambala.

In 1939 he was hospitalised with stomach trouble, and it was discovered that he had only one kidney. Despite the fact that war was just around the corner, the Central Medical Board immediately grounded him.

After six months' non-operational duties, Sinclair's full medical category was restored in May 1940. He was promoted wing commander and posted to 110 Squadron at Wattisham. "Pussy" Foster, the CO, he knew by reputation. Some years earlier, Foster had had the ill fortune to crash on the North-West Frontier in the middle of a tribal war. Dragged from his plane and brought before the tribal gathering, he had faced them all with a smile and a wave, shouting "Shabach!"(or "Jolly good show!") The tribesmen showed their sense of humour by applauding this with enthusiasm and, much against the odds, Foster had been released unscathed.

The squadron at Wattisham was flying Blenheims, and suffered heavy casualties covering the Army's retreat into Dunkirk. Shortly after the exploit for which he won the George Cross, Sinclair was awarded the DSO.

In March 1941 he was posted to the Operational Training Unit at Bicester, before being promoted group captain and taking command of No 2 Group Station at Watton, in Norfolk. The Blenheims were deployed on daylight low-level attacks against enemy merchant shipping and against major strategic targets in Germany. In August 54 Blenheims attacked the power stations at Cologne, and 12 aircraft were lost. Hardened as he was to casualties, Sinclair was shaken by this terrible attrition. Of his aircrew, few survived to complete 25 sorties, and most did not reach half that number.

In October 1941 he was posted as senior air staff officer to No 6 Group at Abingdon, where he introduced new training methods and cut the accident rate dramatically.

In 1943 Sinclair was promoted air commodore and posted to North Africa as commander of the Allied Tactical Bomber Force. After the surrender of the German forces, he was awarded a Bar to his DSO and the American Legion of Merit. The King paid a visit to his squadron, and Sinclair served as his ADC for the next six months.

In July 1943 Sinclair set up his headquarters on Malta for the invasion of Italy. Six months later, he established it on the side of Vesuvius. During this period he was the local Enigma contact.

In 1944 he was posted to Bari to form a Balkan Air Force, which was engaged mainly in attacking the Romanian oilfields. He was awarded the Yugoslav Partisan Star and the Légion d'honneur.

Life at Bari was lived at high pressure. Senior officers had a disconcerting habit of flinging open Sinclair's door with a crash and storming into his office. He trained his dog, Husky, to get up silently, go to the door and quietly close it behind the visitor.

In 1947 he attended the first post-war course at the Imperial Defence College. The following year he was posted as senior air staff officer to HQ No 84 Group at Celle, in Germany. When the group closed down he took command of RAF Gutersloh before being posted to Sundern as OC No 2 Light Bomber Group.

In 1949 Sinclair was appointed assistant commandant at the RAF Staff College at Bracknell before returning to Cranwell as commandant. In 1952 he was commandant of the School of Land/Air Warfare at Old Sarum, before being posted to the Air Ministry as assistant chief of staff. He was posted to Aden in 1955 as commander of the British forces in the Arabian Peninsula. Three years later he was appointed commandant of the Joint Services Staff College at Latimer.

On his retirement from the RAF in 1969 after a year at the Ministry of Aviation, Sinclair was appointed controller of National Air Traffic Control Services on a six-year contract.

Sinclair was a fine-looking man with an enormous enthusiasm for life and a gift for making friends. At the same time he was a man of high principle, who believed in doing whatever he undertook to the best of his ability.

He retired to a village in Oxfordshire where his recreation was fishing – he landed his last salmon on South Uist at the age of 90. In 1992 he privately produced 50 copies of his memoirs, *Strike to Defend*.

Laurie Sinclair was appointed CBE in 1943; CB in

1946; and KCB in 1957. He served on the Victoria Cross
and George Cross Association committee from 1965
until his death.

He married, in 1941, Valerie Dalton White, who died
in 1990. They had a son and a daughter.

SQUADRON LEADER
SIDNEY WILTSHIRE

Squadron Leader Sidney Wiltshire, GC (who died on
September 29 2003, aged 93) won the Empire Gallantry
Medal, later exchanged for the George Cross, for rescuing
his flying instructor from a burning plane.

On October 21 1929 Pilot Officer Wiltshire was flying
an aircraft under instruction with the No 2 Flying
Training School in Lincolnshire. The plane crashed on
landing at Temple Bruer landing ground, near Sleaford,
and immediately caught fire.

After extricating himself from the machine, Wiltshire
found that his instructor, Flying Officer H E Power, was
trapped by his foot in the wreckage.

Although under no illusions about the risk he ran,
Wiltshire went back into the flames to drag his companion clear, but was badly burnt on his face and neck.

Both officers were flown to Cranwell Hospital; the
aeroplane was completely burnt out.

The citation declared: "Power would undoubtedly have
lost his life but for the prompt and courageous action
taken by his pupil." Wiltshire was invested with the
Empire Gallantry Medal by King George V at
Buckingham Palace on March 4 1930.

Fourteen years later he was re-invested with the
George Cross by the Governor-General of New Zealand,
Marshal of the Royal Air Force Sir Cyril Newall, at
Government House, Wellington.

Sidney Noel Wiltshire was born on December 12 1909, one of eight children born to the founder of a company which supplied bicycles, and later repaired motors, at Farnham, Surrey. He was educated at Farnham Grammar School, where he boxed and played cricket.

At the age of 20 Sidney followed the example of his two elder brothers and joined the RAF on a short service commission. Four months later Pilot Officer Wiltshire won the Empire Gallantry Medal. In December 1930 he was promoted flying officer and served with No 4, Army Co-operation Squadron at Farnborough. On completion of his service, he transferred to the RAF Reserve of Officers.

It was difficult to obtain employment in England as a commercial pilot, so Wiltshire followed his brother Bill to the South Pacific to work for a short period for a gold-prospecting company on the construction of a jungle airfield in Papua. When this project was abandoned, he joined North Queensland Airways as a pilot before moving to Guinea Airways, which used New Guinea landing strips cleared by the natives.

In September 1938 Wiltshire went to New Zealand, where he joined Union Airways (later New Zealand National Airways Corporation and now Air New Zealand). He was working for Cook Strait Airways, based at Nelson, when war was declared, and like other pilots in the reserves, found himself posted to the regular list.

He was appointed to a temporary commission in the Royal New Zealand Air Force with the rank of flight lieutenant, and posted to the Air Observers' School at Ohakea; his brother Bill joined the RAAF while brother Norman, who remained at home, was in the RAF.

In January 1941 Wiltshire was posted to No 2 Squadron, based at Nelson. He then moved to Wigram as OC Signals Flight and the following year was promoted to squadron leader.

He attended a course of the Royal Australian School of

Army Co-operation in Canberra, returning to take up an appointment as commanding officer of the Royal New Zealand Air Force station at Milson, near Palmerston North. In May 1943 Wiltshire attended a 16-week course at the Army Staff College, Palmerston North, before being appointed CO of Seagrove Station on the Manukau harbour, where No 25 Squadron was being formed.

In September he moved to Delta Station, near Blenheim, as CO Elementary Ground Training School. In January 1944 he was posted to Wellington, where he was stationed at Rongotai.

Wiltshire was now aged 34, and had logged some 5,300 flying hours. Realising that there was little prospect of employment matching his experience, he approached the RAF, and was offered duties with Transport Command, provided that he reverted to his reserve rank of flying officer and left New Zealand.

He served with the RAF until December 1945, when he returned to New Zealand and rejoined Union Airways. In 1952, on finishing flying duties, he became the passenger services manager for National Airways Corporation for about 18 months. He worked in the antiques business, then was employed by Hutchinson Motors in Christchurch for some years before retiring in December 1978 to Waikanae, outside Wellington, where he built a house called Touchdown.

In 1960 and 1972 he attended the reunions of the Victoria and George Cross Association, on the first occasion as the sole living holder of the GC in New Zealand.

A tall, good-looking man with a quiet sense of humour, he spent the last years of his life at Hunterville, on the North Island, where he enjoyed playing golf and was looked after by his wife's niece.

Wiltshire married, in 1940, Gretchen Guy (née von Dadelszen), who predeceased him.

AIR MARSHAL
SIR JOHN ROWLANDS

Air Marshal Sir John Rowlands (who died on June 4 2006, aged 90) was awarded the George Cross for his work in bomb disposal over a period of more than two years.

By the end of the Second World War, RAF bomb disposal personnel had dealt with some 175,000 weapons of British, Allied and enemy origin in Britain and Europe. The BD squads were in the front line of a battle between the British and German scientists, and sometimes enormous risks had to be taken in order to provide the information on which the British could base their strategy for handling unexploded bombs. In the first year of the war the life expectancy of a BD officer was about ten weeks.

In 1940 Flying Officer Rowlands was posted to the Air Ministry to join T Arm 4, the branch of the RAF responsible for bomb disposal policy. In April the next year an RAF BD squad reported the discovery of an unexploded bomb with some unusual features. Certain members of the Air Ministry staff were deployed operationally from time to time on some of the more difficult and hazardous tasks, and Rowlands was sent to take charge.

The bomb was at a depth of about six feet. It had a Type 17 delayed-action fuse at the nose end which was governed by a clockwork mechanism set to ignite at a pre-determined moment within a period of 72 hours. In the rear end there was a Type 50 anti-handling device. A movement of less than a millimetre would be enough to activate the trembler-switch and ignite the fuse.

Without disturbing the bomb, Rowlands inserted a solution of alcohol, benzene and salt – known as a Liquid Fuel Discharger – into the 50 fuse. After the required waiting period of 30 minutes the fuse was neutralised.

The 17 fuse was discharged in the same way.

A magnetic clock-stopper, known as "Kim", was then applied to the 17 clockwork fuse. BD personnel withdrew to a safe distance and the bomb was given a tug, which proved that the 50 fuse was inert. The bomb, fitted with the clock-stopper and a microphone, was then loaded on to a lorry and driven to a specially designated area where the explosive could be steamed out.

The steam steriliser was designed to cut a hole in the top of the bomb casing and emulsify the explosive before forcing it out under pressure. On the way frequent stops were made to ensure that the clock in the 17 fuse had not re-started. After the steaming-out operation, the bomb was finally rendered harmless.

On June 19 1943, at 9pm, the duty officer at the Air Ministry was informed that there had been a serious explosion at the RAF station at Snaith, in Yorkshire. Eighteen men were missing. A bomb in a large ammunition dump had accidentally detonated, damaging large numbers of incendiary and high explosive bombs. Many of these were already fully fused for operational use.

Rowlands was visiting another RAF station nearby at the time and hurried to Snaith. A reconnaissance of the site revealed a number of dead and no survivors, and no firm figures could be given of the number of bombs involved or of those that had detonated. What was certain was that some were fitted with delayed-action fuses and others with anti-disturbance devices. Many incendiaries had burnt, and the heat from the fire was intense; there was a constant danger from exploding ammunition.

Rowlands allowed a few days to elapse to provide a safety period. He and his colleagues then started to clear the area. A large number of bombs were dealt with. Some fuses were removed by remote control; others, more seriously damaged, had to be neutralised where they lay. By June 29 the work was finished.

The citation for his George Cross declared: "For over

two years, Wing Commander Rowlands has been employed on bomb disposal duties and has repeatedly displayed the most conspicuous courage and unselfish devotion to duty in circumstances of great personal danger." He was invested with the GC by King George VI at Buckingham Palace on July 20 1945.

John Samuel Rowlands was born on September 23 1915 at Hawarden, in Flintshire, and educated at Hawarden Grammar School and the University of Wales, where he took a degree in Physics. He captained the university football side and was in the tennis team.

At the outbreak of war Rowlands joined the RAF Volunteer Reserve. He did his armament engineering training at RAF Manby, in Lincolnshire, and his pilot training at Tern Hill.

From early 1940 to October 1943 Rowlands was with T Arm 4 (later re-designated 0.10 BD) at the Air Ministry, dealing with the organisation and direction of RAF bomb disposal. During this period he dealt with several hundred weapons of different kinds. His duties included dismantling and making safe new types of enemy weapons, and dealing with Allied weapons in crashed aircraft.

Rowlands also attended meetings of the Unexploded Bomb Committee. Inventions by civilian and military scientists were being produced very quickly in response to the challenge posed by the German weapons. The committee, chaired by Dr H J Gough, the Director General of Scientific Research and Development, was formed to co-ordinate these developments.

In 1943 Rowlands was posted to Fort Halstead, in Kent, to attend the Advanced Armament course. At the end of the course he became superintendent of fuse design at their armament design department. Over the next two years he travelled to North Africa, Italy and Germany, working just behind the Allied forces' front line, examining and reporting on German bombs and fuses.

Rowlands obtained a permanent commission in the RAF in 1945. Shortly after the end of the war he attended an RAF Staff College course at Haifa, in Palestine. On returning to England he was posted to head an RAF team to participate in the development of the British atomic bomb. He was in the High Explosive Research Department, also situated at Fort Halstead, and from 1947 to 1952 at the Atomic Warfare Research Establishment at Aldermaston.

In 1952 Rowlands attended the first British atomic tests in the Monte Bello Islands as the senior RAF officer. He had personally taken charge of the radioactive assembly of the bomb. Shortly afterwards he commanded the first atomic weapons unit in Bomber Command, before being posted to a bomber station at RAF Binbrook. In 1958 he was promoted to group captain and returned to the Atomic Warfare Research Establishment to work on the H-bomb, remaining there as the senior RAF adviser until 1961.

Rowlands was then posted to the British Embassy in Washington as a specialist attaché on nuclear matters. In 1964, now an air commodore, he attended the Imperial Defence College course in London. The following year, and for the next three years, he directed the technical training of cadets at RAF Cranwell. While there he visited the US Air Force Academy at Colorado Springs and Princeton University.

He was promoted to air vice-marshal in 1968 and appointed the first Director General of Training at the Air Ministry. Promoted to air marshal in 1970, he served for the following three years as AOC-in-C RAF Maintenance Command at Andover. He retired from the RAF in 1973.

From 1974 to 1980 Rowlands was assistant principal at Sheffield Polytechnic. For several years he was a consultant with the Civil Aviation Administration. He was a life vice-president of the Air Crew Association, and president of the Sheffield branch, to which he gave unceasing support.

A man of great modesty who never trumpeted his achievements, Rowlands retired to a village near Sheffield. His recreations were photography, tennis and motoring.

John Rowlands was appointed OBE in 1954 and KBE in 1971.

He married, in 1942, Constance Wight, with whom he had two daughters.

DISTINGUISHED LEADERS

AIR CHIEF MARSHAL
SIR CHRISTOPHER FOXLEY-NORRIS

Air Chief Marshal Sir Christopher Foxley-Norris (who died on September 28 2003, aged 86) was an exceptional low-level ship-busting pilot and squadron commander during the Second World War, and later the RAF's commander-in-chief in Germany.

Serving briefly as a Hurricane fighter pilot with No 3 Squadron at the tail end of the Battle of Britain, Foxley-Norris, although subsequently chairman of the Battle of Britain Fighter Pilots' Association, was unnecessarily modest about his own combat role in that conflict. "My failure to distinguish myself in the Battle," he said, "was by no means as uncommon as many people would imagine. Particularly, one's shooting was haphazard and untutored, most of us having been thrown in quite without adequate training in that highly scientific art.

"We did not often get into an attacking position, and when we did we missed, firing at too long range and without enough deflection. Those who survived eventually learned by experience, but in 1940 the success went to the few old hands, the naturally gifted and the lucky."

Certainly, Foxley-Norris's apprenticeship in 1940 helped to set him up for the rest of the war, though he still considered himself a learner when, after moving on February 26 1941 to No 615 (County of Surrey) Auxiliary Air Force Squadron, stationed at Northolt, he was surprised by Bf 109 fighters and shot down in flames. Foxley-Norris baled out of his Hurricane and came down near Ashridge, in Kent. After a heavy parachute landing he was delivered to the local police by a farmer wielding a pitchfork. "Got one of the bastards for you," the triumphant farmer declared, convinced that he had captured an enemy pilot.

Little the worse for this encounter, Foxley-Norris "rested" in Canada as a Commonwealth Air Training Scheme instructor. He also ferried Lockheed Hudsons across the Atlantic until mid-1943, when he returned to operational flying. Posted, as a flight commander, to No 143, a Bristol Beaufighter anti-shipping squadron, Foxley-Norris gained his first experience of the perils of strikes against enemy shipping in the North Sea.

Then, following an unpleasant interlude in which he was court-martialled for an alleged breach of security (of which he was acquitted), in the early autumn of 1943 Foxley-Norris was posted to serve as a flight commander in No 252, a Beaufighter squadron based in the Middle East.

Flying from Cyprus, Foxley-Norris was involved in what he described as "the disastrous and ill-conceived attempt to invade the Aegean islands of Cos and Leros". Characteristically forthright, he noted that the Beaufighter crews, who were operating at maximum range and were facing defenders superior in numbers and performance, "got a bloody nose".

Foxley-Norris and his fellow crews retired to Egypt's Canal Zone, where 252's Beaufighters were fitted with rockets in preparation for the squadron's next operational role − interrupting supplies to German garrisons on the Aegean islands.

On one memorable occasion Foxley-Norris encountered a 16-oared boat, "straight out of Homer", as he put it. Refraining from attacking, he skimmed the wave tops and yelled (not that anyone apart from his navigator could hear him), "Come on Leander!" and "Give her ten Argonauts!" (A classical scholar, Foxley-Norris had been captivated by the Aegean, the start of a lifelong love affair with the islands, where he was later to build a house.)

With a constant flow of enemy supply shipping to

intercept and destroy, Foxley-Norris was promoted wing commander and led No 603 (City of Edinburgh) Auxiliary Air Force Squadron on convoy patrol and sweeps over the enemy-held Greek islands.

Christopher Neil Foxley-Norris was born at Birkenhead, Cheshire, on March 16 1917 and educated as a scholar of Winchester and of Trinity College, Oxford, where he joined the University Air Squadron (OUAS). Destined for a career at the Bar, he won a Harmsworth Scholarship to Middle Temple; but this coincided with the outbreak of war, when, along with the future Group Captain Lord Cheshire VC, a fellow member of OUAS, he was ordered to No 9 Flying Training School at Hullavington, in Wiltshire.

After getting their wings, the two men parted – Cheshire went to Bomber Command, and Foxley-Norris to Army Co-operation Command. Posted to No 13 Squadron at Douai, in France, he flew the slow and vulnerable Westland Lysander on spotting sorties for the British Expeditionary Force.

Following the fall of France, Foxley-Norris transferred to Fighter Command. He converted to the Hawker Hurricane and, on September 27 1940, joined No 3 Squadron at Turnhouse in Scotland, taking part in the last few weeks of the Battle of Britain.

After his service over the North Sea and in the Middle East and the Aegean, in early 1945 Foxley-Norris received command of No 143 Squadron's anti-shipping strike wing at Banff, Scotland. Having exchanged its Beaufighters for the faster, more powerful de Havilland Mosquitoes, the squadron ranged the Skaggerak, Kattegat and Germany's north-western seaboard for naval and other maritime targets.

Foxley-Norris's "Mossies" were described as "pushing and shoving like housewives in a bread queue" to get their unfortunate targets, which were "plunging into the sea in all directions". On one sweep, Foxley-Norris and his fellow pilots shot down 11 out of a force of 18 enemy aircraft. Thus he rounded off an excellent wartime operational record, and accepted a permanent commission.

With the return of peace, Foxley-Norris began to scale the rather more mundane ladder which led to air rank and high command, beginning with a spell at HQ No 2 Group and a course at RAF Staff College which equipped him for increasingly important station commands and staff appointments.

In 1948 there came a pleasant interlude when he was posted to command the Oxford University Air Squadron, where he was able to identify and encourage such potential future leaders as David Craig, who was eventually to outstrip Foxley-Norris as a marshal of the Royal Air Force. In 1951 Foxley-Norris returned to the staff college as a member of the directing staff, and then in 1953 went to the Far East, where the Malayan Emergency offered an opportunity to advance his career on the planning staff of HQ Far East, Singapore.

After three years he returned home, taking up planning duties at HQ Fighter Command and then commanding fighter stations at Stradishall, Suffolk, and (from 1958) West Malling in Kent. In 1960 he was called to the Air Ministry as director of organisation and administrative plans, moving up three years later to become Assistant Chief of the Defence Staff (General).

The next year Foxley-Norris was promoted air vice-marshal and returned to the Far East as air officer commanding (AOC) No 224 Group, which comprised a force of fighters, bombers, helicopters and flying boats supporting the Army in the campaign known as the Indonesian Confrontation.

Foxley-Norris returned home again in 1967 as director of RAF organisation for a year until being appointed commander-in-chief Germany and commander of NATO's 2nd TAF. This was a considerable fiefdom, in which the RAF retained a sizeable presence as NATO faced the powerful Warsaw Pact forces.

He encouraged a tactical leadership programme which not only sharpened the RAF's effectiveness, but also later made an important contribution towards educating aircrew in the composite tactics which did so much to shape the air campaign during the Gulf War of 1991. Finally, Foxley-Norris served as chief of personnel and logistics from 1971 to 1974, when he retired.

Since their Oxford days, he had kept in touch with Leonard Cheshire. He had done what he could to support the Cheshire Homes, and was now free to devote more time to them. He was president of the Leonard Cheshire Housing Association from 1978, and chairman of the Cheshire Foundation (1974-82), and later its president.

Equally important to Foxley-Norris was his chairmanship of the Battle of Britain Fighter Pilots' Association. He strove to perpetuate the memory of the Battle and of those who had died in the course of it, and he promoted the welfare of the diminishing number of "the Few" when they needed assistance.

Foxley-Norris was awarded the DSO in 1945. He was appointed OBE in 1956; CB in 1966; KCB in 1969; and GCB in 1973.

On the occasion of the 60th anniversary of the Battle of Britain in 2000, Foxley-Norris publicly criticised the prime minister, Tony Blair, for not replying to, let alone accepting, an invitation to attend a service of commemoration in Westminster Abbey.

Foxley-Norris was a vice-president, from 1979, of the Royal United Services Institute, to whose journal he was a contributor. He was the author of a book, *A Lighter Shade of Blue* (1978).

He was chairman of the Ex-RAF and Dependants Severely Disabled Holiday Trust from 1984; of Gardens for the Disabled from 1980; and of the Trinity College, Oxford, Society from 1984 to 1986.

A keen pipe-smoker, Foxley-Norris served as chairman of Forest, the Freedom Organisation for the Right to Enjoy Smoking Tobacco.

He married, in 1948, Joan Lovell Hughes. There were no children.

MARSHAL OF THE RAF
SIR JOHN GRANDY

Marshal of the RAF Sir John Grandy (who died on January 2 2004, aged 90) was the only chief of the air staff to have commanded a fighter squadron throughout the Battle of Britain.

As chief he presided over some of the most difficult transitions of the post-war period for the RAF. These included withdrawal from bases east of Suez; the cancellation of major aircraft projects; and the dismantling of the strategic nuclear bomber force which he had done so much to nurture. (The cut had been made so that the Navy's Polaris submarines could take over Britain's nuclear responsibility.)

In May 1940 Grandy formed No 249 Hurricane squadron, which he trained and then led in action from Boscombe Down. One of his pilots, Flying Officer James Nicolson, was awarded Fighter Command's only Victoria Cross.

In early September 1940 Grandy was wounded in an attack by a Bf 109, but managed to bale out, landing in a field near Maidstone. His leg wounds prevented him flying on operations for two months, but he continued to command the squadron, which ended the battle as one of Fighter Command's most successful units.

After a spell as a staff officer he was appointed to RAF Coltishall, from where he led his Spitfires at low level to challenge German fighters defending the battle-cruisers

Scharnhorst and *Gneisenau*, which were making their successful Channel Dash; poor visibility, low cloud and rain thwarted his attempts to engage the enemy and made it one of his most dispiriting sorties.

When Grandy received a call that evening telling him to leave for Duxford, he wondered if he was being relieved of his command, and he asked: "What to do?" "You are going to command it, you BF, as from tomorrow," barked Air Vice-Marshal R E Saul.

RAF Duxford had certainly changed since Grandy had piloted a British Movietone News cameraman in a Hart biplane during the 1935 review of the RAF by King George V. Grandy found himself responsible for the introduction of the Typhoon, which had already resulted in the loss of several pilots; but he set about improving morale, not least by inviting the catering officer to provide fare superior to the normal rations. He participated in the test flying himself, and later flew a Typhoon on the Dieppe Raid, an operation which gave him considerable insight into the limitations of the aircraft, which afterwards became a useful fighter-bomber.

Grandy was next sent to command No 210 Air Defence Group, charged with the defence of Tripoli, then moved to the Suez Canal Zone to command No 73 Fighter Operational Training Unit. He tried to return to fighter operations, but instead was given command of No 341 Wing in Burma. This comprised four Dakota transport squadrons which penetrated mountainous areas in monsoon storms to drop supplies to the 14th Army.

On May 4 1945 he flew over Rangoon, where PoWs had painted on the roof of their prison "JAP GONE, RAF HERE, EXTRACT DIGIT". Grandy dropped some Allied flags before landing at Mingaladon and evacuating the weakest prisoners.

John Grandy was born on February 8 1913 and educated at University College School, London. He joined the RAF on a short service commission and flew

Bulldogs, Harts and Demons with fighter squadrons. In 1936 he completed a flying instructors' course at the Central Flying School, the prelude to four years of instructor duties. After being awarded a permanent commission, he served as adjutant of the London University Air Squadron, gaining the rarely awarded A1 instructor category.

Shortly after the outbreak of war he commanded No 219 Squadron, operating the outclassed Blenheim, and was not slow in alerting his AOC to the aircraft's unsuitability as a fighter. Soon afterwards he was given command of No 249 Squadron.

After the war Grandy was heavily involved in the evacuation of civilians during the bloody fighting in the Dutch East Indies, then attended the Army staff college course. He had a two-year spell as air attaché in Brussels before returning to Fighter Command, where he rose to become commandant of the Central Fighter Establishment. Here he was much concerned with developing the tactics of the new Hunter and Javelin fighters.

Thoughtful, reflective and blessed with an original mind, Grandy was clearly destined for higher rank. He started to attend the Imperial Defence College course in 1957, but was plucked out to take over command of the second phase of Operation Grapple, the hydrogen bomb tests on Christmas Island.

By the end of 1958 he was Assistant Chief of Air Staff (Operations) in the Air Ministry, where he was required to oversee the draconian cuts ordered by the 1957 Sandys Defence Review. As C-in-C of RAF Germany and commander of NATO's 2nd Allied Tactical Air Force, Grandy had to deal with the tensions caused by the building of the Berlin Wall while at the same time reluctantly implementing a contraction of the RAF's strength in Germany.

When he took charge of Bomber Command in 1963, Grandy found himself involved in the cancellation of the air-launched Skybolt missile, and in changing tactics to low-level flying in order to counter his V-Force's growing vulnerability to the increasingly effective air defence radar system of the Warsaw Pact.

Grandy's appointment in 1965 as the Commander-in-Chief of Far East Command during the period of confrontation with Indonesia gave him responsibility for the three British services and several Commonwealth countries. As British military adviser to the South-East Asia Treaty Organisation, he enjoyed exposure to joint military operations and high-level politics, which made him an ideal candidate for the post of chief of the air staff.

Grandy took office on April 1 1967, the 49th anniversary of the formation of the RAF. When he had to oversee the transfer of the strategic nuclear role to the Navy, he characteristically paid tribute to the RAF's long hours of "arduous duty in cockpits, crew rooms, dispersals, hangars and operations rooms". He was confronted with the Labour government's cancellation of both the Anglo-French variable geometry aircraft and the order for the American F-111, the replacement for the already cancelled TSR2.

But he also had charge of the introduction of the vertical take-off and landing Harrier, together with the decision to collaborate with the Germans and Italians in the development of the multi-role combat aircraft which later became known as the Tornado.

After retiring in 1971 Grandy served, from 1973 to 1978, as the Governor and Commander-in-Chief of Gibraltar, the first RAF officer to fill the post; he was then Constable and Governor of Windsor Castle for ten years. He served as chairman of the Trustees of the Imperial War Museum from 1978 to 1989. He was a trustee of St Clement Danes, the RAF church; the Prince Philip Trust Fund; the Burma Star Association; and the Shuttleworth Remembrance Trust. From 1984 to 1987 he was president of the Air League, of which he was made a companion in

2001. He was also a vice-president of the National Association of Boys' Clubs, a life vice-president of the RNLI and a patron of the Polish Air Force Association.

John Grandy was a keen golfer, and enjoyed sailing his ketch, *Astra Volante*, at Cowes, where he was a member of the Royal Yacht Squadron.

He was awarded the DSO in 1945 and twice mentioned in dispatches. He was appointed CB in 1956; KBE in 1961; KCB in 1964; GCB in 1967; and GCVO in 1988.

In 1937 John Grandy married Cecile Elisabeth Florence Rankin, younger daughter of Sir Robert Rankin, Bt, with whom he had two sons. She died in 1993.

———

AIR CHIEF MARSHAL
SIR DAVID LEE

Air Chief Marshal Sir David Lee (who died on February 13 2004, aged 91) began his 40-year RAF career patrolling the rugged terrain of India's North-West Frontier in the 1930s.

Flying Wapitis of No 60 Squadron and Harts of No 39 Squadron, Lee learned to cope with the most arduous and testing conditions. One of his most difficult missions ("providing a glimpse of Everest") was to deliver urgently required bubonic plague serum to Gilgit, the mountain outpost astride the route from the plains of India to Chinese Turkestan.

After the 1935 Quetta earthquake, in which 55 RAF personnel and dependants died, Lee dispensed with his air gunner to bring medical staff from Kohat. In December his squadron took part in the annual exercise to Singapore, a distance of 4,000 miles which took six days and ten intermediate stops.

Many years later Lee recalled that it was the custom for newly-arrived junior officers to call on the main service and government residences in married quarters to drop an elegantly engraved visiting card. He discovered that, when making these calls, he could dispense with his regulation sola topi for the more elegant "Bombay bowler". On operational flying duties, he also carried the RAF-issued "goolie chit", a promissory note offering gold to tribesmen who returned intact flyers falling into their hands.

David John Pryer Lee was born on September 11 1912. He was educated at Bedford School and RAF Cranwell before joining No 35 Squadron, flying Fairey Gordon biplanes at Bircham Newton, Norfolk.

After his four years in India, Lee completed a flying instructor's course at the Central Flying School, then became a visiting examiner at the reserve flying schools. When war began he was posted to No 144, a twin-engine Hampden bomber squadron.

Later he transferred to No 61 Squadron, also flying Hampdens. During the "phoney war" they flew daylight shipping searches over the North Sea and dropped leaflets by night, disparagingly described by aircrew as "bumf bombing". On the night of March 19 1940, the Hampdens bombed the seaplane base at Hornum on the island of Sylt; this first bombing raid on a German land target was retaliation for the German attack on the fleet at Scapa Flow, in which a civilian on land was killed.

After being posted to the Air Ministry, Lee attended the RAF Staff College, then briefly returned to desk duties. In early 1945 he was posted to the Far East to take command of No 904 (Fighter) Wing. After Japan capitulated, Lee was given the vital task of assisting in the rescue and repatriation of PoWs and allied internees in the Dutch East Indies; this involved parachuting intelligence officers into remote PoW camps. The situation was fraught with difficulty, and Lee's Thunderbolt fighter squadrons had to provide support for a landing by 49 Brigade, which fought its way to Surabaya. The Thunderbolts were also called in to provide air strikes against Indonesian positions.

The task of protecting and evacuating the PoWs and civilian internees did not appeal to many of Lee's Burma veterans, who regarded themselves as due for repatriation. But thanks to his leadership, No 904 Wing made an outstanding success of a dangerous assignment.

After a spell on the directing staff of the RAF Staff College, Lee assumed command of RAF Scampton, home of a wing of Canberra bombers. In 1956 he commenced a three-year appointment as secretary to the Chiefs of Staff Committee at the MoD.

Three years later, Lee moved to Aden as Air Officer Commanding Air Forces at the HQ British Forces Arabian Peninsula, where he distinguished himself by flying a white Canberra bomber on station visits.

When, in 1961, Iraq threatened Kuwait, Lee moved swiftly, ordering two Hunter fighter squadrons and two Shackleton reconnaissance aircraft to Bahrain.

To supplement Aden's Beverley and Valetta transports, he commandeered a passing Britannia airliner and chartered a Comet from East African Airways. Troops en route to Kuwait were astonished to be served jet passenger cuisine by attractive stewardesses. Lee's response made a crucial contribution to the peaceful outcome of the crisis.

In 1962 he returned to the RAF Staff College as commandant before promotion to air marshal. After joining the Air Force Board as Air Member for Personnel, he spotted an error in a portrait of Prince Philip in the Royal Academy exhibition; the artist, Norman Hepple, had demoted the prince from marshal of the RAF to air chief marshal, until Lee ensured that an extra ring was added to his sleeve. Finally, Lee was UK military representative on the NATO Military Committee from 1968 to 1971.

After retiring, he was the author of three official histories of the post-war RAF: *Flight from the Middle East* (1978); *Eastward: a History of the RAF in the Far East* (1984); and *Wings in the Sun: a History of the RAF in the Mediterranean* (1989). Lee also wrote an engaging memoir about the North-West Frontier, *Never Stop the Engine When It is Hot* (1983), and an account of Java, *And We Thought the War was Over* (1990).

He was a vice-president of the RAF Benevolent Fund in 1988, and chairman of the trustees of the Nuffield Trust for the Armed Forces. He was president of the Corps of Commissionaires.

David Lee was appointed OBE in 1943; CBE in 1947; CB in 1953; KBE in 1965; and GBE in 1969.

He married, in 1938, Denise Hartoch, with whom he had a son and a daughter.

AIR VICE-MARSHAL
JOHN BARKER

Air Vice-Marshal John Barker (who died on May 7 2004, aged 93) had the rare distinction of commanding in action both a Spitfire squadron and a four-engine heavy bomber squadron; later he took the surrender of the Japanese forces in Kowloon, served during the Palestine conflict and arrested the ringleaders of an attempted coup in Ceylon.

For most of 1944 Barker was a member of the War Cabinet plans team making preparations for the forthcoming invasion of Normandy, for which his expertise as an Army co-operation pilot was invaluable. Offered the chance at the end of his tour of duty in London to select his next appointment, he returned to operational flying.

Barker was given command of No 625 Squadron,

flying Lancaster heavy bombers from RAF Kelstern in Lincolnshire; this was a remarkable position for a man who had previously flown only single-engine aircraft. He arrived on the squadron in November 1944 after completing a one-hour flight to familiarise himself with the Lancaster; but he immediately endeared himself to his men by insisting on flying on the next operation over Germany with a junior crew. As squadron commander, he was expected to fly on operations occasionally; but that was not Barker's way, and he attacked many heavily defended targets. A fellow pilot recalled that "he was incredibly brave, and always put himself on the most dangerous sorties".

By the end of April 1945 a large pocket in western Holland was still occupied by the Germans, and the Dutch population was close to starvation. A truce was arranged, and the squadrons of Bomber Command mounted Operation Manna to drop food supplies. Barker, with his air officer commanding as co-pilot, led his squadron on the first drop on April 29. Shortly afterwards, he was awarded the DFC for "his keenness to operate and setting an inspiring example to all under his command".

As the war in Europe drew to an end, Barker joined the staff of Tiger Force, the Bomber Command contingent earmarked for operations against the Japanese. He was immediately promoted group captain to command Shield Force; the advance party, with which he sailed for the Pacific, consisted of a force of 3,000 men.

On approaching the Admiralty Islands in the *Empress of Australia* he received a signal from the Joint Chiefs of Staff in London ordering him to go immediately to Hong Kong. He commandeered a USAAF Dakota and flew to the Philippines, where he boarded *Anson*.

When the Royal Navy task force arrived on August 29, Rear Admiral C H J Harcourt took the Japanese surrender of Hong Kong on Victoria Island, and sent

Barker to the former RAF airfield at Kai Tak. There he took the surrender of the Japanese forces occupying Kowloon, hoisted the white ensign and set about restoring the runways.

On his return to England six months later, an administrative officer rebuked him for not hoisting the RAF ensign. Barker replied: "I am not in the habit of carrying one in my personal kit when on operations." For his services in the Far East, he was appointed CBE.

The son of a doctor who had served at the Battle of Jutland, John Lindsay Barker was born at Hull on November 12 1910. He was educated at Trent College, Nottingham, and Brasenose College, Oxford, where he read Law and joined the University Air Squadron. After gaining his degree, he entered the RAF in February 1934.

On completing his advanced pilot training, Barker joined No 26 (Army Co-operation) Squadron flying Atlas and Audax biplanes before converting to Lysanders. With war imminent, he was told to write the squadron's mobilisation plan, and on September 2 1939 he found himself implementing it when he took his flight of aircraft to France, where he took photographs for the British Expeditionary Force. In January 1940 he returned to England to be chief instructor at the School of Army Co-operation at Old Sarum.

Barker returned to operational flying in August 1941 with No 241 Squadron, operating in the tactical reconnaissance and fighter-bomber roles with the Hurricane. The next year he was appointed the commanding officer as 241 prepared to move to Algeria following the successful Operation Torch landings. Re-equipped with the Spitfire, he led his pilots on intensive operations against enemy tanks and convoys as the Allied army advanced towards Tunisia.

When General George Patton, the US Army commander, asked Barker to attack a target near the Kasserine

Pass, Barker annoyed the American by pointing out that it was too heavily defended for light fighter-bombers, and should be attacked by medium bombers flying above the heavy and accurate German flak. The fiery Patton questioned Barker's resolve; but Air Marshal Tedder's swift intervention, endorsing Barker's decision, defused an unpleasant incident.

Returning from the Far East in February 1946, Barker embarked on a series of appointments that kept him overseas for most of the next 17 years. Appointed to the staff of Air HQ Levant in Jerusalem at the height of the conflict in Palestine, he was responsible for all personnel matters, and was heavily involved in preparing the withdrawal plans.

Barker next assumed command of RAF Ismailia in the Suez Canal Zone in August 1950, a time when Anglo-Egyptian relations were tense. Egypt's abrogation of the Anglo-Egyptian Treaty in 1952 resulted in serious rioting in Ismailia, and Barker lost most of his large Egyptian civil labour force.

After three difficult years in Egypt, Barker moved to the tranquillity of Rome as air attaché. His success in this appointment resulted in the Italian government appointing him a cavaliere of the Italian Order of Merit.

In 1958 Barker was appointed to command the embryonic Royal Ceylon Air Force. When two senior Army officers attempted to stage a coup d'etat, the prime minister, Mrs Bandaranaike, ordered Barker to arrest them, which he did, accompanied by his former ADC, Squadron Leader Samarasinghe.

A disciplinarian, though also an understanding man, Barker was a very popular commander who attracted the nickname "Bouncer" because of his energy. Mrs Bandaranaike was impressed by him, and invited him to extend his tour beyond the normal four years; but Barker decided to retire after spending almost five years in Ceylon, during which time he steered the air force into the jet age to become an effective force. For his services in Ceylon, he was appointed CB.

Barker worked in the City before retiring to Dartmouth, where he sailed his own boat. In his younger days he had represented the RAF at rugby and cricket, and played rugby for Oxford Greyhounds and Leicester Tigers; in later life he took up golf. He never forgot his formative years with 26 Squadron, and was the squadron association's president.

Until shortly before his death, Barker was still able to unnerve his neighbours by driving down the narrowest of Devon lanes, just inches from craggy outcrops of rock, with a degree of speed and verve that was the envy of those many years younger.

John Barker's first marriage was dissolved in 1942, and six years later he married Eleanor Richards, with whom he had a son. She died in 2001.

AIR CHIEF MARSHAL
SIR JOHN AIKEN

Air Chief Marshal Sir John Aiken (who died on May 31 2005, aged 83) was commander of the British forces on Cyprus when the Turks invaded the north of the island in July 1974; he immediately had to organise and implement the evacuation of civilians, and by the end of August the RAF had brought out some 20,000 British dependants.

Aiken had been appointed to Cyprus 12 months earlier, and his role included command of the RAF's largest airbase, at Akrotiri. Following the Turkish invasion he recognised that his first priority was to move the 10,000 British service dependants living in local and dormitory accommodation to the two sovereign base areas (SBAs); in addition, he had to gather the many

British tourists on the island and shelter them in the Episkopi and Dhekelia base areas, which were 60 miles apart in the south and east of the island.

His second priority was to defend the two bases. Royal Marine Commando forces and three squadrons of armoured cars were airlifted to Cyprus from Britain to augment the British Army units serving with the United Nations force on the island. Other commando units remained embarked off shore, and 12 RAF Phantoms flew to RAF Akrotiri to reinforce the resident air defence and bomber squadrons, which were assigned to the Central Treaty Organisation (CENTO).

Within hours of the invasion, Aiken decided to broadcast on the local British Forces radio network, to reassure the garrison of 8,000 and their families. He also robustly denied Greek claims that Britain had played a part in the Turkish action. In the tense days that followed, his unflappable and determined attitude served him well. By the middle of August, he had not only organised the evacuation by RAF aircraft of 20,000 dependants, but also provided shelter for 35,000 refugees, some accommodated in his own residence, who had flooded into the SBAs.

With the evacuation complete, Aiken turned his attention to negotiating the safe return of British nationals to their homes on the island.

The partition of Cyprus also saw the effective end of CENTO, and Aiken oversaw the withdrawal of the RAF's V-bomber force and other fixed-wing squadrons by the end of the following January, leaving only a helicopter squadron in residence at Akrotiri.

Generally, he earned high praise for his cool and authoritative handling of one of the most difficult peacetime international crises faced by Britain after the Second World War.

John Alexander Carlisle Aiken was born in Belfast on December 22 1921. He was educated at Birkenhead

School, and at 17, with war imminent, he joined the Liverpool Scottish. In September 1939 he was commissioned into the Queen's Own Cameron Highlanders.

Aiken transferred to the RAF in April 1941 and trained as a fighter pilot before joining No 611 Squadron, flying the latest Spitfire IX from Biggin Hill. The squadron was employed on high-level escort duties for the RAF's light bomber force attacking targets in northern France and the Low Countries. In 1943 the squadron began flying low-level intruder sorties over France.

The next year Aiken left for the Pacific theatre, and became a flight commander on the newly-formed No 548 Squadron flying Australian-built Spitfires in the defence of Darwin, in northern Australia. At the end of the war he became a flying instructor at RAF Cranwell.

After commanding the Birmingham University Air Squadron, and a period as the personal staff officer to the Commander-in-Chief, Fighter Command, Air Marshal Sir Dermot Boyle, he commanded No 29 Squadron flying the Meteor night fighter jet. In 1958 he started a two-year appointment on the operations staff at NATO's Allied Headquarters, Northern Europe.

In 1960 Aiken was promoted to group captain, and took up the first of three important appointments in the military intelligence community. The rapidly expanding Soviet Air Force had started to deploy large batteries of surface-to-air missiles, together with an increasing number of air defence fighter squadrons, throughout the Warsaw Pact area. The Cuban missile crisis also occupied much of his attention. Never frightened of hard work or of putting in long hours, Aiken had a particularly busy time.

After commanding the V-bomber base at Finningley in Yorkshire, he returned to the intelligence world. The Ministry of Defence had recently been established, following the Mountbatten reforms, and this had resulted in the formation of the Defence Intelligence Staff.

For many years, the three services had nurtured and protected their individual intelligence capabilities, and the amalgamation of the three highly independent organisations proved a difficult, and at times unhappy, marriage. In an attempt to allay single service fears, and to "safeguard" each service's interests, an appointment at one-star level (brigadier) was established for each service at the end of 1964. Aiken was appointed as the first RAF officer to the new post, and his quiet authority and tact did much to limit the many problems encountered.

After completing the Imperial Defence College course in 1968, Aiken became the Deputy Commander-in-Chief in RAF Germany at a time of great change in the RAF's operational capability. The obsolescent Canberras and Hunters were replaced by the new generation of Harriers, Phantoms and Buccaneers, together with a much-enhanced air defence capability provided by the Bloodhound surface-to-air missile, making RAF Germany one of NATO's most potent air forces.

Following his demanding tour in Cyprus, Aiken was appointed to the Air Force Board as Air Member for Personnel in June 1976. Having successfully managed one crisis, he found himself having to oversee a previously approved, but highly unpopular, compulsory redundancy scheme. After two years in the appointment he became head of the Defence Intelligence Staff as Director General Intelligence in the Ministry of Defence.

His experience on intelligence matters, and the steady hand he provided, proved a great asset. The deployment of Soviet long-range ballistic nuclear missiles was creating tension, and the Soviet invasion of Afghanistan in 1979 and the Polish crisis of December 1980 added to the concerns.

A quiet, serious-minded and somewhat austere man, Aiken had a deep loyalty to the RAF. After retiring in 1981, he continued to give unstinting support to the

RAF family and immersed himself in administering service charities. He was chairman of the central council of the Royal Air Forces Association for three years before serving as its president for two terms.

In 1988 he was appointed chairman of the Grants Committee of the RAF Benevolent Fund, a post he held for six years. Described by a colleague as "a most committed and respected chairman", he presided over the award of £56 million to beneficiaries, all members of the RAF community in need.

Aiken was a member of Chatham House and served for a time on its council.

He was appointed CB in 1967 and KCB in 1973.

John Aiken married, in 1948, Pamela Bartlett, with whom he had a son and a daughter.

AIR MARSHAL
SIR EDWARD GORDON JONES

Air Marshal Sir Edward Gordon Jones (who died on February 20 2007, aged 92) commanded a squadron of outdated Gladiator biplanes in the ill-fated Greek campaign, in which he was credited with shooting down five Italian fighters; his dashing leadership earned him the DSO, DFC and the Greek DFC.

Gordon Jones was a flight commander with No 80 Squadron operating in the Western Desert when he was ordered to take his flight to Trikkala in central Greece in November 1940. Within days he was in action, engaging a formation of Italian Fiat CR 42 fighters, and he shot one down on November 27.

The next day he was leading a formation of six Gladiators when they encountered at least ten enemy fighters. In the ensuing battle he drove several Fiats off the tails of his colleagues and shot down two. He himself then came under attack; his aircraft was badly damaged and he took a bullet in the neck. He managed to return to base and spent the next month recovering from his injuries.

On December 21 Gordon Jones returned to take command of No 80 after his CO had been killed by fire from an enemy fighter as he descended in his parachute. During a particularly severe winter, he and his pilots continued to fly patrols.

On February 28 1941 the RAF enjoyed its most successful day of the Greek campaign. Operating from a forward airstrip close to the Albanian border, Gordon Jones was leading his Gladiators on a patrol when they encountered a superior force of Italian bombers and fighters. In the battle that followed Gladiators – and Hurricanes, arriving as reinforcements – shot down a number of aircraft. Two Fiats were the victims of Gordon Jones, and he was awarded an immediate DFC. He also received a DFC from the Greek government.

No 80 was re-equipped with Hurricanes, and on April 6 the Germans invaded Greece; the RAF losses increased and the squadron was forced to withdraw to Crete. Finally, on April 29, Gordon Jones and most of the survivors left for Egypt before moving to Aqir, in Palestine, where the job of rebuilding the squadron began.

The third of four sons of Lieutenant-Colonel Dr Albert Jones DSO, MC, Edward Gordon Jones was born on August 31 1914 at Widnes and educated at the local grammar school. His early childhood had been spent in India, where his energy caused his three brothers to christen him "Doolally Tap", a vernacular expression meaning "slightly mad"; the nickname "Tap" remained with him for the rest of his life.

After school he entered Liverpool University to study Medicine before deciding to pursue Veterinary Science. Although he loved shooting, gun dogs and the outdoor life he had no real interest in being a vet, his sole ambition being to fly with the RAF. He neglected his studies, concentrating on rugby and courting his future wife, a fellow student. Eventually, his powerful mother gave up and let him join the RAF.

Gordon Jones joined the service in 1935 and trained as a pilot at Netheravon before going to No 17 Squadron to fly Gauntlet fighters at Kenley, Surrey. Six months later his flight was detached to form 80 Squadron, which soon re-equipped with the Gladiator, the last of the RAF's biplane fighters. In May 1938 the squadron moved to Egypt, and within a few months was in action in Palestine.

When the Italians declared war on June 10 1940 Gordon Jones was commanding A Flight, and the squadron flew its first patrols from Amriya, in Egypt. In late November came the order to move to Greece. After the Greek debacle Gordon Jones and his surviving comrades went into action against the Vichy French in Syria. He finally left 80 Squadron after four years, and was awarded the DSO.

Following a year with the Rhodesian Air Training Group, Gordon Jones returned to England to command the fighter airfield at Hawkinge, Kent. In July 1943 he was promoted to group captain and joined the staff preparing the tactical air plan for the invasion of Europe, responsible for co-ordinating fighter operations in No 83 Group. The group's headquarters moved to France within days of the invasion to establish fighter strips and co-ordinate the close support operations of its Spitfire and Typhoon squadrons. As the land battle moved eastwards, Gordon Jones and his staff followed immediately behind. On his departure after 18 months he was appointed OBE.

In December 1944 Gordon Jones returned to operational flying, having been given command of No 121 Wing of four Typhoon squadrons. During constant action against ground targets, the rocket-firing Typhoons became the scourge of enemy transport on roads, railways and canals. As the war in Europe ended, Gordon Jones left to join the disarmament staff.

He enjoyed a glittering post-war career, almost all in the operational arena; uniquely, he never served in the Air Ministry or Ministry of Defence. After serving at the School of Land/Air Warfare he commanded a jet flying school before moving to operational duties at the HQ Second Tactical Air Force. He was attached to the HQ Air Task Force in charge of operations during the Suez crisis, and in 1957 took command of RAF Wyton, the home of the RAF's strategic reconnaissance force.

On promotion to air commodore in January 1959, Gordon Jones was appointed AOC the Central Reconnaissance Establishment. He then became AOC, RAF Germany, at a time when the Cuban missile crisis brought his squadrons to a high state of readiness. After two years at the Imperial Defence College, he was made AOC Malta and Deputy Commander-in-Chief (Air), Allied Forces, Mediterranean.

On promotion to air marshal in November 1966 he was appointed AOC-in-C Near East Air Forces and administrator of the sovereign base areas in Cyprus. From 1967 to 1969 he was commander of British Forces, Near East. He retired in August 1969.

Gordon Jones was appointed CBE in 1956, CB in 1960 and KCB in 1967.

A handsome man with a commanding presence, Gordon Jones was a keen sportsman, having represented Liverpool University, Lancashire and the RAF at rugby in his younger days. He remained passionate about rugby and cricket and enjoyed watching sport on his 42in plasma television screen.

"Tap" Gordon Jones married, in 1938, Margery Hatfield. They had met on St David's Day 1934, when he borrowed money from his ever-generous eldest brother to buy her a large bunch of daffodils. For the 63 years of their marriage a similar bunch arrived every St David's Day. She died in 2002, and the couple had two sons.

INDEX OF PERSONALITIES

(Italics denotes main entry)